The Quality of Democracy in Latin America

edited by
Daniel H. Levine
José E. Molina

LYNNE
RIENNER
PUBLISHERS

BOULDER
LONDON

Published in the United States of America in 2011 by
Lynne Rienner Publishers, Inc.
1800 30th Street, Boulder, Colorado 80301
www.rienner.com

and in the United Kingdom by
Lynne Rienner Publishers, Inc.
3 Henrietta Street, Covent Garden, London WC2E 8LU

Library of Congress Cataloging-in-Publication Data
The quality of democracy in Latin America / Daniel H. Levine and José E.
   Molina, editors.
       p. cm.
   Includes bibliographical references and index.
   ISBN 978-1-58826-761-0 (hardcover : alk. paper)
   ISBN 978-1-58826-786-3 (pbk. : alk. paper)
   1. Democracy—Latin America. 2. Political indicators—Latin America.
3. Quality of life—Latin America. 4. Latin America—Politics and
Government—1980– I. Levine, Daniel H. II. Molina, José Enrique.
   JL966.Q35 2011
   320.98—dc22

                                                        2010038600

British Cataloguing in Publication Data
A Cataloguing in Publication record for this book
is available from the British Library.

Printed and bound in the United States of America

⊗   The paper used in this publication meets the requirements
    of the American National Standard for Permanence of
    Paper for Printed Library Materials Z39.48-1992.

       5 4 3 2 1

Contents

Acknowledgments

THIS BOOK BEGAN WITH A CONVERSATION ABOUT HOW BEST TO understand the quality of democracy, and with our shared dissatisfaction with much recent scholarship that addresses this issue in general and specifically in Latin America. With the goal of providing something better, we gathered a group of scholars from Latin America, Spain, and the United States, and together we exchanged ideas, papers, and comments. So our first debt of gratitude is to the contributors to this volume, who worked with us over the past five years. We are also grateful to the Latin American Studies Association, the International Political Science Association, and the Latin American Association of Political Science (Asociación Latino America de Ciencia Política), which provided occasions for discussions.

We gratefully acknowledge support from the University of Michigan (the Department of Political Science; the Center for Latin American and Caribbean Studies; and the College of Literature, Science, and the Arts) and from the Universidad del Zulia. Earlier versions of parts of Chapters 1, 2, and 11 appeared in *The Quality of Democracy in Latin America: Another View,* Kellogg Institute Working Paper No. 342, University of Notre Dame (November 2007), and "La calidad de la democracia en América Latina: Una visión comparada," *América Latina Hoy Revista de Ciencias Sociales* 45 (April 2007). An earlier version of parts of Chapter 5 appeared as "Voz y voto: Participación política y calidad de la democracia en Mexico," *America Latina Hoy* 25 (April 2007). We also gratefully acknowledge support from Sanford Thatcher and Lynne Rienner in bringing this project to a successful conclusion.

—*Daniel H. Levine*
José E. Molina

1

Evaluating the Quality of Democracy in Latin America

Daniel H. Levine and José E. Molina

SCHOLARS OF DEMOCRACY IN LATIN AMERICA, AND OF DEMOC-
racy and democratization in general, agree on a few important facts. There is
agreement that the current wave or cycle of democracy has been more durable
and has more depth and better prospects for survival than others in recent historical experience (Smith 2005). There is agreement that the origins of this new
or renewed set of political systems can be attributed more to the operation of political variables—the discredit of previous authoritarian governments, qualities
of leadership and pact making, and extensive social support—than to economic
or purely institutional factors. Indeed, many of the new Latin American democracies emerged in the midst of economic crisis and have survived severe downturns that might have endangered their survival in earlier times (Levitsky 2005;
Mainwaring and Hagopian 2005; Roberts forthcoming). As political realities
have changed, the predominant focus of analysis has followed the course of
events and moved from the concerns with regime change, transitions, and consolidation (but see Roberts forthcoming) that dominated earlier scholarship to
more detailed consideration of the *quality* of these democracies. Analysis of the
quality of democracy means examining the extent to which in theory and practice citizens are provided with a full range of rights and opportunities, and with
the institutions and effective political rights to ensure that these are realities
(Diamond and Morlino 2005; Mainwaring 2003; Mainwaring and Hagopian
2005; Morlino 2004; Munck 2007b; O'Donnell 2004a, 2004b; Smith 2005).

How to understand the origins, workings, and quality of democracy is a
question that has occupied scholars of politics since Aristotle. In the context of
the current cycle of democracy in Latin America, analysis of the quality of
democracy has become something of a growth industry. There is an abundance
of studies on issues ranging from the specifics of institutional formation, electoral systems, and political parties; to efforts to identify minimum "requisites for

democracy"; to governance and public policy; and to efforts to set political democracy in a general context of rights and liberties (Munck 2007b; Munck and Verkuilen 2002; Tilly 2007). The existence of rights and the degree to which rights are effective are often central to these discussions, particularly to the analysis of accountability, itself a central feature of the quality of democracy. Much of the literature considers rights and the rule of law as separate dimensions of the quality of democracy (Diamond and Morlino 2005; Mainwaring, Scully, and Vargas Cullell 2010; Munck 2007b; O'Donnell 2004a, 2004b). In our view, each of the dimensions of democracy has specific rights associated with it. Therefore, for present purposes, we consider rights as an integral part of the area of democracy they are intended to protect, and not as elements of a separate, distinct, and general dimension of rights. The advantage of treating rights in this way is that the rights included in the analysis are those directly and explicitly related to the quality of democratic processes and to specific areas of the political process.[1] Thus, in contrast to scholars like Diamond and Morlino (2005), Mainwaring, Scully, and Vargas Cullell (2010), and O'Donnell (2004b) for whom the quality of democracy depends on the extent to which civil rights in general are effective, we believe that the rights in terms of democratic procedure that should be taken into account in determining the quality of democracy as conceived here are those civil rights that are specifically linked to the making of political decisions and their control by citizens. Certainly all civil rights are important, but if we wish to distinguish the quality of democracy from an overall evaluation of the performance of government, then it is necessary to identify the quality of democracy by evaluating only those rights strictly linked to political decisions in a democracy, while others, such as social, economic, and religious rights, should be considered as part of the evaluation of governmental performance or of social life in general.

Democracy and the quality of democracy are of course closely related, but they are not identical. An extensive literature and a large number of indices exist that classify countries on a scale whose core lies in a distinction between *nondemocracies* and *democracies*, with intermediate categories added in some cases. The indices analyzed by Munck and Verkuilen are mostly of this type (2002). The aim of this chapter and the studies collected in this volume are different. Our goals are (1) to distinguish clearly between democracy and the quality of democracy, (2) working with a procedural definition of democracy, to provide an operational definition of the quality of democracy, and (3) to specify core empirical dimensions on which the quality of democracy can be measured. Although in some accounts there are important democratic or democratizing elements even within authoritarian regimes (Tilly 2007), we begin with the assumption that any analysis of the quality of democracy requires that a country be at least minimally democratic, that an index of democracy has already been applied. This assumption is also shared by Altman and Pérez-Liñán (2002) and Diamond and Morlino (2005). The next step is to consider and to classify these democratic countries according to the quality of their democracy on a core group of theoretically derived dimensions.

Most indices of democracy, following the pioneering empirical classification of democracies by Dahl (1971: 231–249), work on two dimensions: contestation and participation (Munck and Verkuilen 2002). Much of the literature, such as the emphasis on general issues of rights and liberty, is also heavily influenced by and dependent on indicators and concepts provided by the United Nations Development Program (2005) and by Freedom House with data from panels of experts.[2] There is also emphasis on effective governance and public policy (Kurtz and Schrank 2007) and on the ups and downs of citizen satisfaction with democracy and views on alternative regimes.[3]

We take a different approach. In our view, there is an important distinction to be made between the effort to differentiate democracy from other political systems (dictatorship, for example) or to specify minimum requisites for democracy (inclusive citizenship, for example) and the analysis of the quality of a functioning political system that we can evaluate on the basis of a range of theoretically significant indicators. We coincide with the growing literature that considers the quality of democracy to be a distinct issue from analysis of the difference between democracies and nondemocracies (Abente 2007; Altman and Pérez-Liñán 2002; Andreev 2008; Berg-Shlosser 2004; Diamond and Morlino 2005; Morlino 2004; O'Donnell 2004a, 2004b; Smith and Ziegler 2008; Vargas Cullell 2004).[4]

In this chapter we clarify the concept of quality of democracy as different from the concept of democracy itself, and we consider the dimensions on which the quality of democracy should be measured. Working within the tradition of procedural democracy, we anchor the concept of quality of democracy in a compact group of theoretical and empirical dimensions that center attention on the quality of political processes (Tilly 2007: 7–10), on how democracies work as political systems, and on the rights and opportunities essential to the ability of any democracy to function, survive, and remain democratic.

There is broad agreement among scholars of democracy on the attributes identified by Dahl, whose work takes the understanding of democracy beyond a simple listing of social requisites or specifying the requirement of competition—which may or may not be democratic—to something more nuanced and dynamic. In *How Democratic Is the American Constitution?* Dahl writes that

> to be fully democratic a state would have to provide rights, liberties and opportunities for effective participation; voting equality; the ability to acquire sufficient understanding of policies and their consequences; and the means by which the citizen body could maintain adequate control of the agenda of government policies and decisions. Finally, as we now understand the ideal, in order to be fully democratic, a state would have to ensure that all, or at any rate most permanent adult residents under its jurisdiction would possess the rights

of citizenship. . . . There is no need to describe here the basic political institutions of a modern democratic country; but it should be obvious that just as in the ideal, so too in actual purpose democratic government presupposes that its citizens possess a body of fundamental *rights, liberties, and opportunities.* These include the rights to vote in the election of officials in free and fair elections; to run for elective office; to free expression; to form and participate in independent political organizations; to have access to independent sources of information, and to have rights to other freedoms and opportunities that may be necessary for the effective operation of the political institutions of large-scale democracy. (2002: 136–137)

These reflections provide the basic elements for our understanding of what a procedural definition of democracy must include: (1) free, fair, and frequent elections; (2) untrammeled equal access to voting and to institutions; (3) information that is accessible and sufficient for citizens to make a reasoned judgment; (4) elected officials empowered to govern, but also accountable and responsive to their constituents; and (5) an inclusive definition of citizenship. These are not all-or-nothing conditions, but continuous processes that may be expanded or contracted in a given political system. They also do not necessarily all move and change in the same direction. Countries that have a strong record on free and fair elections may be weak on accountability or responsiveness.

Much recent scholarship and commentary on democracy in Latin America has argued that the quality of these political systems is low because they have not generated effective governments, have not substantially reduced inequality and raised standards of living, and have not generated more widespread and meaningful participation (Diamond and Morlino 2005: xviii; Morlino 2004; Tendler 1997; United Nations Development Program 2005). This inappropriately conflates the quality of democracy with governance and effectiveness of government, as manifest in good or bad public policy, and conditions the success of democracy on the implementation of policies that promote development, social justice, and civil rights beyond those linked to the political process. But these issues are analytically distinct: authoritarian regimes can deliver good policies without thereby acquiring democratic legitimacy; democracies may deliver bad policies, but are not therefore less democratic. The quality of democracy and good government are certainly both desirable, but the value of each is best understood if they are analyzed as distinct concepts.[5] As treated here, the quality of democracy depends on the operation of processes whereby the population selects and controls its government and influences public policies, and not on the efficacy of government in the solution of the problems of the country.

Procedural definitions of democracy run a serious risk of formalism by confusing the identification of the existence of elections and formal democratic rules with what may be a very different reality. What makes and keeps the political process *democratic* is the extent to which access and participation by individuals and organized groups, directly or through representatives, are available on an unhindered basis throughout the social order. This directs attention to how political institutions are situated within a broader social context, to the strength of civil society, and, even more broadly, to conditions of organization and access to public life,[6] as well as to formal institutions of participation, such as electoral systems and legislatures and local governments.

A Procedural Definition of Democracy

Procedural definitions of democracy rest on a liberal and pluralist understanding of politics and the political process. Democracy is conceived as a system of representation with universal adult participation according to open and equal rules. In this vein, our analysis of the quality of democracy centers attention on procedures and on the rights required for them to operate as designed, and on the ways in which groups and individuals can exact accountability and help to shape and monitor policies. For a procedural democracy to function effectively, with procedures that can be described as fully democratic, some basic conditions have to be met: (1) inclusive citizenship, (2) free and open access to the political arena for all groups and individuals subject to transparent rules, (3) freedom of information and organization, and (4) formal as well as informal means of ensuring accountability. In the current literature, with rare exceptions (Beetham 2004; Hagopian 2005; Mainwaring 2003; Munck, 2007b; Powell, 2004; Rueschemeyer 2004), these are left as untheorized elements of a list of desirable traits. To theorize the question means to take the connection between political processes and the surrounding social order not as given, but as a prime focus of inquiry. This requires that we examine prevailing conditions of organization, including formal rules; cultural norms; and access to organization beyond the local level, including national and transnational links, the nature of public space, and barriers to access. The availability of a space that is public and open to all is central to citizen participation and engagement and can be self-sustaining. The ways in which emerging patterns of public participation and the use of space reshape the meaning of representation, both informal and official, are a central question for analysis (Anderson and Dodd 2005; Conaghan 2005; Hagopian 2005).

Procedural definitions of democracy have the attraction of clear analytical boundaries and portability across cases. Nevertheless, they can easily run into difficulties if the motivations and institutional channels specified in the definition are not linked explicitly with the surrounding social context. Elections and electoral systems provide such a link and are, of course, central to any definition of democracy, but the analysis required to address these issues satisfactorily has to reach beyond institutional rules and formal details to examine conditions of registration, access to voting, participation as individuals and through groups, and the flow of information.

How representation is provided for is also critical to the operation of any democratic society of a scale greater than a small group or town meeting. Conventional arrangements for representation—electoral rules, district magnitude, requirements for parties to register and present candidates—continue to play a central role in the quality of democracy (Snyder and Samuels 2001), along with recent innovations intended to multiply instances of citizen participation, including provisions for recall, referenda, rights to petition, participatory budgeting, and some formalized incorporation of civil society into government structures and operations (Avritzer 2002; Mendoza-Botelho 2009; Zovatto 2006). What we term *conventional arrangements* include formal, legal, and, occasionally, constitutional provisions, as well as informal rules and norms that give meaning to the ties between representatives and electors. Important issues here include possible elements of discrimination such as race, gender, and ethnicity; district magnitude and shape; the extent to which electoral rules translate votes into seats in an unbiased manner; the number and depth of offices actually open to election; and the neutrality, transparency, and efficacy of institutions that have the official responsibility of supervising and conducting elections and vote counting (Kornblith 2005; Levitsky and Way 2002).

Assuming universal suffrage and elections that are free, fair, and frequent (all matters for empirical verification), representation that is authentic and of high quality requires lowering barriers for registration, organization, and access to the voting process; multiplying instances and arenas of political action; making voting easier; and ensuring that representatives are more accessible and accountable. Reforms in this vein are intended to link up emerging groups and social networks with formal political institutions in ways that allow social energies to find expression, and affect policy in clear and transparent ways. This is no easy task and cannot be solved simply through measures of decentralization or devolution, although they represent a possible beginning. Decentralization by itself may simply multiply hierarchical units and proliferate subnational authoritarian enclaves (Gibson 2005, 2008). The theoretical challenge is to rethink the relations between the state and society, social movements and institutions, in ways that counter tendencies to group disempowerment and institutional isolation. The experience of Bolivia's Law of Popular Participation is instructive. The political process following the enactment of this law effectively changed a highly centralized prefect-based system into one with widespread popular participation. Central here was the combination of decentralization with lowered barriers to organization that elicited new kinds of participation and new strata of local and regional leaders while facilitating the incorporation of indigenous forms (this volume Chapter 7; Mendoza-Botelho 2009).

Issues of participation are not limited to elections: social movements of all kinds present opportunities for citizens to participate, such as mounting pressure on public officials and placing issues on the national agenda. A broad range of social movements played an important role in Latin America's most recent round of transitions to democracy, but widespread expectations in many countries that these movements would provide the basis for a different and more participatory kind of politics in the new democracies generally have not been met. Indeed, the contrary has often been true because civil society has become fragmented and weakened, with many groups unable to survive, let alone create enduring connections to formal institutions of representation.[7] There has also been a notable drop in indicators of social participation in many countries, which is perhaps not surprising once the immediate issue of restoring or improving democracies was achieved. One result visible in much of the recent experience of the region has been a pattern of social mobilization marked by sporadic outbursts of activism with continued vulnerability and dependence on populist leaders (Feinberg, Waisman, and Zamosc 2006; Piven and Cloward 1998; Roberts 2006; Schonwalder 2002).[8]

Electoral Decision, Participation, Accountability, Responsiveness, and Sovereignty

In earlier work (Levine and Molina 2007a, 2007b), following what has become a norm in the literature on the quality of democracy (Altman and Pérez-Liñán 2002; Morlino 2004; Munck 2007b; Smith and Ziegler 2008), we took as our starting point a procedural definition of democracy derived from the work of Dahl (1971, 1998). We constructed an operational definition of democracy in terms of a collection of procedures—and the rights that sustain these procedures—through which citizens of a country are able to elect those who govern, influence the decisions of those elected, and hold them accountable. This operational definition and the idea of quality that we derived from it allowed us to establish what a democracy of maximal quality would look like, while at the same time recognizing that countries will differ from one another in terms of how and how much they achieve in any particular dimension.[9] These differences respond to the particularities of each country's political history and do not prevent the use of a common criterion of evaluation.

Working from this understanding of democracy, we conceive of the quality of democracy not as an all-or-nothing phenomenon, but rather as a multidimensional continuum. We specify the quality of any democracy in terms of the degree to which its rankings vary from minimally acceptable to best possible conditions. In summary, democracies meet the following requisites:

1. Elections are free, fair, and frequent;
2. Government is effectively in the hands of those elected;
3. There is freedom of expression;
4. Citizens have effective access to alternative sources of information;

5. There is freedom of organization and of assembly, and associations have autonomy from the government; and
6. Citizenship is broadly inclusive with universal adult suffrage and no discriminatory barriers to electoral and political participation.

When democracy is understood as a group of procedures with the rights that sustain them, through which the citizens of a country can elect those who govern, influence their decisions, and hold them accountable, then the level of quality of any specific democracy can be determined by *the extent* to which citizens can participate in an informed manner in processes of free, fair, and frequent elections; influence the making of political decisions; and hold those who govern accountable. Determination of the level of quality of a democracy also involves *the extent* to which those who govern are those who really make decisions and do so in a way that is responsive to popular will. Given these determinants, the quality of democracy yields five empirical dimensions that together provide the basis for evaluation: (1) electoral decision, (2) participation, (3) responsiveness, (4) accountability, and (5) sovereignty. Each of these dimensions has a distinct set of empirical indicators and a clear relationship to the core theoretical understanding of democracy on which our analysis is founded. The following paragraphs elaborate on each dimension. In Chapter 2 we provide a more detailed exploratory analysis of indicators for each dimension as an illustration of how an index of the quality of democracy may be built on the basis of this conceptual scheme.

Electoral Decision

The requirement that elections be free, fair, frequent, and competitive, and that they lead to the designation of officials who have real power to act, is at the heart of any definition of political democracy and of its quality. This is a multidimensional requirement, which ranges from minimal to optimal on each component. One area that lends itself to measures of variation—and hence of quality—concerns free access to multiple sources of information and the provision of cognitive resources through the diffusion of education to allow for what Dahl refers to as "enlightened understanding" on the part of the voters (1998: 97).

A high quality of democracy depends directly on the degree to which citizens have access to ample and diverse sources of information on an equal and untrammeled basis (Rodríguez Arechavaleta 2010). If formal political equality, that is, one person, one vote, is a minimal condition for political democracy, in the same way, substantive political equality, which has as one of its essential components an equitable distribution of cognitive resources, contributes to a greater quality of democracy by enhancing the possibility of informed decisionmaking among the electorate (Dahl 1998: 97). The more diverse, abundant, and egalitarian the distribution of cognitive resources through education and the lower the barriers to accessing information, the greater the probability that the political decisions of citizens accord with their interests and are taken with awareness of their possible consequences. The extent to which cognitive resources are equally available is thus a good indicator of substantive equality, not only in politics, but also in economic and social life (Diamond and Morlino 2005; Lijphart 1999: 182; Rueschemeyer 2004).

Intense electoral competition and close results are not sufficient for defining conditions of democracy: what makes a system democratic is that conditions exist (as defined by Dahl 1971) for competition that is free and fair. Analysis of levels of the quality of democracy thus entails evaluation of the effective conditions of organization, access, and competition, but not the *level* of competition as such. In contrast to Altman and Pérez-Liñán (2002), we do not take intensity of competition as a dimension of the quality of democracy, although certainly it is a factor that affects our participation dimension, in the sense that the more intense and close the electoral competition is, the larger the expected voting turnout and political participation (Blais and Dobrzynska 1998).

The quality of electoral institutions is also critical to the quality of electoral choice (Hartlyn, McCoy, and Mustillo 2009).[10] This is partly a matter of oversight and accountability, but since elections are so critical to political democracy, separate comment is warranted here. The national and regional commissions that manage electoral processes and oversee voting and vote counting in Latin America have a mixed record. Where democracies are strongest, as in Costa Rica, electoral institutions are well established and independent (Molina and Hernández 1999; Picado León 2009). In some cases, as with the last presidential vote in Mexico, they have refereed exceptionally close elections amid allegations of fraud by the losing side (Schedler 2009). In others, for example in Venezuela (Alvarez 2009; Kornblith 2005, 2007; Pereira Almao and Pérez Baralt Chapter 10) or Nicaragua (Martí i Puig Chapter 8), the autonomy required to manage elections in an impartial and equitable fashion has been challenged or entirely overcome by official pressures or under-the-table deals between major political forces.

Participation

Political participation includes both participation in formal political processes like voting or access to government offices and membership in groups that exercise such participation collectively, for example, political parties. It is through participation that citizens choose their government, control it, and influence policymaking either directly or through representatives. The greater the participation, the higher the probability that government and its decisions are responsive to the will of the people. The quality of democracy is therefore influenced directly by the level and character of citizen participation in areas from voting and lobbying to membership in social and political party organizations (Araya and Barría 2009).

Effective opportunities to vote are another important component of participation. This refers to lowered barriers and greater ease of access to registration and voting, to the sheer number and variety of offices open to election, and to the opportunities to vote. These vary substantially across political systems. Federal systems have something of a built-in advantage insofar as they offer more levels of electoral choice. Recent trends to more independent municipal and regional governments, and moves to decentralization, can also enhance participation, although there is evidence that many neoliberal reforms, by removing functions from the state, also remove incentives for organizing and lobbying the state. The ironies are apparent: reforms ostensibly intended to promote individual participation end up reducing opportunities or confining them to the least effective and most sporadic forms of participation (Holzner Chapter 5; Kurtz 2004).

In most political systems over a minimal size, participation is organized through formal systems of representation. But as noted earlier, formal arrangements for participation do not tell the whole story. Formal political representation gains in quality to the extent to which it is situated in a rich and open context for citizen activation in groups and movements independent of the state, which is a core element of most definitions of civil society. There has been much interest lately in Latin America in the promotion of *direct democracy*, such as citizen forums, roundtables, referenda, and recalls, as alternatives to more conventional arrangements for representation. These and related provisions intended to multiply opportunities for citizen participation and enhance citizen influence over decisionmaking are potentially valuable additions to the democratic repertoire (Mendoza-Botelho Chapter 7; Van Cott 2000, 2008). But as a practical matter, it has been difficult to implement direct democracy schemes in ways that can overcome the peril of state and leadership manipulation, and to get around the problems that size alone creates for direct political participation. The level and quality of education, the level of freedom of information and of the press, and the extent of citizen engagement are critical to the possibility of neutralizing or reducing the danger of manipulation. In this sense, the quality of the electoral decision is closely tied to the quality of participation.

Accountability

The term *accountability* directs attention to a range of social and institutional means available for making public officials, whether elected or appointed, subject to control and possible sanction (Mainwaring 2003). Accountability can be both formal and informal: formal means of accountability are institutionalized in laws, administrative norms, and independent or semi-independent offices specifically charged with ensuring accountability, such as attorneys general, ombudsmen, oversight committees, public defenders, and independent electoral commissions. Accountability can also exist without formal sanctions, as in cases where accountability is demanded by public pressure or press or media campaigns. Peruzzotti and Smulovitz (2006a) call this *societal accountability*, and point to a range of social movements, for example, pro–human rights and anti-corruption, that aim to mobilize public pressure to judge and sanction officials.

The common spatial metaphor of horizontality or verticality calls attention to alternative and sometimes complementary aspects of accountability. Horizontal accountability is exercised by elements within government explicitly charged with review of the actions of officials and government offices, for example, judges, accounting offices, investigative services, and oversight committees. Vertical accountability is exercised by citizens through regular elections along with referenda and recalls (O'Donnell 1994a, 2003). Core elements of horizontal accountability are recourse to the rule of law and to sanctioned judgments about the legality of official actions. The validity of vertical accountability obviously depends on the quality of the electoral process, which links this dimension with the previous two of participation and electoral decision.

Although they are analytically distinct, vertical and horizontal accountability are related and interdependent. Our understanding of both is enriched to the extent that we can situate them in a context of societal accountability, where citizens and organized groups and elements of civil society raise issues, change public agendas, press for redress of grievances, organize demonstrations and campaigns to keep cases alive, and occasionally provide alternative means to monitor official activities. Societal accountability is highly flexible and not constrained by official calendars or routines. It may be "activated on demand, and can be directed toward the control of single issues, policies or functionaries . . . without the need for social majorities or constitutional entitlements" (Peruzzotti and Smulovitz 2006b: 150).

Responsiveness

Powell defines *responsiveness* as "what occurs when the democratic process induces the government to form and implement policies that citizens want" (2004: 91). He points to a chain of responsiveness that links leaders, citizens, and policies together over time and across levels of government. A higher degree of responsiveness distinguishes democratic leadership from those who remain in the traditional mode of bosses or *caciques* and from those who say one thing in electoral campaigns, but later do the opposite without bothering to convince the public of the wisdom or need of doing so (O'Donnell 1994a; Stokes 2001). The concept is not without complications. A government could prove itself to be highly responsive by enacting policies that have majority support, but which produce bad or even disastrous results, undermining the very popularity it sought to maintain. Issues of timing are also relevant. Some policies might not pay off in the short term, and by the time results did come in the government could be doomed. In line with our general orientation, we use "responsiveness" here to refer to policies and not necessarily to results.

Sovereignty

Sovereignty is rarely considered in discussions of the quality of democracy, but the requirement that those elected really have the power to govern means that democratic governments not be puppets, and not be so constrained by nondemocratic forces, whether domestic or foreign, that their independence is in question (Dahl 1971: 191). The concept of sovereignty includes formal political independence, which was accomplished a long time ago in Latin America, but goes further to encompass a measure of the extent to which a government is actually able to rule. An elected government faced with an aggressive, powerful military veto player, or forced to operate under a burden of debt and financial constraints so powerful as to preclude policy independence, is not effectively sovereign. Diamond and Morlino treat sovereignty as a minimal requirement for democracy rather than a dimension of its quality (2005: xxix). But this makes sovereignty an all-or-nothing phenomenon, rather than something that varies from greater to lesser along a range of indicators. In contrast, we define sovereignty in terms of the extent to which those elected are able to make decisions, substantially free from control, direct or indirect, by sources outside the democratic process, such as foreign powers, transnational public or private economic institutions, or the military. This is not a zero-sum proposition: all governments are constrained in some ways, and thus democracies may be said to be more or less sovereign. The less autonomy a government has with respect to external pressures, such as financial or diplomatic and internal forces, such as religious, military, or financial, the lower the quality of democracy.

The Quality of Democracy: Distinguishing Political Process from Results or Governance

As we suggested at the outset, each of these dimensions presupposes the existence of rights specifically associated with the activities involved, and which are considered integral to each area. An advantage of treating rights in this fashion and not as a distinct and separate dimension (Diamond and Morlino 2005) is that the rights included are those directly linked to the quality of democracy. Making rights in general a separate dimension runs the risk of stepping over into evaluation of government policies and quality of governance, and thus beyond the quality of democracy. The difficulties associated with a general focus on rights are visible in Freedom House, whose indicators are commonly used in evaluations of the quality of democracy (Altman and Pérez-Liñán 2002; Diamond, Hartlyn, and

Linz 1999: 62; Inglehart and Welzel 2005: 173–209; Mainwaring 1999: 22; Smith 2005). Freedom House considers economic freedom and private property as one of the "civil liberties" it uses for its evaluation of freedom and democracy. However desirable full economic freedom might be—and this is a basic element of disagreement between left and right—it is better regarded as a field for policy decision and evaluation of government performance, and not as inherent to the quality of democracy. Linking democracy to a particular economic system could unfairly reduce the chances of polities with leftist parties in government being considered high-quality democracies. The same could be said about other freedoms as long as they are not directly linked to the procedural components of democracy.

The preceding definition of quality of democracy and its dimensions centers attention on procedures and not results. This distinguishes our approach from that of authors like Abente (2007), Berg-Schlosser (2004), Diamond and Morlino (2005), Morlino (2004), Munck (2007b), or Ropelato (2007). These authors include level of socioeconomic equality as an indicator of the quality of democracy, and Morlino also includes the level of development of civil rights in general terms. Diamond and Morlino include the extent to which democracy "satisfies citizen expectations of governance (quality in terms of results)" within their definition of the quality of democracy (2005: xii). As stated earlier, we take a different position. A central point in our analysis is the need to distinguish the procedures by which decisions are taken from the results of those decisions. If the procedures involve free and fair elections and full citizen participation, respond to the predominant view of the citizenry, and can be subjected to institutional social and electoral control and accountability, then the quality of democracy would be high, even if the results of the policies do not resolve the problems at hand, including social inequality. To include the level of socioeconomic equality and the development of rights not strictly linked to the political process is to enter into the area of policy evaluation, judging what is and is not good policy or effective governance, and this runs the risk of infusing judgments about the quality of democracy with ideological criteria. A case in point might be the decisions taken in some states within the United States concerning gay marriage. One might support one or another outcome, but if the decision is taken following democratic procedures and with guarantees of the rights attached to these procedures, then whatever the outcome, this neither adds to nor reduces the quality of democracy in that country.

The question of levels of social and economic equality warrants further comment. Morlino includes this within his dimensions of the quality of democracy (2004). In our view, the level of political equality is an element of the quality of democracy and forms part of one of its dimensions. Political equality is demonstrated by the extent to which citizens enjoy equal resources for political action and decision. Among these basic resources are level of education and level of information. The socioeconomic resources available to the population and the degree to which these are distributed equally are factors that may influence levels of education and information, but which are not equivalent to them. Socioeconomic differences do not translate automatically into differences in education, information, or political resources. Populations and governments can develop social, educational, or communications policies that may reduce the differences in political resources between social groups, and, in this way, reduce political inequality even in conditions of broad socioeconomic inequalities. We do not suggest that reducing social inequality, eliminating extreme poverty, and promoting economic development are not worthy goals or that they are not important as elements of the quality of governmental performance in a democracy (see Mainwaring, Scully, and Vargas Cullell 2010). They are indeed important, but we believe that they must be kept conceptually distinct from the quality of democracy. Depending on one's point of view, a democratic government may be good or bad in terms of the results of its socioeconomic policies, but this does not necessarily imply that it is more or less democratic.

In our view, the quality of democracy is more than a measure of the development of basic elements of democracy. Altman and Pérez-Liñán conceptualize the quality of democracy as a measure of the extent to which the basic elements of democracy have been developed in a particular country (2002: 86). In contrast, for us, the quality of democracy involves other dimensions than those included in the minimal definition of democracy. Dimensions such as accountability and responsiveness, or elements like level of representativeness, are not, strictly speaking, minimum requisites of democracy, but they are fundamental for determining the level of its quality.

Vargas Cullell presents a definition that differs considerably from ours. He conceptualizes the quality of democracy from the perspective of what are known as "citizen audits." In this view, in accord with the logic of the citizen audit, the level of the quality of democracy is given by the extent to which the performance of institutions coincides with the aspirations of citizens.[11] This definition includes our dimension of responsiveness and corresponds to an evaluation of the quality of democracy from the point of view of citizen satisfaction with democracy.

There is a considerable body of work that relies on qualitative analysis of elections and rights to classify democracies as either liberal or illiberal (Smith 2005). An important antecedent of this dichotomy, and indeed of most studies of the quality of democracy, is the classification made by Dahl that used two dimensions—participation and contestation—to distinguish among polyarchies as either "totally inclusive polyarchies" or "quasi polyarchies" (1971: 248). Others rely on Freedom House scores of political and civil rights as the basis for classification (Altman and Pérez-Liñán 2002; Diamond, Hartlyn, and Linz 1999: 62; Inglehart 2003; Inglehart and Welzel 2005: 175). Freedom House rankings are themselves derived from qualitative analyses carried out by panels of experts on ten political rights items and five civil rights items. Diamond, Hartlyn, and Linz (1999) used Freedom House rankings to classify Latin American democracies as liberal or electoral, a dichotomy broadly equivalent to that proposed by Smith (2005).

The problem with this body of work is that a dichotomous scheme of analysis does not capture the full range of issues involved in understanding the quality of democracy. A twofold classification based on whether there is partial or full respect of civil liberties omits important dimensions, such as responsiveness, accountability, and sovereignty, and also leaves out elements of political equality, such as values. In contrast, Inglehart (2003) uses Freedom House rankings as indicators of the level of democracy reached in each country by adding up the scores in political rights and civil liberties. The result is an operationalization of the quality of democracy along a continuum that goes from 2 (best) to 14 (worse).[12] We think this method better captures the differences in the quality of democracy among the countries than using only a twofold classification. Polity IV also presents a scale that goes from –10, full autocracy, to +10, full democracy (Polity IV 2009). This scale addresses the extent to which the minimal institutional requirements for democracy are fulfilled, covering only partially the dimensions of the quality of democracy. It does not cover critical dimensions or aspects of dimensions concerned with the interaction between society and institutions such as responsiveness, electoral participation, social accountability, and level of equality in political resources.[13]

Our approach to quality of democracy also differs from the concept of democratic governance proposed by Mainwaring, Scully, and Vargas Cullell (2010). These authors propose an index to evaluate the success of governments in creating well-being for the population. The resulting index of Success in Democratic Governance is based on an evaluation of the results of public policies. In contrast, our index of the quality of democracy evaluates the process by which political decisions are taken. The Success in Democratic Governance index includes as one of its nine dimensions one relating to the *level* of democracy, but this element is different from the concept of quality of democracy we present here. As we show in this chapter and in Chapter 2, it is this process, and not the results of policies, that determines the quality of democracy. In effect, for Mainwaring, Scully, and Vargas Cullell (2010) the level of democracy is another result, one that forms part of the overall level of well-being of the population, along with the other eight dimensions. The only indicator they use to measure the level of democracy is the Freedom House index of freedom, which includes political rights and civil rights in general.

On closer inspection, therefore, our evaluation of the quality of democracy differs from the Mainwaring, Scully, and Vargas Cullell index of the level of democracy in the same way that it differs from the Freedom House index. Our index is specifically directed to the quality of democracy, while Freedom House is designed primarily to indicate the level of freedom, and includes neither the dimension of responsiveness, which is demonstrated by an evaluation of the extent to which the population is politically informed as indicated by level of education, nor an analysis of electoral decision, which in our view is essential to any definition of the quality of democracy. Not being a specific index of the quality of democracy, the Freedom House index includes an evaluation of rights that goes beyond those linked to the democratic process. The global evaluation of rights may be adequate, we think, for a Success in Democratic Governance index that focuses on results, but not for a specific evaluation of the quality of democracy that focuses on the decisionmaking process, in the way we do in this volume.

We believe that it is preferable to maintain a conceptual distinction between the process by which decisions are made in a democratic regime, which represents the quality of democracy, and the results of these decisions in terms of the well-being of the population. That particular policies of a democratic regime may not be successful in solving a given problem does not imply that the process for arriving at those decisions was not democratic in character. The Success in Democratic Governance index proposed by Mainwaring, Scully, and Vargas Cullell (2010) tries to consolidate in a single evaluation both democratic processes and the results of public policies. For the reasons we have outlined here, it is better to maintain a conceptual distinction between these two dimensions. Maintaining this distinction helps avoid the error of criticizing democracy per se for the possible failure of any given public policy. The quality of democracy and governmental performance are different issues, and we believe it is necessary and valuable to evaluate the quality of democracy on its own, without in any way undermining important efforts by other authors to carry out a thorough evaluation of the policies undertaken by democratic governments.

The Evolution of This Project

This volume is the culmination of a multiyear effort directed at achieving a richer and more accurate understanding of the quality of democracy. We wanted to find a way of approaching the issues that would respect the importance of political processes and clearly distinguish the quality of democracy from both the minimal existence of democracy and the evaluation of governance or public policies. Our dissatisfaction with much of the literature led us to develop an alternative schema, centered on the five dimensions of the quality of democracy discussed here. We worked with an international group of scholars who exchanged ideas at a series of conferences and workshops beginning in 2005. Our goal from the beginning has been to combine a clear and straightforward approach to the quality of democracy with in-depth studies of a representative range of cases in the region. The cases represented here include countries with new democracies, such as Nicaragua; countries in which democracy was restored after extended and often violent bouts of military rule, including Argentina, Brazil, and Chile; and those engaged in extended efforts to expand and deepen democracy, with varying results to date, such as Mexico and Bolivia. Two cases represent examples of continuity of democratic institutions with deep problems. In Colombia, the quality of democracy is hindered by the impact of continuing and extensive violence. In Venezuela, a long-standing democracy has experienced severe decay in terms of accountability, access to information, and the openness and fairness of electoral institutions.

Of the three cases in which democracy has been restored following military rule, Argentina has gone the furthest in confronting this unfortunate legacy, in a series of trials and convictions of high-ranking officers from the last regime for violation of human rights. In the process, Argentine democracy has survived economic and political crises that would likely have doomed earlier regimes. Democracy also has survived and has been consolidated in Chile with a slow, but steady, dismantling of Pinochet-era rules. In Brazil, there has been a continuing struggle to make democracy work in the context of great inequalities. In Nicaragua, a competitive, mass democracy emerged and was consolidated in the wake of the defeat of the Sandinistas in the 1990 elections. This democracy owed much to the social openings of the Sandinista revolution, but has lately shown evidence of institutional weakness and possible decay.

The emergence of democracy at the national level in Mexico following more than seven decades of one-party rule is highly significant, although it continues to coexist with subnational pockets of authoritarianism and with the effects of inequality. Bolivia offers perhaps the most striking case in the entire region of reforms that have succeeded in opening and extending opportunities for popular participation in what remains a highly unequal, ethnically divided, and multilingual country.

Our last two cases, Colombia and Venezuela, share the distinction of democratic longevity. In each case, democracy and democratic institutions date back to the late 1950s, albeit with notable institutional reforms and political changes along the way. But in both countries, the pressures on democracy and the signs of democratic decay are evident. In Colombia, as noted, these are the result of pervasive violence that undermines accountability and participation and reduces the effective sovereignty of the regime as it struggles to control all the territory of the nation. In Venezuela, the aggressive implementation of "revolutionary" measures under the several governments of Hugo Chávez, who has been in power since 1998, has undermined accountability and freedom of information, while raising serious questions about whether elections can any longer be regarded as free and fair.

The next chapter provides a detailed exposition of the way in which we and our authors have gone about measuring the concept of quality of democracy. Together with the conceptual analysis of this chapter, it provides a basis for what is distinct about the analysis of quality of democracy that inspires this volume. Following the presentation of the separate dimensions and how they combine into an overall index of the quality of democracy, subsequent chapters are grouped in terms of the quality of democracy, ranging from highest to lowest. We begin with Chile, which is commonly ranked highest in the region, along with Costa Rica and Uruguay. We continue with a middle group of cases in which democracy has been restored or created anew and efforts to expand and deepen it are under way despite continuing challenges. This group includes Argentina, Mexico, Bolivia, Brazil, and Nicaragua. The last two cases presented in detail are Colombia and Venezuela, representing the lowest rankings. A concluding chapter reviews the issues, assesses the overall strengths and weaknesses of democracy, and sets the case studies in a regional context.

Notes

1. See Munck, who speaks of a "robust procedural conception" of democracy that "justifies the inclusion of standard political rights associated with the election of representatives, such as universal and equal voting rights, the right to run for office, the right to free and fair elections, and the right to regular elections." He goes on to suggest the inclusion of three other classes of rights: (1) rights exercised within the process of decisionmaking; (2) civil rights, such as freedom of movement, association, and information; and (3) rights surrounding equal participation, including such social rights as access to adequate work, health, and education (2007b: 35).

2. Freedom House, "Methodology," 2006, http:// www.freedomhouse.org/ template .cfm?page=35&year=2006.

3. Latinobarómetro, "Informe Latinobarómetro," 2005, http://www.latinobarometro .org/uploads/media/2005.pdf.

4. See also Chris Armbruster, "The Quality of Democracy in Europe: Soviet Illegitimacy and the Negotiated Revolutions of 1989," *Social Science Research Network,* 2008, http://papers.ssrn.com/sol3/papers.cfm?abstract_id=1153416.

5. See Kurtz and Schrank (2007) as well as the ensuing response and rejoinder and Mainwaring, Scully, and Vargas Cullell (2010) for a thorough review of studies of governance and good government.

6. Anderson and Dodd make this point in their analysis of citizen attitudes and citizen voting decisions in Nicaragua (2005). Holzner shows how structural changes following neoliberal so-called reforms in Mexico undercut the availability of information and restrict participation for poor people (Chapter 5).

7. See Levitsky, who argues that the diffusion of civil society has been critical in preserving Argentine democracy (2005).

8. The experience of sustained indigenous movements in Ecuador and Bolivia is a counterexample that underscores the importance of institutional factors in facilitating participation. Representation and the extension of effective citizenship have been critical issues in the effort to construct democracies in both countries (Mendoza-Botelho 2009; Yashar 2005).

9. Distinct from Armbruster, as cited in endnote 2, but in accord with the rest of the literature, we seek to establish an operational definition of democracy that can be used to evaluate the political systems in Latin America and in the world.

10. See the papers collected in *América Latina hoy* on *gobernanza electoral* (electoral governance) for a comprehensive survey (April 2009: vol. 52).

11. Vargas Cullell (2004: 96) gives the following definition of democracy: "For the purpose of the audit, the *quality of democracy* was defined as the extent to which political life and institutional performance in a country (or part of it) with a democratic regime coincides with the democratic aspirations of its citizens."

12. A similar scale based on Freedom House scores is used by Mainwaring, Scully, and Vargas Cullell to evaluate the level of democracy as one of the nine components of their index of success in democratic governance (2010).

13. See Chapter 2 for a comparison of the Freedom House index, the Polity IV (Polity) scale of autocracy-democracy, and our exploratory index based on the five dimensions of quality of democracy discussed in this chapter.

2

Measuring the
Quality of Democracy

Daniel H. Levine and José E. Molina

THIS CHAPTER EXPLORES DISTINCT OPERATIONAL MEASURES FOR each of the five dimensions outlined in Chapter 1. The indicators suggested here and the index developed with them are provided as an illustration of how future research can work with these dimensions to construct a specific index of quality of democracy. The data used here are for 2005 or for the closest previous year for which information is available. The analysis includes those Latin American cases that could be considered minimally democratic as of 2005. For this purpose, we accept the listing of "electoral democracies" provided by Freedom House for that year, with the exception of Ecuador.[1] In our view, Ecuador in 2005 did not meet minimal standards for democracy, which require that those who govern the country be chosen in free and fair elections, and that the elected officials actually govern the country. None of the three presidents elected in 1996, 1998, and 2002 managed to complete his term; all were ousted by events in which the military played a key role even though they did not resemble traditional models of a coup d'état. Because our data are for 2005, the 2006 election of Rafael Correa and his government are not part of our analysis. Nevertheless, we provide data on Ecuador at the bottom of the tables.

At this point of our research, we find no compelling theoretical reason to weight any particular dimension more than others.[2] Each dimension therefore has an equal value in the composition of the index, which is calculated as an average of the scores attained by each country on the five dimensions: (1) electoral decision, (2) participation, (3) accountability, (4) responsiveness, and (5) sovereignty. Scoring is presented on a scale from 0 to 100, and is constructed for each dimension as indicated below.

Electoral Decision

The quality of elections can be measured on a continuum from minimally acceptable to optimal. The range and rankings on it are determined by three basic aspects: (1) the quality of electoral institutions, that is, the extent to which these agencies provide for a free and equal competition between different groups and prevent public resources from tilting the scales in favor of official candidates; (2) the extent to which multiple sources of information exist and are accessible to the public so that they can freely and fully evaluate the options before them; and (3) the level of political equality among citizens. Equality has different aspects: as a summary measure here we use level of equality in cognitive resources. To arrive at a measure of the quality of electoral decisions, we use the average of the following indicators that correspond, respectively, to each of these variables.

- Freedom House Index of Political Rights. We use the Freedom House scores for each country on political rights as determined by their panel of experts.[3] This is a global indicator that includes electoral institutions along with the rights linked with them.
- Freedom House Index of Press Freedom. This Freedom of the Press index gives each country a score that runs from 0 (maximum) to 100 (total absence of press freedom). To translate this into an index that runs from least to most, we invert Freedom House scores.[4]
- Cognitive resources. To measure the extent to which an adequate level of cognitive resources is shared equally among the population, we use the rate of secondary school enrollment (those enrolled as a percentage of the school-age population) as provided by UNESCO.[5] In much of the world, secondary schooling represents a level that can serve as a measure of comparison of cognitive capacities relevant to politics. Data on the rate of secondary school enrollment are available for all countries in Latin America and for much of the world, and provide a convenient indicator of equality of cognitive resources.

Table 2.1 displays results on each of our three indicators of the quality of electoral decision; the fourth column gives a general score for this dimension, as an average of the three indicators.

Participation

To measure quality of participation, we use an average of four variables: (1) electoral participation (turnout), (2) opportunities to vote, (3) participation in po-

Table 2.1   Quality of Electoral Decision

Country	Level of Political Rights	Cognitive Resources[a]	Level of Freedom of the Press	Quality of Electoral Decision
Argentina	83.3	86 (2004)	55	74.8
Bolivia	66.6	88 (2003)	67	73.9
Brazil	83.3	100 (2004)	61	81.4
Chile	100.0	91	74	88.3
Colombia	66.6	78	39	61.2
Costa Rica	100.0	79	82	87.0
Dominican Republic	83.3	71	63	72.4
El Salvador	83.3	63	57	67.8
Guatemala	50.0	51	42	47.7
Honduras	66.6	65	48	59.9
Mexico	83.3	80	52	71.8
Nicaragua	66.6	66	56	62.9
Panama	100.0	70	57	75.7
Paraguay	66.6	64 (2004)	43	57.9
Peru	83.3	92	61	78.8
Uruguay	100.0	100 (2003)	72	90.7
Venezuela	50.0	74	28	50.7
Average	78.4	77.5	56.3	70.8
Ecuador	66.6	61	59	62.2

Notes: a. Information corresponding to 2005 or to the closest year for which data are available as indicated. In cases where the number of enrolled students exceeds the putative school-age cohort, we use 100 to keep the scale at 0 to 100.

litical organizations, and (4) representativity of institutions. Together these four variables provide a view of the overall level of participation, taking into account both individual political behavior and the characteristics of institutions.

Voting and involvement in political parties are important aspects of participation, but they present varying levels of difficulty to the average citizen (Verba, Nie, and Kim 1978). For this reason, we believe that the extent of popular involvement in both activities is a good way to evaluate the intensity of the incorporation of the population in the electoral process. Our two institutional indicators—representativity of institutions and opportunities to vote—point to the other side of participation, which is the extent to which institutions effectively channel citizen participation by providing for balanced representation and by ensuring an abundance of and accessibility to opportunities for the intervention of citizens in politics, and the degree to which these are actually used. The greater the degree of representativity and the broader the opportunities for participation that are effectively put into practice, the greater the likelihood that decisions taken will be responsive and accountable, thus the greater the quality of democracy. The overall results are provided in Table 2.2, based on the following indicators of participation discussed below: electoral participation, voting opportunities, participation in political organizations, and representativity by party and gender.

Electoral Participation

The proportion of the population of voting age that actually votes is reported (Payne, Zovatto, and Mateo Díaz 2006). We do not distinguish between countries with mandatory and those with voluntary vote systems because in our view the key factor in quality of democracy is level of participation, independent of its possible stimulus, as long as the voting process is democratically acceptable and does not violate human rights (Lijphart 1997).

Table 2.2   Participation (in percentages)

Country	Participation in Presidential Elections[a]	Participation in Political Organizations[b]	Representativity	Voting Opportunities[c]	Participation
Argentina	77.3 (2003)	3.4	88.2	50	54.7
Bolivia	62.2 (2002)	6.1	80.6	60	52.2
Brazil	76.3 (2002)	7.1	78.6	65	56.8
Chile	73.7 (1999)	1.9	79.7	25	45.1
Colombia	40.8 (2002)	7.2	79.3	60	46.8
Costa Rica	60.0 (2002)	2.7	90.4	25	44.5
Dom. Rep.	63.9 (2004)	21.8	81.2	25	48.0
El Salvador	57.7 (2004)	4.5	77.5	25	41.2
Guatemala	48.1 (2003)	2.2	74.3	25	37.4
Honduras	65.7 (2001)	6.7	85.8	25	45.8
Mexico	62.8 (2000)	9.1	83.4	45	50.1
Nicaragua	75.4 (2001)	3.7	83.1	25	46.8
Panama	74.4 (2004)	3.6	77.8	25	45.2
Paraguay	47.2 (2003)	8.5	76.0	45	44.2
Peru	77.1 (2001)	3.8	79.9	65	56.5
Uruguay	90.6 (2004)	6.6	79.1	45	55.3
Venezuela	56.3 (2000)	8.3	87.0	65	54.2
Average	65.3	6.3	81.3	41.2	48.5
Ecuador	70.8 (2002)	2.6	79.1	45	49.4

Sources: The source on national referenda is Zovatto (2006); for primary elections for presidential candidacies, it is Zovatto and Freidenberg (2006).

Notes: a. Year of election in parentheses.

b. Percentages include the responses "very often" and "often" to the question posed by Latinobarómetro in 2005: "How frequently do you do each of the following: work for a candidate or political party. Very often, often, almost never, never?" Percentages refer to valid cases.

c. The source on national referenda is Zovatto (2006); for primary elections for presidential candidacies, it is Zovatto and Freidenberg (2006).

Voting Opportunities

We construct a scale of effective voting opportunities, taking into account mechanisms for popular participation that have actually been put to use, considering also the intensity of this use. For present purposes, we do not enter the debate about differences in quality between presidential and parliamentary regimes, and we do not take into account whether people can vote for both president and members of congress or parliament, or only for members of parliament. We also do not score separately for the election of national authorities, which we consider inherent to democracy. Our concern is with the extent to which other opportunities exist and are used.[6] Therefore, we provide points for the following on a scale of 0 to 100:

- National referenda: One to three national referenda called in the last five years, 20 points; four or more national referenda called in the last five years, 30 points
- Subnational referenda: One to three subnational referenda called in the last five years, 10 points; four or more subnational referenda called in the last five years, 15 points
- Election of regional authorities: 20 points
- Election of municipal authorities: 20 points
- Election of other authorities: Judges, submunicipal authorities, or presidential primaries conducted for at least one of the principal parties, defined as those that obtain 10 percent or more of the vote in presidential elections, or in concurrent legislative elections, between 2001 and 2005, 5 points for each type, up to a maximum of 15 points

Participation in Political Organizations

As an indicator of participation in political organizations, we use the following question from Latinobarómetro (2005): "How frequently do you do one of the following: Work for a candidate or political party: very often, often, almost never, never?" Table 2.2 gives the percentage who responded "very often" or "often." This percentage is calculated on the basis of valid cases.

Representativity by Party and Gender

The proportionality of party representation is calculated for the lower or sole chamber of the national legislature for the latest election up to June 2005. The index of proportionality is obtained by subtracting the level of disproportionality from 100 (Rose 1984). The level of disproportionality is calculated using the Gallagher Least Square Index of Disproportionality (LSq) (Lijphart 1994:

61). We measure the level by which the genders are fairly represented in the national legislature by the level of proportionality between the percentage of members of each gender in the lower or sole chamber of the national legislature and the percentage of each gender among the population. Proportionality would be 100 when each gender gets a percentage of seats that is equal to its percentage of the population. We first calculate to what extent gender representation is disproportional, applying the LSq Index of Disproportionality.[7] Once the level of disproportionality is established, the level of proportionality is calculated by subtracting the LSq Index of Disproportionality from 100 as suggested by Rose (1984). Representativity of parties and representativity by gender are averaged to provide an overall measure of quality of representation. See Table 2.3 for the proportionality of representation by gender and party and the resulting representativity measure.

Table 2.3 Representativity by Party and Gender

Country	Proportionality of Representation by Gender in National Legislature (100-LSq)	Proportionality of Representation by Parties in National Legislature (100-LSq)	Representativity
Argentina	85.2	91.1	88.2
Bolivia	66.7	94.4	80.6
Brazil	58.0	99.1	78.6
Chile	64.5	94.8	79.7
Colombia	61.5	97.0	79.3
Costa Rica	86.0	94.8	90.4
Dominican Republic	68.1	94.3	81.2
El Salvador	59.9	95.1	77.5
Guatemala	57.0	91.6	74.3
Honduras	73.8	97.7	85.8
Mexico	73.6	93.1	83.4
Nicaragua	70.7	95.5	83.1
Panama	67.2	88.4	77.8
Paraguay	60.5	91.5	76.0
Peru	68.6	91.1	79.9
Uruguay	59.7	98.5	79.1
Venezuela	80.1	93.8	87.0
Average	68.3	94.2	81.3
Ecuador	66.2	91.9	79.1

Accountability

The literature on accountability points to three areas that need to be measured separately and then brought together for an integral evaluation of this dimension: (1) horizontal accountability, (2) vertical accountability, and (3) societal accountability. Indicators for each of these areas are discussed below and presented in Table 2.4, which provides the results for each indicator and an overall averaged score on accountability for each country.

Horizontal Accountability

The presence of an independent national legislature and of an honest and independent judiciary are critical elements of horizontal accountability; honesty and independence overlap. An honest and effective judiciary should reduce corruption, while an elevated level of corruption is a sign of a judiciary that is incapable of requiring accountability and is disinclined to do so. The level of corruption in the administration is also an indicator of the effectiveness of the institutions that should oversee it. The higher the level of corruption among government officials, the less efficient one would expect the institutions charged

Table 2.4   Index of Accountability

Country	Horizontal	Vertical	Social	Index of Accountability
Argentina	28	40.8	13	27.3
Bolivia	25	14.4	26	21.8
Brazil	37	20.8	14	23.9
Chile	73	42.0	12	42.3
Colombia	40	27.0	25	30.7
Costa Rica	42	55.0	15	37.3
Dominican Republic	30	36.0	32	32.7
El Salvador	42	33.0	13	29.3
Guatemala	25	23.0	13	20.3
Honduras	26	25.0	12	21.0
Mexico	35	13.2	33	27.1
Nicaragua	26	16.8	9	17.3
Panama	35	43.2	19	32.4
Paraguay	21	27.2	36	28.1
Peru	35	10.4	20	21.8
Uruguay	59	69.6	15	47.9
Venezuela	23	29.4	21	24.5
Average	35.4	31.0	19.3	28.6
Ecuador	25	20.0	10	18.3

with oversight and sanction of corruption to be. Those institutions include the legislature and the judiciary—the institutions through which horizontal accountability takes place. For this reason, we take as our indicator of horizontal accountability the Corruption Perception Index developed by Transparency International using data for 2005.[8] It measures to what extent public officials are prone to take bribes. Scores for each country run from 0, representing greater corruption, to 10, representing free of corruption. For equivalence with our other measures, we multiply these scores by 10.

Vertical Accountability

This is made effective through voting and depends on the frequency with which officials are subject to elections and on the fairness and impartiality of the elections themselves. We measure vertical accountability in the following manner. We take the length of the term of national officials or institutions subject to election, weighted by the proportion of the population that considers the elections to be clean. This yields an indication of how frequently people in elected office are subject to judgment by the population. It can be assumed that the more often elections take place, the more intensified is the control over government by the people. But frequency alone is not enough; therefore, we weight it by a measure of whether the elections are fair using the proportion of the population that considers the elections to be clean. Although this is no guarantee that they are clean, it does provide a window on how citizens judge the process and, in this way, on how they may exercise accountability through voting or through pressures for reform.

Length of term is the average of the terms of the president and the legislature. If there are two chambers with different terms, we first take the average of the two chambers' terms, add the length of the presidential term, and then divide by two. For countries with an average term for elected officials of four years or less, the score is 100; for those with between four and five years, the score is 80; between five and six years, 60; between six and seven years, 40; and average terms of more than seven years are scored as 20. This result is multiplied by the proportion of the population that considers that elections in their country are clean (Latinobarómetro 2005).[9] For details on the calculation of this indicator see Table 2.5.

Societal Accountability

As a summary indicator of societal accountability, we use the proportion of respondents in the 2005 Latinobarómetro study who state that they "frequently or very frequently engage in work on community issues." Engaging in collective and voluntary work on community issues implies demanding that public officials resolve problems, fulfill electoral promises, respect citizen rights, and be

Table 2.5 Vertical Accountability

Country	Presidential Term	Term of Lower House or Sole Chamber	Term of Senate or Equivalent	Scoring for Term on Scale of 0 to 100	Proportion That Considers Elections Clean	Index of Vertical Accountability
Argentina	4	4	6	80	0.51	40.8
Bolivia	5	5	5	80	0.18	14.4
Brazil	4	4	8	80	0.26	20.8
Chile	6	4	8	60	0.70	42.0
Colombia	4	4	4	100	0.27	27.0
Costa Rica	4	4	—	100	0.55	55.0
Dom. Rep.	4	4	4	100	0.36	36.0
El Salvador	5	3	—	100	0.33	33.0
Guatemala	4	4	—	100	0.23	23.0
Honduras	4	4	—	100	0.25	25.0
Mexico	6	3	6	60	0.22	13.2
Nicaragua	5	5	—	80	0.21	16.8
Panama	5	5	—	80	0.54	43.2
Paraguay	5	5	5	80	0.34	27.2
Peru	5	5	—	80	0.13	10.4
Uruguay	5	5	5	80	0.87	69.6
Venezuela	6	5	—	60	0.49	29.4
Average						31.0
Ecuador	4	4	—	100	0.20	20.0

subject to accountability and popular pressure. Greater citizen involvement reduces the impunity of officials and makes possible greater societal influence or control over governments. For these reasons, we consider this a useful indicator of the level of societal accountability.

Responsiveness

To measure responsiveness, we use a question from the 2005 Latinobarómetro survey on the "efficacy of the vote," which is "Some people say that how one votes can make things different in the future. Others say that regardless of how one votes, things will not be better in the future. Which of these is closest to your way of thinking?" We present the percentage of valid cases that indicate agreement with the statement: "The way one votes can make things different in the future." See the Responsiveness column in Table 2.7. We assume that those who consider that their vote is efficacious are implicitly recognizing that politicians are responsive to the popular will as expressed in elections. This is a more direct indicator of responsiveness than questions about satisfaction with the general functioning of democracy (Diamond and Morlino 2005; Powell 2004). The latter runs the risk of being more a measure of approval or disapproval of a particular government than a measure of the extent to which the policies put into practice are actually those supported by citizens.

By tapping citizen perception about whether politicians act in accordance with the direction indicated by the vote, whether for elections or referenda, our indicator measures the extent to which the politicians are doing what their voters want them to do, or, in other words, the extent to which policies correspond to citizen preferences.

Sovereignty

Two issues, in particular, are relevant in any effort to measure the extent to which public policies are under the effective control of elected officials in Latin America: economic policy and control of the military. Given the role that the weight of external debt has played in forcing countries to follow internal economic policies prescribed by international organizations controlled by lenders as a condition for refinancing debt and obtaining new capital, economic policy autonomy is an important indicator of effective sovereignty. At the same time, Latin America's long tradition of military intervention in politics makes it important to evaluate the degree of influence military leaders and institutions exercise over political decisions (Kooning and Kruijt 2003; Smith 2005: 101).

Economic Autonomy

This is measured by using as an indicator of economic dependence total external debt service as a percentage of exports for each country for 2005 (World Bank 2007). The greater the weight of debt on the economy, the more likely it is that a country will be obligated to follow economic policies dictated by its creditors or by international financial institutions. The indicator of economic autonomy provided in Table 2.6 is calculated by subtracting the level of economic dependence from 100, that is, 100 minus external debt service as a percentage of exports.

Autonomy Vis-à-Vis the Military

We use a qualitative indicator of civilian control over the military based on the typology provided by Smith, who classifies countries as follows: (1) *Military Control*, when there is a nominal civilian government, but political decisions are under military control; (2) *Military Tutelage*, marked by active military participation in the formation of public policies and military capacity to intervene in politics; (3) *Conditional Military Subordination*, when there is no direct intervention in public policy formation, but the military retains veto power and reserves the right to intervene in what they consider to be the national interest; and

(4) *Civilian Control,* which involves subordination of the military to civil control and oversight in all areas (Smith 2005: 101, 103). To make this scale equivalent to the others used here, we allocate scores to each category as follows: Military Control, 0 points; Military Tutelage, 33 points; Conditional Military Subordination, 66 points; and Civilian Control, 100 points. For the evaluation of each case, we follow Smith (2005: 103). The index of sovereignty in Table 2.6 is the average of the two component indicators of this dimension.

The Quality of Democracy Index: Correlations Among Dimensions and Comparison with Other Indices

Overall results are summarized in Table 2.7, which provides scores on each of the dimensions of quality of democracy, as well as the overall score for each country and the relative ranking of the countries, using data from 2005. We compare the results from our index for the quality of democracy with a consolidated score for each country derived from rankings on Freedom House scales of Political Rights and Civil Liberties. There is a high correlation between the two indices (Pearson's $r = -.895$, significant at 0.01) that affirms that despite differences in method and theoretical focus—one focused on quality of democracy, and the

Table 2.6 Quality of Sovereignty

Country	Civil Control of the Military	Economic Autonomy	Index of Sovereignty
Argentina	100	79	89.5
Bolivia	66	85	75.5
Brazil	66	55	60.5
Chile	66	85	75.5
Colombia	66	65	65.5
Costa Rica	100	94	97
Dominican Republic	66	93	79.5
El Salvador	33	91	62
Guatemala	33	94	63.5
Honduras	66	93	79.5
Mexico	100	83	91.5
Nicaragua	66	93	79.5
Panama	100	83	91.5
Paraguay	66	89	77.5
Peru	66	74	70
Uruguay	100	61	80.5
Venezuela	33	91	62
Average	70.2	82.8	76.5
Ecuador	33	69	51

other more generally concerned with liberty and rights——they tap an underlying common reality. Table 2.7 also presents the 2005 scores for Latin American countries in the Polity IV scale of autocracy-democracy, which runs from –10, full autocracy, to +10, full democracy. The correlation between this Polity IV index and our index of the quality of democracy is 0.686, which is also substantial (Polity IV 2009).[10]

Bivariate correlations (Pearson's r) among the dimensions range from 0.011 (Participation with Accountability) to 0.657 (Electoral Decision with Accountability). The only two-tailed statistically significant correlations, $p < 0.05$, are Electoral Decision with Accountability, 0.657, and Responsiveness with Accountability, 0.532, which are also the highest correlations between the dimensions of quality of democracy in our data. Only two of the correlations are negative, but they are not statistically significant: Responsiveness with Sovereignty at –0.113 and Participation with Sovereignty at –0.017. These findings indicate, as the literature expects (Diamond and Morlino 2005), that there is overlap among some of the dimensions of quality of democracy, but it does not reach the point at which one could assume that any two of them are measuring the same phenomena. We found statistically significant correlations only between accountability and both electoral decision and responsiveness. This is not unexpected, because to a certain extent the indicators of these three dimensions all deal with the electoral process, although from different perspectives. Nevertheless, it is also clear that the overlaps are low enough to leave us satisfied that each one of our dimensions is distinct from the others. The correlations that are significant are positive, suggesting that there is no trade-off between accountability and either electoral decision or responsiveness. Improvements in the former seem to be associated with enhancements in the latter. As stated above, there are two negative correlations, but they are not statistically significant. Therefore, we cannot conclude from our data that any trade-off occurs between sovereignty, on the one hand, and participation and responsiveness, on the other. Further research is needed into the correlation between the dimensions of quality of democracy before we can definitively discard that the improvement in one dimension comes at the cost of deterioration in others, but our data do not indicate that this is so.

In the recent literature on democracy, and specifically on democracy in Latin America, numerous distinct indices and databases have been created that provide a foundation for alternative views of the situation of democracy—and of governance and good government—in specific countries and, in some cases, over time. After an exhaustive and detailed comparison, Munck and Verkuilen conclude that "this review shows that no single index offers a satisfactory response to all three challenges of conceptualization, measurement and aggregation. Indeed even the strongest indices suffer from weaknesses of some importance" (2002: 28). They also note a high intercorrelation among almost all the indices, and wrote regarding the results of comparison tests: "For all the

Table 2.7 Index of Quality of Democracy, 2005

Country	Electoral Decision	Participation	Accountability	Responsiveness	Sovereignty	Quality of Democracy	Ranking on Quality of Democracy	Freedom House Political and Civil Liberties Combined Total	Polity IV Scale of Autocracy-Democracy
Uruguay	90.7	55.3	47.9	85	80.5	71.9	1	2	10
Costa Rica	87.0	44.5	37.3	51	97	63.4	2	2	10
Chile	88.3	45.1	42.3	65	75.5	63.2	3	2	9
Argentina	74.8	54.7	27.3	67	89.5	62.7	4	4	8
Mexico	71.8	50.1	27.1	66	91.5	61.3	5	4	8
Panama	75.7	45.2	32.4	61	91.5	61.2	6	3	9
Dom. Rep.	72.4	48.0	32.7	67	79.5	59.9	7	4	8
Brazil	81.4	56.8	23.9	67	60.5	57.9	8	4	8
Peru	78.8	56.5	21.8	56	70	56.6	9	5	9
Bolivia	73.9	52.2	21.8	50	75.5	54.7	10	6	8
Nicaragua	62.9	46.8	17.3	60	79.5	53.3	11	6	8
Colombia	61.2	46.8	30.7	62	65.5	53.2	12	6	7
Venezuela	50.7	54.2	24.5	74	62	53.1	13	8	6
El Salvador	67.8	41.2	29.3	64	62	52.9	14	5	7
Paraguay	57.9	44.2	28.1	57	77.5	52.9	14	6	8
Honduras	59.9	45.8	21.0	49	79.5	51.0	16	6	7
Guatemala	47.7	37.4	20.3	54	63.5	44.6	17	8	8
Average	70.8	48.5	28.6	62.1	76.5	57.3	—	4.8	8.1
Ecuador	62.2	49.4	18.3	48	51	45.8	—	6	6

differences in conceptualization, measurement, and aggregation, they seem to show that the reviewed indices are tapping into the same underlying realities" (Munck and Verkuilen 2002: 29). As noted, our index also shows a high correlation with the results of Freedom House, by far the most widely referenced of all the indices available, and to lesser but sizable extent with the Polity IV index.

If most available indices measure, in effect, the same phenomenon, what is the value of yet another index? Most of the indices and databases in the literature (including those reviewed by Munck and Verkuilen) are directed to very general issues about democracy, including broad distinctions between democracy and dictatorship, or the extent to which a given case meets a minimal level of requisites of democracy. But as a rule they do not focus specifically on the quality of the political processes of democracies. For example, the variables examined by Munck and Verkuilen in their review of indices of democracy include only two of our five dimensions; those two are participation and electoral decision (2002).

The index of quality of democracy presented here is not about democracy in general, but, rather, is centered on political processes and is based on concepts directed specifically at the quality of democracy. For this reason, it moves debates beyond simple binary choices, for example, democracy vs. dictatorship, liberal democracies vs. illiberal democracies, to a more nuanced understanding of the multidimensional character of democracies. Democracies can clearly take hold first in some dimensions—such as electoral choice or voting opportunities—creating opportunities and institutional interests that can be extended and expanded in the future. Because we focus directly on issues of the quality of democracy, the index can build on closer links to social science theories about democracy.

With respect to indices that address mainly whether countries are democratic or authoritarian, such as the Polity IV scale, or that are not specifically made to measure the quality of democracy, such as the Index of Freedom by Freedom House, if we consider the overall rankings of Latin American countries in Table 2.7, an index like the one presented has the advantages of being more precise in the classification of the countries and of establishing differences between them more clearly.

The quality of democracy index, which provides the basis for the analysis of this volume, establishes clear distinctions among countries that Freedom House and Polity IV score equally, which makes it possible to evaluate the similarities and differences among the countries. It also makes possible a detailed specification of variation in elements of the quality of democracy *within* countries. Freedom House has Uruguay, Chile, and Costa Rica tied for top rank in quality of democracy. Polity IV has Uruguay and Costa Rica tied, with Chile one point behind. But although these three cases clearly demonstrate a higher quality of democracy than the rest of the region, measured on our index notable differences emerge among them, with Uruguay having a level of democratic quality superior to the other two. The distance between Uruguay at a ranking of 71.9 and Costa Rica at 63.4 is greater than the difference between the second and the ninth ranked case, which is Peru at 56.6.

The difference in quality of democracy between Uruguay, on the one hand, and Costa Rica and Chile, on the other, rests on the fact that Uruguay outranks the other two on four of the five dimensions, and does so by differences of 10 points or more on participation, accountability, and responsiveness. Uruguay also stands out in terms of the cognitive resources of its population, with a level of secondary school enrollment that is basically universal, and the highest level of electoral participation in the entire region, easily outstripping Chile and Costa Rica, which it also outranks in opportunities to vote given the holding of a national referendum in the period under study. This helps Uruguay compensate for the fact that its level of representativity is lower than Costa Rica's, given that nation's implementation of gender quotas for candidacies. Uruguay also has the highest overall accountability score in Latin America, while ranking second on horizontal accountability—surpassed only by Chile—and ranks highest in vertical accountability. This is an item in which Uruguay easily outranks the rest of the region. Uruguay also outranks all other countries in the region on responsiveness, affirming the high confidence its citizens have in the efficacy of their votes in shaping the politics of their country.

Below the top level, our rank ordering also differs from the one that Freedom House provides, with differences particularly evident for Panama, El Salvador, and Venezuela. According to Freedom House, Panama outranks both Argentina and Mexico, but working with specifically political measures, our index ranks it slightly lower. Although the three countries look more or less the same in overall terms, on closer inspection, Argentina and Mexico easily outscore Panama on opportunities to vote and representativity. The results on electoral decision, as shown in Table 2.1, reveal with particular clarity the advantage of the indicators that our index adds to Freedom House. As measured only by the items Freedom House uses, which are political rights and freedom of information, Panama outranks the other two countries, but when an important and theoretically relevant dimension like cognitive resources is added, Argentina and Mexico far outrank Panama; thus the final result is more balanced and realistic.

The preceding discussion shows that the index of quality of democracy presented here does not merely provide a global comparison among countries, but also offers greater depth and specificity, with data on the strengths and the weaknesses of each country on each dimension of analysis, along with its component elements. Clearly, countries that regularly top the rankings of democracies may lag in some significant areas and almost all countries need to strengthen accountability. This opens the way to a more nuanced understanding of areas where institutional reform is needed and possible. Within a group of countries that shares as many broad characteristics as Latin America, a nuanced analysis of this kind helps isolate the most and the least successful aspects on each dimension, and opens possibilities for research on likely and probable sequences of reform.

Notes

1. A discussion of the methodology used by Freedom House can be found at http://www.freedomhouse.org/template.cfm?page=35&year=2006.

2. We follow here the decision taken by Dahl when constructing a scale of Opportunities for Political Opposition. Dahl argued: "Since there was no a priori or theoretical reason for weighting the variables unequally or assigning a greater weight to one category or another, the variables were all handled the same way" (Dahl 1971: 237). Altman and Pérez-Liñán also give the same weight to their dimensions of quality of democracy and take an average of them for their index (2002).

3. Cf. Freedom House, which uses a scale from 1, maximum democratic political rights, to 7, absence of democratic political rights. To translate this into a scale comparable to the others, we convert this to 0–100 using the following procedure: the Freedom House scale is inverted, so that the 7 becomes 1, 6 becomes 2, etc. Then we subtract 1 from each score, so that the resulting scale goes from 0 to 6; then this scale is transformed proportionally to a scale from 0 to 100.

4. Http://www.freedomhouse.org/template.cfm?page=271&year=2006.

5. Http://stats.uis.unesco.org/unesco/tableviewer/document.aspx?ReportId=143.

6. Opportunities to vote are taken as follows: Argentina, provincial and municipal elections, local elections in some provinces (e.g., school boards in Buenos Aires), and primaries. Bolivia, municipal elections, voting for departmental prefects, and the 2004 referendum on energy policy. Brazil, regional and municipal elections, the 2005 referendum on firearms sales, primaries. Chile, municipal elections, primaries. Colombia, departmental and municipal elections, the 2003 referendum on institutional reforms. Costa Rica, municipal and primary elections. Dominican Republic, municipal and primary elections. El Salvador, municipal and primary elections. Guatemala, municipal and primary elections. Honduras, municipal and primary elections. Mexico, state, municipal, and primary elections. Nicaragua, municipal and other elections; according to Zovatto and Freidenberg (2006: 213) the "popular consultations" on the Sandinista National Liberation Front (FSLN) candidacies in 2001 were subject to ratification by the party's national leadership, which modified some results such as the vice presidential candidacy, and for this reason they are not properly considered to be primary elections. Panama, municipal and primary elections. Paraguay, departmental, municipal, and primary elections. Peru, regional, municipal, and primary elections, the 2005 subnational referenda on constitution of regions, the 2004 and 2005 municipal and regional recall votes, elections for local coordinating councils. Uruguay, municipal and primary elections, the 2003 national referendum on the autonomous agency for combustibles and its possible links to private enterprise. Venezuela, municipal and regional elections, the 2004 presidential recall, elections for parish boards (*juntas parroquiales*). Ecuador, provincial and municipal elections, elections for parish boards.

7. Data on representation by gender in national parliaments are taken from the Inter-Parliamentary Union, "Women in National Parliaments," 2006, http://www.ipu.org/wmn-e/classif.htm; updated through January 31, 2006. Population data are from Economic Commission for Latin America and the Caribbean (ECLAC), 2005, http://www

.eclac.cl/cgi-bin/getProd.asp?xml=/publicaciones/xml/1/21231/P21231.xml&xsl=/
deype/tpl-i/p9f.xsl&base=/tpl-i/top-bottom.xsl.

8. Http://www.transparency.org/policy_and_research/surveys_indices/cpi/2005.

9. The question used is: "In general terms, do you believe that elections in this country are clean or are they fraudulent?"

10. Significant at 0.01.

3

Chile: A Model Case?

Leticia M. Ruiz Rodríguez

SINCE ITS TRANSITION TO DEMOCRACY IN 1989, THE CHILEAN political system has shown all the signs of a rapid and successful democratic recovery. The improvement in civil-military relations, the slow but sure treatment of human rights violations, and the 1980 reform of the Constitution are just some examples of democratic consolidation. Nevertheless, there is no shortage of voices proposing that these conclusions should be reviewed and reappraised, together with other elements, to obtain a comprehensive diagnosis of the overall situation of democracy in Chile. This is the context of this study, which aims to analyze the quality of democracy in present-day Chile. It is based on the theoretical model proposed by Levine and Molina, in which the measurement of democracy centers more on processes than on the outcomes they generate (2007a, this volume Chapter 2).

According to Levine and Molina the highest quality of democracy in Latin America is to be found in Chile and Uruguay (2007a, and this volume Chapter 2). In this chapter, I argue that in the case of Chile, the quality of democracy would be even better if certain reforms were carried out, and that the impediments to this are mostly institutional. Despite their important role, not all institutions have been given the attention in academic and political circles that is in keeping with their impact on the quality of Chilean democracy. While it is true that any institutional reforms would require a concerted and coordinated effort on the part of the political elite, their impact on the quality of democracy would be felt in a relatively short space of time. They include recognizing the vote of Chileans living abroad, the introduction of changes in the voter registration system, appointments to regional authorities by universal suffrage, and modification of the electoral formula. Another element that has a negative effect on democracy, related more to the options of the political elite than to institutions, is the redistribution of income. Dealing with this problem has traditionally proved to be more difficult because of its multicausal nature, although this does not preclude a solution. It will be broached here by looking at how the decisions of democratic governments have perpetuated, and even compounded, such inequality, and how the lack of receptivity to popular demand undermines the quality of Chilean democracy. At the same time, other elements will be analyzed, such as the present state of civil-military relations and the ideological concentration of the media, which, although still significant, does not have the same impact on Chilean democracy in the twenty-first century.

The sections that follow will examine the five core elements at play in the politics of a democratic regime: electoral decision, participation, accountability, response to popular will, and sovereignty. The aim is to assess in which of these Chile emerges as a democratic political system, and in which its procedures and institutions are democratically deficient. The concluding section will assess the prospects for change in the elements affecting the quality of democracy in Chile. It will be argued that some of the handicaps affecting Chilean democracy are already undergoing change, but that others show no sign of being tackled in the near future.

Electoral Decision

The 1988 Referendum reopened the possibility for Chileans to express themselves by ballot. Since that time, a total of twenty-two electoral contests have taken place (twenty-five if three second rounds are included).[1] It can safely be said that elections in Chile have more than surpassed the minimum threshold for qualifying as democratic, with the exception of the 1988 referendum marking the beginning of the transition, in which competition between political options was not evenly matched.[2] Nevertheless, there are four limiting factors that prevent Chilean elections from being of a higher quality: (1) the right to vote for Chileans living abroad, (2) the fact that important regional government authorities are not democratically elected, (3) equality of party access to electoral competition, and (4) the restrictions on freedom of the press. Each of these is discussed in more detail below.

The first limit is nonrecognition of the right to vote of Chilean nationals living abroad. This situation puts restrictions on the meaning of the universal suffrage that Chile enjoys today, as it means that election results are not as representative as they could be.[3] It is one of the reforms promised by Michelle Bachelet, president from 2006 to 2010, in her electoral campaign of 2005. Nevertheless, there is marked reluctance on the part of right-wing parties to introduce these changes, and neither has the Concertación (Concert of Parties for Democracy, a center-left coalition that ruled the country from 1990 to 2010) encouraged any speeding up of the legislative agenda on this point. As a result, the Chamber of Deputies and the Senate were still debating this reform in the final stages of the Bachelet mandate (elections took place in December 2009 and

January 2010, and the presidency was won by Sebastián Piñera, the opposition candidate of the Coalition for Change [Coalición por el Cambio, the coalition of right-wing parties that was previously called Alliance for Chile, Alianza por Chile, and renamed for the 2009 presidential elections]). Many Chileans currently living abroad went into exile prior to or during the authoritarian Pinochet regime, or else they are the children of exiles.[4] Their votes would probably be of no benefit to right-wing forces, which for a time were identified with Pinochet's legacy, the theory being that most of these votes would be cast for parties of the center and the left, although no rigorous systematic studies have been done that might confirm this hypothesis. Opposition to change by right-wing parties was made evident in the Congress of Deputies in May 2007, when the bill to amend this point was rejected.[5]

The second limit is related to the fact that important regional government authorities are not democratically elected. As part of the unfinished process of decentralization that is slowly taking place in Chile, an amendment to the regulations introduced in the Law of Municipalities, No. 18.695, has given Chileans more scope for participation in elections for local authorities. The 2004 elections were the first to be held under the new electoral system, in which mayors and councilors were elected separately. In the three local elections held prior to that, only councilors were elected.[6] Mayors are now elected by a majority vote system, and councilors by a proportional system. Nevertheless, this process of decentralization coexists with appointments to regional office designated by central government, which limits the scope of electoral decisions. The highest regional authority is the regional governor. The regional governors are appointed by the president of the Republic, which means that ordinary citizens are unable to express any sort of preference. Given the importance of the role of these governors, it would be reasonable to expect changes in the way they are elected. Only in this way can regional governors counterbalance any actions on the part of the presidency of the Republic that might jeopardize the interests of the regions that the governors serve; at the same time, their own actions can be controlled by the citizens. In the immediate future, this change is not among the priorities of Piñera's government. In addition, this reform is feared by senators who see governors as potential political contenders in their districts, who would be reinforced if they were to become democratically elected.[7]

Until 2009, there was a similar situation regarding the CORES (regional councils), whose members were elected by the councilors of each province, who made up a regional *electoral college*. In this case, there was indirect suffrage, since the electors chose the councilors, who then voted for the CORES. Following a debate in the Senate, Law 20.334 was passed in 2009. This modified Law 19.175 on regional government and administration and introduced direct suffrage for the CORES. Nevertheless, this specific reform does not include the election of regional governors.

The third consideration regarding electoral decision mechanisms concerns equality of party access to electoral competition. There is a limited offer of political parties in Chile. Few parties put candidates up for elections, and there is little variation from one election to the next. Although independent candidacies are permitted, the possibilities of winning are low unless one is put up for election under a major political party label. The combination of small-sized districts and a high threshold for representation encourages the joining of forces. Parties compete in coalitions to reap maximum benefit from the number of seats gained. A multiparty system, such as Chile's, with support spread over a very broad spectrum and low-magnitude (two-seat) districts, means that it is only worthwhile for a political party to compete if it can rally enough support. In fact, since the first elections, congressional representation has been practically limited to parties that come under the umbrella of the Coalición por el Cambio or the Concertación. This is why only a few independent candidates and political parties not belonging to a coalition have achieved a seat without being launched as part of a political pact. In the 1997 elections, two seats were obtained by the Progressive Center Union Party (Partido de Unión de Centro Progresista) and one by the Party of the South (Partido del Sur). In the 2005 elections, the Regionalist Action Party (Partido de Acción Regionalista) obtained one seat.[8]

Other electoral issues needing attention are the question of equal conditions for parties competing in Chilean elections and the suspicions that have arisen with respect to transparency in campaign financing. Law 19.884 on Transparency, Limits and Control of Electoral Expenses, passed in 2003 and amended in 2004, establishes that approximately 30 percent of campaign financing should derive from public sources, with the specific amount based on calculations of votes obtained in the previous election of the same type.[9] The rest of the money should come from the party's own contributions and those of third parties, which may be public or private, depending on the total donated. Private contributions are controlled by the Electoral Service (Servicio Electoral) and are distributed to candidates and parties without the source being disclosed. Such private campaign financing may account for as much as 20 percent of the total.[10] In the year previous to the 2009 election, the Concertación, which had governed since the transition to democracy, was at the center of a storm because of its alleged use of public funds beyond the amount it is entitled to for financing its parties and electoral campaigns. Two cases debated in public were ChileSports (Chiledeportes) and the General Employment Plans (Planes Generales de Empleo), examples that reflect the lack of transparency in the practices of the coalition in power.[11] Added to this are declarations from different leaders on a possible ideology of corruption within the Concertación, which Bachelet denied.[12] Such an ideology appears to attempt to justify the use of public funds for financing the center-left coalition to counterbalance the fact that the alliance of the right has private sector resources at its disposal for party and campaign funding. This will probably be met with a judicial response, which shows that accountability between powers does exist and that the judiciary works efficiently in cases where irregularities have been found. Therefore, although the electors' trust in electoral processes is undermined, the effects of this are ameliorated because the system is proving itself capable of correcting its own deficiencies through legal action, at the same time as laws regulating electoral campaigns and party financing are gradually being improved.

The fourth factor that limits the quality of elections in Chile involves the media. Since the return to democracy, there have been considerable restrictions on freedom of the press. This is most marked in the written press, where the market is monopolized by two major groups, El Mercurio and Copesa. As Sunkel and Geoffroy point out, this concentration is accompanied by an ideological monopoly that probably has no parallel in Latin America (2001). A notable consequence respecting the quality of democracy is that the media is perceived as representing big business and people with certain prestige. Ordinary citizens do not consider the media to be a mechanism for transmitting and representing their own interests. The authors also point out that no action has been taken by the state to rein in this situation, and that the ideological monopoly seems to be gradually contaminating radio and television.

Given this situation, it might seem that informed decisions among the Chilean electorate were not very frequent. Nevertheless, if electoral results are anything to go by, for many Chileans, the main effect of this ideological monopoly in the media industry has more to do with disenchantment and disaffection with the system than with election results. Despite a press bias in its favor and notable performances in elections, until its victory in the 2009 election, the right did not defeat the center-left coalition in any of the presidential elections after 1990. Until now, the effects of this monopoly have been less direct and more diffuse than the other three aspects described above, which is why this study argues that the political elites must give priority to reaching agreement about voting rights for residents abroad, election to regional posts by popular vote, and equal access to electoral competition for all parties. Nevertheless, the fact that the Chilevision Television Channel is owned by the winner of the 2009 presidential election, Sebastián Piñera, should mean that greater attention is paid to ideological concentration in the media in future analyses of democratic performance and quality. Along these lines, there are some who already acknowledge that ideological concentration in the media is having a growing impact on the political game. The lead-up to the campaign for the 2009 presidential elections provided one of the best examples of this tendency when it was publicized in different media by specialists of the stature of Carlos Hunneus that the media clout of the candidacy of Marco Enriquez Ominami, former member of the Socialist Party (Partido Socialista; PS), now independent, in the presidential elections formed part of a right-wing strategy to take away votes from the progovernment candidacy of the Concertación, headed by ex-president Frei.

Along with these limitations are two aspects of the electoral dimension in which Chile has improved the quality of its democracy. This has been possible due to a package of constitutional reforms in 1980 that were introduced toward the end of the government of President Lagos in mid-2005. In the first place, the elimination of designated senators means that all senators currently in the upper house have been elected exclusively by means of elections, thus increasing control over this body of representatives.[13] Second, in the 2005 reforms the presidential term was reduced from five to four years, with no possibility of immediate reelection.[14] As a consequence, presidential and congressional elections now take place concurrently, a more convenient solution that avoids constant mobilization of the people in successive calls for different types of elections. This measure also has an impact on the quality of democracy. According to the proposal of Levine and Molina, quality is enhanced when the mandate is reduced; since the government is controlled by popular vote, the shorter the mandate, the greater the accountability (2007a). Nevertheless, despite this positive reading, in Chile the measure has originated a debate on the feasibility of implementing long-term policies in such short periods of time. For example, policies involving the redistribution of income need long-term planning, although there has been little change of direction by the present government in economic matters, something that will be considered again later since it affects the degree of democracy. At the same time, the impossibility of reelection has given rise to a race that begins practically the day after elections to define those in each electoral pact who will be the contenders for the presidency in the next elections. There have been times when a mandate is about to expire that this has affected governability, because of the feeling of temporariness that prevails in the perception of the existing government.

Participation

There are two aspects of participation in Chile that limit the quality of democracy: the electoral arena and the party arena. Although participation in the electoral arena is a concern that is repeatedly voiced, it has an apparently easier solution, since to a large extent it is embodied in institutional reforms. As a result, it will probably undergo more rapid changes than participation in the party arena.

Electoral abstention in the last elections was 13.11 percent based on the people registered to vote. This was higher than in 1999, when it was 10.05 percent, and considerably higher than 1993, which was 5.27 percent. Nevertheless, various factors must be taken into account before these apparently low levels of participation are evaluated.

The first factor has to do with traditional levels of participation in Chilean elections. Chile is usually classed as a country with a strong tradition of participation and, when analyzed diachronically, figures show that this has fallen off considerably. Nevertheless, this argument does not take into consideration the fact that between 1970 and 2010, there has been a variation in institutional requirements for the right to vote, and that as a consequence any comparability of tendencies is not methodologically accurate. The 1973 coup interrupted a process that only some years previously had seen the first elections held under universal suffrage and the promise of a sequence of electoral processes of higher quality. Prior to that, the number of people with the right to vote had been extended several times since the beginning of the Republic. A large part of the population had been excluded by property rights until 1874, when this requirement was abolished and the right to vote was extended to all males over the age of twenty-five who could read and write. As for women, they were able to take part in presidential elections for the first time in 1952 and in municipal elections some years earlier. The illiterate population was finally included in 1970, at the same time that the voting age was lowered to eighteen. Although these were the first elections held under universal suffrage as it is understood today, many who previously had been deprived of the vote did not exercise their rights because they had not registered on the voter registration lists.[15] It was not until the eve of the coup that a system of universal suffrage in the strictest sense was in place. It is therefore impossible to compare participation levels prior to Pinochet's coup with those registered in the period that followed. Even so, certain features of the political culture of Chile have been identified by authors, who have analyzed patterns of participation prior to 1973 in detail. For example, Navia maintains that levels of participation have not fallen when looked at from a historical perspective, that is, beyond the exceptionally high level of participation in the first elections held in the democracy (2004).

A second note of caution against an alarmist interpretation of electoral participation levels relates to the institutional framework in place in 2005. Apart from the high number of calls to election that have provoked a sense of surfeit in the electorate, especially when elections for deputies and senators do not coincide with presidential elections, the compulsory voting system is another highly significant factor. This system, regulated by the 1980 Constitution, is combined with a voluntary registration mechanism in such a way that the citizen who does not register is not obliged to vote, but, once registered, voting becomes a permanent obligation. Therefore, in any analysis of electoral participation, the number of registered voters should be taken into consideration. If this type of de facto abstention were taken into account, the levels of participation in relation to the population of voting age as a whole would be higher. For example, in 2005 only 78.71 percent of potential voters were registered.[16] This meant that when both sets of data were taken into account, only 69.15 percent of the potential electorate took part in the last elections.[17] It could therefore be argued that de facto abstention may be high, but that institutional conditions are not conducive to it being any lower.

If we analyze political actions to reduce the disincentives to participation generated by the institutional framework, two recently implemented strategies stand out. In the first place, in view of the aging of registered voters, a campaign has been initiated to encourage young people to register on voter registration lists under the slogan "I have power, I vote." Second, there is a proposal to introduce automatic registration and voluntary voting. This reform, discussed but not passed into law by the previous Congress (2006–2010), would make it easier to vote, especially for younger people, but it is not at all clear what effect it would have on the degree of abstention. While automatic registration would increase participation, making voting voluntary could have the opposite effect in that currently registered citizens would be freed from the obligation to vote. Viewed from the perspective of quality of democracy as a procedure, quality would be enhanced with the introduction of automatic voter registration. Viewed in terms of results, however, a downward trend in levels of participation as a consequence of voluntary voting could well diminish the quality of democracy in Chile. See Table 3.1 for levels of participation.

Together with these considerations on the number of people participating, it is necessary to reflect on the quality of participation. In the electoral arena quality participation is that which does not translate into too much of a distortion of the will of the electorate and includes all ideologies in proportion to their strength in society and decisionmaking bodies. Therefore, another aspect included in Levine and Molina's concept of participation is representativity of electoral results (2007a).

In the case of Chile, the electoral formula works against a proportional translation of votes into positions of power. The main elements of the presidential elections are:

- A second round is held when none of the competing candidates obtains more than 50 percent of the votes. This reform was introduced in the 1980 Constitution.
- The term is for four years. This mandate reduction was introduced as part of the package of reforms to the 1980 Constitution passed in 2005.
- There is no immediate reelection.

The main elements for election of deputies are:

- There are 60 binominal districts, resulting in 120 deputies.
- Each list (the slate of candidates nominated by a party or a coalition) for each specific pact, party, or coalition contains two names from which the voter elects only one.
- The distribution formula is a corrected majority formula: the plurality party wins both seats if it doubles the vote of the runner-up; otherwise

Table 3.1   Levels of Participation in Chile, 1989–2005

Year and Type of Election	Population Registered to Vote	Valid Votes	Percentage Participation of Registered Population
1989 P	7,557,537	6,979,859	92.36
1989 D	7,557,537	6,797,122	89.94
1989 S	7,557,537	6,800,410	89.98
1992 M	7,840,008	6,410,906	81.77
1993 P	8,085,439	6,968,950	86.19
1993 D	8,085,439	6,738,859	83.35
1993 S	8,085,439	1,874,127	a
1996 M	8,073,368	6,301,298	78.05
1997 D	8,069,624	5,795,773	71.82
1997 S	8,069,624	4,239,366	a
1999 P 1st round	8,084,476	7,055,128	87.27
1999 P 2nd round	8,084,476	7,178,727	88.74
2000 M	8,089,363	6,515,574	80.54
2001 D	8,075,446	6,144,003	76.08
2001 S	8,075,446	1,732,415	a
2004 M councilors	8,012,065	6,123,375	78.76
2004 M mayors	8,012,065	6,310,206	76.43
2005 P 1st round	8,220,897	6,942,041	84.44
2005 P 2nd round	8,220,897	6,959,413	86.07
2005 D	8,220,897	6,601,811	80.31
2005 S	8,220,897	4,770,981	a

Notes: P = President; D = Deputy; S = Senator; M = Municipal.

a. The participation percentages for elections of senators are not given because officially only half the population is called to vote in each election since only one-half the Senate is renewed at any one time.

one seat goes to the party with the most votes, and the other seat is gained by the runner-up.

- There is a high electoral threshold; that is, for the same list—whether pact, coalition, or party—to obtain both seats in a district, it has to double the votes gained by the list in second place. Otherwise, the second seat goes to the second most-voted list.
- The elections for all deputies are every four years.
- There can be immediate and indefinite reelection.
- The elections are held at the same time as elections for senators.

The elements for election of senators include:

- There are nineteen binominal districts resulting in thirty-eight senators.

- There is the same distribution formula and barrier as in elections for deputies.
- Senators are elected for an eight-year term.
- One half are voted on every four years.
- There is immediate and indefinite reelection.
- The senators for life and designated senators have been abolished as part of the package of reforms to the 1980 Constitution passed in 2005.

Under the binominal electoral system, which has been in place since 1989, only rarely has a pact doubled and gained both constituency seats. On the other hand, there have been occasions when a list has obtained a very high percentage of votes (though less than 66.7 percent), and the list next in line, with a much lower electoral performance, has achieved identical congressional representation (one deputy for each list). It is difficult for those with the most votes to obtain a sufficient margin to win two seats, while the one with the second most votes secures a seat practically automatically.[18] This is how the forces of the right were able to artificially secure at least one seat in each district, with much less support at the time. It can be demonstrated empirically that, although both coalitions are overrepresented under this system, as a report by FLACSO shows,[19] the coalition that has benefited the most is the Alianza (now Coalición por el Cambio), especially with regard to the election of senators, where the Concertación is overrepresented by an average of 0.76 percent and the Alianza by an average of 8.58 percent (see FLACSO 2006: 12 and 13). Furthermore, the report continues, the Alianza is the coalition that loses the fewest seats when its volume of votes drops off and gains the most seats when it rises. By parties, the one most favored by this system in the last elections was the Independent Democratic Union (Unión Democrática Independiente; UDI) and the worst affected was the Christian Democratic Party (Partido Demócrata Cristiano; PDC). With 22 percent of the vote, the UDI achieved thirty-four deputies, which was 28.33 percent of the seats; the DC achieved twenty-one deputies, with 20.78 percent of the vote representing 17.5 percent of the seats.

Like the electoral formula, constituency design has also contributed to distortion. Under the present system, rural areas are overrepresented with respect to urban centers, which generally have more progressive tendencies. A good example is that of District 59 in the Ninth Region: its population is eight times lower than District 29 in the Metropolitan Region, yet both have the same number of representatives (Boeninger Commission 2006). As well as benefiting from conservative forces, configuration of the map of constituencies creates a fourth effect in that it generates deep inequality in the vote between different geographical areas of the country.[20]

In this situation, neither the electoral formula nor the distribution of districts will be modified in the short term. The Boeninger Report, developed during Bachelet's presidency, brought together extracongressional experts, deputies, and consultants to address the effects of the electoral system. Since then, a project has been initiated aimed at constitutional reform of the electoral system, which is in progress as of 2010.

Another notable effect of the electoral system on representativity of results is the high percentage of votes without congressional representation. In the 2005 congressional elections, almost 14 percent of the votes only gained one deputy, and most of them were to parties with no seats; see Table 3.2. Such a system of exclusion is very inaccurate when it comes to translating votes into seats. As a result, the institutions constituted by it, that is, the Chamber of Deputies and Chamber of Senators, are hardly representative, and this becomes an impediment for reflecting the country's ideological diversity. Particularly noticeable was the absence in the 2006–2010 Congress of any representation of the Communist Party of Chile (Partido Comunista de Chile; PCCh). Despite being an institutionalized party that periodically stands for election and with support that never falls below 5 percent, up to 2009 it was deprived of congressional representation since the return to democracy by the new electoral system, whereas in the past it was a prominent player in Chilean party politics.

As was pointed out at the beginning of this section, the shortfall in the quality of participation is not confined to the electoral arena. Participation at party levels is considered by some to be a second crisis of participation. There is a marked elitism present in the internal workings of political parties, which limits the quality of participation by citizens. As Valenzuela and Dammert assert, to have a more open system, it is not enough to reform the electoral system; it is up to the parties to renew themselves and foster participation (2006). The maximum expression of this lack of transparency with respect to citizens' participation is the candidate selection procedure, which is tightly controlled by the party machinery. This centrality of party leadership with respect to choosing candidates gives rise to a system that distances itself from the electorate in that it is hierarchical, exclusive, and hardly democratic. At present, only the Party for Democracy (Partido Por la Democracia; PPD) elects its candidates by means of relatively competitive internal elections. Although electoral polls are increasingly used to choose candidates in the constituencies, the whole process is conditioned by the decision as to which party the candidate should belong to. It often happens that the candidate chosen is not the one who enjoys the most popular support, but rather is the one from the party with the quota in that particular district.[21] The maximum expression of manipulation by the parties is when there is only one candidate on the list.[22] At the same time, these dynamics are not conducive to renewal of the elites. The arrival of new names is practically impossible in a system where options are conditioned by agreements within the coalition and the accompanying estimates of survival. This has raised the level of mistrust toward the parties, which is presently high and increasing (Angell 2006).

The driving force behind this manipulation is the existence of coalitions. In each district, the electoral lists have two names each for every party or coalition

Table 3.2 Electoral Performance of Parties with Independent and Noncoalition Candidates in Deputy Elections, 1989–2006

Parties	1989		1993		1997		2001		2005	
	% Votes	Seats	% Votes	Seats	% Votes	Seats	% Votes	Seats	% Votes	Seats
Independents, Concertación	9.12	9	0.74	1	0.81	0	2.20	3	2.00	0
Others, Concertación	0.99	1	0.79	0	0	0	0.06	0	0	0
Independents, Alianza	6.09	8	4.81	4	4.67	6	5.32	8	2.23	0
Others, Alianza	0	0	3.45	2	0	0	0	0	0	0
Other political parties	12.43	2	6.13	0	12.90	3	6.33	0	8.55	1
Independents not in the Pact	1.88	1	0.11	0	0.69	2	1.42	1	0.94	0
Total	30.51	21	16.03	7	19.07	11	15.33	12	13.72	1

Source: Author's own based on data from the Interior Ministry. I am indebted to Rodrigo Bugueño and Mauricio Morales who kindly provided the data.
Notes: "Independents" are those candidates who do not take part in coalitions or political parties but who may later join a coalition; "Others" are members of minority parties in the coalitions.

of parties;[23] thus, belonging to a coalition means there is an automatic reduction in the number of candidates a party could potentially field. Parties have to share the total number of candidacies (120 deputies and 38 senators) with the rest of their colleagues in the coalition. This is particularly difficult in the case of the Concertación, which comprises five political parties. The decision as to which party will stand in which district is a task that involves a considerable amount of political engineering and electoral calculations. To date, the PDC, a party within the Concertación, has fielded sixty candidates for deputy in each of the sixty districts, and the rest of the parties, forming the progressive subpact, have shared the sixty remaining places based on the electoral weight of each party in previous elections. The Coalición por el Cambio currently allocates deputies for each constituency equally between the National Renovation (Renovación Nacional; RN) and UDI, although in the first two congressional elections it was the RN that fielded a greater number of candidates. Allocation was subsequently modified as the UDI gradually acquired greater electoral clout.[24]

The shortfalls outlined so far relate to conventional participation. With respect to the issue of parties, it seems there is a long way to go in the development of more democratic practices. For the time being, parties share the same diagnosis as conventional participation, but are still seeking solutions to their poor democratic performances. Given this situation, changes to the electoral formula and the system of compulsory voting would raise the quality of electoral participation. While these solutions seem to be more likely, a formula has yet to be found.

It is worth mentioning that, apart from the conventional forms of participation, there was a series of initiatives introduced in 2006 that was intended to broaden the concept and context of participation beyond electoral and party considerations. In September 2006, Bachelet's government presented a citizens' Proparticipation Agenda, embodying four core issues: (1) the citizen's right to information, (2) citizen participation in public administration, (3) nondiscrimination and multiculturality, and (4) the empowerment of associations. A different plan of action was envisaged for each of these aspects, and in all of them the Internet was designed to play a key role in the exchange of ideas, particularly for consultation and communication of information. It is too early to assess this initiative, and it is not a substitute for electoral and party reform. Nevertheless, the creation of citizens' forums already forms part of the action plans of progressive governments in the region, although the proposals they put forward are never binding and, in many cases, concern matters that are marginal to national politics. Pilot programs operating along these lines that help to propagate the concept of participation include the Participatory Budgets (Presupuestos Participativos), developed in the Cerro Navia municipality. In the case of Chile, however, it is not clear that the spread of this concept reduces the level of dissatisfaction with the way conventional participation works, judging from public opinion. In fact, criticism has been voiced concerning the impact of this kind of refocusing of participation without, at the same time, reviewing other formal petitions for participation appropriate to a representative democracy. Valenzuela and Dammert argue that no reform involving participation will be complete until legislative powers and prerogatives have been restored (2006). They go on to say that the place for seriously debating public policies on key issues is not a collection of ad hoc citizens' commissions that report to a dominant executive power, but the corridors of the Chamber of Deputies or public hearings.

Responsiveness

In Chile the democratic government agenda has been dominated by two issues that have alternated in importance throughout the sixteen years of democracy. As far as response to the popular will is concerned, these have been treated with different degrees of success.

The first concern is the issue of human rights. This was a core issue particularly during the Aylwin administration when, within the possibilities of the context, it obtained a response that has subsequently followed its own path in the courts as a gradual strategy. As Valenzuela points out, in Chile the strategy to recover the capacity of the law to resolve cases has been slow but systematic (2006). Moreover, it has not reduced the issue of human rights to the courts; rather, each government has tackled different issues: judicial renewal, the reconstruction of memory, victim compensation, and civil control over the military. In their dealings with these matters, successive governments have found solutions that respond to the demands of society, taking into consideration the context that generated them and the government's ever-increasing margins for maneuvering, which have made a more vigorous treatment of these issues possible.

The second issue dominating the agenda of Chile's democratic government concerns the economic model, which occupies center stage in the citizens' debate. Responses from political parties are not diametrically different; they all move within a certain neoliberal orthodoxy, with adjustments that are appropriate to each case. Aylwin, Frei, and Lagos all continued the neoliberal politics that had been established and maintained by Pinochet. These brought about considerable economic growth, but this has not been accompanied by income redistribution. In the report on human development drawn up by the United Nations Development Program (UNDP) for the year 2008, Chile was in second place in the Latin American region.[25] Nevertheless, it continues to be a country with great disparities in its distribution of wealth.

Some programs have made adjustments to the neoliberal model. The Plan AUGE for the reform of public health services is an example. This was later replicated in the private sector by the Isapres de Salud system, the Chile Solidario program, and the Chile Crece Contigo (Chile Grows with You) program, a system of comprehensive social protection for children. Regulations on labor, the environment, and consumer rights have also been introduced that have softened the hard line in economic affairs that was a legacy of the dictatorship. In this regard, however, it could be said that Concertación governments have been less receptive to citizens' demands than might have been expected. Furthermore, no formula has yet been found that will make the Chilean economic model more people-oriented or eradicate poverty and social inequality. Consequently, the most urgent social agenda, which can no longer be delayed, is the implementation of redistribution policies.

Other important issues that persist from the past are reforms to the social security system, which came into force with Law 20.255 on March 17, 2008, and to the educational and health systems. Until now, despite their importance, programs involving reform seem to have included large doses of continuism. The shorter presidential mandate of four years has been considered, perhaps exaggeratedly so, as too short a period to bring about any substantial changes. This reinforces the argument that it is unlikely that there will be a Bachelet era, in the sense of a legacy characterized by very different public policies. The idea of a new style of government, which is what brought Bachelet to power, proved to be only partially true because the driving force behind citizen participation was not given the prominence, nor did it yield the returns that were expected. Much more serious was the fact that this progressive aesthetic was not accompanied by progressive policies. Failures in the neoliberal economic model that Pinochet imposed threaten to spawn a new form of government with respect to content. One such failure became evident when riots by high school students (the so-called Penguin Revolution) broke out just weeks after Bachelet's government took power, which led to the first changes in the team of ministers.

The electoral system is another dimension in which receptivity to popular demand would be considerably enhanced if changes were put into practice. These would entail a thorough reform of the system, which some consider is in need of a complete transformation. On this point, there is strong disagreement between political elites and the electorate. The majority of citizens are in favor of change because they are disaffected with the system and see change as a path toward recovering hope for the future. On the other hand, party politicians and congressional members are deeply distrustful of changing a system from which they have benefited. This is one of the topics in which the conduct of the political classes is poorly rated.

Accountability

Social and institutional conditions exist in Chile that place accountability mechanisms on a par with other consolidated democracies. The possibility of demanding official accountability is a reality embodied by the judiciary and society; nevertheless it has little impact in the electoral context.

At a judicial level, there have been some important proceedings in Chile demanding accountability for corruption involving civil servants. Two of the most notorious cases of recent times are the Chiledeportes case and the accusations of illicit personal enrichment against Pinochet and his family during the authoritarian period. Both cases are being followed up judicially and are examples demonstrating that accountability exists, although this is irrespective of the fact that the workings of the judicial institution have been called into question over their lack of transparency and secrecy, practices that undermine the chances of achieving greater accountability. This has been helped by significant institutional reform: the renewal of the Supreme Court of Justice after the dictatorship by means of a system of incentives for early retirement, the penal procedural reform (Reforma Procesal Penal) initiated by the Frei administration that created the Ministry of the Public, and the creation of a judicial academy that has begun to mold a culture of autonomy and independence in the judiciary.[26]

In a societal context, there is increasing awareness that the political elite and civil servants can be held accountable. In Transparency International's Annual Reports, Chile repeatedly appears as a country with low levels of corruption. Nevertheless, these data contrast sharply with the perception obtained from the Social Research Institute (IPSOS) and Chile Transparente barometers, in which 55 percent of those surveyed in 2009 responded that Chile was a very corrupt country. This apparent contradiction might suggest that a mentality of zero tolerance toward corruption has been instilled in the population, so that any cases that do exist, although fewer in number than in other democracies, would have a greater impact on public opinion. Together with questions relating to public opinion, accountability has developed rapidly at a societal level. Since the mid-1990s there has been a proliferation within civic society of different organizations engaging in supervisory tasks associated with societal or social accountability.[27]

This would appear to strengthen the hypothesis that on both an institutional and societal level, mechanisms are in place in Chile that make the question of accountability less of a problem than the other aspects related to improving the quality of democracy examined here. Nevertheless, demand for accountability is not reflected in the electoral arena. The existence of a highly institutionalized party system should guarantee the possibility of demanding of the leaders some commitment to their promises (Torcal and Mainwaring 2005). In reality, this option is not used by the electorate to sanction or reward their leaders, as illustrated by the low levels of electoral volatility in Chile, although decreasing levels of participation and voter registration could possibly be interpreted as a form of protest and, indirectly, control over political representatives.

Sovereignty

Sovereignty is one aspect that has not traditionally been included in measurements of the quality of democracy, but, as Levine and Molina point out, it is a facilitation condition. In their model, sovereignty is understood to be a measure of the effectiveness of political decisions taken by elected civil servants; the less autonomy a government has with respect to external forces (military, financial, or diplomatic) or internal ones (religious, military, guerrilla fighters, drug cartels, etc.), the lower the quality of democracy (2007a, and this volume Chapter 1).

Chile is not faced with any threat from guerrillas or drug cartels that question the state's autonomy and power over the territory comprising the Republic. Any threat to state sovereignty following the transition to democracy has come from relations between civilians and the military, owing to the character of the transition negotiations that allowed the latter to hold on to substantial power. Since then, civil-military relations have evolved to adapt to democratic normality.[28] In 2005, in the package of reforms to the 1980 Constitution, the president of the Republic was once more given the power to remove commanders-in-chief, who, until then, had been immovable. The role and composition of the National Security Council (Consejo de Seguridad Nacional) were also modified, making it a purely advisory body. With this measure, former president Lagos's administration removed the bulk of the remnants of authoritarianism.

As Agüero points out, these reforms touched on the core aspects of any system embodying supremacy of political power over the military. Nevertheless, Agüero continues, despite notable advances, some issues are still pending (2006b). Of these, the most important are the composition of the National Security Council (in which the president of the Supreme Court and the comptroller general are unjustifiably present, yet the minister of defense is absent, even though part of the council is made up of commanders-in-chief), the reform of military justice, the level of military control in states of emergency, and the continuation of the assignation of the copper funds that have contributed to the autonomy of the military.

In the case of Chile, it is precisely this last point that introduces a limitation on sovereignty. The Copper Reserve Law, 13.196, states that 10 percent of the revenue obtained from sales by the state-owned copper company must be divided into equal parts and allocated to the three branches of national defense, and that this money will be used solely for the purchase of arms. As a result of this law, enacted in 1976, the armed forces have had considerable margin for maneuvering that has increased when profits from copper have risen. Moreover, they are under no obligation to justify their expenditure, although the Lagos administration introduced modifications that require arms to be purchased through an agency presided over by the Ministry of Defense in conjunction with the Treasury Department (Hacienda).[29] An autonomous initiative by a group of deputies to present a bill to repeal it was quashed without even being debated.[30] The main argument was that this law was based on an initiative that was exclusively governmental and that it was actually a secret law whose complete contents were unknown. The fact that a body exists that autonomously controls a sum of money without being accountable to anyone is an attack on the sovereignty of the government-elect, even more so when the body in question is in charge of national defense, when in a democratic regime it should be subordinate to civilian power.

The second point regarding sovereignty that is worth considering concerns Chile's relationship with Bolivia with respect to the latter's historical demand for an exit to the sea. There are fluctuations in coverage of this topic in the media and in political circles. Chile has skillfully tried to implicate Peru in this process by pressuring for the Bolivian exit to be in Peruvian territory. Needless to say, this option has generated strong opposition in Peru, which has culminated in their taking the territorial conflict to the International Court at The Hague, although officially the Peruvian petition is more concerned with the directive establishing the division of waters between Chile and Peru than with Bolivia's landlocked condition. If Bolivia finally acquires an exit to the sea through Chile, it could well lead to a scenario in which sovereignty in that part of Chilean territory is shared with Bolivia. Unlike the previous point respecting civil-military relations, such a solution would not affect the quality of Chilean democracy as understood here. Although sovereignty would be shared with Bolivia, it would be accepted within a legal framework.

Conclusions

The reforms to the 1980 Constitution at the end of the Lagos mandate significantly enhanced the quality of democracy in Chile, which in comparative terms is one of the highest in the region. In this context of marked improvement, this chapter has highlighted certain aspects that still pose a challenge to attaining an even greater degree of democracy. Most of these challenges are of an institutional nature, and the effects of any reforms would be closely interwoven with the electoral and participatory dimensions; see Table 3.3. This study has drawn particular attention to recognition of the right to vote of Chileans living abroad; election of regional authorities through universal suffrage (recently introduced with Law 20334); and changes in the electoral formula and the registration system, which should be automatic, not voluntary, to eliminate technical barriers to the right of suffrage. These are all changes entailing low-cost institutional reforms that would bring about great benefits within a short time.

With respect to the participatory and electoral dimensions, the institutional measure that would have the most effect on the quality of democracy would be

Table 3.3 Institutional Achievements and Pending Reforms

Institutional Measures	Prospects for Change	Aspect of Democracy Affected
Abolition of designated senators	Measure introduced in the 2005 constitutional reform	Electoral
New forms of participation	Introduced under Bachelet's government	Participation
Reduction of presidential mandate	Measure introduced in the 2005 constitutional reform	Electoral
Faculty for removing commanders-in-chief restored to the president	Measure introduced in the 2005 constitutional reform	Sovereignty
Right to vote for Chileans living abroad	Bill rejected in May 2007; another one discussed in 2009 and in process in 2010	Electoral
Democratic election to regional office	Introduced in 2009 and in process in 2010	Electoral
Electoral system: party offer restricted; no representativity; participation not encouraged	This was discussed in 2007, but no agreement was reached; no prospects for change	Electoral and participation
Party elitism	Isolated minor modifications	Participation
Ideological concentration of the media	None	Electoral
Allocation of copper funds for autonomous management by the military	Under discussion; has received a first rejection in Congress; awaiting an executive bill	Sovereignty

a change in the electoral system. Among the consequences would be greater representativity implicit in the translation of votes, which would encourage more sectors to participate in elections, as both electors and candidates (the present system hinders the entry of new parties). Nevertheless, this is also the measure with the least probability of being implemented. The Concertación is a powerful political actor with clear preferences that would influence outcomes. Nevertheless, within the coalition, the absence of a consensus due to internal divisions, the presence of *rebel* deputies, and the fact that the support of the right-wing coalition is required for approval of any reform make the prospect of change highly unlikely.[31] Many consider this aspect to be the last vestige of a dying authoritarianism, and that it will not be reformed anytime soon as there is little likelihood of change in the Constitution.

Reform of the right to vote for Chileans abroad, automatic registration, and voluntary voting were measures that seemed to be close to the final discussion stage in the 2006–2010 Congress; nevertheless they were left still pending. Another institutional challenge that was still pending in 2010 concerns sovereignty, in particular, the autonomy the military has for managing part of the budget. Although considerable progress has been made in relations between civilians and the military, certain changes have yet to be implemented.

With respect to noninstitutional challenges, the most pressing issue that is still unresolved is that of greater receptivity to the popular will regarding plans for the redistribution of income. This is one of the banes of democratic governments that has not found a solution to the continuance of the economic model by correcting its growing deficiencies. The fact that this problem characteristically has multiple causes does not temper the assertion that the political elite has taken decisions since the transition that have perpetuated, and even exacerbated, high levels of inequality. In comparison, the issue of human rights is a good example of a gradual and effective response that is in tune with citizens' demands. A similar response to matters of inequality, together with the constitutional reforms described above, would considerably enhance the already high quality of democracy in Chile. Concertación governments have repeatedly stressed their social vocation as an element that distinguishes them from the right-wing coalition, but policies on these issues during its two decades of government were neither forceful enough nor effective.

This study has shown that the quality of democracy in Chile could be even greater than it is at present if certain institutional reforms were put into practice. What is clearly required is consensus among the main political forces on reforms that would be highly effective in the short term. In other words, with a concerted effort to coordinate Chile's political elites, the quality of democracy would rapidly improve. Some important steps have already been taken in this direction. If these changes became effective, issues such as falling levels of participation and mistrust of various governmental institutions, two aspects of Chilean democracy that are traditionally described as deficient, would start to undergo improvements and lead to a reformed institutional framework.

Notes

An earlier version of this study was presented at the Congress of the Latin American Studies Association (LASA) in Rio de Janeiro in 2009. I gratefully acknowledge the comments I have received and would like to give special thanks to José E. Molina (University of Zulia, Venezuela), Cristian Beltrán (former Chilean cultural attaché in Peru), and Alejandro Turis (Chamber of Deputies' Library, Chile) for reading the text and offering their valuable advice. The research for this chapter and the translation into English were made possible thanks to financing from the "Instituciones y rendición de cuentas en regímenes parlamentarios y presidencialistas: Los casos de Argentina, Chile, España, Francia, Gran Bretaña, y Hungría" project (SEJ2007-67995/CPOL).

1. Of these, six have been to elect deputies and six to elect senators (1989, 1993, 1997, 2001, 2005, 2009), five to elect presidents (1989, 1993, 1999, 2005, 2009—the last three with second-round runoffs), and five to elect municipal officers (1992, 1996, 2000, 2004, 2008).

2. For more detail on these issues, see Fernandois and Soto (2005).

3. According to the census of Chileans abroad, it is estimated that there are presently 857,781 Chileans and their children living abroad. Of these, 56.8 percent were born in Chile and 43.2 percent abroad.

4. With the Reform of the Constitution in 2005, the number of people who could opt for Chilean nationality was extended. Prior to this, only foreign-born sons and daughters of Chileans had this option, but this has now been extended to include grandchildren born abroad of Chileans. Furthermore, before the reform, at least one year's residency in Chile was required to become a Chilean national. This requirement has now been abolished.

5. In May 2007, Congress rejected a bill to modify a law that would have allowed Chileans abroad to vote. Sixty-three Concertación congressional members were in favor of the initiative, while in the Alianza por Chile, twenty-three voted against it and twenty abstained. Since it involved the amendment of a constitutional law, the bill required the backing of four-sevenths (sixty-nine votes) of the congressional members.

6. Until the amendment applied to the 2004 elections, the mayor was the candidate who obtained the first majority in the municipality and who also belonged to a list or pact with at least 30 percent of the valid votes in that election. Otherwise, the mayor was the candidate for councilor who obtained the first majority and whose list or pact had been the most voted in the municipality. If neither of the above conditions was fulfilled, the mayor was the most voted of the list or majority pact in the municipality. This system was used in the 1992, 1996, and 2000 elections.

7. For example, Enríquez Ominami, the candidate who came in third place in the 2009 presidential election, made the election of regional governors and decentralization issues part of his main electoral discourse.

8. This does not include the left-socialist party, PAIS, that obtained two deputies in 1989 after it agreed to be represented, along with the PRSD, in a coalition called Unity for Democracy (Unidad para la Democracia). The PAIS was an instrumental party enabling the Communist Party (Partido Comunista) to run in the first elections, although it did so under another label as it had not been legalized at the time.

9. Law No. 19.884 on Transparency, Limits and Control of Electoral Expenses was published in the official state gazette, *Diario Oficial* (D.O.), on August 5, 2003, and amended by Laws No. 19.963 and 19.964, both published in the D.O. on August 26, 2004, and by Law No. 20.053, published in the D.O. on September 6, 2005.

10. For an analysis of the funding of political activity in Chile, see Chile Tranparente, "Financiamiento político en Chile: Documento de trabajo," No. 4, May 2008, Santiago de Chile, http://votainteligente.cl/index.php?option=com_phocadownload&view=category&id=6:documentos&Itemid=93.

11. In the Chiledeportes case, it was established in the courts that some members of the institution had misappropriated funds through the concession, often to relatives, of projects that were not executed, with contracts for services that were paid for and not rendered.

12. Schaulsohn, for the period he presided over the PPD, and Boeninger, a member of the PDC and ex-minister.

13. The 1980 Constitution established three ways of electing senators. Under the bi-nominal system, thirty-eight senators were elected by vote in nineteen constituencies, with majority distribution and the same electoral threshold as in the case of deputies. These senators held office for eight years and could be reelected indefinitely. The upper house was to be partially renewed every four years in half the regions. There were also nine senators designated by different institutions. Finally, the third group consisted of senators for life. This varied in number and comprised ex-presidents of the Republic, who had held the office for six consecutive years. The reform of the Constitution elim-inated the nine designated senators and the senators for life, reducing the number of members of the Senate from forty-eight to thirty-eight. Under this system of renewal by half at a time, in the 2009 elections, nineteen senators stood for election and the rest will remain for four more years.

14. The duration of the presidential term has changed three times since the 1980 Constitution was passed. Unlike the 1925 Charter that preceded it, this extended the mandate to eight years with presidential elections taking place at the same time as con-gressional ones, held every four years, so that one congressional election would coincide with the presidential election, while the following would not, and so on. In 1989, a pack-age of constitutional reforms was introduced, still under the authoritarian government, with the aim of adjusting the constitutional text to the minimum demands of the inter-nationally recognized democratic standard. One of these reforms, which was provisional, established that the first presidential mandate would be four years to facilitate the tran-sition process. For this reason, in 1989 and 1993 both congressional and presidential elections were held simultaneously. The second change to the presidential mandate took place in 1994 with the Constitutional Reform Act (Ley de Reforma Constitucional), which reduced the mandate to six years, meaning that after that the presidential and con-gressional elections ceased to be held simultaneously. Therefore, in 2000 only presi-dential elections were held, with congressional elections held the following year in 2001. The final reform of the Constitution in 2005 further reduced the presidential mandate from six to four years to make elections coincide once more with congressional elections. In 2009, both presidential and congressional elections took place at the same time.

15. See Navia for a detailed account of this (2004).

16. Although voting is compulsory, electoral registration is not. This means that a citizen who has never registered on the voter registration list is not obligated to vote.

17. Nevertheless, these data are much less dramatic when compared to those of other countries in the region.

18. Until the 2010 elections, the Concertación succeeded in doubling the votes of the former Alianza (now Coalición por el Cambio) in 11 electoral constituencies in 1989, 11 in 1993, 9 in 1997, and 4 in 2001. During this time, the Alianza por Chile only dou-bled on two occasions, once in 1993 and once in 2001 (Siavelis 2004: 60).

19. According to this FLACSO report, both coalitions have benefited in the elec-tion of deputies by a similar percentage (an average of about 4 percent of overrepresen-tation). This conclusion was reached by calculating the average differences between the percentages of votes and of seats in the whole sequence of elections for deputies and sen-ators for each of the coalitions (see FLACSO 2006).

20. The design of constituencies was based on the results obtained by Pinochet in the referendum. The aim was to guarantee representation in all of them by designing them artificially.

21. As Siavelis states: "Voters perceive that the ultimate victory in elections comes about as the result of the strategic machinations of party elites, rather than an expression of the will of the people" (2005: 223).

22. See Cea Egaña for precedents of this practice (2002).

23. Each list contains two names, and the voter elects one of them. To determine which of the lists has won, the votes obtained for the candidates on the same list are added together, even though the voters may have decided to vote for only one of them. After estimating whether a list wins one or two seats, these are assigned to specific candidates in accordance with the popular vote.

24. In an enlightening article on this matter Siavelis points out that in any district, when doubts are raised over the winner, the candidates of both coalitions are required to choose between a weak colleague on the list (which may allow them together to reach the threshold of 33.33 percent plus one vote that guarantees winning one seat, but not with more votes individually) and a colleague who holds a lot of power (2005). This second option would allow a doubling of the vote of the electoral list, and both candidates on the list would each gain a seat because the 66.7 percent threshold that guarantees two seats would be exceeded. This becomes more of a risk when the candidate considers the likelihood of winning to be only probable, not guaranteed. As for strong candidates, they are usually unwilling to compete against other strong candidates on the same list. There is also an interesting analysis on negotiations during successive elections between the RN and the UDI in Morales (2005).

25. Of the 177 countries classified by the UNDP according to the level of human development, in Latin America the list is headed by Argentina (thirty-eighth place), followed by Chile (fortieth) and Uruguay (forty-sixth).

26. On the transformation of the judiciary, see Hilbink 2007.

27. For more detail on these issues, see the numerous studies by Peruzzotti and Smulovitz.

28. For more detail on this issue, see Agüero (2006a).

29. In 2006, Codelco's contribution to the armed forces was US$1,311 billion.

30. In June 2006, the bill in question was rejected after its proposal by Enrique Accorsi (PPD), Marco Enríquez-Ominami (PS), Tucapel Jiménez (Independent), Alejandro Sule (PRSD), Patricio Vallespín (DC), and Clemira Pacheco (PS).

31. With respect to the viability of the changes, Electoral Law Reform involves amending the Constitution and Constitutional Laws, in which case two-thirds of the votes of senators and members of the Chamber of Deputies are required to reform the Constitution, and four-sevenths of both of them are needed to modify Constitutional Laws. Neither the Coalición por el Cambio nor the Concertación has such a majority.

4

Argentina: Resilience in the Face of Challenges

Mark P. Jones and Juan Pablo Micozzi

THIRTY YEARS AFTER THE INITIATION OF THE *THIRD WAVE* OF democratization in Latin America (Huntington 1991), evaluations of democratic performance in the region have been decidedly mixed. While some scholars have highlighted that the risks of democratic breakdown are minimal today in the region, others have a more sanguine opinion regarding the region's prospects for democratic breakdown given the continued presence of underdevelopment, inequality, and political instability (Coppedge, Alvarez, and Maldonado 2008; Mainwaring and Hagopian 2005; Munck 2007a). Ironically, both of these positions appear to be correct in their assessments, and are best viewed as complementary, rather than competing, arguments. Specifically, Levine and Molina make a major theoretical contribution to the study of democracy in the region, reconciling these diverse assessments of democracy by distinguishing democratic quality from democratic governmental performance (Chapter 1).

Levine and Molina develop a set of conceptual dimensions, variables, and indicators to assess how well democracies, rather than governments, are performing (Chapter 2). In this chapter, following the methodology suggested by Levine and Molina, we provide an empirical assessment of democratic performance in Argentina. After reviewing aggregate- and individual-level information, we highlight the current democratic system's commendable ability to survive severe challenges over the past two and one-half decades that in the past would have resulted in the breakdown of democracy, and conclude that there is good cause to be moderately optimistic about the future of democracy in Argentina.

Argentina is a federal republic that suffered the same patterns of instability as the rest of the region during most of the twentieth century (Rock 1987). Beginning with the 1930 military coup against democratically elected president Hipólito Yrigoyen (1916–1922, 1928–1930), the country experienced a pattern of alternation between elected civilian and military governments, a pattern that appears to have ended in 1983 with the return of democracy to the country. Of course, many things have happened in Argentina between 1983 and 2010. Two massive financial meltdowns, two confiscations of bank deposits, a bout of severe hyperinflation, and several serious political crises—including five presidents holding office during a chaotic fortnight at the end of 2001 and beginning of 2002—characterized the convoluted performance of the third-wave Argentine democracy. Based on the experience of Argentina's democracy since 1983, many would posit that the democratic system possesses many serious defects. Nevertheless, others might quite reasonably conclude that while democracy is not fully consolidated in the country, at the same time the country's democratic system has proven capable of enduring severe political and financial crises that in the past generally resulted in a breakdown of the democratic system of government (Rock 1987).

In this chapter, we conform Argentina's case to Levine and Molina's framework, and evaluate the empirical evidence regarding democratic quality in the country. For the empirical analysis, we employ several data sources. For public opinion–related indicators, we rely on three principal sources: Latinobarómetro survey data from 1995, 2001, and 2005; World Values Survey (WVS) data from 1991, 1995, 1999, and 2006; and Latin American Public Opinion Project (LAPOP) data from 2008. In addition to these individual-level data, we utilize aggregate-level information (e.g., national- or province-level data, such as election returns) drawn from the Ministry of Internal Affairs (Ministerio del Interior) and from the Argentine Chamber of Deputies' Office of Parliamentary Information (Dirección de Información Parlamentaria).

Finally, before moving on to the empirical analysis, it is important to note that over the twenty-seven years of uninterrupted democracy in Argentina from 1983 through 2009, the principal democratic institutions have remained relatively unchanged. Although the constitutional reform of 1994 introduced some important modifications to the Argentine Constitution (e.g., immediate presidential reelection, shorter Senate terms, the direct election of the president and senators), the major democratic institutional structures for allocating power remained constant (Jones 1997; Spiller and Tommasi 2007). In sum, any changes in democratic quality observed over time in Argentina cannot be attributed primarily to any institutional reforms, with the single exception of the dramatic increase in the percentage of women legislators, which was a result of the 1991 adoption of the world's first gender quota law.

Empirical Analysis

Levine and Molina highlight three principal areas that constitute the foundation of a democracy: the election of the rulers, popular influence over public policy decisions, and accountability. Within these areas, five major dimensions have been identified for empirical analysis: "electoral decision, participation, accountability, responsiveness, and sovereignty." Each of these dimensions has a set of indicators designed for cross-national analysis. As mentioned above, we will approach each dimension by selecting the data that we consider to be the most valid measures for Argentina of the theoretical concepts articulated by Levine and Molina (Chapter 2).

Informed Electoral Decision

Information is a key component of any democratic decision, simply because the more knowledge citizens have, the better they can evaluate the competing electoral options and make the best possible decision in regard to their votes. Therefore, the more informed citizens are, the better the expected quality of democracy. We rely on Latinobarómetro data for 1996, 2001, and 2005 to empirically assess this assertion. The survey question utilized is "How many days did you obtain news from TV/newspapers/radio last week?" A separate question exists for each of the three news sources. Responses range from zero to seven in each case. See Table 4.1 for a summary of responses for prior week news consumption.

Looking at Table 4.1, we can verify that people are very well informed in Argentina, at least in regard to their consumption of television news. Almost 50 percent of the sample population watches news daily, and an average of approximately 90 percent does at least once every seven days. Nevertheless, it must be taken into account that an overwhelming majority—approximately 95 percent—of Argentines have a television in their home and that TV news shows are provided free of charge, in contrast to newspapers. Despite the existence of

Table 4.1   News Consumption Percentages During the Prior Week: TV, Newspaper, Radio

Number of Days	TV			Newspaper			Radio		
	1996	2001	2005	1996	2001	2005	1996	2001	2005
0	9	18	8	29	47	36	22	35	24
1	2	3	3	14	12	17	3	3	4
2	6	8	8	11	11	14	4	5	7
3	6	8	7	8	7	9	4	5	6
4	6	5	4	5	2	3	5	3	3
5	10	13	13	2	5	4	6	6	9
6	4	4	5	2	2	2	3	2	2
7	57	40	53	30	15	15	53	41	46

some cross-temporal variation in the extreme categories (i.e., both zero and seven days a week), the tendency in TV news consumption did not vary notably for the 1996 to 2005 period; in all years, a substantial percentage of Argentine citizens watch the news on TV every day of the week.

A review of newspaper consumption provides a finding notably distinct from that for TV news consumption among Argentine citizens; see Table 4.1. In contrast to TV news viewership, on average over one-third of the Argentine population does not read news in a newspaper any day of the week, while only around one in seven read a newspaper on a daily basis. The low value for 2001 showing that nearly one-half of Argentines did not read news in a newspaper at all during the prior week is most likely due to the severe economic crisis that year.

Unlike newspapers, but similar to television, radio news broadcasts are free. Table 4.1 underscores the fact that Argentine radio news consumption is much more similar to that of TV news viewers than to newspaper readers, with essentially one-half of the population listening to news on the radio every day of the week. However, regarding the distribution of the extreme categories, the columns are more similar to those for newspaper readers, with a concentration in the two most extreme values. Of particular note is the fact that approximately one in four Argentines does not utilize the radio as a news source. Looking at intertemporal performance, once again, 2001 shows a different pattern, with many more people in the zero category than in 1996 and 2005.

Public opinion data available on news consumption for 2008 (LAPOP 2008) are in line with the data presented here. People who report having watched TV news broadcasts seven days a week represent 58 percent of the population. Those who listen to news broadcasts daily on the radio represent 45 percent, while the percentage of Argentines who read the newspaper on a daily basis is a mere 22 percent.[1] LAPOP also reports information on citizen access to news through the Internet, with 16 percent of the respondents obtaining news from the Internet on a daily basis.

Another proxy for the level of information possessed by citizens is related to the consumption of news from any of the sources mentioned above. How common is it for Argentines to inform themselves (from one or more sources) on a daily basis? Taking a simple aggregate measure of the aforementioned media (LAPOP 2008), we find that 80 percent of Argentines consume news reports of some type, whether television, radio, newspaper, or Internet, on a daily basis. Therefore, relying on all the reviewed evidence, we conclude that most people have been regularly informed in the period analyzed. The implications for this first dimension of democratic quality are straightforward: the Argentine democracy seems to have been performing quite well.

In a related vein, Levine and Molina point out that information is a key resource for good decisions, but that this might not be enough (Chapter 1). In their perspective, and that of Zaller (1992), among others, cognitive capacities are the flipside of the informational coin. People lacking cognitive resources may have trouble processing information and transforming such inputs into conscious decisions. Despite the fact that detailed data about cognition would require a more complex data-gathering strategy, a good proxy for this variable is a person's level of educational attainment.

The distribution of Argentines' educational background has two clear peaks: one at seven years of education, which is the completion of primary school, and the other at twelve years, which is the completion of secondary school (Latinobarómetro); see Table 4.2. In addition, a considerable percentage of the sample has some level of postsecondary education, either technical or university. Relevant cross-temporal variation in educational attainment is not present for the 1996–2005 period. In fact, most of the categories remain virtually identical across time, with the only exception the university level, where the percentage of citizens with a university degree declined over this time frame.

Overall, how should we judge the levels of education in Argentina based on the empirical evidence? An overwhelming majority, 89 percent, of Argentines have completed at least elementary school, which is a very high value for Latin America. In addition, 60 percent of the population has at least some secondary-level training, with more than 40 percent graduating from high school. Finally, between 20 percent and 25 percent of the population has at least some university or technical college training. In sum, overall, the Argentine citizenry possesses a relatively high degree of educational attainment, especially within the context of the Latin American region.

After analyzing news consumption and educational attainment as key components of an informed electoral decision, an almost obvious question emerges: are these two variables not highly correlated? Even though the goal of this chapter is not statistical inference, we run a simple bivariate model to determine to what extent the aforementioned relationship is true. We computed a multinomial logit to observe the likelihood of the members of each educational category to

Table 4.2   Education Attainment (maximum level reached as percentage of the population, by year)

Education Attainment	1996	2001	2005
None	0	1	2
Primary incomplete	10	10	11
Primary complete	23	25	26
Secondary incomplete	18	17	18
Secondary complete	23	22	23
Technical incomplete	2	3	4
Technical complete	5	5	5
University incomplete	10	12	9
University complete	9	5	4

be informed at each of the frequencies.[2] For the sake of simplicity and clarity, we report only some of the most relevant categories for one of the dependent variables, news consumption from newspapers. As can be seen in Figure 4.1, the probability of people reading newspapers with a different frequency does change as levels of education vary. For instance, the different curves show that a person who has obtained a university degree is 800 percent more likely to read a newspaper daily than a person lacking even a primary level of education. It is noteworthy how the five curves behave differently as they reach the extreme values, something quite expected, considering that most of the cases are concentrated in these categories.

Education and information appear to be correlated. This finding illuminates our understanding of the informed electoral decisions dimension, but also points to an interesting direction for future analysis. Overall however, we can state with considerable confidence that Argentines have considerable levels of information and acceptable degrees of education; thus, it can be assumed that they can make informed decisions at the ballot box. In sum, on this dimension, we can rate Argentina's democratic system as being of a reasonably high quality.

Democratic Participation

Levine and Molina define democratic participation as the means by which "citizens choose their government, control it, and influence policymaking either directly or through representatives" (Chapter 1). The direction of the hypothesis is clear: countries where citizens have higher degrees of political participation are more likely to have a higher-quality democracy. To empirically assess the degree of democratic participation in Argentina, we rely on several indicators. First, we assess the level of voter participation measured by turnout for the most relevant election, which is for president, and the most frequent elections, which are for national deputies. We also calculate the representativeness of the different political options in the elected bodies via a measure of disproportionality in the translation of electoral votes into parliamentary seats (Payne, Zovatto G., and Mateo Díaz 2007). Finally, we examine the degree of popular participation in the country's political parties and the evolution of the election of women to the Argentine Chamber of Deputies.

Voter turnout must be analyzed within the correct institutional context: Argentina is a country with automatic voter registration, mandatory voting for those under seventy, and elections held on Sunday—procedures that the literature suggests should foster electoral participation (Franklin 2002; Massicotte, Blais, and Yoshinaka 2004). Restricting the analysis of voter turnout solely to the national level would open up the possibility of systematic bias in the interpretation of trends over time in Argentina, given the country's robust federal system, concurrent and nonconcurrent national and provincial elections, and

69

Figure 4.1   Probability of Reading Newspapers x Times a Week, by Education Attained

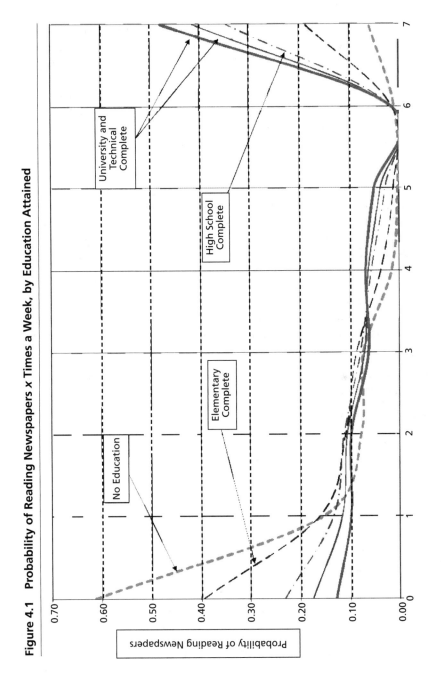

Number of Days

tremendous variation in provincial population sizes. For instance, something as simple as a concurrent gubernatorial and a national congressional election in the province of Buenos Aires, which is the country's most populous province, could theoretically compensate for a generalized decrease in turnout across Argentina's other twenty-three districts. For this reason, we focus our examination of turnout for the 1983–2009 period at the provincial level, which includes twenty-three provinces and the autonomous Federal Capital.[3]

In Argentina, voter turnout in presidential elections is high in general, even though exhibiting some cross-temporal and cross-sectional variation; see Table 4.3. The average using the arithmetic mean of the twenty-four districts, without weighting by population, is 80 percent during this time frame, a number that is comparable to that found in European parliamentary elections (Rose 2004). An examination of the turnout data for the 1983, 1989, 1995, 1999, 2003, and 2007 presidential elections indicates that during this time period, voter turnout has decreased over time, with an 8 percent difference between 1983 and 2007. A crisis of representation would be one of the most common explanations to account for this negative trend. Nevertheless, some other factors, such as a change in the frequency of concurrent presidential and provincial-level elections or a degree of waning of voter enthusiasm over time as the Argentine democracy has matured, may also have contributed to this decline (Calvo and Micozzi 2005).

Moving down to the district level, the aforementioned regional differences become evident. Overall, most districts are centered on the mean, with small deviations in general. Nevertheless, differences between the extreme provincial

Table 4.3   Presidential and Legislative Voter Turnout: National and Provincial Average (percentage of registered voters)

Election Year	Legislative National	Legislative Provincial	Presidential National	Presidential Provincial
1983	86	83	86	83
1985	84	81	—	—
1987	85	83	—	—
1989	85	83	85	83
1991	80	78	—	—
1993	82	78	—	—
1995	75	80	83	80
1997	80	78	—	—
1999	82	80	82	80
2001	78	75	—	—
2003	68	71	78	76
2005	73	69	—	—
2007	76	74	77	75
2009	72	72	—	—

Note: The provincial average is based on the mean for twenty-four provinces.

cases are noteworthy, reaching a value of 17 percent. Taking the temporal performance into account, we realize that the slope is negative in almost every case. Should we be concerned about a progressive decline of democratic quality based on these data? Six data points are insufficient to maintain such a statement with any confidence. Furthermore, even with the decline, turnout levels in the Argentine provinces remain in the 75–80 percent range, levels that are still indicative of a reasonable level of participation when placed within the international-regional context (Payne, Zovatto G., and Mateo Díaz 2007; Rose 2004).

In contrast to the presidential elections, which have been held every six years from 1983 to 1995 and every four years starting in 1999, since 1983 one-half of the Chamber of Deputies has been renewed every two years, leading to a much larger number of data points for fourteen elections in total for the 1983–2009 period. This sequence allows for a superior evaluation of the evolution of turnout than in the case of presidential elections. Overall, the mean level of turnout differs only 2 percent from the executive elections on average, with off-year elections normally representing valleys between the sexennial and quadrennial concurrent presidential and legislative elections. Since 1989, turnout across the twenty-four provinces has progressively declined in Argentina, dropping from an average of 83 percent in the 1980s, to an average of 79 percent in the 1990s, to an average of 73 percent during the 2000s.

At the provincial level, average turnout rates are relatively stationary during this time frame. A few provinces do have clearer lower peaks, especially after 2000, but overall, as in the case of presidential elections, participation in legislative elections continues to be quite respectable in Argentina, suggesting that democratic quality in the area of participation continues to remain at acceptable levels in the country.

Another way to analyze the linkage between participation and democratic performance is by examining the manner in which voter preferences are accurately translated into representation of those interests in the legislature. The more proportional this translation, the greater the quality of representation, while conversely the more disproportional the outcome of this translation, the weaker the quality of representation in the country (Payne, Zovatto G., and Mateo Díaz 2007).[4] The data for the 1983– 2009 Chamber of Deputies elections underscore some intertemporal variation in the level of disproportionality in Argentina; see Table 4.4. After the lowest value of 1983,[5] disproportionality started increasing, until reaching a level greater than 20 percent in 1995, before beginning a slow decline (except in 2001 and 2009).[6] Thereafter, the formation of a coalition by the two largest parties in the opposition depressed disproportionality briefly, a process that reversed notably in 2001 as the party system atomized. On average, disproportionality in Argentina during this period was 17 percent, which serves as an approximate measure of the distortion between popular preferences and the partisan composition of the year's class of deputies. Looking at the tempo-

Table 4.4   Disproportionality in Chamber Elections Across the 24 Provinces

Election Year	Mean Level of Disproportionality	Standard Deviation
1983	0.11	0.05
1985	0.16	0.07
1987	0.14	0.07
1989	0.18	0.09
1991	0.17	0.06
1993	0.17	0.07
1995	0.21	0.11
1997	0.17	0.09
1999	0.15	0.07
2001	0.31	0.14
2003	0.13	0.06
2005	0.13	0.05
2007	0.17	0.07
2009	0.27	0.14

ral performance of the curve in Figure 4.2, it becomes evident how large the increase in disproportionality was in 2001 and 2009, and also how wide the dispersion is across the twenty-four provinces (i.e., the 95 percent confidence interval that surrounds the mean level of disproportionality). As mentioned, the decomposition of the traditional patterns in the party system starting in 2001 fostered a high degree of party-system fragmentation. Given the systematic majoritarian bias in the legislative institutions of Argentina, the result was an enormous majority-party bonus for the only stable actor, Peronism, in 2001, as well as, to a lesser extent, in 2009.[7] However, with the exception of 2001, the level of disproportionality in Argentina has remained relatively constant across the twenty-four provinces during the 1985–2009 era.

As mentioned previously, district magnitude can exert a strong influence over the level of disproportionality. Following this reasoning, if this measure is employed as an indicator of the quality of democracy, then district magnitude should be carefully controlled for. Does magnitude directly affect disproportionality? In that case, could there exist some provinces that are more *democratic* than others? A review of the twenty-four Argentine provinces makes evident that districts with the highest disproportionality also have the lowest district magnitudes. However, not every district with those characteristics is highly disproportional, nor are provinces with higher magnitudes necessarily less proportional. Results of a simple linear regression show a weak −.003 coefficient for each unit increase in district magnitude.

In sum, disproportionality remained moderate throughout most of the democratic period. There were spikes in the level of disproportionality during peri-

Figure 4.2   Index of Disproportionality

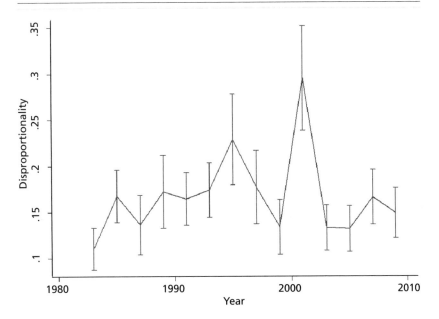

ods of electoral realignment and turmoil—1995, 2001, and 2009—but overall a relatively stable pattern existed with disproportionality levels normally in the 13 percent to 17 percent range.

Argentina lacks salient racial and ethnic cleavages, but, along with all other Latin American countries, has historically suffered from a severe underrepresentation of women in its national legislature. With the explicit goal of increasing gender equality, in 1991 Argentina passed a bill that set a mandatory 30 percent gender quota for legislative elections (Jones 1996). The effects of this institutional innovation are clearly demonstrated in Figure 4.3. Before 1993, the percentage of women elected barely surpassed 5 percent. In 1993, the curve rises substantially, and remains above 25 percent for all of the following elections. In this aspect, it seems that Argentina made considerable advances in gender parity via the adoption of gender quotas. In sum on this indicator, Argentina has quite high levels of democracy.

Finally, we use a fourth indicator for the dimension of representation: participation in political parties. Respondents were asked in the WVS whether they were "active, moderately active, or not at all participants in a political party."

Overall, only a minute segment of the population was either active or moderately active in a political party—8 percent in 1991, 10 percent in 1995, 5

Figure 4.3   The Election of Women to the Argentine Chamber of Deputies, 1983–2009

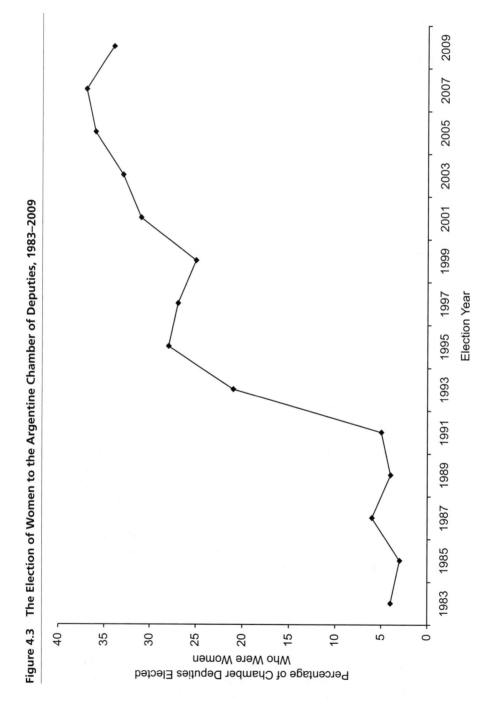

percent in 1999, 9 percent in 2006—with the remaining population having no ties of any type to a party.[8] In all, Argentine citizens are not active participants in the internal life of their parties.

The 2008 LAPOP survey provides a different lens from which to view the relationship between Argentine citizens and the country's political parties. Asked whether they feel close to a party, 25 percent of the sample agreed. However, *closeness* can have a variety of different meanings. Asked about the intensity of their party attachment, the one-quarter of the population who identify with a party varied in terms of the intensity of their attachment, with 47 percent possessing a moderate degree of attachment, 35 percent a strong degree, 9 percent a very strong degree, 8 percent a weak degree, and 1 percent a very weak degree. Summing the moderate, strong, and very strong partisans, 91 percent of this subgroup of respondents (which is one in five Argentine citizens overall) can be considered to possess some type of noteworthy attachment to a political party.

Accountability

Levine and Molina rely on a definition of the concept of accountability that highlights "the extent to which political figures and public officials are subject to control, sanction, and regular reporting and inspection." They distinguish among three types of accountability: horizontal, which includes checks and balances among the branches of government; vertical, whereby citizens are using devices of direct and indirect democracy; and societal, consisting of social mobilization and organization to pursue specific goals (Chapter 1, Chapter 2). In regard to measuring these three concepts empirically in Argentina, we are unsure how well the indicators suggested by Levine and Molina represent valid measures of these concepts within the Argentine context.[9] As a consequence, in this chapter we do not attempt to empirically measure horizontal, vertical, or societal accountability. Our qualitative understanding of Argentina does nonetheless lead us to conclude that the democratic system suffers from severe flaws in terms of relatively limited levels of horizontal and vertical accountability in particular, flaws that have become more severe and pronounced during the reign of the Kirchners (former president Néstor Kirchner, 2003–2007; President Cristina Fernández de Kirchner, 2007–).

Responsiveness

Levine and Molina underscore that congruence between citizen preferences and public policies enacted by governments is a central component of democracy.

We use the Latinobarómetro survey and the question "How satisfied are you with democracy in your country?" As Levine and Molina caution, such a question can induce either performance- or quality-based answers from respondents, but in aggregate this measure does help to shed some light on this key dimension (Chapter 2).

The results in Table 4.5 do not provide a particularly optimistic portrayal of Argentine citizens' opinion of their democracy. The percentage of respondents who indicate that they are "very satisfied" is by far the lowest among all of the potential options, with a satisfied/dissatisfied ratio of approximately 1 to 2 at best and 1 to 4 in the worst year, which was 2001. We concur with Levine and Molina that there is an important performance component in a citizen's response to this question. To test to what extent that intuition is right, we decided to include another indicator as a control. We analyzed the responses to the question "Do you always prefer democracy over any other regime?" to see whether it confirmed the weak value captured in the previous question.

On the basis of the Latinobarómetro question regarding regime support, we created a binary variable that groups answers that always prefer a democratic regime in one category, and those answers that do not indicate a full degree of support for the concept of democracy in another. In 1995, 2001, and 2005, 73 percent, 59 percent, and 70 percent of the respondents respectively preferred a democratic regime to any other regime. In this case, the results demonstrate a strong degree of support by Argentines for the general democratic regime type over its undemocratic alternatives, such as a dictatorship. Even at the nadir of the post-1983 Argentine democracy, which was the 2001–2002 crisis, three in five Argentines still expressed the belief that democracy was preferable to any other regime alternative. The differences between these two sets of answers—satisfaction with democracy and regime preference—are sufficiently strong that we are comfortable in inferring that the reported dissatisfaction with democracy

Table 4.5   Degree of Satisfaction with Democracy

Degree of Satisfaction	1996	2001	2005
Very satisfied	7	4	5
Somewhat satisfied	27	17	30
Somewhat unsatisfied	51	42	49
Not at all satisfied	15	37	16
Total satisfied	34	21	35
Total unsatisfied	66	79	65

detailed above has much more to do with governmental performance, rather than with support or opposition to a democratic regime of government.

The 2008 LAPOP survey provides additional evidence related to popular support for democracy in Argentina. The LAPOP survey asks three similar questions in this thematic area, which we analyze separately from those of Latinobarómetro, as the wording of the questions and the sample population are not comparable. The first question inquires "Are you very satisfied, satisfied, dissatisfied, or very dissatisfied with the way Argentine democracy is performing?" More than one-half of the respondents are either "very satisfied" at 4 percent or "satisfied" at 50 percent with the country's democratic performance. It is noteworthy to point out that the question directly assesses the regime's functioning in the country. A similar concept is measured by the question "How democratic is Argentina?" which also has four ordinal response choices: "very democratic, reasonably democratic, poorly democratic, not democratic at all." This and the preceding question are highly correlated at 0.6, but the distribution is more positive regarding the performance of the Argentine democratic system for the latter question. In all, over two-thirds of the respondents consider Argentina to be at least reasonably democratic—11 percent "very democratic," 60 percent "reasonably democratic"—while only a miniscule proportion (3 percent) believes Argentina is "not democratic at all." Do these results suggest a dramatic shift in the quality of democracy in Argentina after 2005? As mentioned above, wording and framing may have affected the way respondents have chosen their answers. In addition, a complete understanding of this issue requires a multivariate analysis, something that is not within the scope of this chapter. However, the partial reversal of the pre-2008 negative attitudes toward democracy is highly germane, and is meritorious of more intensive analysis in the future.

Finally, a question about a respondent's preference for democracy over any other regime is also included in the LAPOP survey. Nevertheless, instead of offering a binary choice, the LAPOP survey allows the respondents the ability to assess their level of agreement with the statement "Democracy is the most preferred regime" on a seven-point ordinal scale. When focusing on the three extreme categories of each end of this seven-point scale as a single group, perspectives for regime support are notably high in Argentina, with 91 percent of respondents agreeing with the statement, while only 5 percent would appear to prefer an alternative regime type.[10] As a consequence of the review of the LAPOP data in particular, at present it is accurate to state there is no doubt about the Argentine population's firm and widespread support for the maintenance of the democratic system in Argentina.

Overall, what can we say about responsiveness based on the indirect inferences made in this section? If we thought that dissatisfaction with performance is partly due to a lack of congruence between citizens' and elected officials' respective policy preferences, then we would say that responsiveness is in deficit. However, if we judged preference for democracy as the product of policy congruence, among other factors, then we would assign a positive value to the indicator. At this stage, though, it is not possible to make more conclusive inferences without controlling for additional factors as well as employing a longer time series of comparable public opinion data, which, unfortunately, does not yet exist.

Sovereignty

This final dimension assesses the extent of autonomy enjoyed by the democratic political system from other political power brokers in the country, for example, the church, foreign powers, large corporations, and the military. As Levine and Molina highlight, a host of measures should be included to capture the relative autonomy of governments vis-à-vis these different groups (Chapter 2). Considering the availability of data, we preferred to rely on citizens' perceptions about the relative strength of the country's democratic institutions compared to other actors. We hypothesize that the higher the perception of the supremacy of democratic institutions over other domestic or international political actors, the higher the quality of democracy. We assume that people's opinions somehow reflect the true situation, which is not a trivial assumption. However, to some extent, the concepts of sovereignty and autonomy always involve some degree of subjective perception, as both scholars and ordinary citizens usually disagree on their meaning.

As Table 4.6 shows, citizen perceptions demonstrate considerable temporal coherence. We utilize the Latinobarómetro's question "Which of the following actors do you think has more power in your country?" and report the result of the first answer of each interviewee. For every year, more than 60 percent of the sample agreed that large firms are the most powerful actor in Argentina. This reality has considerable implications for the concept of sovereignty and also for the quality of democracy. If a large majority of the people believe that economic interests have more power than the democratic institutions of government, the quality of democracy would correspondingly be considered to be low. A visual comparison between the place occupied by large firms with government, political parties, and Congress provides an accurate perspective of how severe the characterization is; see Table 4.6. In particular, Congress, the body that represents people's preferences by definition, is considered the most powerful body by less than 1 percent of the citizens. Conversely, private firms, whose main interest is profit, are considered dominant by about two-thirds of Argentineans. This contrast may have several implications for perceptions of democratic quality. First, if public officials are not believed to have real power, or at least fail to demonstrate that they possess it, high levels of support for democratic institutions on other dimensions might be interpreted as being of little

Table 4.6   Popular Perception of the Most Powerful Argentine Actor for 1996, 2001, and 2005 (in percentage)

Actor	Perceived as Most Powerful
1996	
Large firms	64.0
Government	13.0
Multinationals	10.0
Political parties	6.0
Banks	3.0
Military	3.0
Labor unions	1.0
Mid-sized firms	0.4
Congress	0.4
2001	
Large firms	60.0
Labor unions	8.0
Government	7.0
Multinationals	6.0
Political parties	5.0
Military	5.0
Courts	4.0
Banks	4.0
Congress	0.4
2005	
Large firms	67.0
Labor unions	10.0
Military	6.0
Mass media	5.0
Political parties	5.0
Government	4.0
Banks	3.0
Congress	1.0

value. Even though we do not take this type of mechanical approach to the evaluation of these results, this does provide some cause for concern. Second, these perceptions have remained relatively constant over time (before, during, and after the 2001 crisis). In sum, unlike previous dimensions examined above, this evidence raises more serious questions about the performance of Argentine democracy, at least from the perspective of the country's citizens.

Conclusion

The underlying goal of this chapter has been to provide an empirical assessment of democratic quality and performance in Argentina, utilizing the guiding theory provided by Levine and Molina and those empirical measures that are the most valid indicators for the distinct concepts articulated in Chapter 1 and Chapter 2. This chapter on Argentina provides vital information regarding citizen behavior captured by public opinion surveys and also by their electoral decisions. Far from reaching irrefutable general conclusions, we focus on the provision of an overview of how the different dimensions that comprise Levine and Molina's general theory of democratic quality have evolved over time in Argentina.

Our overall findings suggest that the quality of democracy in Argentina is, in general, acceptable, although not without flaws. In particular, the popular belief that sovereignty lies more in powerful business actors than in democratic institutions represents a noteworthy deficiency in the functioning of the Argentine democratic system. Nevertheless, we do not forget what these conclusions would have implied in different historical periods. The fact that none of these perceived pitfalls ended up in massive claims for or the effective arrival of the armed forces is a trigger of satisfaction. Future work and additional data are needed to deepen our understanding of democratic quality in Argentina, as well as how the level of quality varies across both geographic regions and social classes within the country. However, it is crucial to place this specific evaluation of the quality of Argentina's democracy within the context of the Latin American region, since countries such as Chile, Colombia, and Mexico are the principal comparators for Argentina, and not, for instance, Scandinavian democracies, such as Denmark, Norway, and Sweden. All the same, the evidence reviewed here provides a relatively positive portrayal of the Argentine democratic system.

While far from ideal in regard to its performance, in the eyes of the Argentine citizenry, the Argentine democratic system has, at a minimum, achieved a satisfactory performance grade. This performance is all the more impressive when one considers the resilience of the Argentine democratic system, which since 1983 has faced numerous challenges in the forms of attempted coups, severe economic crises, political instability, and societal protest, and, admirably, come through all of these challenges intact. This resilience in the face of extreme adversity not only reflects positively on the Argentine democratic system's past performance, but also provides considerable hope for the continued successful performance of the system in the future.

Notes

1. At the other extreme, 6 percent, 15 percent, 20 percent, and 52 percent of the population did not access news via television, radio, the newspaper, and the Internet respectively.

2. We could have run an ordered logit model, considering that categories in the dependent variable mostly reflect one-unit increases. Nevertheless, the first category of no education and the last four categories covering postsecondary education are intervals that become immeasurable in terms of years. Considering that these groups are central

components of the statistical analysis, we preferred to use a model that does not induce any bias in the estimation and the interpretation.

3. National-level turnout data for presidential and legislative elections are also provided in Table 4.3.

4. We measure disproportionality (D), where $D = \dfrac{\left(\sum_{i=1}^{n} abs(v_i - s_i)\right)}{2}$. V_i is the ratio of votes of each party; s_i is the ratio of seats of each party, i, in the Chamber of Deputies elections for twenty-four electoral districts (Loosemore and Hanby 1971).

5. In 1983, each district chose all its legislators, unlike all the other elections where half of the legislators were elected. Given that increases in district magnitude should make the allocation of seats more proportional, it is to be expected that disproportionality was significantly lower in that election than in subsequent elections.

6. It is important to remember that the electoral rules governing Chamber elections remained essentially constant throughout this period. The principal explanation of the 1995, 2001, and 2009 peaks is the interaction between a heightened level of partisan fragmentation with very low district magnitudes (median of three) in the country's electoral districts (provinces).

7. For more detail, see Calvo and Abal Medina (2001); Calvo and Escolar (2005). The official name of the Peronist Party is the Partido Justicialista; however, Peronism frequently participates as part of larger multiparty alliances in which it is the dominant player. In 2009, coalitions of anti-Kirchner opposition parties won substantial vote shares in many provinces with low district magnitudes, which provided them, as well as the territorially dominant allies, pro-Kirchner Peronists in low-district-magnitude provinces, important seat bonuses, which resulted in a higher than normal level of disproportionality.

8. A comparable percentage of Argentines (10 percent) reported working for a presidential candidate during the 2007 presidential election campaign (LAPOP 2008).

9. We are not persuaded that patterns of interbranch cooperation and conflict reflect variation in democratic quality rather than simply a measure of the tenor of relations between the government and opposition. Only one referendum took place in Argentina between 1983 and 2010; however, we do not read this as an indication of weak democracy, as it is not a necessary condition for a healthy political regime. Finally, counting strikes and protests may be useful for the study of social movements, but we are uncertain if this activity reflects an active civil society or is merely a consequence of the mobilization capabilities of organized groups.

10. The remaining 4 percent occupy the midpoint, which is four, on this seven-point scale.

5

Mexico:
Weak State, Weak Democracy

Claudio A. Holzner

MEXICO'S TRANSFORMATION FROM A HIGHLY INSTITUTIONALIZED authoritarian regime dominated by a single political party, the Institutional Revolutionary Party (Partido Revolucionario Institucional; PRI), to a multiparty democracy was a remarkable achievement two decades in the making. Now that opposition parties have won two successive presidential elections; Congress can check the power of Mexico's once all-powerful president; and the outcomes of virtually all federal, state, and local elections are uncertain, the time is ripe for an assessment of the quality of democracy in Mexico. The picture that emerges is quite complex and inconsistent. From a strictly procedural standpoint, there is little doubt that Mexico's democratic transition and consolidation have been successful. In addition to free, fair, and frequent elections, the protections of freedom of the press, of expression, and association have been strengthened; the military is under civilian control; and there are no significant formal barriers to electoral or political participation for any group. However, Levine and Molina are right to argue that assessments of the quality of democracies need to pay attention to how they actually work, that is, whether rules are actually implemented, enforced, and produce desirable outcomes (Chapter 1). From this practical standpoint, the quality of democracy in Mexico is still lacking.

Jonathan Fox makes a useful distinction between transitions to democracy, which involve changes in the rules that determine who governs, and transitions to accountability, which involve more thorough changes in state institutions and their relationship to groups in society (Fox 2007). In many new democracies reforms of the state often lag behind reforms of the rules of the game, creating a disconnect between what political regimes aspire to and what they actually achieve. This is the case in Mexico. The primary strengths of Mexican democracy lie in institutional structures and laws that guarantee, at least in theory, civilian control over the military, protection of human rights, respect for freedoms of speech and

83

association, free and fair elections, and equal opportunities for all citizens to participate in the political process.

The primary weaknesses occur in the ways that the political system functions in practice, largely as a result of weak institutions that do not adequately enforce the rule of law, protect civil and political rights, combat corruption, collect taxes, or restrain powerful business and rent-seeking interests. As a result, the significant reforms that established the institutional foundations for an electoral democracy have not delivered adequate levels of accountability, responsiveness, rule of law, and political equality, doing great harm to the quality of democracy in Mexico.

It is also the case that Mexico's democratic consolidation is still very much a work in progress, haunted and hampered by deeply entrenched authoritarian legacies. While some have written about the persistence of authoritarian enclaves in Mexico, the word *enclave* understates just how pervasive, deeply rooted, and powerful authoritarian practices, institutions, and elites are in Mexico. Authoritarian legacies persist in a multitude of federal agencies, thrive in local- and state-level institutions, and thoroughly permeate the criminal justice system, seemingly immune to pressures from electoral competition. Many of the most egregious flaws with democracy occur at the subnational level, where vote buying, official violence and repression, and the intimidation of journalists and opposition supporters are still common. These authoritarian subnational practices have proven to be extremely resilient despite a strengthening civil society and significant democratic progress at the national level.

As we will see, Mexico's poor are much more likely to experience the authoritarian dark side of the political system, meaning that their opportunities for political participation are much narrower than the opportunities available to more affluent actors, their political and civil rights are more likely to be violated, and the elections they participate in are more likely to be marred by fraud. As a result, political inequalities tend to overlap with socioeconomic ones, further harming the quality of democracy in Mexico.

Strengths of Democracy in Mexico

Reforms of the Electoral System and the Rise of Political Competition

One of the defining characteristics of Mexico's political system between the 1930s and 1980s was the lack of meaningful political competition in elections at any level. The PRI regularly won local elections with 100 percent of the vote;[1] it never lost a presidential or gubernatorial election and won every single Senate seat before 1988. The National Action Party (Partido de Acción Nacional;

PAN), a probusiness party established in the 1920s in northern Mexico, has been the most consistent challenger to the PRI. But until it won the 2000 elections it rarely received more than 20 percent of the vote in presidential elections. Numerous other parties, particularly on the left of the political spectrum, have come and gone during these six decades; some even won municipal elections, but none of them ever posed a serious challenge to the PRI's electoral hegemony. Many of these small parties, such as the Popular Socialist Party (Partido Popular Socialista; PPS) and the Authentic Party of the Mexican Revolution (Partido Auténtico de la Revolución Mexicana; PARM) during the 1960s and 1970s, and later the Labor Party (Partido del Trabajo; PT) and the Green Party of Mexico (Partido Verde Ecologista Mexicano; PVEM) in the 1990s, made up a loyal opposition that exercised little autonomy from the PRI.

Most explanations of the PRI's electoral dominance emphasize the party's corporatist structure, which allowed it to control the political activity of labor, peasants, and state employees; its use of electoral fraud to pad its own votes; and occasional, but decisive, use of violence to repress groups that challenged the state or sought to democratize the political system. However, these strategies alone could not have preserved the legitimacy and stability of Mexico's one-party authoritarian regime for so long. The legal foundation for Mexico's electoral authoritarianism and PRI's ability to monopolize state offices were set in place with the electoral law passed in 1946 (Levy and Székely 1987).[2] Key features of this electoral system included (1) a single member, simple plurality (SMSP) electoral system to elect representatives to the Chamber of Deputies;[3] (2) the self-certification of elections through which newly elected members of Congress confirmed the election results that put them into power; (3) provisions that made it difficult for new political parties to emerge;[4] (4) the organization of elections and the counting of votes by the Ministry of the Interior, which, of course, were under the control of the PRI; and (5) an absence of real campaign finance laws, which allowed the PRI to use its almost unlimited access to state resources to outspend opposition parties by a huge margin. Each of these five features would have to change before elections in Mexico could become free, fair, and competitive.

The most important initiative for the long-term prospects of democracy in Mexico was the creation of the Federal Electoral Institute (IFE) in 1990, a decentralized entity in charge of organizing federal-level elections. Though at first the IFE remained under the control of the Ministry of the Interior and had little independent power to organize and monitor elections, over time its power and autonomy were bolstered in ways that produced free and fair elections by 1997, making possible the PAN's landmark victory in the 2000 presidential elections (Crespo 2004; Gómez Tagle 2004). The first reforms to strengthen the IFE occurred in 1994, giving citizen councilors more power and eliminating electoral self-certification by granting the IFE and the Federal Electoral Tribunal

(TEPJF), created in 1996, the power to certify the election of federal deputies and senators. Though the PRI could still—and did—outspend all other parties by a large margin, and though it received a disproportionate share of the media coverage, the victory of the PRI's presidential candidate, Ernesto Zedillo, in 1994 is generally regarded as legitimate. Today it is the institutional keystone of Mexican democracy.

The final bastions of the PRI's electoral authoritarianism crumbled with electoral reforms proposed in 1996 and passed by Congress in 1997 that finally eliminated all government control over elections, placing them fully in the hands of a strengthened IFE. The 1997 law also changed the way campaigns were financed to level the playing field between the PRI and the opposition. The new law set upper limits for campaign spending, limited private sources of financing to 10 percent of total campaign expenditures, established a new oversight mechanism for campaign spending, greatly increased public financing for campaigns, and expanded access to radio and television for all parties (Domínguez 1999; Gómez Tagle 2004). Because it was still the largest party in the country, the PRI received a larger share of this public funding and media coverage than the PAN or the left-of-center Party of the Democratic Revolution (Partido de la Revolución Democrática; PRD). However, under the new proportional financing formulas both the PAN and the PRD saw huge increases in public financing, giving them the resources with which to mount effective electoral challenges to the PRI (Bruhn 1999).

As important as these reforms were for establishing truly free and fair national elections in Mexico, other reforms were necessary to increase their competitiveness. Though it receives relatively little scholarly attention, Mexico's SMSP electoral system was a key institutional underpinning of Mexico's electoral authoritarianism that allowed the ruling party to convert its dominance at the polls into hegemonic control over the state. The SMSP system is not inherently undemocratic, but it does give important advantages to national parties that can organize effective campaigns and run candidates in all electoral districts. Since parties can only win seats in Congress by actually winning elections, small parties without a national presence can hope to win representation only if their support is concentrated in geographic regions that overlap with district boundaries. If their support is dispersed, as was the case for most opposition parties in Mexico, they may fail to win any seats in Congress even if they capture a substantial portion of the national votes, and even if the regime does not resort to any kind of electoral fraud.[5] By amplifying the representation of the PRI well beyond their actual vote count—and doing so legally and legitimately—the SMSP system was an important institutional foundation for the PRI's monopoly over government offices.

The first serious efforts to increase the competitiveness of elections in Mexico can be traced to the 1977 reforms of the electoral system that modified the

SMSP system by creating 100 proportional representation seats in the Chamber of Deputies, increasing the total number of seats to 400 from 300.[6] The intention of the reform was to create incentives for small parties to participate in elections by reserving all of the 100 proportional representation seats for minority parties, assuring them at least minimal levels of representation. In addition, the new electoral law made it easier for small parties to register and compete in elections, and guaranteed them free radio and television time.[7] The law had an immediate effect on political competition. Three new parties formed and competed in the 1979 midterm elections,[8] and by 1985 nine parties competed in national elections— five more than before the reforms. Nonetheless, the electoral rules still ensured that the PRI would retain control of all branches of government.

After the collapse of the economy in 1982 and the severe economic crisis that lasted past the middle of the decade, the PRI faced a crisis of legitimacy and increasing electoral challenges from both the left and the right. In response to these mounting challenges, the de la Madrid administration enlarged the lower house once again in 1986, creating an additional 100 proportional representative seats in the Chamber of Deputies, bringing the total number of seats to 500 (Crespo 2004: 69–70). Political competition was further enhanced in 1996 with reforms that adopted a formula for allocating proportional representation seats in the Chamber of Deputies that ensured that no party would be overrepresented by more than 8 percentage points, eliminating the PRI's ability to achieve an absolute majority without actually winning a majority of seats. It further reformed the way senators are elected, introducing a complex system of proportional and minority representation that reduced the chances that a majority party would be overrepresented in that chamber (Gómez Tagle 2004: 94–95).

By lowering the threshold for representation in both the chambers of Congress, the transition from an SMSP to a mixed proportional system in both houses created important incentives for small parties to compete in elections, and for voters to actually vote for them. Early electoral victories gave opposition parties opportunities to govern and raised their visibility with the public, making them more credible alternatives to the PRI (Magaloni 1999). The result is that Mexico now has a robust three-party system in Congress, with several small parties winning a handful of seats as well.

In addition to these reforms that guaranteed free, fair, and competitive elections at the national level, in 1997 residents of Mexico City were finally allowed to elect their mayor and local representatives.[9] The importance of this reform for the quality of democracy in Mexico is hard to overstate. It not only gave opposition parties a prominent stage where they could challenge the ruling party's grip on power, it also created brand new opportunities for more than 10 million Mexican citizens to vote, lobby, and otherwise influence local government decisions. Citizens of the capital city are now among the most engaged and politically active in the country, never shy about demanding the responsiveness of their elected leaders and holding them accountable for their decisions.[10]

The cumulative effect of three decades of electoral reforms on the quality of democracy in Mexico has been substantial. Mexico's electoral system has successfully minimized the chances that fraud will affect election results, ensures the competitiveness of elections, and enables parties to compete on a more or less level playing field (Schedler 2008). The victories of the PAN in the 2000 and 2006 presidential elections, along with the strengthening position of the PRD in parliamentary elections, have produced a balance of power between the executive and legislative branches that ensures much higher levels of both horizontal and vertical accountability. In fact, the same party has not controlled the executive and legislative branches since 1996, allowing the Mexican Congress to finally fulfill its constitutional role as a check on presidential power—historically one of the pillars of authoritarianism in Mexico. Optimists can also point to the 2009 midterm elections as evidence that citizens have learned to use elections to punish incumbents that underperform. After a dismal showing in the 2006 presidential and congressional elections, the PRI staged a remarkable comeback in the 2009 midterm elections, when it increased the number of seats it held from 104 (21 percent of the total) to 237 (47 percent), once again becoming the largest party in the Chamber of Deputies. In contrast, the PAN lost 63 seats, garnering only 28 percent of the vote. To the extent that the Mexican Congress is willing and able to exert its constitutional powers, congressional elections will become more important and meaningful, providing additional opportunities and stimuli for citizens to become involved in politics.

Decentralization and Subnational Participation Opportunities

Decentralization in Mexico was another institutional innovation that enhanced political competition and created new incentives for citizens to become involved in politics. Referenda are not common in Mexico, but the state's federalist structure; opportunities to elect mayors, city councils, governors, state senators, and deputies; and recent efforts to devolve power to state and local governments provide many opportunities for citizens to vote along with multiple mechanisms for demanding accountability and responsiveness from elected officials (Cabrero Mendoza 1998).

This was not always the case. Although Mexico's Constitution outlined a federal system similar to the one that exists in the United States, during the PRI's dominance almost all power was concentrated in the federal government, with most of that in the hands of the president.

> Each successive level of government is weaker, more dependent, and more
> impoverished than the level above. Since the municipality is at the bottom of
> the federal-state-local chain, it is in reality . . . the least autonomous unit of

government in the republic. An *ayuntamiento* or municipal government is normally constituted at the pleasure of state authorities, is in the control of very
few funds, and is limited juridically and politically to caretaker and administrative functions. (Fagen and Tuohy 1972: 20–21)[11]

Given this rigid power hierarchy, the political energies of political parties and
of ordinary citizens were often focused on state and national politics, hindering the
development of alternatives to the PRI at the municipal level. Serious efforts to decentralize power began under the de la Madrid administration with reforms that
granted municipal governments the capacity to raise revenues on their own
through property taxes and from the provision of public services (Rodríguez 1997:
73–76). Former president Zedillo (1994–2000) made decentralization a priority in
his administration and designed a program, called New Federalism, to further
strengthen the financial and administrative capacity of municipalities (Rodríguez
1997: 83–88).

In the same way that centralization of power and resources at the national
level reinforced and was, in turn, bolstered by one-party dominance, decentralization and increasing political competitions worked synergistically to dis-
mantle authoritarianism in Mexico. It is probably fair to say that
democratization in Mexico during the decade between 1989 and 1999 was
pushed forward by a rising tide of opposition-party victories in key state and
municipal elections. By the time Fox became the first opposition-party president
in seven decades, the PAN and the PRD had governed in most of Mexico's
largest cities, including Mexico City, and controlled the governments of nearly
half of Mexico's states. As more and more opposition parties gained control of
local and state governments, they individually and jointly pressured the federal
government to devolve more power and resources away from Mexico City. This
devolution of power was intended not merely to enhance governmental efficiency, but also as a means for furthering democratization by distributing power
and resources away from the presidency, away from the ruling party, and opening new channels for citizen voice.

Decentralization and competitive local elections have done much to enhance the functioning of democracy in Mexico. Local election victories have
been important launching pads for small new parties, giving citizens new
choices at the polling booth. Similarly, the ability of opposition parties to win
elections at the state and local levels has forced local governments to become
more responsive to citizen preferences, has allowed local legislatures to become
more professional and powerful, and has pushed parties to recruit candidates
that are better qualified and that have stronger local connections (Beer 2003).
Nevertheless, as we will see below, decentralization has also strengthened the
hand of authoritarian elites in many states and localities across Mexico, allowing a large number of authoritarian subnational regimes to survive within a
much more democratic national context.[12]

Weaknesses of Democracy in Mexico

Weaknesses in the Electoral System

Democracy has been firmly established in Mexico, built upon the bedrock of free, fair, and competitive elections overseen by the IFE. This is no small feat in a country where elections were synonymous with fraud, carried out not to elect leaders, but to legitimize an authoritarian regime. Still, electoral politics in Mexico has done little to produce a high-quality democratic system in which citizen voices are heard, elected representatives are responsive to citizen demands, and public officials are regularly held accountable for their actions. This is not only the fault of Mexico's electoral system. Even in the best of cases competitive elections are blunt instruments with which to hold leaders accountable (Fox 2007; Przeworski, Stokes, and Manin 1999). Nonetheless, Mexico's electoral democracy still has many flaws that hinder competition and impede accountable governance.

First among these is the constitutional ban against immediate reelection to any elected office. Elected officials are much more likely to be responsive to the public will if their permanence in office depends on voters' choices. However, the ban on reelection delinks politicians from voters while tying the politicians' political futures much more closely to their parties. Indeed, in Mexico, building a political career depends primarily on fulfilling the demands of party higher-ups than on fulfilling the demands of constituents, making elections a very indirect and often ineffective instrument for vertical accountability. Moreover, without the possibility of reelection, even well-intentioned officials will have trouble delivering on campaign promises because their one term in office makes it impossible to develop the relationships, experience, savvy, and political power necessary to get things done. In the case of mayors and federal deputies, who each serve three-year terms, it is often the case that as soon as they've learned the ropes of their new office, it is time for them to vacate it.

Under these institutional constraints, electoral accountability operates through the collective performance of all of a party's incumbents. This is not necessarily bad. Party discipline and party accountability to voters are core features of parliamentary democracies in Western Europe. However, political parties in Mexico are not nearly as coherent, organized, or disciplined as parties in Europe. All three major parties have transformed themselves into catchall parties, for whom ideological consistency matters less than winning elections. This ideological flexibility reached a new peak in 2010 when the right-of-center PAN and the leftist PRD—parties that have almost nothing in common ideologically—entered into a series of unlikely electoral alliances with the sole goal of defeating the PRI in state and local elections held that year. Smaller parties, such as the PVEM, the PT, Convergencia, and Nueva Alianza, too often either play the role of loyal opposition or are vehicles for the personal and political ambitions of their leaders. Most have little or no independent ideological identity. The result is that political parties, elected officials, and many political institutions have lost the trust of the vast majority of Mexicans. This distrust spawned a well-organized campaign during the 2009 midterm elections that encouraged Mexicans to abstain or to spoil their ballots.[13]

Though there is a growing consensus among Mexican politicians and analysts that the electoral system needs a major overhaul, political parties lack the political will or the incentives to bring about such a change (Dresser 2008). The reforms passed in 2007 have received mixed reviews. On the one hand, the reforms set new lower limits on campaign spending and private contributions while also cutting the length of campaigns in half. These changes are positive since campaigns had become unreasonably expensive, media driven, and vulnerable to the pressure exerted by powerful interest groups. On the other hand, critics argue that key aspects of the reforms served to further entrench existing parties and elites in power while failing to tackle tough issues like the constitutional ban against reelection.[14] According to Castañeda and Morales, the new rules will harm both the fairness of elections—favoring already existing parties and incumbents—and electoral accountability since citizens' access to information concerning the performance of incumbent parties will be limited precisely when they need it most. "By attempting to patch up the law and making simplistic reforms based on a flawed logic, elections will remain inequitable. This is certainly an undesirable outcome for citizens seeking to enhance the democratic character of the political system" (Castañeda and Morales 2008).

Uneven Subnational Democratization

Despite advances at the national level, subnational autocracies endure in many states and hundreds of municipalities in Mexico. Though studies have argued that political competition at the subnational level has been an important catalyst for democratic changes at the national level (see Beer 2003), the subnational political arena is also where authoritarian leaders are making rather successful last stands. The strongest resistance to democratization typically comes from state governors who use the power of their position to perpetuate local autocracies even as national politics are becoming more competitive and open (Gibson 2005). Though opposition parties compete for power in such settings, the dominant party typically wins a very large majority of legislative seats—in addition to its control over the executive—that enables it to exercise unchecked influence over political institutions and processes. As a result, electoral fraud and misconduct, along with other abuses of power and challenges to the rule of law, go largely unchecked (Magaloni 2006: 32–36).

Indeed, fraud is still a common occurrence in many state and local elections across Mexico. Though the bolstered IFE has been able to guarantee free and fair elections at the federal level, state and local elections are still under the responsibility of State Electoral Institutes whose quality, professionalism, and independence from state authorities are uneven. Many of them are still susceptible to manipulation from powerful governors and frequently enable electoral mischief (Gómez Tagle 1997; Peschard 2010). As a result, vote buying, stolen ballot boxes, coerced or mobilized voting by local bosses, and even computer crashes when the PRI is losing are still part of Mexico's electoral landscape.

Public opinion surveys that ask respondents whether or not they thought elections were conducted cleanly and fairly are a good way to measure the pervasiveness of authoritarian practices at the local level. The 2006 CSES-CIDE[15] asked people to evaluate the 2006 presidential elections on a 5-point scale according to whether they were "clean, somewhat clean, neither clean nor fraudulent, somewhat fraudulent, or totally marred by fraud." Overall perceptions of fraud were quite high (32 percent) and nearly twice as high as in 2000. Nevertheless, perceptions of fraud varied significantly across states, ranging from a low of 4 percent in Nuevo León to a high of 61 percent in Mexico City; see Figure 5.1.[16] Perceptions of fraud were highest in southern states, particularly in states where the PRD won the largest share of the vote. In Chiapas, Guerrero, Mexico City, state of Mexico, Oaxaca, Tabasco, and Tlaxcala—all states carried by the PRD—more people doubted the cleanliness of elections than thought they had been free and fair.[17]

Another pattern that stands out is that electoral irregularities appear to be much more common in poor states, towns, and neighborhoods (del Pozo and Aparicio 2001), which means that the poor experience the authoritarian side of Mexico's political system more consistently than higher-income citizens. Indeed, according to CSES-CIDE survey results, the poor consistently perceive elections as more fraudulent than the more affluent. Figure 5.2 compares the perceptions of electoral fraud across income groups between 1997 and 2006, precisely the period *after* elections were supposed to have become free and fair in Mexico. In 1997, 2000, and 2003 perceptions of fraud were highest among low-income respondents (people earning 0–3 times the minimum wage), although perceptions of fraud spiked for the most affluent (those earning 7 or more times the minimum wage) in 2006. This perception gap across income groups may account for lower turnout rates by the poor since perceptions of fairness of elections are among the most powerful predictors of turnout (Domínguez and McCann 1996; Lawson and Klesner 2004). What is perhaps most troubling for the consolidation of democracy in Mexico is that after declining between 1997 and 2000, as we would expect given the strengthening of the IFE, perceptions of fraud increased sharply for all income groups in the 2003 and 2006 elections.

It would be naïve to dismiss these subnational autocracies and authoritarian practices as anachronistic remnants of Mexico's authoritarian past, destined to wither away as democratic rules, norms, and practices take root and strengthen elsewhere. On the contrary, perceptions of fraud increased in all but

93

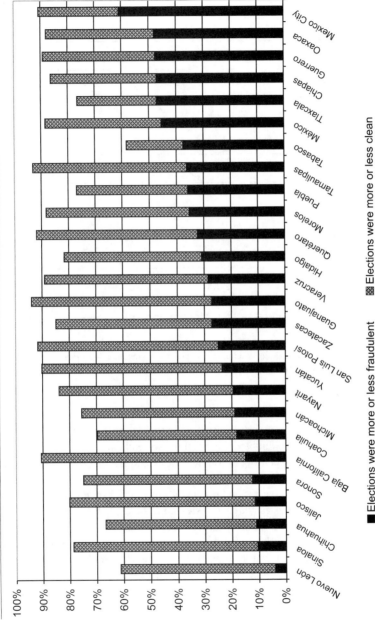

Figure 5.1 Perception of Election Fraud, by State (2006)

■ Elections were more or less fraudulent   ▨ Elections were more or less clean

Source: CSES-CIDE 2006.

Figure 5.2   Percentage of Respondents Who Thought 1997–2006 Elections Were Not Clean

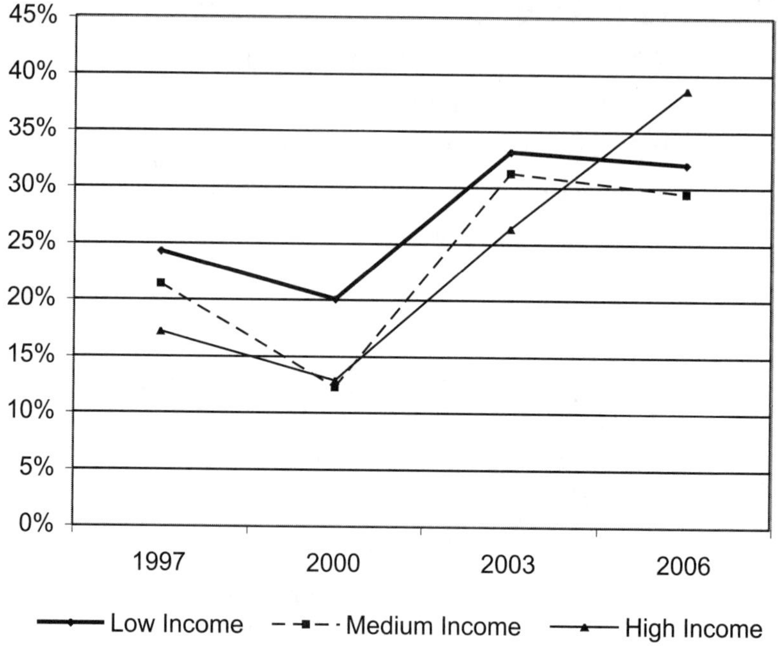

Source: CSES 1997–2006.
Notes: Low income: 0–3 times minimum wage; middle income: 3–7 times minimum wage; high income: 7+ times minimum wage.

three states included in both 2000 and 2006 CSES-CIDE surveys, in some cases by as much as 40 percent; see Figure 5.3. In the nation's capital, more than 60 percent of respondents doubted the elections were clean. Clearly, authoritarian practices are not disappearing in Mexico. Levy and Bruhn (2001), among others, point to several reasons to expect state-level autocracies to endure. First, the strength of opposition parties and organizations in civil society is very uneven across Mexico, leaving vast areas of Mexico to be captured and controlled by a dominant party organization—not necessarily the PRI—that will be able to govern with few if any checks on its power. Second, severe poverty and growing income inequality leave millions of Mexicans vulnerable to clientelist manipulation, so that they may actually choose to support authoritarian elites instead of more democratic alternatives. Third, decentralization policies have significantly strengthened state governments vis-à-vis both the local and national administrations, giving governors significant financial and political autonomy to pursue their own self-interested ends (Cabrero Mendoza 1998;

Figure 5.3   Change in Perceptions of Fraud Between the 2000 and 2006 Presidential Elections

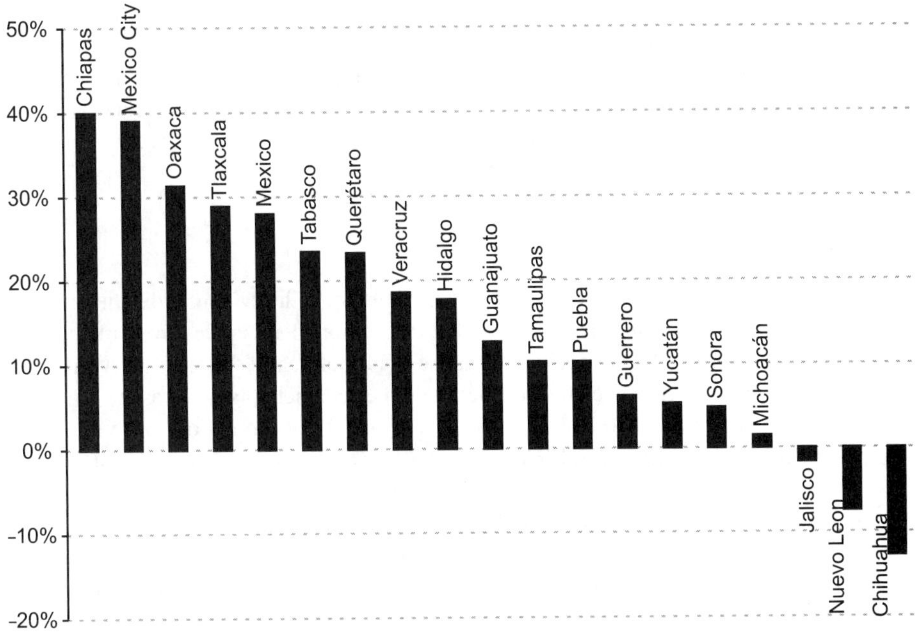

Source: CSES-CIDE 2000 and 2006.

Díaz-Cayeros 2004; Rodríguez 1997). Though these initiatives were supposed to reduce the power of the president and increase the quality of democracy, in many cases they have strengthened the hand of local authoritarian elites, who now have more resources with which to consolidate their power, leaving many state governments in the hands of people who have no intention of governing democratically (Gibson 2005; Levy and Bruhn 2001: 107).[18]

These local variations are immensely important for political participation and political attitudes, since it is at this level where people have their most frequent and meaningful experiences with the political process, form their ideas about how the political system works, and learn how to participate (Hiskey and Bowler 2005). In a study of local politics in Mexico, Hiskey and Bowler found that direct experiences with a subnational opposition government during the 1990s cultivated beliefs among Mexicans in those areas that elections were fair and the political system was democratic. However, citizens living in places where the opposition had never governed were much more inclined to view the system as fundamentally flawed, and consequently many chose to disengage from political life during the 2000 presidential elections (Hiskey and Bowler

2008: 67–68). Indigenous groups and the poor were the most likely to live in such towns, so it is their political participation that suffered the most from enduring local-level autocracies. The authors also warn that national-level processes of democratization can potentially be derailed by subnational authoritarian practices. While truly democratic local environments may help convince citizens that the system as a whole is improving, "an authoritarian, one-party local environment, on the other hand, will potentially undermine any impact positive national-level changes may have had on levels of system support in society" (Hiskey and Bowler 2008: 58).

Sovereignty and Rule of Law

Unlike most other Latin American countries where the military's subordination to civilian rulers has been an ongoing point of contention, democratic governments in Mexico have not had to deal with a legacy of a politically active military. Indeed, one of the defining features of Mexico's "perfect dictatorship" was the limited political influence of the military and its clear subordination to civilian political leaders (Camp 2004; Córdova 1972). To the extent that the military played a political role—by collecting political intelligence, repressing autonomous unions and political organizations that challenged the regime, and suppressing armed uprisings—it served the interests of Mexico's civilian authoritarian leaders. As a result, the autonomy of elected governments was never in doubt during Mexico's protracted democratic transition, and is surely one of the most important institutional strengths of democracy in Mexico (Camp 2007).

However, this does not mean that democratically elected governments, especially at the state and local levels, are free from the influence of nondemocratic actors. The financial, military, and political strength of drug cartels has increased significantly during the past decade, and they have not been shy about wielding this power to constrain the actions of elected officials. Of course, drug cartels can't threaten the sovereignty of civilian governments in the same way or as directly as the military can, but it is clear that when their economic interests are threatened, they act as aggressive veto players in ways that undermine Mexico's fragile democracy.

In the past, organized crime groups in Mexico channeled many of their resources toward battling the state, either through direct confrontation with the army and police forces or by bribing and co-opting them. Drug cartels have successfully infiltrated or rendered ineffective police forces and judicial systems in important cities, such as Tijuana and Ciudad Juárez, and wield enormous political influence in states like Guerrero, Michoacán, Sinaloa, Quintana Roo, and Tamaulipas. More recently, drug cartels have also begun trying to control the state itself by influencing the outcome of state and local elections. In the state and municipal elections held in fourteen states on July 5, 2010, cartels used a combination of strategies, including bribes, financing politicians' campaigns, hijacking party primaries, running their own candidates, intimidation, and outright assassination of unacceptable candidates to ensure that trusted allies were elected into positions of political power.

For example, on May 27, 2010, the PRD's gubernatorial candidate in Quintana Roo, and former mayor of Cancun, was arrested on suspicions of money laundering and ties to drug cartels. In the northern state of Tamaulipas, neither the PAN nor the PRD was able to recruit candidates to run in three municipal elections because all of their candidates faced death threats from drug traffickers. As a result, the PRI candidates ran unopposed in these elections. In the same state, the PAN suspended all of its local-level primaries, deciding instead to appoint all of its candidates directly from its national headquarters because of fears that drug cartels would influence the selection of the party's own candidates. Then, on June 28, less than one week before the elections, Rodolfo Torre, the PRI's gubernatorial candidate in Tamaulipas, was gunned down, allegedly by hit men from one of the drug cartels vying for control over key smuggling routes through the state. At least eleven other candidates and party officials were killed nationwide in the run-up to the local elections.

There appears to be little the Mexican state can do to prevent drug cartels from hijacking local-level democratic process. Though the IFE argued that the 2007 electoral reforms provide sufficient safeguards against the infiltration of drug money into political campaigns, in reality it has no way to track the cash payments, bribes, and business opportunities that cartels routinely offer political candidates. The federal government has on occasion arrested candidates with ties to cartels, but many more with clear ties to organized crime groups go free and win elections. Since declaring a war on drug cartels in 2007, President Felipe Calderón has deployed 45,000 troops and 5,000 federal police officers in eighteen states, often to replace local police forces who either resigned en masse, were too corrupt to be trusted, or lacked the resources to fight the cartels. Even so, this massive deployment of troops has not prevented electoral violence or adequately protected political candidates and elected officials.

It is also increasingly clear that where they are strongest, drug cartels threaten the capacity of the state to rule and protect basic civil and political rights, especially freedom of speech and of the press. According to some estimates, more than 22,000 people have been killed in drug-related violence since January 2007.[19] Freedom of the press is also severely restricted by drug cartels in certain states and municipalities, where journalists are routinely bribed, threatened, kidnapped, or killed. Editors of local newspapers admit to self-censoring when reporting news about drug cartels.[20] Their fears are well justified. Mexico is one of the most dangerous countries in the world for journalists, more dangerous even than Iraq and Afghanistan. According to the International Press Institute, eleven journalists were killed in 2009, up from five in 2008; ten journalists were killed by July 2010, more than in the rest of Latin America or in the entire continent of Africa. Ironically, all of this means that the quality of democracy in Mexico suffers not at the hands of an oppressive leviathan, but because a relatively weak state is unable to protect its own citizens, guarantee political and civil liberties, or ensure the integrity of local elections.

The rising power of organized crime points to other serious weaknesses with the rule of law in the country. Mexico's criminal justice system is woefully incapable of dealing with the challenges of increasing criminal activity in the country, creating conditions in which citizens' political and human rights are not consistently protected, government officials are not held accountable, and corruption undermines the strength of the state.[21] However, deep structural reforms of the criminal justice system are only in their infancy, while other reforms designed to bolster the rule of law and fight organized crime have been ineffective, shortsighted, and ultimately damaging to democratic rule in Mexico.[22]

The federal government's efforts to fight the violence and corruption caused by the drug trade have had their own harmful effects on the quality of democracy in Mexico. Forced to respond to a mobilized and restless electorate, democratically elected presidents have strong incentives to ignore the deep structural reforms that are necessary to improve the rule of law in Mexico, and pursue instead policies that are politically expedient in the short term even if they harm the quality of democracy in the long term. The militarization of public security and crime fighting under Fox and Calderón is one such initiative that responds to public pressure to do something about the growing strength of drug cartels, but does little to improve the functioning and capacity of existing organizations nor does anything to improve institutional accountability or citizen's access to justice (Arzt 2007). Analysts are especially concerned about potential and actual human rights abuses committed by the military,[23] the lack of transparency and accountability in military operations, increasing corruption within the military, declining capacity in both the police and armed forces, and negative long-term consequences for civilian-military relations (Arzt 2007; Camp 2007). In the worst-case scenario, the militarization of public security may produce more corruption, more impunity, more human rights abuses, with little or no improvements in the capacity of local police or prosecutors to fight crime.

The growing economic and political power of drug cartels, coupled with the obvious weakness of key state institutions, has raised concerns that Mexico could become a failed state. Though Mexico is not likely to collapse like Afghanistan, the fight against drug cartels has revealed with great clarity and tragedy that Mexico's political and judicial institutions are very weak. As one moves from the federal to the state and the municipal levels, the weaknesses become more apparent and systematic. Decentralization reforms that gave state and local governments more power of the purse without strengthening key governing institutions are partly to blame for this situation.

Rather than collapsing from the center, a more likely scenario—and in some places already a reality—is that the Mexican state will crumble from the bottom up, failing first where it is weakest: at the local level. In large municipalities like Ciudad Juárez, and smaller ones like Tancítaro, Michoacán, the state and federal governments have had to take over public security from local police forces deemed ineffective or too corrupt. In Tancítaro the entire local government resigned in December 2009, leaving the town without a government or a police force for weeks. Thus far, the relative strength of federal institutions—the IFE, the military, the economic bureaucracy—is sustaining Mexico. But President Calderón is being forced to deploy more and more federal resources to buttress the weakness of local governments. These are steps toward a recentralization of power, which may be necessary in light of the inability of local institutions or governments to resist the influence and strength of drug cartels. But the danger remains that Mexico will become a fragmented state with large pockets of ungovernability, authoritarianism, and institutions that cannot cope with the challenges they face.

Political Participation and Political Inequality

Because the intrinsic equality of each citizen is a fundamental assumption of democracies, any assessments of the quality of democracy must consider the equality of political voice, that is, whether a political system provides citizens with more or less equal opportunities for effective political participation and political access to decisionmakers during and between elections (Dahl 1989a; Verba, Schlozman, and Brady 1995). Without such effective participation the other four conditions for democratic rule highlighted by Levine and Molina—accountability, electoral decision, responsiveness, and even sovereignty—necessarily suffer.

It is tempting to conclude that the transition from autocracy to democracy in Mexico created political openings and opportunities for participation for all. But there are good theoretical and empirical reasons to expect democratic systems not to be neutral in their participatory effects, but to bias political opportunities toward some groups and away from others.[24] Thus, whether citizens are able to exercise their voice equally in a democratic political process is an empirical question, not an intrinsic characteristic of democracies.

Most attempts to assess levels of political equality focus on *who* participates and *how much*. Inequalities of voice, especially systematic inequalities that overlap with social cleavages (income, gender, religion, etc.), damage democracy by affecting the messages that politicians hear and diminishing the incentives they have for responding to the needs and preferences of certain groups. Despite two decades of economic reforms designed to grow the economy and alleviate poverty, Mexico still has one of the most unequal distributions of income of any country. Rural residents and members of indigenous groups are the most likely to both live in poverty and face exclusionary political practices. Thus, extreme poverty, social marginalization, and gaping socioeconomic inequality are among the greatest threats to political equality in Mexico.

A quick look at Figure 5.4 shows that political inequality based on socio-economic inequalities is a potential problem in Mexico. Overall, the poor participate less than middle- and high-income groups, while citizens with less than a high school education, who make up a majority of the population, are much less active than high school and college graduates. Men are slightly more politically active, and, as in other democracies, the elderly participate more than the young. The CSES-CIDE survey did not have information about rural and urban residents, but it is quite clear that residents of Mexico City are more active than residents of other states. Though this is not surprising, given that most federal government offices are located in the capital city, residents' political activism magnifies even more the political importance of the city's local politics.

Though it is important to know who participates, a full assessment of political equality needs to also consider variation in the *kinds* of political activities individuals and groups attempt. Much of the literature equates elections and the principle of one person, one vote with political equality.[25] However, the link between elections and governmental accountability and responsiveness is actually rather weak. Voting is simply too infrequent and conveys too little information to act as a reliable check on the behavior of elected and appointed government officials. In places where the democratic rule of law is compromised, elections may have the opposite effect: they can serve to affirm the power and impunity of a small number of undemocratic actors (O'Donnell 2004a). Other kinds of political acts, such as protests or the direct contacting of government officials are just as, or more, crucial for influencing policy decisions, holding political representatives accountable, and ensuring that governments are responsive to the needs and preferences of citizens between elections.

Political acts serve different purposes within the political process. Some forms of political participation, such as elections and referenda, provide opportunities for citizens to make collective decisions, while others are more important for placing issues on the decisionmaking agenda or for influencing the behavior of government officials. In practice, direct contacts, letter writing, protests, and public-opinion campaigns, more than voting itself, are the means by which citizens convey specific information to state actors and hold democratic governments accountable. Distortions of the principle of political equality also arise, therefore, when some social and economic groups are better able to participate in activities that convey detailed information about policy matters and place significant pressure on politicians, even if they vote little or not at all (Holzner 2007b).

While Figure 5.4 looks at overall levels of participation for different groups, Figure 5.5 uses data from three national-level surveys to compare political activism by income group across a wide variety of political activities, from donating money to campaigns to protesting and contacting local and national government representatives. It is evident that for most activities, the poor now

Figure 5.4   Political Participation: Mean Number of Acts by Mexicans, 2000

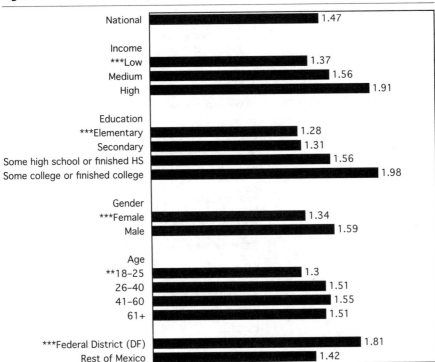

Source: CSES-CIDE 2000.
**Indicates that differences are statistically significant at .05 level; ***indicates that differences are statistically significant at .01 level.
Notes: Income categories are based on household income: Low income = $0–3,384; Middle income = $3,385–7,896; High income = $7,897 or more.

participate less than the most affluent, and usually less than all other income groups. For some activities, such as signing petitions and talking about politics, which always followed class-based patterns, the participatory gap between the rich and poor widened. For other activities, such as joining strikes, contacting government officials, and participating in protests and marches, in which the poorest citizens used to outparticipate the most affluent, the pattern is now reversed, with the poor now being the least active (Holzner 2007a). The poor participate more frequently than middle- and high-income individuals in only two political acts: working together with neighbors to solve community problems and contacting local government officials. This predilection for political contacting does not extend beyond the local level, however, since the poor contact national-level representatives or government offices at much lower rates than higher-income individuals.

Figure 5.5   Frequency of Political Activity by Income

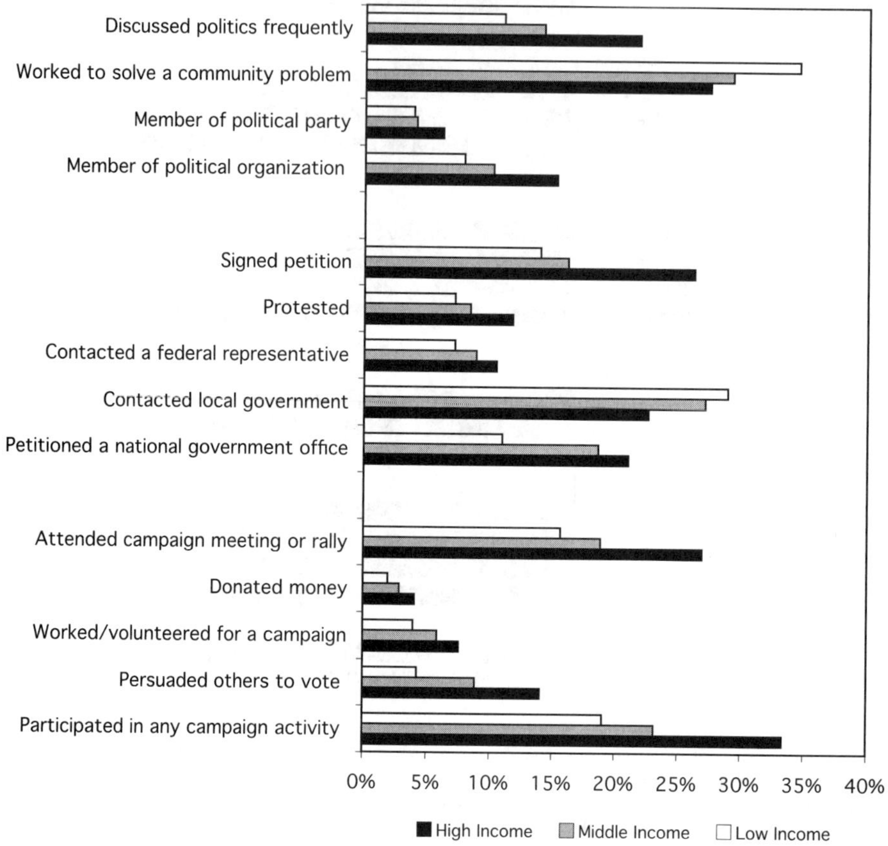

Sources: CSES-CIDE 2000; World Values Survey 2000; LAPOP 2004.

Voting and turnout in federal elections follow a similar pattern. Though the difference in turnout between income groups reported in the CSES-CIDE survey does not show a clear stratification by social class,[26] others have found a large and growing income gap among voters (Klesner and Lawson 2000; Lawson and Klesner 2004). The wealthy did not always vote more than the poor in Mexico. Quite the contrary: research into voting behavior in Mexico has shown that during the 1960s, 1970s, and 1980s the poor and relatively uneducated were more likely to vote than the rich (Craig and Cornelius 1980). The stratified voting pattern, with wealthier, more educated citizens voting more regularly, did not become established until the 1990s and continues into the present (Lawson and Klesner 2004).

Implications for Voice and Equality in Mexico

Voting and campaign activity. The establishment of regular, competitive elections in Mexico, where electoral fraud and clientelist mobilization practices were common, has been justly celebrated.[27] Voting is now the most common political activity for Mexican citizens, and given the competitiveness of elections and the guarantees against fraud, it is now also meaningful since it provides a credible mechanism for removing incumbents from power. However, compared to other kinds of electoral and government-directed activities, the vote is a weak tool for influencing the decisions of policymakers. Though available to all, unless votes are organized in large, disciplined blocks around policy issues, elections convey little information to elected officials and exert even less pressure on their decisions (Piven and Cloward 1997: 281). In fact, one of the core findings of political participation research in democratic systems is that effective participation in the electoral process requires resources, skills, and organizational ties that the poor do not possess in abundance. We might, therefore, think of a political system that relies primarily on voting as a means to ensure government responsiveness and accountability as a *thin democracy*, because there will be few opportunities for citizens to put pressure on government officials between elections.

Campaign activities, such as attending rallies, volunteering for political candidates, and donating money, hold more potential for voice than voting alone. Though citizen participation in electoral campaigns has always been important in Mexico,[28] given how expensive, sophisticated, and organizationally complex electoral campaigns have become, candidates depend more than ever on citizen support to run successful campaigns. Volunteering for campaigns or donating money to candidates gives participants multiple opportunities to meet with political candidates and their advisors. In turn, candidates have more incentives to listen and respond to the messages they hear from these activists. Just as importantly, campaign activity, unlike voting, can be multiplied in frequency and intensity, so that citizen inputs are not counted or weighed equally (Verba, Schlozman, and Brady 1995: 45–46). We have already seen that in Mexico the affluent are about twice as likely to participate in campaign activities as the poor and much more likely to donate money to campaigns. This creates the potential for severe inequalities in voice that overlap with Mexico's severe income inequalities, producing candidates that are less responsive and accountable to the poor. Unless the poor are able to participate in ways that send clearer messages to government officials and put more pressure on them in between elections—by contacting them directly or carrying out protests and marches—they may have little voice in policymaking.

Petitioning and protest activity. Like campaign activity, petitioning of government officials and participation in protests can be used by individuals to send precise messages about their needs and opinions about issues, and can be multiplied in ways that increase the pressure individuals can place on policymakers. Both these characteristics make such activities powerful vehicles for citizen voice and accountability, which can be used by the poor to mitigate the class biases generated by the electoral process. Petitioning party and government officials for assistance has been one of the most common and meaningful forms of participation for Mexico's poor. However, petitioning among the poor has declined since the democratic transition, so that now they petition much less frequently than before and about half as often as the most affluent (Holzner 2007a).

This somewhat counterintuitive finding makes more sense if we consider how democratic and economic reforms in Mexico affect the capacity and incentives of citizens to contact government officials. Contacting government officials has become an increasingly costly and ineffective strategy, requiring a significant investment in time, money, and lost wages. On the one hand, declining incomes during the 1980s and 1990s mean that the opportunity cost of political participation is higher now than during the prereform era, discouraging the poor from attempting political contacting on their own. On the other, during the 1990s, policy and distributional decisions became more centralized in distant ministries, while many budgetary decisions are now insulated from political pressures from below by using fixed formulas to determine spending levels for education, health care, and poverty alleviation programs. To be effective, contacting activities require the support of important allies within government ministries and from local organizations that subsidize the cost of travel or whose leaders carry out the petitioning activity on behalf of local groups. However, traditional worker and peasant organizations have been severely weakened as a result of economic crises and free-market policies that reduced their access to government patronage. Many new independent organizations now populate Mexico's civil society, but these tend to be small, weak, and fragmented. So while it is true that clientelist and corporatist organizations during the rule of the PRI tended to demobilize popular groups by fragmenting them and forcing them to compete against each other for patronage, civil society in Mexico today is no less fragmented, and organizations face different but still strong pressures to compete against each other for resources and access (Kurtz 2004). We might expect that because of worsening grievances and the closing of conventional channels of access, there would be an increase in protest activity. However, poor people's predilection for disruptive acts is often overstated in the literature. The incidence of protest in Mexico, as elsewhere, responds more to the actions of the state and of political entrepreneurs and to the strength of organizations than it does to societal grievances (McAdam, McCarthy, and Zald 1996; Tarrow 1998).

Many, if not most, of Mexico's poor see protest as a risky, dangerous, and not very effective strategy, to be attempted only after all other options have been exhausted (Holzner 2004). This should not be interpreted as an attitude rooted in a political culture characterized by deference to authority, as some have argued (Almond and Verba 1963; Stokes 1995). Rather, it is rooted in a clear recognition of the risks, difficulties, and unlikelihood of success of protest activity. In fact, because of the centralization of policymaking in Mexico protest campaigns must target the highest levels of government over a sustained period of time to be successful. Of course, these are exactly the kinds of protests that are most visible and receive the greatest media coverage, but are practically impossible for increasingly unorganized and resource-poor actors to undertake. Given that the affluent were nearly twice as likely to attempt protests in Mexico, we would be right to suspect that they are better able to bear the risks and costs of protesting and have more opportunities and incentives to target the state than the poor (Holzner 2010).

Exit. Though much of the demobilization and depoliticization of the poor occur at the level of groups, affecting their capacity to undertake collective action, the voice of the poor is silenced just as much by the cumulative effect of individual decisions to simply drop out of politics. That does not mean that the urban and rural poor are becoming an apathetic mass. On the contrary, popular urban neighborhoods and small rural towns in Mexico are alive with community activity, ranging from juntas and *asambleas* (meetings and assemblies), to cooperation among neighbors to supply themselves with water and electricity, to negotiations with local officials about pressing problems, to membership in numerous civil society organizations (Fox 2007; Gutmann 2002; Rubin 1997). Though such activities may be interpreted as a kind of civic activity, they are also the result of a learned pessimism that government-directed activity will not work (Dietz 1998; Holzner 2010). Though in the long term self-help strategies and community politics may produce a more active citizenry, they are not an effective means for citizens to communicate preferences to political leaders or to put pressure on government officials to be more responsive. On the contrary, rather than demanding accountability from the state, self-help activities let the state off the hook.

Conclusion

What does all this mean for the quality of democracy in Mexico? Although national-level elections are competitive, free of fraud, and inclusive, electoral competition has not been enough to ensure the responsive, accountable, and transparent functioning of state institutions and elected governments. In addition, the spread of political competition and democratic political practices has been very uneven in Mexico, creating a complex mix of pluralist enclaves coexisting with authoritarian strongholds and semidemocratic, subnational regimes (Beer 2003; Fox 1994, 1996). Optimists consider the spread of political competition across cities and states as beneficial for the consolidation of democratic practices in Mexico. Increasing political competition, openness and transparency of administrations, and opposition victories teach residents about democratic practices and send citizens signals that change is possible and political participation worthwhile (Beer 2003). By the same logic, however, the survival of authoritarianism at the state and local levels means that undemocratic practices are also constantly reproduced and reinforced. Thus, Mexico's mottled, uneven, and incomplete transition to democracy simultaneously encourages democratic practices and allows authoritarian ones to thrive.

The principle of political equality of citizens is also under threat. On the one hand, increased political competition has not empowered the poor during or after elections. The decline of corporatism tied to the former ruling party has helped spawn a more independent and active civil society, but it has not resulted in an end to clientelism or in the emergence of organizations capable of mobilizing the poor into politics on a consistent basis. The political process and systems of representation in Mexico are organized in ways that privilege established political parties, making it difficult for citizens, groups in civil society, and new social movements to press their claims in representative arenas in ways that preserve their autonomy. On the other hand, neoliberal reforms have reduced the number of institutional sites available where citizens can exercise their political voice and, in many instances, raised the barriers and costs of political participation to levels that make it especially difficult for the poor to contemplate political activity (Holzner 2010; Kurtz 2004). Together, the political and economic reforms of the past decade have created a political process that translates economic inequalities into political ones.

Many of the weaknesses of democratic rule in Mexico do not have their origins in faulty rules of the game, but in institutional weaknesses within the Mexican state that make the implementation of those rules inconsistent, unpredictable, and, in some cases, nonexistent. The weakness of the Mexican criminal justice system, which includes police forces, prosecutors' offices, and the court system, stands out as a key source for low levels of accountability. But weaknesses in electoral and human rights oversight agencies, in local state institutions, and in institutions that guarantee the transparency of government operations also create the conditions under which corruption, abuse of power, and human rights abuses flourish.

The combination of weak state institutions, the persistence of subnational authoritarianism, and high levels of economic and political inequality have trapped Mexico's democracy in a self-enforcing, low-accountability equilibrium, where weakness in one set of accountability institutions and actors perpetuates weaknesses in others (Fox 2007). A strong civil society can counterbalance some of these weaknesses and enhance the vertical, horizontal, and societal dimensions of accountability, but only to a point (Fox 2007; Peruzzotti and Smulovitz

2006b). "When ineffective official human rights defenders fail to stop or sanction violations of basic political freedoms, they also weaken civil society's capacity to exercise vertical accountability over the state. The weakness of governmental electoral and human rights agencies generates a downward spiral; persistent electoral and human rights violations in turn weaken civil society capacity to pursue all kinds of accountabilities, which in turn weakens the official horizontal accountability agencies" (Fox 2007: 34).

A key question raised by the Mexican case is whether democracy is even possible where the state is weak. Iraq and Afghanistan are evidence that where states fail, democracy is little more than theater. Though it is safe to say that the Mexican state is not on the verge of collapsing,[29] the prognosis is very different at the provincial and local levels. In many of Mexico's most modern cities, crime is rampant, kidnappings and murders are commonplace, and police forces are outmanned and outgunned by drug cartels. During the past decade, dozens of local governments have collapsed under the pressure of fighting drug cartels operating in their territory, leaving citizens with no government and no police force. What is worse, these institutional weaknesses at the state and local levels have provided drug cartels with multiple opportunities to hijack the electoral process for their own ends. The worrisome prospect is that drug cartels will use Mexico's democratic process to gain control of key parts of the Mexican state.

Are these weaknesses large enough to call into question Mexico's democratic credentials? The answer depends, of course, on how one chooses to define a democracy and on what evidence one chooses to focus. Advocates of procedural definitions tend to see the glass as half full, arguing that Mexico is a competitive electoral democracy by virtue of free, fair, and competitive *national* elections. If one prefers instead a dichotomous definition of democracy, does Mexico meet a minimum threshold of democratic governance? How much corruption, impunity, or fraud can exist before we begin to question the democratic credentials of a regime? Can we tolerate more corruption and less accountability at the local level if national-level elections are free, fair, and competitive? Unfortunately the literature does not provide clear answers. Certainly some kinds of corruption—petty corruption among police and graft among politicians—are common to all democracies. But dichotomous definitions of democracy don't allow for many nuances: a half-empty glass is just that, half empty. Political systems in which citizens cannot hold government officials accountable, cannot request information with guarantees that it will be provided in a timely manner, where the rule of law is tenuous and corruption rampant, where human rights abuses go unpunished, and where local authoritarian leaders manipulate elections before and after ballots are cast are not very democratic.

The answer is further complicated by the coexistence of authoritarian, subnational regimes with truly democratic ones. Though democratic local and state governments exist in most states, it is probably safe to say that at least a quarter of the population lives under authoritarian provincial governments (especially in rural states like Oaxaca, Guerrero, and Chiapas); it is probably also safe to say that many millions of others live in urban settings where the rule of law is under serious threat. Additionally, leaders of all three parties have at various times shown dubious commitments to democratic rule, particularly when it conflicts with their personal interests or the interests of their core constituencies. Given these realities, the existence of free and fair elections every three years at the national level is an important but increasingly tenuous basis for claiming democratic credentials. Democracies cannot live by elections alone, at least not for very long.

Notes

1. Because of the PRI's practice of inflating voter rolls and sending teams of supporters to vote multiple times in different locations, the party sometimes won with more than 100 percent of the vote. See Preston and Dillon for anecdotal descriptions of these practices (2004); Molinar Horcasitas for a more systematic analysis of fraud in the 1986 gubernatorial election in Chihuahua (1987).

2. For more details on the election system and electoral competition before 1946, see Crespo (2004); González Casanova (1965, 1985).

3. This system is more commonly known as a winner-take-all system, or a first-past-the-post system, which is very similar to the electoral system in the United States. In such a system, candidates compete for a single seat in each of the federal districts. The candidate with the most votes, even if it is less than an absolute majority, wins the seat. It is a system that favors large, well-organized parties that can field candidates in all districts and tends to produce fewer parties than proportional representation systems.

4. To register, new political parties had to register 30,000 members nationwide, with 1,000 more distributed in at least two-thirds of the thirty-one states and Mexico City. The Communist Party was not allowed to participate in elections (Levy and Székely 1987: 65).

5. For example, in 2005 in Great Britain, which also has an SMSP system, the Labour Party won a majority of the seats in the House of Commons with less than 40 percent of the vote.

6. A reform implemented in 1963 allocated thirty to forty seats to minority-party candidates on the basis of their national vote totals, but it was not a proportional representation system. For more detail on these reforms and their consequences, see the essays by Middlebrook, Cornelius, and Molinar Horcasitas in Drake and Silva (1986).

7. See Levy and Székely (1987: 66–67) for details on this reform.

8. The 1977 reforms made it possible for the left to reorganize and compete again in national elections. Between 1977 and 1985, the PSUM, PMT, PRT, and PST all formed and achieved a national registry. In addition, the conservative PDM gained legal status.

9. Up until that point, the mayor of the city was appointed by the president, which meant he was not just a PRI loyalist, but a close and trusted ally of the president.

10. For example, between 1997 and 2006 the average turnout in federal elections for Mexico City was 62.5 percent, compared to 55.5 percent nationally. In the 2006 presidential elections, turnout in Mexico City was 10 percentage points higher than the national average.

11. See Rodríguez for further elaboration of the capacities of local governments in Mexico during the 1970s and 1980s (1997).

12. For more detailed discussions of the relationship among federalism, democracy, and accountability, see Eaton (2006); Fox (2007); Gibson (2005).

13. Overall, approximately 5.5 percent of the ballots were nullified during the 2009 election, up from 2.5 percent in 2006. In Mexico City more than 10 percent of the ballots were spoiled, up from about 1.8 percent.

14. Some of the key provisions of the new law included: (1) a prohibition on negative campaigning; (2) shortening the length of presidential campaigns to three months; (3) a requirement that television and radio stations broadcast free political advertising; (4) a ban on candidates, political parties, and party supporters from buying political advertisements on radio and television; (5) a lower cap on the amount of money parties can raise from private sources; (6) a reduction in public financing for parties; and (7) the removal of some of the IFE leadership before their term was due.

15. For most of the analysis I use data from the Mexico waves of the Comparative Study of Electoral Systems (CSES) surveys. In addition to the standard CSES survey questions, which are the same for every country, each country collaborator can add additional questions to the end of the questionnaire. I rely on the full Mexico version of the CSES surveys, which are housed at the library of the Center for Economic Research and Teaching (Centro de Investigación y Docencia Económica; CIDE). I refer to these as CSES-CIDE surveys to distinguish them from the narrower CSES surveys.

16. In most cases, the sample size collected in each state ranges from about 50 to well over 200, giving us greater confidence in these numbers. However, in certain states such as Morelos, San Luis Potosí, Tabasco, Tlaxcala, and Oaxaca, sample sizes ranged from twelve to twenty-five. We should be much more cautious when making inferences about these states based only on the survey evidence.

17. There is a significant amount of variation within states as well. For example, within the state of Mexico, which is the most populous, perceptions of fraud ranged from a low of 26 percent to nearly 80 percent in some municipalities.

18. Cornelius sees local- and state-level governments as "the principal source of inertia and resistance to democratization, rather than the prime breeding ground for democratic advances" (Cornelius, Eisenstadt, and Hindley 1999: 11). See also Fox (2007, especially chapters 3, 5, and 7).

19. "Mexico Under Siege: The Drug War at Our Doorstep," *Los Angeles Times,* July 26, 2010; http://projects.latimes.com/mexico-drug-war/#/its-a-war.

20. In September 2010, after one of its photographers was killed, the newspaper *El Diario de Juárez* published an editorial in which it pleaded with drug cartels "to explain what you want from us, what you would like us to publish and not publish so that we can abide by that."

21. Transparency International, an international organization that evaluates levels of corruption across the world, gives Mexico a score of 3.6 out of 10 on its Corruptions Perception Index, where 10 is least corrupt. Mexico ranks seventy-second out of 180 countries on this index, above Brazil and Argentina, on par with China and Peru, and well below Costa Rica and Uruguay (www.transparency.org).

22. See the essays in Cornelius and Shirk (2007). However, it is worth noting that some reforms, particularly reforms that increased the independence of the Supreme Court (see Magaloni 2003) and that mandate increased institutional transparency (see Fox et al. 2007), have had positive consequences for horizontal and vertical accountability.

23. According to national and international human rights organizations—such as Mexico's National Human Rights Commission (Comisión Nacional de Derechos Humanos; CNDH), Amnesty International, and Human Rights Watch—police torture; ille-

gal search, seizure, and arrests; and impunity for military and police officers who commit human rights abuses are persistent problems with Mexico's criminal justice system.

24. See Campbell (2003); Gaventa (1980); Holzner (2010); Houtzager and Kurtz (2000); Verba, Nie, and Kim (1978).

25. See Verba, Schlozman, and Brady for a review of this literature (1995: 12–14).

26. Overreporting of voting behavior is a common problem with survey research, including the CSES-CIDE surveys.

27. This section draws from Holzner (2007b).

28. Even if only to ritualistically confirm the legitimacy of the electoral process (Adler Lomnitz, Lomnitz Adler, and Adler 1993).

29. Indeed, many federal institutions are quite strong and have recently shown encouraging resilience in the face of potentially devastating political and economic crises.

6

Brazil:
The Persistence of Oligarchy

Alfred P. Montero

BRAZIL HAS ALWAYS BEEN A PUZZLING CASE WITHIN LATIN America. This is no less true about Brazil's present-day democracy, which at twenty-five years, represents the longest period of liberal democratic rule in the country's history. In January 2003, then-president Fernando Henrique Cardoso (1994–2002) passed the presidential sash to newly elected president Luiz Inácio da Silva (2002–2010)—commonly called Lula. Although it occurred eighteen years after the transition to democracy, it was the first time two directly elected presidents made this exchange.[1] By this time, many dimensions of Brazilian democracy were consolidated, including civilian control over the armed forces, most of the procedural aspects of political contestation such as free and fair elections, and robust levels of participation, both at the ballot box and in the form of continued organization of civil society. Yet Brazilian democracy also evinces many characteristics of its oligarchical and authoritarian past. Political identities remain weak, and voters are typically unknowledgeable about politics, allowing elites to "manage" the voting of the poor, especially in the more rural areas of the country in the northern and northeastern regions. While Brazilian civil society has been successful in mobilizing on behalf of democratization and human rights, conservative elites continue to mobilize the poor as well, often in support of policies and politics that disempower them. Corruption, the politicization of the courts, and even political violence play a role in protecting these domains of oligarchical rule.

The main argument of this chapter is that the quality of liberal democracy in Brazil is, to follow Levine and Molina (Chapter 1), a multidimensional, composite concept. Some aspects of the quality of democracy may advance while others erode. This is true of Brazil's democracy on two dimensions: (1) the level of participation versus elite accountability and responsiveness, and (2) procedural democracy and good governance. The first dimension refers to the puzzle of why, after more than twenty-three years of extensive mobilization and consistently strong participation, civil society has not more fundamentally transformed the political elite or the procedures that govern the political system in Brazil. This chapter argues that the institutions and practices of democracy reinforce the rule of oligarchical and clientelistic elites even while they expand opportunities for the organization and participation of a growing diversity of social groups. This is possible because two dimensions of the quality of democracy—electoral decisionmaking and political participation—have not evolved in ways that develop coherent, autonomous, equitable, and sustained forms of civil societal action. That is not to say that periodic, anomic, and even more institutionalized efforts have not borne fruit. But these experiences are too local or sui generis to become systemic and transformative. As a consequence, two other aspects of democratic quality have suffered: elite accountability and government responsiveness. Both have evolved unevenly and without lasting institutional changes to guarantee that periodic reforms consolidate.

The other dimension of the puzzle of Brazilian democracy refers to the experiences of the Cardoso and Lula administrations. These governments have demonstrated through their competent management of economic and social policies that good *governance* is possible. Yet these governments have done so without notably strengthening *procedural democracy.* Worse still, good governance has served to veil the slowness of progress on the quality of democracy. As Levine and Molina argue, the quality of democracy may stagnate or suffer even as government performance improves (Chapter 1). The covering-up effect of good governance has been especially egregious under the Lula government. Lula, the longtime leader of the Workers Party (Partido dos Trabalhadores; PT), was for two decades the prime leftist opposition to the center-right governments that ruled Brazil from 1985 to 2003. The PT itself was regarded as an agent of competent and clean government, as it proved during the 1990s through its management of hundreds of municipalities and a few states. Incongruously, Lula's first term became mired in a vast corruption scandal implicating his party and individuals working closely with him in the presidential palace (Planalto). First, the *mensalão* scandal, involving monthly payments to deputies in return for their votes, was linked to the top officials in Lula's administration, including his chief of staff, José Dirceu, and the head of the PT, José Genoino. The story broke spectacularly in June 2005 through the testimony before a congressional board of inquiry of Roberto Jefferson, a leader of the right-wing Brazilian Labor Party (Partido Trabalhista Brasileiro; PTB), a sometime ally of the government in the Chamber. But the alleged malfeasance was more extensive than even Jefferson revealed. Other cases of wrongdoing exploded thereafter, including the *caixa dois* (second cashbox) scandal, which implicated dozens of PT mayors in the use of kickbacks from municipal service contracts to finance the party's campaign activities. Despite all of this, Lula was reelected in 2006.

Lula's return to power was the result of his strong support among the poor. His lead over his rival from the centrist Party of Brazilian Social Democracy (Partido da Social Democracia Brasileira; PSDB), Geraldo Alckmin, was determined largely by this advantage among poor households, especially in the less developed north and northeast of the country, where Lula's margins were the highest (Hunter and Power 2007: 4–5). Poor voters, most of whom had fresh and ongoing experiences with the benefits of Lula's social policies, drew a direct link between his continuation in power and their own improvements in household income. In rewarding Lula, did Brazilian voters undermine further the quality of their own democracy? Or, by following their pragmatic interests in rewarding realized good government, did voters reinforce the principle that elite responsiveness enhances the value of political representation? It is questions like these that epitomize how the quality of Brazilian democracy is multidimensional and composite. The rest of this chapter analyzes each of the five dimensions of the quality of democracy in Brazil, highlighting the contradictions between oligarchical and participatory dimensions as well as the effects of good governance under Cardoso and especially Lula.

Electoral Decision Without Partisan Decisiveness

Electoral participation is one dimension of the quality of democracy in Brazil that is strong on the surface level. Voters have many opportunities to vote at every level of the federation (municipal, state, and federal). Political rights are defended and practiced routinely. Yet the quality of the decisions Brazilian voters make is questionable. In this section, I argue that the poor quality of electoral decisionmaking in Brazil is the result of the weakness of political ideological and partisan identities. This weakness is institutionally embedded in an electoral system that undermines the capacity of parties to organize electoral behavior. Instead, candidates cultivate a personal following among the electorate, and voters respond to offers of particularistic, material rewards. While robust partisanship is not necessary for the quality of democracy, the extreme weakness of partisanship and the dominance of personalism in Brazilian politics hurt the link between citizens and programmatic government.

One of the central challenges in studying the electoral behavior of Brazilians is the paucity of empirical work on the subject (Ames, Baker, and Rennó 2008b; Carreirão and Kinzo 2004: 131–132; Singer 1999: 49). Samuels, in a comprehensive review of the literature, opines that this lack of scholarship contrasts with the extraordinary amount focused on the Brazilian party system and the legislature (2006a). Much of what is known about electoral behavior is derived from this work. The relevant literature has focused on two dimensions: (1) the coherence of ideologies in the electorate, and (2) partisanship, which looks at to what extent voters identify with particular parties.

Brazilian voters fail to follow coherent left-right ideologies. Some empirical work using surveys of voters done between 1989 and 2000 shows that Brazilian voters situate themselves on a left-right scale and vote in ways that are consistent with their ideological self-identity (Singer 1999). Subsequent work, however, has failed to confirm this pattern. In an empirical evaluation of responses to the first two iterations of the Brazilian National Election Study (Estudo Eleitoral Brasileiro; ESEB) in 2002 and 2006, Carreirão finds that 58 percent of the electorate self-identify on the left-right scale (2007a: 313–314). However, the comparison of the two ESEB data points reveals a decline of 24 percent, mostly on the more defined ends of the spectrum of left and right, suggesting a degree of volatility on this variable that is not typical of coherent political identities elsewhere. One may even question the validity of self-identification on the left-right scale, as most voters do not understand this gamut (Almeida 2001, 2006). For example, fewer than 20 percent of respondents to the ESEB surveys could correctly place the major parties on the left-right spectrum (Carreirão 2007a: 316). Empirical evidence from elections between 1994 and 2002 suggests that Brazilian voters are largely nonideological, preferring candidates based on information they gather from friends and relatives in their immediate social context (Baker, Ames, and Rennó 2006).

The causal significance of self-identity in voter choices is also questionable. When control variables such as education, social class, and religion are added to the statistical models, the importance of ideological self-identity for predicting voter choice evaporates (Carreirão 2002, 2007b). Party identifiers' ideological proclivities do not even coincide consistently with their partisan choices. More voters who self-identify as centrist or right-wing report a preference for the PT than for any of the parties that complement their ideological predispositions (Carreirão 2007a: 318).

Concerning partisanship, the balance of scholarship demonstrates that Brazilians have weak connections to parties, even when controlling for class, age, race, and religion, factors that in older democracies form the social bases for affiliation to parties (Lipset and Rokkan 1967). Studies consistently demonstrate more than 60 percent or more of Brazilian voters evince no partisan identity (Carreirão 2007a; Carreirão and Kinzo 2004). Work on electoral volatility—defined as half the sum of the distribution of party vote shares between electoral cycles (Pedersen 1990)—shows that Brazil has one of the highest levels in the world, suggesting that patterns of party identity remain highly fluid in the electorate (Baker, Ames, and Rennó 2006; Nicolau 1998; Peres 2000). Consequently, over two-thirds of the electorate regularly engage in split-ticket voting, selecting candidates from different parties, and sometimes diverse ideologies, on the same ballot (Ames, Baker, and Rennó 2008a). Brazilian voters harbor preferences for *politicians* rather than their parties, so partisan sentiments tend to fail as accurate predictors of their choices (Carreirão and Kinzo 2004: 156). Attitudes concerning parties underscore these results. According to the 2007 Brazil survey conducted by the Latin American Public Opinion Project (LAPOP), 51.7 percent of respondents expressed the opinion that democracy would do fine without political parties of any kind.[2]

If Brazilians evince any degree of partisanship it is mostly among the supporters of the PT. When compared to the ideology of the other major parties—Liberal Front Party (Partido da Frente Liberal; PFL) on the right, Party of the Brazilian Democratic Movement (Partido do Movimento Democrático Brasileiro; PMDB) of the center-right, and Party of Brazilian Social Democracy (Partido da Social Democracia Brasileira; PSDB), a centrist/center-left party—*petismo* (the PT's ideology and following) is more substantive and widespread while voters for conservative parties tend to identify less with the organization and more with the individual candidate (Ames, Baker, and Rennó 2008a; Mainwaring, Meneguello, and Power 2000: 196–197; Samuels 2006a). However, even that is in decline, as fewer voters identified with the PT in 2006 (27.4 percent) than they did in 2002 (35.3 percent) according to the ESEB (Carreirão 2007a: 319). The balance of the evidence from electoral polling confirms the expectations of weak partisanship, though this may simply be a reflection of the better and more consistent polling done in recent years. While studies of the 1989–2002 period have found stronger correlations between partisanship and vote choice and declining Pedersen volatility scores,[3] empirical work on the post-2002 period shows that this has declined significantly.

The causes of weak ideological and partisan disposition among Brazilian voters have been blamed on educational and institutional factors. The inequalities of the educational system severely skew the availability of cognitive resources, but the upshot of this finding in Brazil is debatable. Scholars are not agreed on the proposition that education correlates with voter partisanship. Generally speaking, more educated Brazilians evince a greater preference for party, and particularly for the PT, but this tendency is conditional (Carreirão and Kinzo 2004: 147–150). Samuels detects no correlation except a weak one ($p < 0.1$) for the PT, which disappears when control variables are added to his models (2006a). Mainwaring, Meneguello, and Power show that education is an inconsistent predictor of identification with conservative parties (2000). Kinzo finds that education matters in multivariate models when the cases are coded as *high* and *low* education, thereby inviting grouping error (2005). Carreirão finds more consistent correlations between partisanship and education level for the 2002 than for the 2006 ESEB (2007a: 322–325). Thus, overall, empirical support for the role of education is mixed at best.

Institutional characteristics in the Brazilian electoral and legislative systems are more likely causes of the continuation of weak partisan and ideological self-identities in the electorate. At the top of the list of factors is the open-list proportional representation electoral system, which places a sometimes overwhelming number of candidates on a single ballot and requires voters to select individuals rather than parties (Santos and Vilarouca 2008). The high number of effective parties and the fact that electoral districts are whole states add to the tremendous range of candidate choices, reinforcing the tendency for voters to discriminate by personality (Ames, Baker, and Rennó 2008b: 109–110). Parties also do a poor job of campaigning on clear programmatic platforms, in no small part because they do not pretend to act on that basis in the legislature. Brazilian parties, with the exception of the PT, are internally undisciplined and ideologically catchall parties (Ames 2001; Mainwaring 1999). To be sure, inchoate parties and party systems redound in inchoate partisan thinking in the electorate. Brazilian voters are not presented with consistent, programmatic, and ideologically coherent options, so they are driven by the incentives presented by clientelistic politicians that particularize their appeal. As I demonstrate below, this can have a profound effect on the quality of participation by making citizens the targets of elite mobilization, rather than the agents of change themselves.

Participatory Democracy *(Ma Non Troppo)*

Despite the evident weakness of partisanship and ideology among Brazilian citizens, they participate extensively in politics. The 1988 Constitution conceived of participation as the lifeblood of democracy, underscoring not just the representative dimension, such as elections of members of the legislature and the president, but also direct democracy through referenda, plebiscites, popular initiatives, and activities through councils (Calvancanti 2006). Brazilian civil society also enjoys a broad diversity of opportunities for organization and mobilization autonomously from the state, including through public demonstrations, official hearings, and legal actions. Elections offer a surfeit of choices for voters, with each four-year electoral cycle producing numerous opportunities to determine leadership on multiple levels. Presidents are elected every four years concurrently with federal deputies, senators, governors, and state legislators. Mayors and city councilors are selected during midterm elections. Brazilians tend to make the most of these opportunities by turning out to vote in large numbers in national, state, and municipal contests. The national turnout rate during the democratic period has averaged around 80 percent, or 100 million voters per election.[4]

With so much emphasis on participation in and between electoral cycles, Brazil can be considered a participatory democracy, but, as I argue in this section, the activism of civil society is curtailed in several ways. First, participation can be captured by political elites and be converted to support for the status quo, particularly when voters hand them their votes in the hopes of receiving material rewards. Second, even the best efforts to expand participation and sustain it in the shaping of public policy can fall short. There are plenty of examples of civil societal mobilization placing previously ignored issues on the political agenda, but being unable to engineer change either because mobilization or political institutions faltered. Third, *who* participates can be as important as *how many* participate. Movements and nongovernmental organizations have proven highly effective for broadening the participation of Brazilian civil society, but many formal institutions still underrepresent women and ethnic minorities.

Having opportunities to participate does not mean that participation itself is the product of autonomous, citizen action. Everyday forms of clientelist mobilization pervade the Brazilian polity. Just as leftists in the highly industrialized areas of São Paulo were able to mobilize partisans of the PT and union members (Keck 1992), so conservatives in the poor northern and northeastern regions of Brazil have been able to send their rural workforce to the polls to vote for rightist candidates. Without access to autonomous organization, both the urban and rural poor are susceptible to being mobilized as clienteles of conservative parties that appeal to the material and short-term interests of the uneducated, landless, and penniless (Gay 1990; Mainwaring, Meneguello, and Power 2000: 170–173).

These patterns of conservative versus more autonomous forms of participation have a geographic dimension, which can be illustrated by comparing subnational political systems in Brazil. Table 6.1 presents several indicators for the political competitiveness, pluralism, and socioeconomic development of the twenty-seven Brazilian states (including the federal district) in the 1982–2003 period. The states of the northern and northeastern regions evince the strongest tendencies to mobilize the poor and powerless on behalf of conservative incumbents and extended political families that tend to dominate political competition. These states are run by many of the same traditional elites who were present before the transition to democracy and who continue to control state legislatures and all-powerful gubernatorial offices (Desposato 2006; Hagopian 1996; Mainwaring, Meneguello, and Power 2000: 193–196). Conservative mobilization from above is captured in first-round vote margins for both gubernatorial and legislative elections that are much greater than those in the southeast and south. Basic indicators of pluralism, which are the effective number of parties (ENP) based on votes in gubernatorial contests and share of seats in the legislature, are lower on the conservative side, denoting the dominance of established elites there. As the mean legislative concentration scores attest, the parties of the winning and rival coalitions garner on average 79 percent of the seats in the state legislature, another reflection of the oligarchical nature of politics in these states. These characteristics of low political competitiveness and pluralism map onto differences in socioeconomic development, as these states are those with the lowest GDPs per capita.

The alternative to being mobilized from above is the development of an autonomous base for self-mobilization. Since clientelist exchange (*troca de favores*) narrows the polity to patrons and their clients, any effort to expand the autonomous organization of a broader network of civic activism challenges these structures (Abers 2000). With the transition to democracy in 1985 came

Table 6.1   Competitiveness and Socioeconomic Development in the Brazilian States, 1982–2003

Region/ State	1st Round Mean Margin Gubernatorial	ENP Gubernatorial Votes	1st Round Mean Margin Legislative	ENP Legislative Seats	Mean Legislative Concentration[a]	GDP per Capita (2003 US$)
North						
Acre	18.3	2.6	11.8	5.1	74.3	2,639
Amapá	13.1	3.2	2.0	7.7	56.8	3,110
Amazonas	18.6	2.2	36.9	5.4	85.5	4,050
Pará	11.7	2.8	8.2	5.5	79.7	2,224
Rondônia	8.4	3.9	4.1	6.9	49.1	3,297
Roraima	7.1	2.7	12.0	7.7	69.0	3,728
Tocantins	22.3	2.2	28.2	4.0	92.8	2,892
Average	14.2	2.8	14.7	6.0	72.5	3,134
Northeast						
Alagoas	25.4	2.0	5.1	5.5	83.9	1,903
Bahia	28.5	2.3	32.2	4.7	79.3	2,516
Ceará	27.4	2.2	28.3	3.9	83.4	2,073
Maranhão	28.0	2.1	37.9	5.4	83.3	1,556
Paraíba	18.9	2.2	16.7	3.5	88.0	1,999
Pernambuco	19.9	2.1	9.2	5.4	83.6	2,387
Piauí	3.7	2.3	12.3	3.5	90.0	1,489
Rio Grande do Norte	9.2	2.4	5.6	3.7	90.3	2,313
Sergipe	21.3	2.2	27.1	5.7	86.8	2,859
Average	20.3	2.2	19.4	4.6	85.4	2,122
Southeast						
Espírito Santo	18.3	2.5	11.0	7.6	48.6	4,713
Minas Gerais	7.2	2.8	6.5	6.8	62.6	3,969
Rio de Janeiro	17.8	3.0	14.1	7.5	56.0	6,257
São Paulo	7.2	3.4	11.8	6.2	56.6	7,394
Average	12.6	2.9	10.9	7.0	56.0	5,583
South						
Paraná	13.7	2.6	15.8	5.4	77	5,468
Rio Grande do Sul	7.1	2.9	1.5	5.4	62.7	5,871
Santa Catarina	9.0	2.6	9.6	4.1	75.4	5,882
Average	9.9	2.7	9.0	5.0	71.7	5,740
Center-West						
Distrito Federal	7.8	2.8	11.2	8.5	63.2	14,141
Goiás	19.5	2.4	15.6	4.5	81.7	3,969
Mato Grosso	29.4	2.1	4.9	4.6	86.9	5,174
Mato Grosso do Sul	13.1	2.3	1.4	5.8	82	4,386
Average	17.5	2.4	8.3	5.85	78.5	6,917

Sources: Author's own calculations for pluralism indicators; IBGE, Contas Regionais do Brasil 2003–2006 for the GDP per capita figures.

Note: a. Defined as the sum of the share of seats of the parties that endorsed the winning and the rival candidates for governor.

a wave of major activism in the form of urban social and landless peasant movements, including women's, Afro-Brazilian, religious workers', environmental, and consumers' movements (Alvarez 1993; Johnson 2008; Keck 1992). These civil societal organizations (CSOs) mobilized on the basis of expanding citizenship (*cidadania*) as a master frame, or, as Dagnino describes it, "the right to have rights" (1998). Social mobilization based on social justice rights claims empowered the poor and oppressed to organize and participate (Avritzer 2002; Friedman and Hochstetler 2002). At the same time, the establishment of popular councils (*conselhos populares*) in major municipalities such as Porto Alegre and Belo Horizonte opened the way for institutionalizing participatory forms of policymaking, including in the budgetary process. Citizens map out priorities for the next budget cycle in what, to date, have been dozens of well-attended meetings. Though the particulars of municipal budgets are drafted by elected state and local officials and regional delegates, participatory budgeting made public accounts more transparent by expanding popular oversight through the development of the abilities of low-income citizens to become involved in public policymaking (Baiocchi 2005; Wampler 2007). These processes cultivate horizontal ties among civil societal groups, thereby weakening their incentives to engage in clientelist exchange and enabling alliances that make social mobilization and participation more robust (Wampler and Avritzer 2004).

The expansion of movements and nongovernmental organizations (NGOs) and processes such as participatory budgeting was promising, but they produced considerable disappointment when compared to their once-high expectations. The activism of the movements dwindled in the years following the transition, in part because individual members branched out into NGOs and other CSOs (Alvarez 1993). Notably, Brazilian CSOs did not fragment, but instead created rich, collaborative networks during the 1990s that held out the hope of more fundamental change (Hochstetler 2000). Lula's election in 2002 galvanized these hopes, as did his promise to listen to the CSOs. However, the new administration's commitment to neoliberal reform with reformist social policies dashed the hopes for more fundamental redistribution held by unions, landless peasant movements, and other CSOs (Hochstetler 2008).

Another disappointment was the popular councils that continued to be lionized abroad as models of good government, but which produced mixed results at home. While some scholars found empirical evidence in Porto Alegre that budgetary policymaking increased civil organization membership (e.g., Abers 2000: 166), studies conducted elsewhere showed inconsistent increases in participation (cf. Baiocchi 2005; Nylen 2002, 2003). The underresourcing of municipalities and the diversion of popularly approved funds for political purposes also undercut the efficacy of participatory budgeting as a pro-poor policymaking device (Goldfrank 2007; Wampler 2007, 2008).

Despite the diversity of opportunities to participate and a history of sustained participation at all levels of the Brazilian federation, there is a persistent inequality in *who* participates. Women, ethnic minorities, and the poor are less likely than men, whites, and the middle and upper classes to participate in organizations such as political parties or run for office. Given that the political class is highly educated in Brazil, with over 80 percent holding advanced university degrees, it is not surprising that the extreme inequalities inherent in the educational and class systems keep most Brazilians out of this class (cf., Araújo and Alves 2007). In this sense, the historical exclusion of Afro-Brazilians from higher education is particularly weighty as an explanation for the paucity of political representatives of black or mixed race (Johnson 2008; Telles 2004).[5] Although they comprise more than half of the population, women have failed to improve their presence in the federal Congress or state legislatures. Since 1997, federal law requires political parties to apply quotas increasing the number of women they place on the ballot for federal deputy, but the parties backslide regularly and enforcement is rare. As a result, Brazilian women enjoy fewer shares of seats in the Congress (only 8.8 percent) than in other countries with quotas and even those without (Araújo and Alves 2007: 535–536).

Part of the problem is the double-edged nature of Brazilian political institutions, which expand opportunities for many, but fail to enable the less well-off to afford the resources needed to sustain participation. In the electoral arena, large district magnitudes, proportional representation, open-list ballots, low thresholds, and many small- and medium-sized parties (including several on the left that are more open to diverse candidate lists) are factors that normally improve the chances that women and minorities can gain seats in the legislature. But these same conditions put a premium on individual politicians mustering ample campaign finance and the support needed within the subnational polity and the party elite to gain a toehold against so much competition (Htun and Jones 2002).

The role of participation in the judiciary is noteworthy, as Brazil has become quite a litigious society. An estimated half million cases are brought against the federal government every year with the total *per judge* rounding out to 5,000 (Arantes 2005: 237). Litigiousness expanded rapidly soon after the democratic transition as civil societal organizations used the judiciary more extensively in a variety of areas to enforce consumer rights, environmental regulations, civil rights, the defense of the rights of children and minors, and to address unequal quality in public education and health care. Many of these cases were intended to overturn or, more frequently, simply delay or delegitimize legislation passed by Congress (Taylor 2008). One of the most commonly used mechanisms, the Direct Action of Unconstitutionality (Ação Direta de Inconstitucionalidade; ADIN), was enacted by the 1988 Constitution to allow prosecutors, the branches of government (Congress and the presidency), state governors, and organizations with a national representative function (e.g., the national bar association, political parties, labor unions) to challenge the constitutionality of any measure.[6] Any political party with as little as one seat in the Chamber retains standing to bring ADINs before the high court.[7]

Whether institutions enable or undermine participation depends also on how much self-confidence and determination to enact change a particular group may have. Elites and the dispossessed evince a self-serving malaise in Brazilian politics that is captured by the pro-incumbency tendency known as *gov-*

ernismo, which pervades alliances. As conservatives and former members of the promilitary National Renovating Alliance/Social Democratic Party (Aliança Nacional Renovadora/Partido Social Democrático; ARENA/PSD) were fond of saying, "*Se ha governo, eu apoio!*" ("If there is a government, I support it!"). This position is strategic, as allying oneself (and one's party) with the government opens up access to patronage (Power 2000).

The *governista* tendency is not limited to the behavior of political elites; it is also evident in mass behavior. The penchant for *governismo* is most apparent in the poorer regions of the country. Analysis of electoral results for the past three presidential contests shows that the less developed municipalities and states of Brazil tend to support the incumbent no matter the candidate or his program (Almeida 2006: 56–57).

Lula's reelection in 2006 confirms the erstwhile tendency of the poor to support incumbents and for the same reasons. In the 2006 elections, the PT suffered setbacks due to the corruption scandals of the first term, losing seats in the Chamber and the Senate for the first time in its history. What is striking about this was that the party did better in the states of the center-west, southeast, and south than their presidential candidate, who won resounding victories in the states of the poor north and northeast, where he garnered 65 and 85 percent of the vote, respectively. This is one explanation why, despite his government's problems with corruption, northern and northeastern respondents (N = 388) to the 2007 LAPOP Brazil survey give Lula more credit on anticorruption efforts than respondents in the south and southeast (N = 701) ($t = 2.99, p < 0.05$).

Lula's electoral success was more consistent with the historical pattern of conservative forces supporting the incumbent, albeit in this case the candidate and not his party (Hunter and Power 2007: 9–11; Zucco 2008b). This support is typically based on a pragmatic response to material incentives, a factor that pervaded the case of the presidential elections of 2006. Lula was closely associated with his signature cash transfer program, the Bolsa Família (Family Grant), an array of social programs originally initiated under his predecessor, Cardoso. As a conditional cash transfer (CCT) program, Bolsa Família grants families earning less than R$120 per month (US$60) a subvention provided they keep their children who are six to fifteen years old in school more than 85 percent of the time. By expanding Cardoso's CCT programs after 2003 and uniting them administratively under a single user-card access system (the Cadastro Único), the Bolsa quickly became Lula's central material argument in favor of a second term (Melo 2008). And the significant correlation between distribution of social spending under the Bolsa Família program in the months prior to the 2006 presidential election and voters' support for Lula confirmed the utility of the tactic (Carreirão 2007c: 104–106; Zucco 2008a). This was also true for turnout, indicating that the poor continue to respond to material incentives to participate, whether those signals are provided by conservative or left-leaning elites (Hunter and Power 2007: 20).

An alternative interpretation of this outcome is more positive for the quality of democracy: poor voters are inclined to vote their interests and this may *weaken* entrenched oligarchies. If we turn to the subnational level, there is evidence for this view in how the electorate in states such as Bahia and Sergipe, which have long been run by oligarchical families, dumped those allegiances in favor of Lula and, in some cases, PT gubernatorial candidates in 2006. One explanation is that poor voters' material interests are broader than the response to *Bolsa* subventions suggests. In the 2006 vote, even non-Bolsa recipients plumped for Lula in areas that benefited indirectly from CCTs (Zucco 2008b). Broad economic improvements, such as a 13 percent real improvement in minimum wages and low inflation for basic foodstuffs, reinforced retrospective voting in favor of the incumbent (Carraro et al. 2007). Notably, middle-class and upper-class voters in the poorest regions supported Lula based on overall improvement in the economy of these areas that saw double-digit growth during the president's first term (Sola 2008: 42). In this sense, then, Lula's good governance was rewarded and in the regions of the country most in need of this performance.

Yet if our concern is with improving the *procedural quality of democracy*, then good governance in this case veiled the persisting defects in Brazilian democracy. Lula's reelection did not strengthen the PT as a national party, mass partisanship, or otherwise reconfigure the political system in favor of programmatic government. Voters' support for the incumbent rewarded demonstrated good government, but did not sustain a form of participation that guaranteed its continuation. Moreover, Lula's success did not guarantee that government would become more accountable; just the opposite. Lula's good governance kept his electoral hopes alive in the face of massive political corruption. In this sense, the exigencies of greater elite accountability parted ways with elements of good governance.

Harder Accountability, Softer Corruption

In liberal democracies, elite accountability is the result of both horizontal and vertical forms of oversight, control of law abidance, and ratification of mandates and power. Horizontal accountability relies on intrastate institutions (e.g., the judiciary, the executive, the legislature, oversight agencies, etc.) that enforce legal restrictions on public authorities and, more broadly, require the answerability of public officials to one another (Mainwaring 2003: 11; O'Donnell 2003). The vertical dimension is based on societal organizations, the media, and voting by citizens (Peruzzotti and Smulovitz 2006a). In Brazil, both dimensions of accountability have become more *institutionally* developed and more *interdependent* during the democratic period, but political interests and technical problems have often undermined the effective implementation of these rules.

The relationship between the presidency and the Congress is a central dimension of horizontal accountability in Brazilian democracy, but it is decidedly indeterminate. The heretofore mentioned weakness of political parties in the electoral arena compels presidents to distribute financial and political benefits to craft a governing relationship with a majority in the Congress. According to the seminal study by Figueiredo and Limongi (1999), this is done through negotiation with the leadership of the main parties that is organized as the Leadership Council (Colégio de Líderes). Presidential-legislative relations are based on coalition patterns that involve extensive formal and informal arrangements, producing the effect of more disciplined parties in the legislature.[8] This has depended on the doling out of key cabinet posts, something that has varied in degree and scope with different governments. Coalition dynamics are said to be relatively stable when cabinet assignments predict the tendency of politicians affiliated with the parties in the cabinet to vote with the government (Amorim Neto, Cox, and McCubbins 2003). When coalition dynamics have achieved some stability, Brazilian presidents have retained a set of understandings with mostly the center and center-right parties. Cardoso's first term was reflective of this set of conditions. Under other administrations (e.g., Fernando Collor 1990–1992 and Itamar Franco 1992–1995) coalition dynamics were unstable. The result is a formula for governance that is highly contingent and therefore hardly sufficient to guarantee collective responsibility between the executive and the assembly (Ames 2001, 2002).

Congress retains direct oversight functions, but these are most typically shaped by the underlying partisan understandings that exist (or do not exist). Since the 1988 Constitution, Congress has had the authority to form Parliamentary Investigative Committees (Comissões Parlamentares de Inquérito; CPIs) to exert oversight on the president and its own members and to report findings to the Public Ministry (Ministério Público; MP) for possible civil or criminal prosecution.[9] Yet the context in which a CPI is formed makes these devices vulnerable to political manipulation. If a strong majority in the Chamber and the Senate support the government, CPIs cannot be initiated, even if the idea gains much citizen support (Sadek and Cavalcanti 2003: 216). Many CPIs are initiated as a bargaining chip with the government or opposition parties; therefore few are concluded with any sort of legal action (Figueiredo 2003: 176).

Further evidence that coalitional dynamics shape oversight functions is the fact that breakdowns in executive-legislative relations have been at the center of corruption scandals involving the PT and the Lula government. Not wishing to follow Cardoso's style of governing too closely, Lula increased the number of cabinet ministries from twenty-seven to thirty-five, but he concentrated appointments in his own PT. Bereft of some of the mechanisms for building legislative backing for reform, some leaders of the PT used bribery to secure this support. The *mensalão* scandal and its associated network of pay-to-play transactions can thus be viewed as a problem emerging from the undermining of coalitional dynamics or a particular problem of a *minoritarian* approach to forming cabinets.

Politics, of course, do not just govern oversight functions; they also determine the kinds of corrupt practices in which public officials engage. These acts are varied, though they most commonly involve exchanges of policy outputs for cash or policy changes meant to enrich the legislators after passage. For example, the *mensalão* scandal was a case of the government buying the support of legislators for policy. Campaign finance has emerged over the years as one of the chief areas of malfeasance, partly because of its importance in engineering political success and partly due to the informal webs of influence and exchange of policy outputs that sustain it beyond the gaze of public or official oversight (Samuels 2006b).

If what is illegal threatens elite accountability in Brazil, what is legal is perhaps more of a threat. Returning to campaign finance, the lack of legal limits on contributions gives individuals with interests in acquiring political support in Congress strong incentives to "invest" large amounts in candidates. Since political careers are long and stretch from local to national and most often back to local and subnational politics, politicians have good reasons to cultivate financiers by providing continued returns on their investment in the form of public policy outputs, or pork (Samuels 2006b). The small and mostly familiar (i.e., family and friends) networks of contributors backing each politician strengthen contributor monitoring and sanctioning of politicians who might otherwise renege on their promises. As a result, the provision of pork and the continuation of campaign finance investment are strongly correlated (Samuels 2002). While not strictly illegal, the incentives this system creates are perverse, and they have been shown in recent years to lead down a slippery slope to more genuinely corrupt practices.

The judiciary is often called upon to sort out the truth and reinforce the citizenry's confidence in democracy. Though the courts are reactive entities that, unlike the legislature, do not have the power to act on policy unless they are called to do so, the judiciary has exerted a critical gatekeeping role on policymaking in Brazil. As already noted, the courts have been a venue for many different political and societal groups that have assembled legal challenges to policy decisions made by the government. Even opposition political parties, having lost on a vote in the legislature, can turn to the courts to challenge laws. Not surprisingly, then, the Supreme Federal Tribunal (Supremo Tribunal Federal; STF) has considered more constitutional challenges to legislation than any other supreme court in the hemisphere (Taylor 2008: 13–14).[10] Injunctions issued by the STF, especially in response to an ADIN, either can suspend implementation of a law or can strike the law from the books if deemed unconstitutional.[11] Such actions are universally binding and are not subject to appeal. Appellate and federal district court dockets are likewise loaded down with challenges to government policies.[12] Indeed, one favorite tactic of the PT when it was in opposition was known as "juridical guerrilla warfare" (i.e., filing broad judicial challenges to policies throughout the lower court system).

While the 1988 Constitution made the judiciary more independent, it did not make it more functional or accountable. First, the weight of escalating caseloads at all levels, but especially at the STF, has produced gross inefficiencies in the judiciary. Since the high court cannot establish precedent that applies to the whole system, the judges of the STF must rule on each and every case brought before it. This can amount to an astonishing burden of hundreds of thousands of cases per annum. Second, the judiciary has increasingly become involved in the electoral process, exposing itself further to political interests wishing to change the rules of the game in their favor. An increasing volume of court cases is brought with each election, often against the application or the content of electoral rules and procedures. Arantes estimates that in the 2002 elections alone, there was an average of thirty-two legal actions for each of the 1,654 executive and legislative positions to be filled by voters (2005: 246). In that same year, the STF ruled that party coalitions across the state and federal levels had to be the same, thereby involving the judiciary in the composition of partisan alliances. Finally, the politicization of the courts has exposed the judiciary to undue influences from other institutions, and especially other branches of government such as the legislature, the presidency, and subnational governments (Arantes 1999: 91–92). In some cases, judges have been influenced by politicians and private business in ways that move beyond a mere conflict of interest to outright corruption of scandalous proportions. One of the most notorious was exposed by a sting operation (Operação Anaconda) that exposed a US$65 million kickback scheme in São Paulo involving a federal judge and private contractors in 2004.

For these reasons, judicial reform has become a major focus of legislative efforts to modernize the Brazilian state's oversight and anticorruption functions. Taylor counts no fewer than forty reforms proposed between 1988 and 2004 (2008: 29–30). The most important of these changes came in December 2004 when a comprehensive judicial reform was passed by Congress. Meant to ease overburdened dockets, especially at the STF and STJ, and reduce the use of the courts as a political weapon, the 2004 reform strengthened upper-court precedent setting and made appeals more difficult.[13] Significantly, it created a National Judicial Council (Conselho Nacional Judicial) to impose greater administrative control on lower courts, particularly on widespread practices of nepotism and other conflicts of interest.

The investigatory and prosecutorial capacity of the state has expanded markedly since the transition to democracy. The 1988 Constitution strengthened the office of prosecutor general, the MP, and with it, an emerging body of civil law in defense of collective rights (Arantes 1999, 2003; Kerche 2007).[14] The MP has responsibility over constitutional matters, individual and group rights, and oversight over the administration of public policy at all levels of the federation. As an assessor of constitutional responsibilities, it is one of the institutional actors that has standing to bring an ADIN to the STF against any of the branches of government. The MP also has at its disposal a host of procedural actions, including civil summary proceedings and public civil actions (class-action lawsuits) that act in defense of the collective rights of citizens. The MP is fully autonomous from the executive and the judiciary, and it retains jurisdiction over all levels of the federation.[15] At present, Brazil has 9,662 state and 338 federal prosecutors (Calvancanti 2006). Appointment of the ministers is based on merit, and job security is guaranteed for life. The MP is also accessible to the citizenry. Individuals' and organizations' access to state-level MPs has been eased significantly by allowing citizens to use the Internet or phone calls to file a complaint and initiate an investigation. This empowers citizens considerably and raises the stakes for dishonest politicians. Since 1999, administrative corruption and malfeasance by politicians have been prosecuted as criminal acts punishable by prison terms (Arantes 2003; Sadek and Cavalcanti 2003: 216).

Elected officials have responded to this increased oversight by generally embracing it and even integrating civil societal organizations in public decisionmaking (Arantes 2005: 253; Calvancanti 2006: 44–45). Congressional politicians have created and used several oversight bodies with governance over ethics rules and the use of public monies. The Federal Accounting Tribunal (Tribunal de Contas da União; TCU) operates independently in an oversight and investigatory function over presidential and congressional accounts. Other mechanisms are the previously discussed CPI and the auditor of state and municipal accounts (Controladoria Geral da União; CGU). These institutions have expanded the transparency of public accounting, making data more easily and publicly available (Figueiredo 2003: 183–186). They have also had their powers enhanced informally by the public. Protests and manifestations during occasional CPIs serve to put pressure on public officials to exert their oversight role in the legislature (Lemos-Nelson and Zaverucha 2006). Media coverage refracts the public's attention onto the larger questions of corruption and the political class during these events.

Even so, the political class has succeeded in curbing prosecutorial bodies such as the MP. According to a law passed in 2002, officials indicted for malfeasance, including mayors, governors, and federal legislators, cannot be prosecuted at any other level than in the high courts. This effectively undermines the ability of the MP's extensive subnational network to bring cases against corrupt officials. It also means that thousands of cases against these figures languish on a long waiting list as the massive backlog in cases at the STF is dealt with. That, coupled with the tendency of political interests to shape investigatory processes such as those governed by the CPI or the TCU, means that only a small percentage of cases of official malfeasance reach the stage of indictment or prosecution (Figueiredo 2003).

Even if the development of new institutions of horizontal oversight are made to work more effectively, these institutional changes would make little difference if Brazilian citizens remain complacent. The experience of participatory budgeting and public protests against corruption during CPIs point to the capacity of civil societal organizations to exercise what Peruzzotti and Smulovitz have called "societal accountability," a nonelectoral form of vertical oversight that can act as an alternative mechanism for enforcing elite accountability, most usefully between elections (2006a). Indeed, Brazilian civil society has pursued all of the major strategies of societal accountability outlined by Peruzzotti and Smulovitz: diverse organizations have mobilized, and they have employed the judiciary and the media to exert pressure on elected officials and bureaucrats. Yet, as I argued in the last section, such bottom-up oversight can be undermined in Brazil by the unsustainability of movements, the tendency of political institutions to protect the interests of incumbents, and the inability of once-empowering participatory institutions, such as those of participatory budgeting and the judiciary, to follow through and actually produce outcomes that encourage citizens to continue their organizational efforts. Blame can also be placed on formal institutions, as the failure of intrastate institutions to exert consistent oversight undermines the capacity of civil society to gain information about malfeasance and corruption (Figueiredo 2003: 191).

Perhaps the factor that most conspires against societal accountability, despite periodic protests and calls for the corrupt to leave office, is the overarching tendency among Brazilian citizens to reward even corrupt politicians who are efficacious. This propensity is captured well by the popular saying "*Rouba mas faz*" (He steals, but he gets things done). According to the ESEB data, voters are more likely to reward a politician who is highly efficacious and steals a great deal than one who steals much less but is not nearly so effective (Almeida 2006: 44–45). Consistent with my findings in the previous section on the geographic dimensions of conservative and *governista* tendencies, the *rouba mas faz* tendency is more acute in the poorer regions of the north and northeast. Using the LAPOP Brazil survey, I assessed the differences in means between the poorer and richer (south and southeastern) respondents in the study who responded to their degree of agreement with the following statements:

1. It doesn't make a difference if a politician steals. The important thing is that he/she accomplishes what the citizens need done.
2. It is better to have a politician who accomplishes a lot and steals a little than a politician who does little and does not steal at all.
3. A politician who accomplishes much and steals a little deserves the support of the people.

On each of these statements, a statistically significant larger proportion of respondents from the north and northeastern regions supported corrupt politicians who get things done than did respondents from the richer south and southeastern regions.[16] These findings are consistent with what we already know about the distinct attitudes concerning corruption among Lula supporters in the 2006 election in the north and northeast.

Citizens have low expectations of elite accountability because they are exposed daily to the other side of corruption: the impunity of the guilty (Morris and Blake 2009). This is especially evident in the behavior of lower-level officials of the government bureaucracy and law enforcement. Human rights violations committed by the police or gangs of off-duty police and security guards known as *milícias* and individual *justiceiros* are well-known and highly publicized examples of abuses of power by officials. These cases are, as Pereira argues, indicative of a generalized "ambiguity of law" that oppresses the poor and landless while protecting the rich and powerful (2000). Police violence is often used for political purposes, especially in the more conservative and underdeveloped states where elite responses to the mobilization of landless peasants and urban shantytown dwellers are particularly brutal (Ahnen 2007; Hinton 2009). The fact that so few of these criminal and corrupt acts are punished confirms for many the fact that justice exists for one class of citizens and not for others.

Seen in light of the culture of impunity, Lula's resuscitation in 2006 underscores some of the consistent themes regarding whether allegations of corruption have consequences in the Brazilian polity. First, contrary to the results shown in the work on mass partisanship, education levels matter in forming these political perceptions. The illiterate are willing to accept patrimonial and even venal actions by their elected officials to a much greater extent than the more educated. Second, social class interacts with education to determine voters' responses to corruption. As education and household income rise, voters are less tolerant of corruption. Lower-class and less schooled voters simply vote their pocketbooks, supporting the incumbent if times have been good or voting for the opposition if times have been bad (Almeida 2008). Accordingly, Lula retained the support of low-income groups, but he lost precipitously the support of middle- and high-income voters in the months following the *mensalão* scandal. Third, press accounts of corruption can sway public opinion against the incumbent. To be sure, education, class, and access to public media interact to explain whether or not voters support a politician tainted by allegations of corruption.

Responsive Government Within Reason

Elite accountability is only possible if citizens are able to detect deviations in policy from previous promises to the electorate and voters retain the means to punish unresponsive government.[17] If responsiveness is defined and measured in terms of citizen preferences for outcomes as opposed to particular policies, then the administrations of Cardoso and Lula have been responsive in providing macroeconomic stability, most notably beginning in 1994 with Cardoso's Real Plan, and modest improvements in social welfare. If the concept is defined and measured in terms of preferred policy—the mechanisms of how to achieve these goals—citizen wants and government responses have not jibed as well in Brazil.

What Brazilian citizens want can be studied in terms of the issues with which they are most concerned and by the broader principles of what they prefer from democracy and the state. Regarding the former operationalization, surveys consistently show a concern with the economy, personal security, and government probity. According to the LAPOP 2007 Brazil survey, these matters were represented well at the top of the list of respondents' definition of the gravest problems facing Brazil: unemployment (20.6 percent), violence (18.8 percent), and corruption (13.6 percent).[18] Table 6.2 lists the salient expectations of respondents regarding democracy and the state. The numbers demonstrate that Brazilians have a strong preference for democracy and for a socially activist state, though not one that undermines the freedom of choice of firms and workers. The theme of personal freedom is especially present in how Brazilians define democracy. The more frequent expressions revolve around personal liberty (e.g., freedom of speech, the vote, freedom to choose leaders, etc.) (LAPOP 2007). The general picture is that Brazilian citizens care profoundly about policy outcomes that affect their economic and personal security, and they are concerned about the means used to produce those policies.

Table 6.2 Salient Preferences of Brazilian Citizens: Respondents Who Agree/Agree Strongly (in percentages)

	Agree/Agree Strongly
On Democracy	
Democracy is the most preferable form of government.	71.5
Sometimes authoritarianism is more desirable than democracy.	19.1
The country's problems can be solved with the participation of all.	93.3
Electoral democracy is more favorable than an unelected, strong leader.	87.4
On the Role of the State	
It is the duty of the state to diminish inequality between rich and poor.	81.6
The government should cut social services to reduce taxes.	15.9
A richer Brazil should not worry about inequality.	24.3
The less the government intervenes in the economy, the better.	40.1

Sources: Latin American Public Opinion Project (LAPOP), Brazil 2007 Survey.

The Cardoso and Lula administrations were able to satisfy citizen prefer-ences concerning policy outputs at an aggregate level by producing and sus-taining macroeconomic stability (especially inflation control) with modest poverty alleviation and redistribution. But the process for arriving at these re-sults depended upon technocrats working out the details ensconced in popular oversight or input. For example, Cardoso's Real Plan was entirely crafted within the economic bureaucracy and issued through a presidential decree, virtually as a surprise tactic on an unsuspecting public. Like many of the ill-fated anti-in-flationary shock plans that preceded it, the government invited no public debate on the matter.

Despite much talk about consulting with civil society on social reform, nei-ther administration created a workable process for doing so. Cardoso placed his wife, Ruth, a well-regarded anthropologist and scholar of social movements, as head of the newly created Council of the Solidarity Community to engage with CSOs. Yet little came of these efforts and subsequent attempts to pass leg-islation to formalize partnerships between the state and CSOs (Friedman and Hochstetler 2002: 29–30). Lula made more of an effort to consult by scaling up the existing Economic and Social Development Council (Conselho de Des-envolvimento Econômico e Social; CDES) and, at least episodically, meeting with dozens of CSOs to iron out the administration's legislative agenda. As with the Solidarity Community, little came of the CDES, as the government felt nei-ther compelled nor constrained by its recommendations. Social actors ranging from the unions to the landless peasant movement defected from CDES, pre-ferring to return to a more fundamental critique of the neoliberal policies Lula's government was pursuing (Hochstetler 2008: 43–44).

What these experiences underscore is that there exists a strong *delegative* element in the relationship between the political class and civil society in Brazil that is at the core of the problem of responsiveness. Brazilian governments are open to talking to civil society, but not to negotiating with CSOs. Even in cases of participatory budgeting, CSOs may voice their ideas, but the details of mu-nicipal budgets are hammered out exclusively by city councils and mayors.

Even if the process is not as transparent or consultative as many Brazilians would like, are the results of policymaking responsive on the output side? Given the complexity of democratic responsiveness in Brazil, any summary of public opinion regarding it is likely to be an incomplete indicator. However, public opinion concerning the efficacy of the vote, particularly the assessment of whether elected officials are carrying out the will of citizens, can be a valid and useful index for responsiveness (Powell 2005: 73). By this measure, Brazilian governments are insufficiently responsive. Figure 6.1 shows results from the LAPOP 2007 Brazil survey regarding the responsiveness of the Lula adminis-tration. More respondents opined that the government was less responsive on the top issues—unemployment, fighting corruption, and improving personal security—than those who believed it was strongly responsive. Notably for a

Figure 6.1 Perceived Responsiveness of the Lula Government (percentage of respondents)

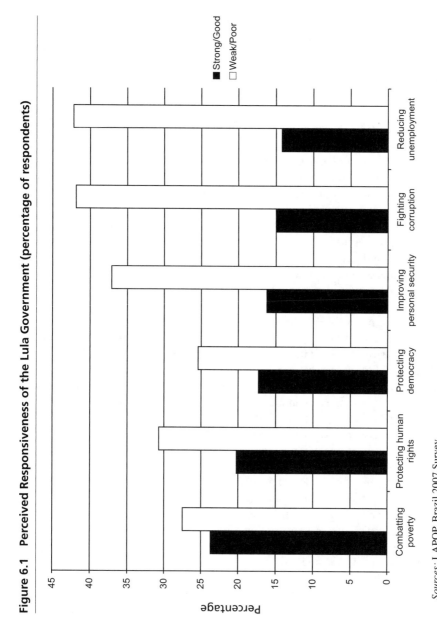

Sources: LAPOP, Brazil 2007 Survey.
Notes: Responses are scaled: 1 "not at all/terrible" to 7 "very much/very good." "Strong/Good" = 7, 6; "Weak/Poor" = 2, 1.

left-of-center government, more respondents felt that Lula's government was not doing enough to protect democracy, human rights, or even fight poverty. So on both the policy output and the process dimensions, the Lula government fell short.

Brazilians want effective, socially responsible, and clean government, but they have been repeatedly frustrated by many of the tendencies discussed in the previous sections on elite accountability and participation. This is one of the main reasons why CSOs have increasingly turned away from seeking partnerships with the federal government.

Sovereignty Unbound?

Sovereignty represents a strong point for the quality of Brazilian democracy. Despite a history of twenty-one years of bureaucratic-authoritarian rule marked by military dictatorship between 1964 and 1985, civilian leaders gained ministerial control over the armed forces several years after the transition (Hunter 1997; Stepan 1988). Though scholars during the early 1990s continued to wring their hands over the survival of democracy in Brazil, it is now apparent to most observers of the country that Brazilian democracy is no longer under any existential threat from the military (Kingstone and Power 2008: 2). As the largest and most powerful country in South America, Brazil has little to fear from foreign governments. The erstwhile rivalry with Argentina, which at one point included an arms race during the period of dictatorial rule in both countries, ended during the early 1990s with a series of accords concerning collective security and the peaceful use of nuclear energy. Cardoso and Lula even implemented a National Military Defense Strategy that calls for the redeployment of troops from the quiet southern border to the north to bolster the Amazonian defense network. Regarding economic constraints, Brazil continues to generate a relatively high debt that stands at 45 percent of the GDP. However, most of the national debt is held by domestic investors in official bonds. Progress on reducing the debt has been steady throughout the Lula years as the government has continued to run a primary surplus. External debt levels have declined under Lula from 14.5 percent of GDP in January 2003 to 4.0 percent in January 2010. And tax revenues have continued their increase from the Cardoso years. In short, the Brazilian state enjoys a great deal of autonomy and is not beholden to any particular veto player, foreign or domestic.

One of the core reasons for high sovereignty in Brazilian democracy is the acceptance of democratic processes by the political right. In the face of both the rise of leftists to power (Lula's presidential near-victory in 1989 and actual victory in 2002) and economic turbulence between 1985 and 1994—two factors that in the past spelled the end of democracy in Brazil—conservative parties and the military retained their acceptance of the democratic rules of the game.

Even conservatives' early opposition during the transition to democracy to consolidating civilian ministerial control over the armed forces faded. After many years of the armed forces having cabinet-level branch ministers, Cardoso was finally able to create a single, civilian minister of defense in 1999 with backing by all of the conservative parties and the armed forces (Mainwaring, Meneguello, and Power 2000: 220).

Nonetheless, the armed forces do maintain reserved veto powers that prevent civilian governments from having the widest possible control over the military. Under the 1988 Constitution (article 142), the armed forces retain ultimate authority to intervene in the democratic process in the face of threats to "law and order." This undermines the president's authority as commander-in-chief, as the unified military may interpret threats to internal security as coming from the actions of the president. Since constitutional law is vague on what constitutes a threat to law and order, the generals are free to interpret a president's actions as being within or outside the boundaries of the law. The generals also claim de facto autonomy over areas of military technology. This is especially relevant to the management of the Amazonian satellite surveillance system known as SIVAM. Congress approves spending on the system as part of the military budget, but it retains little oversight over the network or the building of new weapons systems. The same is true of the national nuclear industry, which politicians do not control directly and understand only incompletely. Such holes in civilian control over the armed forces raise troubling questions about who maintains ultimate authority over the use of military force (Hunter 2000: 119–122).

Conclusions

Reflecting on the quality of democracy in Brazil since the first years following the transition, one must agree with Hagopian that it has improved in some major respects (2005). Nevertheless, Brazil's quality-of-democracy score as calculated by Levine and Molina (Chapter 2) gives the country a decidedly middling ranking within Latin America. This finding, I have argued, is the result of several factors that weigh down the quality of democracy. The most persistent of these are the many tendencies that dilute the otherwise potent mixture of high levels of participation, hardened institutions of elite oversight and prosecution, responsive good government, and high sovereignty over economic and national security areas of public policy. The weakness of programmatic government; the persistence of conservative and oligarchical political interests; the delegative aspect of policymaking; and even the indifference, or simply the numbness, of citizens to the impunity of the few all create a drag on the quality of Brazilian democracy.

Making sense of the Brazilian puzzle requires understanding the core contradiction between the history and institutional mechanisms that enhance participation with all those that make this participation, and the elite accountability and government responsiveness that it should foster, uneven. The Brazilian case confirms Levine and Molina's judgment that the quality of electoral decision-making and participation are closely associated. But the unequal access that Brazilians have to education undercuts the potential for capitalizing on a highly mobilized civil society. The courts, participatory budgeting, and the political parties have proven inconsistent vehicles for channeling popular interests into policy change. More often than not, the opponents of change have superior access to the decisionmaking process, and they are able and willing to use that access to short-circuit the organization of civil society.

This study argues that much of the popular support of recent governments in Brazil is the result of material outputs, especially for the poor. Though these elements of good governance are important, not least to beneficiaries, they obfuscate the need to strengthen procedural and oversight functions of the policymaking process. If policy outputs do not guarantee improvements in democratic practice, it is also true that enhanced democratic process does not necessarily ensure good policy results. Where government has become more accountable and responsive, and where civil society has taken advantage of expanded opportunities for participation, the results are sometimes disappointing nonetheless. For example, recent work on participatory budgeting in Brazil finds little evidence of improved fiscal management (World Bank Report 2008) or sustained welfare-enhancing benefits on any of the indicators of social well-being, including infant mortality, adult illiteracy, the municipal Human Development Index, and the Gini coefficient.[19]

At this point in the research program, one can claim only that the study of the quality of democracy in Brazil has several theoretical and methodological payoffs. First, the differences and sometimes contradictory interactions between democracy and good governance require much more comparative analysis. This study suggests that all good things do not go together, and so it is with democracy and governance. Scholars ought to investigate under what conditions these processes can be made mutually reinforcing. Second, the sometimes stark differences across Brazil's dimensions of democratic quality reinforce the call by theorists such as O'Donnell (1994b) and Schmitter (1997) to disaggregate democratic regimes into component parts. Levine and Molina's (this volume, Chapter 2) treatment of the quality of democracy is actually an evaluation of the *qualities* of democracy, so the present research project is very much in keeping with this line of thinking.[20] One contribution of this chapter underscores that one of these qualities involves a *geographic* component. This is evident in the differences in political attitudes, opportunities for elite oversight, and autonomous participation that exist between the poor northern and northeastern states and the more developed states of the southeast and south. Further exploration of the quality of democracy in Brazil will need to develop an understanding of the geographic dimension using comparative methods.

Notes

1. The last military president, General João Baptista de Oliveira Figueiredo (1979–1985), refused to pass the sash to José Sarney (1985–1990), who had been Tancredo Neves's vice president when Neves died before the inauguration. Neves had been elected indirectly by an electoral college. The directly elected Fernando Collor (1989–1992) received the sash but failed to serve out his term completely as he was impeached for corruption. His vice president, Itamar Franco, passed the sash to Cardoso in January 1995, but it was not until January 2003 that two directly elected presidents exchanged the sash.

2. LAPOP 2007: Q.DEM23.

3. For more detail, see Carreirão (2007b); Carreirão and Kinzo (2004); Hagopian (2005: 139); Kinzo (2005); Reis and Castro (1992); Singer (1999).

4. These numbers are no doubt inflated by the obligatory vote, the statutory requirement that citizens go to the polls.

5. Efforts to correct for this through affirmative action are spreading throughout federal universities in Brazil. See Johnson (2008: 222–227).

6. The extensive use of ADINs is notable. Taylor finds that the measure was used more than one thousand times between 1988 and 2002, though as is noted below, the success rate is low and variable (2008: 78–83).

7. As an indicator of how potentially obstructive the ADIN can be, Arantes estimates that one-quarter of those issued during the 1990–2003 period were brought by parties with fewer than 5 percent of the seats in Congress (2005: 243).

8. This leaves open the question whether, over time, the parties have actually become more internally disciplined. Nicolau presents evidence for that trend during the 1990s (2000), while Ames shows that deputies regularly ignore their party leaders on vote recommendations (2001, 2002). The results of this debate remain, in the words of Amorim Neto, "an unresolved enigma" (2006: 142). See also Amorim Neto (2002); Figueiredo and Limongi (1995, 1997, 1999, 2002); Figueiredo (2001); Pereira and Mueller (2003).

9. CPIs can be formed by either chamber or jointly. Under rules in effect in 2010, the Chamber can only have five CPIs functioning simultaneously. New CPIs are held in abeyance until a spot opens up or if an extra CPI is authorized by majority vote.

10. The STF is one of the five high courts in the Brazilian system, though it is the court of last instance on constitutional questions involving all levels of the federation. The Superior Justice Tribunal is the high court on nonconstitutional questions. The three other courts are limited to particular domains of law: the Superior Military Tribunal, the Superior Electoral Tribunal, and the Superior Labor Tribunal.

11. The chances of either happening are more remote. Taylor finds that injunctions are granted only 24 percent of the time and findings of unconstitutionality are rarer still at 11 percent of the time (2008: 79).

12. The courts of appeal under the Superior Justice Tribunal include five regional federal tribunals staffed by 130 judges. There are 560 courts of first instance, the equivalent to the 94 district courts in the United States, and they are staffed by 990 judges (Arantes 2005: 236).

13. Constitutional Amendment 45 (December 2004) established the *súmula de efeito vinculante* (summary of binding effect)—a power allowing two-thirds of the judges on the STF to establish a precedent binding on all other courts in the Brazilian system. While the restrictions on appeals and the *súmula vinculante* strengthened the higher courts, it did little to reduce the dockets of the lower courts, which still swell with frivolous and politicized cases.

14. Another entity that existed prior to the 1988 Constitution, the Federal Police, has also expanded its role, largely in conjunction with the MP.

15. The structure of the MP follows the divisions in Brazilian court jurisdictions across common law, military justice, and the labor courts with federal and state prosecutors in each of these areas. Only the federal prosecutor can bring cases before the two high courts, the STF and the Superior Justice Tribunal. For a more complete analysis of the MP, see Arantes (2003); Kerche (2007); Sadek and Cavalcanti (2003).

16. The statistics from the independent-sample t-tests in order of the questions 1 (RM9): $t = 7.83$, $p < .001$; 2 (RM10): $t = 8.46$, $p < .001$; 3 (RM14): $t = 6.68$, $p < .001$. Nonrespondents and those who could not make up their minds were removed from the analyzed cohorts.

17. See Manin, Przeworski, and Stokes (1999); Peruzzotti and Smulovitz (2006a); Powell (2000); Stokes (2001).

18. Other national surveys in Brazil confirm this hierarchy. See Almeida (2006: 28).

19. The HDI is an index scaled 0 to 1 based on a composite of three indicators of well-being: life expectancy, per capita income, and educational attainment. The Gini coefficient is a commonly used index for income and wealth inequality. Technically, the number represents the area between the arc and the line of equality in the Lorenz curve. The index ranges from 0 for perfect equality to 1 for a society in which one person has all income or wealth.

20. The disaggregation principle is also underscored by recent studies of Brazil. See Hagopian (2005); Kingstone and Power (2008: 6).

7

Bolivia: The Growth of Grassroots Participation

Martín Mendoza-Botelho

SINCE THE RETURN OF DEMOCRACY IN 1982, BOLIVIA HAS MADE substantial progress consolidating this process. As elsewhere in Latin America, part of the effort has been concentrated around procedural aspects related to electoral and party politics at the national level: the electoral decision. However, an important part of the progress made in this country expanding the quality of democracy, and congruent with the dimensions that Levine and Molina propose in this volume, lies at the grassroots level. Fifteen years into the implementation of decentralization, or the process of Popular Participation (Participación Popular; PP) as it is widely known, have shown that despite its many limitations and drawbacks, this institutional reform not only has transformed the political system as a whole, but also has opened many spaces for political participation, civic activism, and the emergence of a new civic-minded local leadership. Using the five dimensions proposed by Levine and Molina, this chapter contrasts key aspects of the democratic evolution in Bolivia at the national level with those at the grassroots resulting from PP.

Democratic Evolution

Transition and Attempts at Consolidation

On October 10, 1982, Hernán Siles Zuazo assumed the presidency of one of the most unstable countries of the hemisphere, one where democracy finally triumphed after almost two decades of mostly military regimes that reached power through nondemocratic means. Moreover, Siles Zuazo received the presidency after five years of intense turmoil from 1978 to 1982, one of Bolivia's most unstable periods throughout its history, when the country saw the dismissal of one president due to fraudulent elections, the overthrown of two constitutional provisional governments, four military coups d'état, one military junta, two transitional juntas, and three other unconstitutional seizures of the presidency.

The immediate task for Siles Zuazo, therefore, was to consolidate democracy—regardless of its quality—with a strict respect for human rights and civil liberties. Unfortunately, during his time in office, international and national contextual issues conspired against his government, including an already decreasing trend for the prices of Bolivia's most important exports, commodities such as tin and silver, and the noncollaborative, highly impatient, but powerful Bolivian Workers' Union (Central Obrera Boliviana; COB). Despite some democratic gains and some feeble attempts at redesigning the institutional makeup of the country through social and economic plans, the populist and unsuccessful policies adopted by his administration culminated in an economy on the verge of collapse, affected by one of the highest rates of inflation that the world has seen, which peaked at a staggering annual rate of 25,000 percent (!) (Sachs and Morales 1990). In an uncommon gesture for a Latin American politician, Siles Zuazo cut his constitutional mandate a year short.

Democracy in Bolivia survived this initial test through the constitutional transfer of powers to Víctor Paz Estenssoro, the winner of the 1985 elections, who represented once again the emblematic party of the 1952 Revolution, the National Revolutionary Movement (Movimiento Nacionalista Revolucionario; MNR), and Siles Zuazo's old comrade-in-arms. Paz Estenssoro's famous phrase *"Bolivia se nos muere"* (Bolivia is dying) during his inaugural speech reflects the gravity of the crisis. Immediately, he addressed the most pressing economic issues and brought back stability to the country with a strong neoliberal agenda, but at a high social cost. The following three administrations of Paz Zamora, Sánchez de Lozada, and Bánzer/Quiroga,[1] in power from 1989 to 2002, were possible through a series of intraparty accords designed to share power through electoral reciprocity, a Bolivian version of Venezuela's *puntofijismo*[2] (Trinkunas 2002), which in Bolivia had the formal label of *Pacted Democracy* (Democracia Pactada). This agreement was possible due to the characteristics of the Bolivian electoral system of the time that gave Congress (Congreso Nacional) the power to elect the president if a simple majority was not reached during the election, something that Mayorga defined well as a successful implementation of a hybrid (*mestizo*) model of *parliamentarized presidentialism* (1997).

In a simplistic interpretation, two different but interconnected stages can be distinguished for the period 1982–2002, one of democratic transition/consolidation during the administrations of Siles Zuazo, Paz Estenssoro, and Paz Zamora and one of consolidation/expansion under the governments of Sánchez de Lozada and Bánzer/Quiroga. Although it is not the purpose of this chapter to analyze this period in detail, I include some general comments regarding the quality of democracy using Levine and Molina's five empirical dimensions (2007a).[3] First, Bolivia showed an unprecedented level of electoral maturity. For the first time since the introduction of universal suffrage in 1952, this country enjoyed a long and uninterrupted period of democratic practice through free, fair, and competitive elections. This doesn't mean that this process was exempt from faults. There were many, including restrictive entry barriers for the creation of parties, poor registration mechanisms for voters (e.g., absence of proper documentation such as birth certificates, etc.), low levels of education particularly for indigenous peoples and women (including high rates of illiteracy in many areas), a wide urban-rural gap in terms of access to resources and political participation that historically penalized the countryside, minor incidents related to co-optation and purchase of votes, and an unhealthy monopoly of political parties over state powers and oligarchic party structures, which fostered *caudillismo*, clientelism, corporatism, and nepotism. But the existence of frequent and mostly fair elections and the consistently high turnout can be understood as signs of civicness and a regained sense of responsiveness from the state and of political parties to mounting social pressure for higher political participation—the electoral decision dimension—including a relatively neutral involvement of the armed forces and its less interventionist leadership.[4] See Table 7.1.

Despite these positive gains, the quality of democracy did not expand as much as had been expected, in part because of the already mentioned structural constraints, but also because of some specific characteristics of the system itself that distorted representation, giving too much power to a set of institutions that were historically exclusive, such as political parties. In all the cases during

Table 7.1 Electoral Turnout for National and Municipal/ Regional Elections, 1989–2010 (percentage)

Year of the Election	Type of Election	
	National	Municipal/ Regional[a]
1989	73.6	—
1993	72.2	—
1995	—	63.6
1997	71.4	—
1999	—	59.4
2002	63.4	—
2004	—	63.4
2005	84.5	—
2009	94.5	—
2010	—	87.0

Sources: Author's elaboration with data from Bolivia National Electoral Court (CNE) at www.cne.org.bo; Altman and Lalander (2003); Miguel Centellas at http://www.centellas.org/politics/data.html; and Romero Ballivián (2005).

Notes: Turnout is defined as number of votes divided by number of registered voters.

a. Municipal and regional elections for governors were carried out simultaneously for the first time in 2010.

this period, the election of the president was done through political negotiations behind doors, following the corporatist logic of power sharing through political quotas, favoring political opportunism as opposed to thoughtful processes of state planning and reform.

The other dimension considered is participation, which will be explored later in the context of decentralization reforms. But leaving this reform aside, although national participation, such as voting, seemed to be open, most spaces for more meaningful forms of political involvement were closed. It is not a surprise, therefore, that in their pursuance of political goals many unions and non-state social organizations had to seek alternative ways of participation through direct activism in the form of demonstrations, strikes, and blockades. The state response to periods of high social and political unrest was often harsh, including frequent use of exceptional constitutional measures, such as the imposition of a state of siege, which entails the restriction of political rights and civil liberties, thus questioning the quality of democracy in Bolivia. The lack of institutional channels for participation, contestation, and negotiation at the national level, combined with a perceived lack of proper representation in instances such as the national parliament, is one of the factors that explain the proliferation of social movements and all sorts of nongovernment organizations (NGOs) with distinctive sets of political agendas, ideology, membership, and areas of influence; examples include the coca leaf growers (*cocaleros*) in the Chapare region and the autonomy movement in the city of Santa Cruz. It is not a coincidence, therefore, that Bolivia has one of the most politically active citizenries in the hemisphere, and that the "politics of the street," such as marches and blockades, is a regular and expected form of political participation and negotiation, rather than an extreme form of protest. Indeed, Bolivia has had the highest levels of participation in public demonstrations compared to similar countries; see Figure 7.1.

During this period, the other three dimensions of the quality of democracy proposed by Levine and Molina—accountability, responsiveness, and sovereignty at the national level—are much weaker than the two already discussed. Due to the restricted and closed character of partisan politics, accountability of public officials has been restricted to a few highly publicized cases of corruption rather than a constant, institutionalized exercise. Despite some progress made generating transparent and modern legislation to control the functioning of the state and oversight bodies, such as the introduction in 1990 of the Government Administration and Control Law (Ley de Administración y Control Gubernamentales; SAFCO) or the creation of the figure of ombudsman (*defensor del pueblo*) in 1997[5] and the Permanent Commission of Human Rights in Bolivia, a nonpartisan and independent body that oversees government, accountability remained elusive, particularly at the higher levels of the administration.

The responsiveness of the Bolivian state in this initial stage was also limited. The management of the national and regional organs of the state apparatus— such as the central executive and regional prefectures, and prior to Sánchez de

Figure 7.1   Percentage of Participation in Public Demonstrations

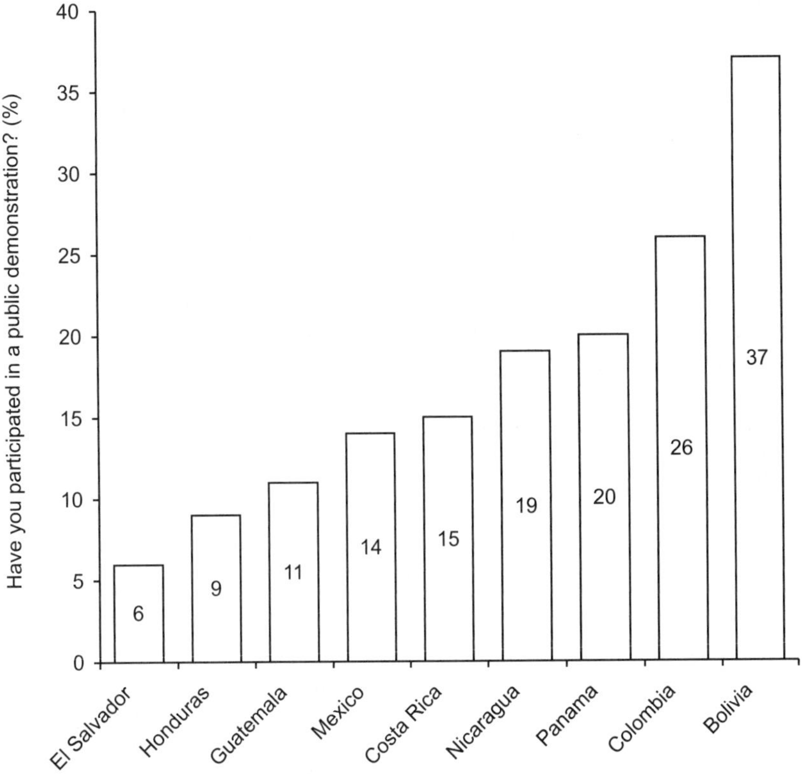

Source: Seligson, Morales, and Blum 2005: 83.

Lozada, the regional development corporations (Corporaciones Regionales de Desarrollo; CORDES)—and the public policies produced by them were mostly developed by closed political circles impervious to external influence. Moreover, the policy of "do now and negotiate later" prevailed in the logic of the state in its approach to society, which paradoxically granted society's informal organizations the legitimacy that its formal institutions lacked. The (un)responsiveness of the Bolivian state was also linked to a chronic lack of political stability, combined with limited bureaucratic capacities and public resources for seemingly endless social and political needs. These arguments also question how much sovereignty these different administrations had at the time of implementing their own set of political goals through policy alone. The lack of internal coherence in the design of public policies and programs and the need for financial resources generated a continuous dependence on "guidance" and support from international organizations and financial institutions (IFIs), which seemed to be the natural repositories of technical skills and an easy mechanism to access those fresh resources that the national state lacked.

In many cases foreign assistance has been beneficial by allowing the modernization of the state, including key infrastructure and catching up with a pending social agenda—such as women, children, and indigenous people's rights and environmental issues. Nevertheless, in other cases, big financial institutions, such as the World Bank and the Inter-American Development Bank, were able to secure the implementation of large adjustment and reform of state programs with little local input and with a general contempt for contextual elements. In addition, the surplus in the production of coca in Bolivia made this country one of the targets of the United States in its antinarcotic hemispheric strategy, resulting in constant and direct US pressure on domestic affairs in the pursuance of antidrug objectives. The lack of sovereignty of the state, internal and external, resulted in serious drawbacks not only for the development agenda but also for the overall quality of democracy.

The 2002–2005 Political Crisis

By 2002 the exhaustion of the Pacted Democracy accord was manifest. Not only were political parties discredited in the eyes of voters due to the minimal economic and social progress and prevalent corruption, but also the lack of internal leadership within these strongman/*caudillista* parties precipitated a larger crisis. For these reasons, the 2002 elections represented a turning point in Bolivia's recent democratic history and the beginning of a period of destabilization and turmoil. MNR's tight victory, with roughly 21 percent of the vote, allowed Sánchez de Lozada to become president for the second time. However, as a result of a bitter political campaign, the MNR had few allies left, which put the government in a feeble position with no room for political maneuvering. In addition, a deteriorating economic situation, mounting pressures of diverse social sectors (particularly the demands of indigenous organizations for a constituent assembly to formally incorporate indigenous claims in Bolivia's magna carta), a controversial plan to export gas through Chile,[6] ill-conceived proposals to introduce income taxes and reform the pension system, and the president's inflexible attitude regarding these issues escalated into social unrest and violence. Finally, in October 2003 (infamously known as Black October after the deaths of dozens of people during intense protests in the cities of La Paz and El Alto), Sánchez de Lozada was forced to resign and fled the country, being succeeded by his vice president, Carlos Mesa. In this period, the strength of ethnopolitical forces and their definitive arrival in mainstream politics were also confirmed (see Van Cott 2005), such as Evo Morales Ayma's party, the Movement Toward Socialism (Movimiento al Socialismo; MAS), which obtained a close second place during the 2002 election, and the Aymara Indigenous Pachakuti Movement (Movimiento Indígena Pachakuti; MIP), which obtained almost 6 percent of the vote.

Democracy again survived another difficult test, but with minimal improvements to its quality. For this reason, the succeeding presidency of Mesa (also short-lived, October 2003–June 2005) attempted to restore order and democratic rule by adopting an apolitical posture (e.g., by appointing a ministerial cabinet mostly composed of professionals and intellectuals with limited ties to political parties). This strategy, however, put the government in an ever weaker position vis-à-vis powerful social movements and regional elites demanding autonomy, particularly in the eastern lowlands in the so-called Half Moon area (Media Luna), composed of the departments of Santa Cruz, Beni, Pando, and Tarija. Some of the important policy efforts during the Mesa administration were the attempts to enhance decentralization reforms, particularly by addressing some of its political shortcomings related to the intermediate level, such as the direct election of prefects (see Barbery 2006), and his promise to carry out a national consultation on departmental autonomies—the responsiveness dimension. An important contribution to the consolidation of democracy during Mesa's administration was the implementation of a constitutional amendment allowing municipal candidates to take part in the 2004 election under the umbrella of citizen groups (*asociaciones ciudadanas*) or representing indigenous groups (*pueblos indígenas*) in addition to political parties, which I will discuss later.

After a difficult eighteen months, Mesa succumbed to social and political pressures and resigned, giving way to the transitional government of Eduardo Rodríguez Veltzé (June 2005–January 2006), a Harvard-educated lawyer, head of the Supreme Court at the time, and the constitutional successor after both heads of the two congressional chambers, the Chamber of Senators (Cámara de Senadores) and the Chamber of Deputies (Cámara de Diputados), refused to accept the presidency. From the beginning, Rodríguez made clear that his main objective was to reinstate institutional order and call for an early election. At the same time, he managed to give continuity to some of the promises made by his predecessor regarding the election of prefects to occur simultaneously with the upcoming presidential election, and the signing of a decree for a national referendum on autonomy also to be carried out by his successor.

This particular and turbulent period shows mixed signals regarding the functioning of democracy in Bolivia—and its quality, for that matter. On the one hand, the fact that all the presidential transitions followed constitutional means was a sign that the rule of law prevailed, despite high adversities. Moreover, all relevant political institutions, including opposing political parties and the military, recognized not only the validity and legitimacy of electoral processes, but also their importance as conflict resolution mechanisms. For observers of this process, the ousting of Sánchez de Lozada accomplished through massive mobilizations, with estimates that approximately one in seven citizens participated actively in the demonstrations,[7] represented a social victory that delivered the powerful message that even the highest leader of the nation can become directly accountable to the people. On the negative side of the ledger, this extended crisis demonstrated once more the chronic institutional weakness that characterizes this country, including a perceived lack of representation in Congress, which was particularly incompetent at this time due to the intransigence of many of the political leaders. In addition, although social movements played an effective role securing the mobilization of protesters and other demonstrations, their presence and strength are signs that Bolivian citizens are still forced to find alternative means to achieve political representation.

Evo Morales and the Movimiento al Socialismo

The historic election of Evo Morales Ayma to the presidency in December 2005, the first fairly elected president of genuine indigenous background, brought many hopes to Bolivia as he and his party, MAS, symbolized not only the arrival to power of indigenous and social groups, but also the emergence of a new paradigm in Bolivian politics.[8] Moreover, Morales was elected with 53.7 percent of the popular vote, a hitherto unseen outcome in Bolivia's recent democratic history, and a result that granted him the presidency without the need to form the customary backstage congressional political alliances. The wide margin obtained in this election guaranteed MAS political control, including a comfortable majority in the lower chamber of Congress, although not in the Senate. In addition, MAS's ethnosocialist ideology was seen as a viable alternative to an already decaying neoliberal economic and political model. Once in office, Morales immediately addressed two important pending issues in Bolivia's complex political agenda. He called for the creation of a Constituent Assembly (*Asamblea Constituyente*; AC), with the mandate to rewrite Bolivia's Constitution, and reluctantly authorized a national referendum on regional autonomy, a process inherited from his predecessors.

The most significant event during Morales's first mandate, therefore, and one with far-reaching implications for democracy, was the rewriting of Bolivia's Constitution. On July 2, 2006, 255 assembly members (*asambleístas*) were elected to the newly created AC. The way in which they were elected, by constituencies and sponsored by parties and civic associations, gave this legislative body a highly partisan character. The results of the election resembled the composition of the Congress's lower chamber, as MAS won 137 seats (53.7 percent), leaving the AC divided between those in power (*oficialistas*) and opposition (*opositores*). During the first year, practically all the AC's political energies were devoted to the futile task of achieving consensus on the number of votes necessary to approve the still-nonexistent articles of the new Constitution. Eventually consensus was reached, but practically a whole year had been wasted, and only a few commissions had met occasionally to discuss substantial issues. To make things worse, the constitutional review process revived the city of Sucre's historical claims as capital of the Republic and its right to host the entirety of the central administration, currently shared with the city of La Paz. Finally, on December 9, 2007, the draft of Bolivia's new Constitution—prepared in semisecrecy by a select group of MAS intellectuals—was approved in the city of Oruro by the 164 assembly members that participated in this historic meeting, after the AC had to be moved because of turmoil in Sucre. Although there was some initial rejection by the opposition, eventually the majority of the AC accepted a revised draft, which was later passed to Congress and was finally approved through a referendum on January 25, 2008, by 61.4 percent of voters.[9] Despite this sound victory for the Morales administration, close scrutiny of the results reveals the sour side of this process, as the geographical electoral results of the Yes and No votes reflected the same political trend of the election of Morales and that of the autonomy referendum. This is strong support for Morales and MAS in the Andean west, where the presence of indigenous groups is more numerous, and strong opposition in the east in the Half Moon departments. Despite some of the drawbacks, the constitutional process showed an unprecedented level of responsiveness from the Bolivian government to a long-standing historical claim through democratic means and high levels of participation.

During the Morales administration, the departmental claims for increased autonomy also received an initial response in the July 2006 Autonomy Referendum, where citizens were asked to express their preferences on their departments to become more autonomous (Yes), or not (No).[10] The results showed that the majority of voters in the traditional and more indigenous-mixed departments of the west rejected autonomy claims (No). In the eastern lowlands, however, most people opted for Yes. Therefore, although slightly more than half of the voters said "No" to autonomies (53.5 percent), the Yes vote prevailed by a considerable margin in four of the nine departments, showing the strong geographical divide in this country.

In terms of the regional agenda, simultaneously with Morales's 2005 election, prefects were also elected for the first time; see Table 7.2.[11] MAS's national triumph, however, was not enough to guarantee regional victories, with two-thirds of prefectures in the hands of the opposition. This scenario has changed after the 2010 regional elections in favor of MAS-IPSP—MAS added the IPSP acronym to its name in that election to emphasize its role as the political force of social and indigenous movements; IPSP stands for Political Instrument for the Sovereignty of the Peoples (Instrumento Político por la Soberanía de los Pueblos)—as this political force gained governors in six of the nine departments. In any case, what is evident is that regional governments became open critics of central government policies, a posture sustained in the legitimacy granted by their direct democratic election.

Table 7.2 Winning Parties in the National and Regional Elections, 2005–2010

Department	Presidential Elections				Regional Elections[a]			
	2005		2009		2005		2010	
	Party	%	Party	%	Party	%	Party	%
La Paz	MAS	66.6	MAS-IPSP	80.3	PODEMOS	38.0	MAS-IPSP	50.0
Oruro	MAS	62.6	MAS-IPSP	79.5	MAS	40.9	MAS-IPSP	59.6
Potosí	MAS	57.8	MAS-IPSP	78.3	MAS	40.7	MAS-IPSP	66.8
Cochabamba	MAS	64.8	MAS-IPSP	68.8	AUN	47.6	MAS-IPSP	61.9
Chuquisaca	MAS	54.2	MAS-IPSP	56.0	MAS	42.3	MAS-IPSP	53.6
Tarija	PODEMOS	45.3	PPB-CN	51.1	ERCC	45.6	CC	48.9
Santa Cruz	PODEMOS	41.8	PPB-CN	52.6	APB	47.9	VERDES	52.6
Beni	PODEMOS	46.3	PPB-CN	53.1	PODEMOS	44.6	PRIMERO	42.5
Pando	PODEMOS	45.2	PPB-CN	51.1	PODEMOS	48.0	MAS-IPSP	49.7
Foreign residents[b]	—		MAS-IPSP	72.9	—		—	

Sources: Based on data from Bolivia's National Electoral Court (CNE) at www.cne.org.bo.

Notes: National parties: MAS-IPSP, Movement Toward Socialism–Political Instrument for the Sovereignty of the Peoples (Movimiento al Socialismo–Instrumento Político por la Soberanía de los Pueblos); PODEMOS, Social and Democratic Power (Poder Democrático y Social); PPB-CN, Progress Plan for Bolivia–National Convergence (Plan Progreso para Bolivia–Convergencia Nacional)—the latter is a coalition of opposition political forces. The other three are regional political organizations: CC, Path to the Change National Alliance (Camino al Cambio Alianza Nacional); VERDES, Green Party; and PRIMERO, First Party.

a. The term "prefect" was changed to "governor" per the new Constitution; however, the significance is the same in terms of describing the highest regional authority.

b. In the 2009 national election, Bolivian citizens residing abroad voted for the first time in selected locations in Argentina, Brazil, Spain, and the United States.

An important governance aspect, therefore, has been the relationship between the central government and the regional prefectures, which has deteriorated progressively after the 2006 Autonomy Referendum. This was partly the result of MAS's intention to recentralize powers through different mechanisms. One of these, a cause of bitter confrontation between national and regional authorities, has been the reduction of the departmental share of hydrocarbon taxes (Impuesto Directo a los Hidrocarburos; IDH)[12] from 56.9 percent to 24.39 percent (a reduction estimated at approximately US$140 million for 2008) in favor of municipalities, which increased their share from 34.5 percent to 67 percent (the other 8.6 percent is allocated to public universities and was not altered). This decree also forced prefectures to share a further 30 percent of their resources to fund an income subsidy scheme for people over the age of sixty, called the Dignity Pension (Renta Dignidad*)*. This reduction greatly affected the operational capacity of prefectures and triggered a fierce political reaction. Moreover, many departments interpreted this policy as a direct threat to their relative autonomy and economies and fueled strong antigovernment sentiments throughout the country. This recentralization of powers contradicts MAS's apparently higher responsiveness to regional claims and has negatively affected the quality of democracy by making the central government less accountable to other echelons of the administration.

Ironically, the intention of the central government to undermine the capacity of prefectures served as a good excuse to move forward the autonomy process in the east. On December 2007, public and civic institutions in Santa Cruz, including the prefecture and the powerful Civic Committee, made public an Autonomy Statute (Estatuto Autonómico), elaborated by a provisional Autonomy Assembly, and a referendum was scheduled for May of the following year. The results of this public consultation were overwhelming, as two-thirds (62 percent) of Santa Cruz's inhabitants participated in this process and 86 percent of them approved this regional legislation; see Table 7.3. The reaction of the central government was swift and as soon as the extra-official results were known, the National Electoral Court (CNE), the president, and other high-ranking public officers declared the referendum illegal and anticonstitutional. Nevertheless, eleven days later, on May 15, Santa Cruz officially promulgated the creation of an Autonomous Departmental Government, headed by a provisional Departmental Legislative Assembly with twenty-eight members, including five representatives of the largest lowland ethnic groups (i.e., Guarayos, Chiquitanos, Ayoreo, Mojeños, and Guaraníes). The departments of Beni, Pando, and Tarija followed the example of Santa Cruz by drafting their own statutes and carrying out departmental referendums that took place in June 2008 with similar results in favor of further autonomy; see Table 7.3. The new Constitution, however, makes explicit the issue of regional autonomy—in addition to municipal and indigenous autonomy—and this topic is not the monopoly of the opposition anymore. Therefore, it is likely that the rest of the departments will draft similar legislation.

Table 7.3   Results of the Autonomy Referenda in Bolivia for Approval of Departmental Statutes, 2008

Department	Number of Voters		Turnout of Registered Voters (%)	"Yes" to Autonomy Statutes (%)	"Yes" in Relation to the Number of Registered Voters (%)
	Registered	Turnout			
Santa Cruz	936,048	558,252	62.1	85.6	51.0
Beni	134,488	88,090	65.5	80.2	52.5
Pando	28,990	15,510	53.5	81.8	43.8
Tarija	173,231	112,946	65.2	78.8	51.4

Sources: Author's extra-official estimates based on data from *La Razón* newspaper, "El sí arrolla con 86% en Santa Cruz," May 5, La Paz, Bolivia; "El sí a los estatutos gana en Pando y Beni; pero el ausentismo es alto," June 2, La Paz, Bolivia; "El sí logra 80% en Tarija y el bloque se hace más fuerte," June 23, La Paz, Bolivia; and Corte Departamental Electoral de Santa Cruz at http://www.corteelectoralsc.com/.

A further complication—and one that jeopardizes the dimension of electoral choice for that of accountability—was the Recall Referendum (Referendum Revocatorio de Mandato), which took place on August 10, 2008.[13] The purpose of this consultation was to ratify (or not) the mandate of the president and the prefects; however, there were no constitutional provisions to support such action. This consultation, therefore, was more a political gamble from both sides to expand an already obtained legitimacy, with the central government on the centralizing offensive, and certain departments pushing forward their autonomy and decentralization agendas. The results of the referendum ratified President Evo Morales and Vice President Álvaro García Linera with 67 percent of the vote, a higher figure than that obtained during the 2005 election; see Table 7.4. From the side of the prefectures, the results favored MAS, as two opposition prefects were not ratified and were forced to resign. These results also confirmed the polarization of the country as the prefects of the Half Moon bloc were ratified with high levels of support in their regions.

But democracy emerged badly bruised, as this process made evident not only the weakness and high dependence from the center of basic democratic institutions, such as the CNE, that had to bend to satisfy the demands of the executive, but also how an apparently democratic gain, the election of prefects, was subject to control from the center. In terms of the quality of democracy, this event can be seen as a loss of internal sovereignty and a certain disregard for the electoral decision. The three conflictive cases were those of La Paz, Cochabamba, and Oruro. In the case of La Paz, Prefect José Luis Paredes accepted his defeat and presented his resignation. Oruro was a bit more difficult, because the initial results were evenly split. Eventually Prefect Alberto Aguilar, originally elected under a MAS ticket, was ratified after parliament accepted an official report from the CNE. The critical aspect of this case, however, was

Table 7.4   Results of the August 10, 2008, Recall Referendum

Level	Yes[a]	No
National results for president and vice president	67.41	32.59
By department for prefects		
La Paz	35.48	64.52
Oruro	50.85	49.15
Potosí	79.08	20.92
Cochabamba	35.19	64.81
Chuquisaca	53.88	46.12
Tarija	58.06	41.94
Santa Cruz	66.43	33.57
Beni	64.25	35.75
Pando	56.21	43.79

Source: Corte Nacional Electoral de Bolivia (CNE), http://www.cne.org.bo/resultadosrr08/wfrmPresidencial.aspx.
Note: a. Yes means popular support for that particular public candidate.

MAS's intention to oust a prefect perceived as hostile to the directives of the party and the president. But the most conflictive case was that of Cochabamba, because Prefect Manfred Reyes Villa, also the leader of one of the strongest opposition parties, the New Republican Force (Nueva Fuerza Republicana; NFR), initially refused to accept the referendum results. Moreover, Reyes Villa's main support rested in the city of Cochabamba (where he had served as mayor for several terms), while his opposition was mainly rural, including the coca-growing (*cocalero*) region and MAS's bastion of Chapare. This situation led to violent clashes between Reyes Villa's urban supporters and his mainly rural detractors. A month later, facing mounting social pressure and turmoil (including a few related deaths) and the constant intervention of the central government, Reyes Villa was forced to resign. The recall referendum, however, did not have clear provisions for the replacement of authorities. For this reason, three months later, Evo Morales signed two presidential decrees appointing two members of his own party as interim prefects of La Paz and Cochabamba.[14] To put the matter bluntly, two democratically elected prefects were replaced by presidential appointees.

Another incident that tested the responsiveness of the Bolivian state and its democracy was a tragic confrontation near the community of Porvenir in Pando, where at least thirteen people were killed during a bloody confrontation between personnel of the prefecture and peasant MAS sympathizers. An important repercussion of this event was the arrest of Pando's prefect, Leopoldo Fernández, for his alleged participation in this incident, which was carried out without proper due process, following a state of siege imposed only on this department. As in the other changes of regional authorities, Evo Morales appointed directly by decree an interim prefect,[15] in this case Admiral Landelino Rafael Bandeiras Arze.

This particular action was highly criticized not only because of the still-pending legal process against Fernández—who ironically became one of the candidates for the vice presidency for the 2009 elections while still in jail—but also because it compromised the political neutrality of the military.

Despite these drawbacks, Bolivians returned massively to the polls in 2009 and 2010 for national, regional, and municipal elections respectively; see Tables 7.1 and 7.2. In 2009, Morales and his vice president, Alvaro García Linera, were reelected with an even higher share of the popular vote (64.2 percent), confirming their popularity and the heavy political weight of their party. Postelectoral evaluations conducted by international observers confirmed that the electoral processes in 2009 and 2010 were carried out in a transparent and fair manner, despite a few insignificant irregularities and noting some improvements to be made, such as the enhancement of registration mechanisms and media regulation, particularly the use of public television during campaigns. These last elections, therefore, support the idea that the electoral dimension of democracy in Bolivia is greatly consolidated.

A varied group of judgments can be made about the quality of democracy in Bolivia during the administration of Evo Morales. There have clearly been improvements in terms of allowing direct participation through democratic channels. The use of referenda is a new phenomenon in Bolivian politics, and the few instances in which they have been used have proven to be relatively effective in addressing political disputes, at least in the short run. But the evidence suggests that referenda by themselves do not provide definite solutions for problems that they are intended to solve. Results are still subject to interpretation by legislative or other institutional bodies that often favor dominant political forces and ideologies rather than assuming a transparent and neutral role. In most cases, therefore, referenda were used as political tools based on calculations of success by political actors as opposed to transparent and institutionalized mechanisms of public consultation. Bolivia's new Constitution has provisions for this type of direct consultation, and it is likely that these instruments will be used again in the future. The new magna carta also brought other important changes that affect the democratic game. One of them is the possibility of consecutive presidential reelection for one additional term, something that favored the reelection of Morales. This is not necessarily a negative element, but it carries the danger of becoming a constitutional advantage for actors and forces in power, who might use and abuse this provision to enhance their hegemonic powers, particularly if future constitutional alterations should permit unlimited reelections. Also, the new Constitution seems more accepting to a globalized notion of citizenship as Bolivians residing abroad were allowed to vote for the first time in a presidential election in 2009, something that evidently makes democracy in this country more inclusive.

On the other hand, in their pursuit of political objectives, the MAS administration has shown, on more than one occasion, a general disregard for the ex-

isting institutional setting, on both the formal institutional side, including legislation, laws, and state institutions themselves, and the informal side by strong
social pressure through affiliated social movements and MAS's political apparatus. The conflictive way in which the relationship between the powerful president and the less powerful prefects (now governors) has been carried out is
another example of how difficult and painstaking is the process of institution
building in this country. Moreover, many institutions have been caught in this
crossfire. It is not a coincidence that since this struggle began, the CNE has
changed four presidents in a period of five years (2004–2009), most of them in
response to strong pressure from the central government.

A direct threat to the quality of democracy in Bolivia is corruption. There
is substantial evidence that the MAS administration, like the preceding governments, has been plagued by cases of corruption, shattering the belief (and
hope) that ideologically driven bureaucracies, such as this one, were more immune to this pernicious practice. One of the most notorious cases was that of
Santos Ramírez, former president of the Bolivian Oil Company (Yacimientos
Petrolíferos Fiscales de Bolivia; YPFB) and Evo Morales's close collaborator
and old union comrade (*compañero*). Ramírez has been accused not only of
embezzling large amounts of money, but also of allegedly direct involvement
in the murder of a local gas entrepreneur, Jorge O'Connor, apparently linked to
Ramírez's network of cronies. The accountability dimension, therefore, is still
highly elusive.

Another weak element of the MAS administration has been the limited
progress, and drawbacks, made in enhancing civic and political rights. A good
example is the perceived deterioration of the freedom of the press, as measured
by Freedom House; see Table 7.5. Bolivia has steadily slipped down in this international ranking from a country with a free press in 2003 to a country with
a partial free press in all the following years. According to Freedom House, a
climate of hostility has developed against the press from both sides: government and opposition supporters.[16] Moreover, many press organizations and civic
groups have shown their dissatisfaction with the negative rhetoric against private media, including harsh criticisms from the president himself and the lack
of adequate legal guarantees. The polarization and discrediting of the press have
resulted in hundreds of physical attacks against journalists, including the death
of a radio broadcaster, many of them carried out by the military and the police,
but also by protesters from all sides of the political spectrum. In addition, the
MAS government has enhanced its share of the media through the expansion of
its own media outlets, polarizing even further this particular aspect, with a
highly MAS-supportive, mainly official, media on one side, and with a critical
one on the other side that constantly punishes the government. This situation has
evidently damaged the quality of information in this country and therefore affected the freedom of expression and the construction of well-informed public
opinion.

Table 7.5   Global Press Freedom Rankings for Bolivia from Freedom House, 2003–2009

Year	Rating[a]	Bolivia Ranking/ Number of Countries Ranked
2003	30	—
2004	37	84 / 192
2005	35	77 / 194
2006	33	76 / 194
2007	37	80 / 195
2008	39	84 / 195
2009	42	89 / 195

Source: Freedom House, www.freedomhouse.org.
Note: a. A rating between 31 and 60 is considered "partly free."

During the past years, the main international influence over the Bolivian government has shifted from that of the IFIs and their multilateral agenda and the US regional policy linked to antidrug efforts, to a more ideological one fostered mainly by the Bolivarian Republic of Venezuela through the active involvement of its president Hugo Chávez, a longtime supporter of Morales. The interaction and collaboration between Bolivia and Venezuela have moved from symbolic gestures to a more substantial and practical agenda that has the clear purpose of expanding political (and to a lesser extent social) ties between these two governments that share a seemingly common ideology. Although the main partnership is between Bolivia and Venezuela, it also extends to other countries such as Ecuador and Cuba and, for the moment, counts on the sympathy of the giant neighbor, Brazil. Despite some positive elements of this partnership, such as humanitarian and development aid, the constant political intervention of Venezuela in internal affairs, including during the AC process, has created a lot of suspicion and dissatisfaction throughout the country, particularly in the east and among the opposition. For example, a controversial measure is the signing of a trade partnership between these countries, the Bolivarian Alternative for the Americas (Alternativa Bolivariana para las Américas; ALBA), as a policy option to the US-sponsored Free Trade Area of the Americas (FTAA), despite the fact that the United States, Brazil, and Argentina remain as Bolivia's main economic partners and that trade between ALBA members is minimal. Another case of increasing foreign intervention is in the energy sector, where technical and political advice from Venezuela's oil company (Petróleos de Venezuela S.A.; PDVSA) is helping Bolivia to redesign its national policies and its institutions, such as YPFB. Venezuela has also been assisting the Bolivian government financially and logistically to enhance various capabilities, including internal security, primarily the police and the military, and the government's media, such as community radio networks.[17] A prevalent official anti-US rhetoric has also brought unlikely partners to Bolivia, such as Iran, China, and, to a lesser extent, Russia, which have been actively lobbying for their areas of interest, such as energy and raw materials and minerals. It is not that Bolivia enjoyed full political sovereignty in the past, but instead that the source of influence has shifted, this time with a strong ideological twist.

Beyond national politics the model of grassroots democracy promoted by this country's decentralization reform, Popular Participation, that began fifteen years ago continues expanding. The following section presents evidence related to this process, which, in contrast to the more complex national scenario, seems to be more successful at enhancing the quality of democracy, at least at the grassroots.

Decentralization and Social Change

The macrovision of democracy presented in the previous section suggests that although there have been substantial improvements in its quality, there are still many structural aspects and problems that hinder its consolidation. But what about democracy at the grassroots? This is the kind of democracy that affects people in their day-to-day activities, where the state becomes tangible through local governments; and in Bolivia, democracy is also expressed through communitarian and indigenous activism. This is precisely the qualitative enhancement brought by PP through a renewed sense of citizenship and social and civic participation. The theoretical dimension, however, remains the same, and the assessment of democracy at the local level is also subject to the same five dimensions presented by Levine and Molina. This section, therefore, describes the vibrant process of PP in Bolivia and its overall effects on the quality of democracy.

Decentralizing Through Popular Participation

President Sánchez de Lozada's letter to parliament in February 1994 introduced Law No. 1551 of Popular Participation as "the most important redistribution of political and economic power since the revolution of 1952" (Grindle 2000). PP's first article describes best the spirit of this reform:

> The present Law acknowledges, promotes, and consolidates the process of Popular Participation, incorporating the indigenous communities, indigenous peoples, rural communities and urban neighborhoods in the juridical, political and economic life of the country. It is aimed at improving the quality of life of Bolivian women and men, through a fairer distribution and better administration of public resources. It strengthens the political and economic means and institutions necessary for perfecting representative democracy, incorporating citizen participation in a process of participative democracy and guaranteeing equality of representation at all levels between women and men.[18]

The reasons to decentralize were as diverse as the models considered. Sánchez de Lozada, for example, wanted to address three main issues: promote national legitimacy and consolidate an elusive nation-state, thus fulfilling the promises of the 1952 revolution; have a positive effect on corruption; and counteract centrifugal regional tendencies, particularly those from the eastern lowlands (Grindle 2000). For others, decentralization was mainly the result of democratization and political opening since 1982 and the response to mounting social pressures at the microlevel (O'Neill 2005). Another plausible reason was the international consensus on decentralization, seen as a viable alternative—particularly by IFIs—to inefficient centralist states and congruent with neoliberal reforms (see Hiskey and Seligson 2003). PP, therefore, was perceived as a social mechanism to enhance public efficiency and counterbalance the implementation of harsh economic measures resulting from neoliberal reforms, and one that also would help to reduce poverty.[19] Hence, the original design of PP was aimed—intentionally or not—at improving the quality of democracy through electoral means but with particular emphasis on the participation, responsiveness, and accountability dimensions.

The implementation of PP brought immediate social, political, and economic transformations. While some readjustments were merely cosmetic, others had a deep impact on society.[20] First, PP fostered the municipalization of the country through the creation, practically overnight, of 250 new municipalities. PP also allowed the consolidation of representative democracy at the local level as mayors and municipal councilors were elected throughout the country for the first time in 1995; prior to PP, the election of municipal authorities was the privilege of cities only. Moreover, in this election, 27 percent of councilors claimed to be of indigenous origin and held a majority in one-fourth of the new municipalities, marking a new trend in the participation of indigenous peoples in formal politics. To enhance local accountability, PP also allowed the creation of participatory democratic structures within the state. A wide array of public responsibilities were also transferred to the local and regional levels, including health, education, infrastructure, and economic development. These responsibilities were accompanied by resources assigned through a transparent, demographically based formula—coparticipation. As a result, social investment as a proportion of total investment tripled in the first three years.[21] In terms of participation, PP allowed ethnic and social groups, such as indigenous groups and women, to gain local spaces of formal representation (see Van Cott 2005).[22]

Institutional Engineering

Perhaps the most innovative element of PP, and one that contributes directly to the quality of democracy through higher participation and accountability, was the formal incorporation of organized civil society and social movements as control mechanisms in public affairs. In addition to the elected municipal government, composed of an executive branch, the mayor and his/her technical staff, and a legislative branch, the municipal council,[23] PP incorporated two new institutional actors.

The first one is the Grassroots Territorial Organizations (Organizaciones Territoriales de Base; OTBs), which are the basic units of social representation through which local communities, indigenous groups, and neighborhood associations can gain legal recognition in a specific territory. By 1997, at least 13,827 OTBs were registered (Ayo 1999), demonstrating not only the public interest in this process, but also the acceptance by the population of newly created—and, in a way, artificial—local institutions. Their creation also represents a positive change as it gives legal recognition to social and indigenous groups, including traditional indigenous authorities, as legal representatives of community interests (Gray-Molina 2002). For other students of this process, however, OTBs are not fully recognized by communities. As Ayo explains, one of the mistakes in the design of PP was to believe that OTBs, with their territorial logic, were going to replace corporatist forms of social organization, in many cases based on economic and other kinds of interests, but they didn't.[24]

Another innovative aspect of this model was the incorporation of Oversight Committees (Comités de Vigilancia; CVs). CVs were created to give representation to "organized civil society" and to insert a mechanism of social control into public affairs. CV members are elected from OTB representatives and can participate in official municipal meetings and may request any sort of financial or technical information. Their innovative character lies in the fact that for the first time the government allows OTBs to monitor the use of public funds through direct participation. According to Tuchschneider, more than 1,600 CVs were created in the initial years of PP (1998). Although CV members are unpaid—at least not directly—there are other social compensations and motivations, such as local prestige and the opportunity to provide community service and demonstrate leadership skills. The law also entitles CVs to submit complaints directly to the central executive, which in turn can refer them to the Senate, which has the authority to freeze municipal accounts if necessary, even if there is no conclusive evidence. According to Grindle, a national survey in 1996 showed that at least one in five CVs initiated such action against their local government (2000).

Another innovative aspect of decentralization has been the use of diverse participatory and planning mechanisms. Every year, each municipal government, in coordination with local OTBs and sectors involved (i.e., education, health, etc.), prepares an Annual Operative Plan (POA), where local projects are listed and funds earmarked. This plan is drafted in response to demands presented by community members or representatives under a participatory planning approach (*planificación participativa*). POAs also need to be consistent with Municipal Development Plans (Planes de Desarrollo Municipal; PDMs), a five-year strategic plan elaborated in coordination with prefectures and following national guidelines provided by the central government. These two plans, the POA and PDM, represent the backbone of the municipality's development agenda and must address social and economic needs as well as those related to infrastructure.

The inclusive and participatory character of PP has had a deep impact in terms of how democracy functions at the grassroots, with clear and tangible efforts to bring accountability to the local level. Nevertheless, an institutional reform like PP per se was not enough to break a deeply embedded political culture. A good example is a controversial measure—considered by some to be one of PP's weakest links—that allows the removal of mayors from office, the so-called constructive censure vote (*voto constructivo de censura*).[25] Once a year, councils evaluate the performance of mayors and have the power to remove them from office under allegations of incompetence or corruption. Although the spirit of this reform was to enhance accountability, by giving local governments a parliamentarian character, political actors soon began to use this legal loophole for their own personal and political advantage, bringing political instability to the municipal level. During the first three years in which this measure was put in place, one-third of the mayors were removed from office. Changes in the Municipal Law of 1999 reduced this tendency[26] and between 2000 and 2001 one-fifth of the municipalities removed their mayors; however, this number has increased again since 2002 to its initial levels. For some analysts the struggle of mayors to remain in power is another teething problem of PP; for others, however, the constant political instability at the municipal level is a reflection of the overall weakness of state institutions and the feeling of lack of respect for electoral decision at the grassroots level.

Another weak element of PP has been the role of prefectures, which were historically dependent on the central state. In 1995 the Administrative Decentralization Law (LDA) that accompanied PP revitalized prefectures by defining them as "deconcentrated powers of the central government." As decentralization consolidated, however, prefectures became competitors of local governments in terms of capturing resources and duplicating functions in a constant political struggle. In this tussle, prefects—appointed directly by the president until 2006—lacked the legitimacy of democratically elected mayors, so they turned to the center as a source of power and thus distanced themselves from the population.[27] As noted earlier, responding to strong regional demands, prefects were elected for the first time in 2006; see Table 7.2.[28] The overall implications for decentralization and democracy are mixed because, on the one hand, an apparent strong influence of national over regional politics remains; on the other hand, regional political agendas, representing autonomy, have captured the attention and passion of voters, granting certain legitimacy to prefects in the process and strengthening their posture vis-à-vis municipalities, which evidently is a new phenomenon in Bolivian politics.

Political and Social Changes

The election of mayors has spawned new political dynamics at the microlevel, the participation dimension. Political parties have been forced to review their strategies, and unprecedented alliances have been formed at the local level based on considerations beyond the clientelistic logic of Bolivian politics. Party nomination practices have also changed, forcing parties to create internal democratic processes. This situation has weakened partisan structures, but at the same time has allowed for a much needed political renovation. This new scenario has had an impact on the way in which mayors are elected—a microversion of Bolivia's presidential election, parliamentarized presidentialism—mainly because it encourages local political forces to create their own alliances. The social effects of PP were mostly indirect and worked gradually through a virtuous circle of increasing participation and opening of the state.

In this sense, although social groups did not participate in the initial design, they swiftly assimilated decentralization through collective action and mobilization. Congruent with social theory, PP opened a local institutional window allowing the efforts of individuals through collective action to reach a previously elusive state, this time in the form of municipal governments. Through the many institutional mechanisms created by PP—for some foreign, but for others complementary to local practices of governance—people and communities found the right incentives to participate, especially in rural areas. The state, therefore, became accountable even in the most isolated areas. Somehow, PP managed to foster local activism and organization, mainly by reducing participation costs, as it became easy to get involved in local public affairs, and maximizing the benefits of becoming active rather than a *free rider*. These arguments suggest, therefore, some positive effects on the quality of democracy.

The Pluralism of the Reform

PP's institutional design, however, was based on a Westernized view of democracy, philosophically constructed from and for individuals for whom an advanced civic behavior was assumed, rather than following the communal logic still prevalent in most of rural Bolivia. As Booth, Clisby, and Widmark argue, "because it creates a new layer of elective local government, PP was envisaged as the framework for blending Western representative democracy and Andean participatory democracy" (1997). But PP also revitalized traditional practices of governance, particularly in rural areas and indigenous communities. Thus, paradoxically, although one of the main objectives of PP was to consolidate representative democracy by devolving powers and to introduce mechanisms of participatory democracy, in the end it promoted a different type of local democracy where consensus, democratic participation, and decisionmaking happen below that of the municipality, in the community.

The kind of democracy that PP promotes assumes that (1) citizens express their preferences at the time of voting, (2) elected candidates cannot be removed from office unless certain procedures are followed, and (3) candidates' legitimacy as expressed by the vote allows them to make decisions individually, and presumably on behalf of their constituency. These points, however, contrast with some traditional governance practices. For example, it is common for indigenous and rural communities as well as some neighborhood associations to gather and select municipal candidates directly in assemblies (*cabildos*), based on their past performance, skills, and services rendered to the community during their *cargo* service.[29] In many cases candidates are selected regardless of their political orientation or party membership, either active or past. Thus, many indigenous groups approach political parties or other groups required for the formal electoral registration once a candidate has been selected. There have also been many cases in which communities presented different candidates to different parties as a way to minimize electoral risk and secure political representation (see Albó 1999). For former congresswoman Erika Brockmann this community assembly system (*asambleísmo comunitario*) to select candidates competes directly with the representative system through political parties (in Ayo 2004). As a result, alternative forms of democracy have also been strengthened by PP, mainly at the grassroots level, but not necessarily in the same direction that orthodox, Westernized democratic theory predicts.

The permanence of elected mayors and councilors in office is also contested in the rural world. Because of the constant rotation in leadership, part of the logic of the *cargo* system, many communities believe that public servants can be removed at any time. This situation helps to explain the wide acceptance of the constructive censure vote in rural areas. When elected officials lose support, communities may mobilize, demanding their dismissal simply because an active minority disagrees with these officials. The co-optation exercised by community leaders, and therefore of those communities that they represent, can be very strong. Common forms of popular protest include street and road blockades, forceful occupation of municipal offices, walling-in of the main municipal building (*tapiado*),[30] social marginalization of local authorities, and acts of aggression against them (destruction of property, etc.). On only a few occasions does local political conflict resort to formal forms of dispute resolution such as the police or the judiciary. For the most part, elected authorities respond to community requests by resigning their positions and thus avoiding confrontation. It is also common for councilors to relinquish their posts to give their elected substitutes the opportunity to gain some experience, following the traditional rotation system. Under this logic, the resignation of a mayor is seen by the community not as an act of humiliation, but as a routine process of participatory decisionmaking, which is opposed to the expected *rational* behavior in which political actors make every possible effort to stay in power. This behavior questions traditional views of democracy, because in the logic of rural and indigenous communities, electoral decision and responsiveness can be sacrificed to achieve higher accountability through participation and consensus.

The legitimacy of elected authorities in rural areas is another important issue. According to Albó (1997, 1999) and Albó and Barrios (2006), in the first municipal election more than five hundred "peasant-indigenous" (p-i)[31] candidates were elected councilors, roughly one-third of the available posts, but only a small fraction secured mayoralties. The fact that many of these predominantly indigenous municipalities did not manage to impose their candidates as mayors was, perhaps, a sign of their incipient power and the continued dominance of local elites. In many cases, elected authorities were recognized as legitimate as long as they responded to community decisions, often made by local councils—such as councils of elders in Aymara Ayllus[32] (Mallkus) or councils of community representatives, Curacas, in Quechua regions—and in open meetings (see Albó et al. 1990), contrasting with the notion that representatives make decisions on behalf of those represented (see Pitkin 1967). This overlap weakens the legitimacy of elected authorities, who, in many instances, had to negotiate with grassroots organizations before decisions were made, putting into question why they were elected in the first place. Reaching consensus at the communal level is not an easy task either, as it requires discussion, agreement, and commitment. Although this has some benefits—such as better informed citizens and opinions shared, rather than imposed—it also has clear disadvantages as consensus is difficult, if not impossible, to achieve.

Shortcomings of the Process: New Institutions, Old Vices?

Although PP opened new spaces for participation, supporting the institution-building process from the bottom up, there were some shortcomings, such as the prevalence of clientelism and elite capture. On the one hand, it seems possible that PP strengthened clientelist networks because it made municipal positions a desired commodity to local elites and political parties, thus reinforcing this intrinsic element of Bolivia's political system and culture. On the other hand, PP weakened many clientelist networks, and local elites were not able to (re)capture power to the extent that many analysts predicted. Decentralization and the prospects of local representation encouraged communities to strengthen their organizations, many with successful results. This gave local leaders a privileged bargaining position at the time of negotiating their participation with political forces. As a result, although PP might be contributing to lessening long-standing political distortions such as clientelism and elite capture, this reform by itself is not enough to alter the dominant political culture, at least not in the short run.

The designers of PP were also aware of the implication that a large transfer of resources would have for corruption—the accountability dimension. For this reason, PP incorporated a wide array of control mechanisms, particularly with the involvement of organized civil society through instances such as CVs, in addition to all sorts of internal bureaucratic controls. The evidence, however, is contradictory. According to Transparency International, the perception on corruption has varied little since the inception of PP, and Bolivia has ranked consistently as one of the most corrupt countries in Latin America; see Table 7.6. Other studies, however, suggest that this perception varies depending on the level of government. Seligson, Moreno Morales, and Schwartz Blum show that the perception is that corruption is lower at subnational levels, municipalities, and prefectures than at the center (2005: 152); see Figure 7.2. A 2002 report from the Comptrollers Office (Contraloría General) stated that there was evidence of misuse of funds in "only" 3 percent of the US$404 million spent by municipal governments between 1994 and 2001, which amounted to a little over US$12 million (Altman and Lalander 2003).[33] Although any level of corruption should be unacceptable, this relatively low percentage—at least the kind

Table 7.6   Transparency International's Corruption Perception Index (CPI) Results for Bolivia, 1996–2008

Year	Ranking	Score CPI[a]	Countries with the Same Ranking	Countries Surveyed
1996[b]	36	3.4	—	54
1997	51	2.05	—	52
1998	69	2.8	Ukraine	85
1999	75	2.5	Armenia	99
2000	71	2.7	Côte-d'Ivoire, Venezuela	90
2001	84	2.0	Azerbaijan, Cameroon, Kenya	91
2002	89	2.2	Cameroon, Ecuador, Haiti	102
2003	106	2.3	Honduras, Macedonia, Serbia and Montenegro, Sudan, Ukraine, Zimbabwe	133
2004	122	2.2	Guatemala, Kazakhstan, Kyrgyzstan, Niger, Sudan, Ukraine	145
2005	117	2.5	Afghanistan, Ecuador, Guatemala, Guyana, Libya, Nepal, Philippines, Uganda	159
2006	105	2.7	Iran, Libya, Macedonia, Malawi, Uganda	163
2007	105	2.9	Albania, Argentina, Burkina Faso, Djibouti, Egypt	179
2008	102	3.0	Djibouti, Dominican Republic, Lebanon, Mongolia, Rwanda, Tanzania	180

Sources: Author's elaboration with data from Transparency International, www.transparency.org.

Notes: a. CPI score relates to perceptions of the degree of corruption as seen by businesspeople and country analysts and ranges between 10 (highly clean) and 0 (highly corrupt).

b. Year in which Bolivia was added to the index.

Figure 7.2 Response to Which Level of Government Is More Corrupt

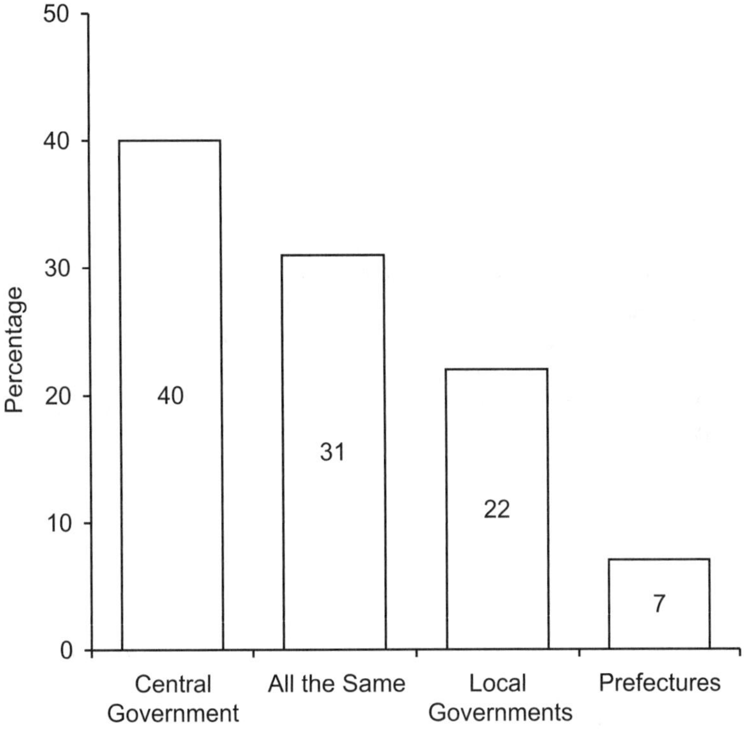

Source: Seligson, Morales, and Blum 2005: 152.
Notes: This graph shows the percentage of people interviewed who responded to the question "Which level of government do you think is more corrupt: central government, local governments, prefectures, or are they all the same?" The survey was conducted in 2004.

of corruption that is captured by national auditing systems—shows that although this evil persists at the local level it is below what some detractors of this process anticipated. This contradictory evidence shows not only how difficult it is to assess this problem, but also how much an artificial institutional design can alter a deeply embodied political culture.

Another notable shortcoming of PP has been the failure to narrow a wide and persistent gender gap. While local spaces for leadership and participation have been opened by this reform, most of them have been appropriated by men. Although electoral laws establish that at least 30 percent of the candidates in party lists and 50 percent in citizen and indigenous groups must be women, these quotas are interpreted as referential, and women are normally placed at the bottom of the lists as substitutes. While in 1993, the year before PP, there were

19 women mayors and 231 women municipal councilors (27 percent of the total), in 1995 this number decreased to 11 and 135 respectively (8 percent); see Table 7.7. The arrival of political power and resources generated a perverse incentive for the marginalization of women in local politics.[34] In 1995 the participation of indigenous women was even more limited, as there were only 22 indigenous women serving as councilors, compared to 464 indigenous men. Although the participation of women improved slightly in 1999, with the election of 252 female municipal councilors (14.9 percent), this percentage was still below the one-third limit set by the law. The fact that 71 percent of all substitutes were women also made evident how female politicians are relegated to nonactive positions. In the 2004 municipal election, women candidates managed to occupy 19.2 percent of available municipal positions (and 1,289 substitute positions, or 73 percent of the total). The number of female mayors, however, decreased considerably to only 13 throughout the country (4 percent); and in 28 percent of municipalities there was no female representation at all! (ACOBOL 2006: 267). Finally, the 2010 elections showed some signs of improvement, not in terms of female mayors elected (only 24 or 7.1 percent of the total), but also in terms of councilors, with women occupying 785 seats in

Table 7.7   Elected Municipal Government Positions, 1993–2010

	1993		1995		1999		2004		2010	
	No.	%	No.	%	No.	%	No.	%	No.	%
Number of municipalities	59		311		314		327		337	
Women mayors	19	3.2	11	3.5	23	7.3	13	4.0	24	7.1
Indigenous and campesino men elected as mayors	—	—	464	28.6	—		—		—	
Indigenous and campesino women elected as mayors	—	—	2	0.6	—		—		—	
Total municipal councillors	858		1,624		1,685		1,750		1,831	
Women elected as municipal councilors	231	26.9	135	8.3	252	14.9	337	19.2	785	42.9
Indigenous and campesino women elected as municipal councilors	—	—	22	1.3	—	—	—	—	—	—

Sources: Altman and Lalander (2003); ACOBOL (2006); http://www.acobol.org.bo/portal/default.asp?cg1 =108; http://www.enlared.org.bo/portal/default.asp?cg2=6998.

municipal councils (42.9 percent), an outstanding victory for women and perhaps a sign that conditions at the grassroots are finally improving. But the political discrimination against women is also visible in other decentralized scenarios. According to Ayo, in 1995 only 11 percent of OTBs' representatives and 4.7 percent of department councilors were women (1999). The limited progress of PP in promoting gender equality, therefore, is one of its shortcomings and one that affects enormously the quality of democracy, although these results are the reflection of a wider cultural pattern rather than a new phenomenon. Paradoxically, therefore, PP diminished the political participation of women, one of the social groups that it sought to empower, although this negative impact may be changing.

Sixteen Years of Popular Participation

The effects of decentralization on the democratic system during the past years can be divided into three periods related to changes in national governments. The first one (1995–1997) is one of invention, experimentation, and an attempt to consolidate this process. The 1995 municipal election brought new political dynamics to the local level and the interest of political parties in gaining some of the 2,900 municipal posts available for mayors and councilors, for which 25,000 candidates participated, until then the largest electoral and political mobilization in Bolivia (Blanes 1998). Although in many places traditional political parties prevailed, in others new leaders were elected. Therefore, PP opened up the possibility for an active and independent role of local political actors and the emergence of a new intraparty competition dynamic. For example, the share of the national vote for MNR (ironically PP's main promoter) fell from 33.8 percent in the 1993 national election to 21 percent in the 1995 municipal election, partly because their local candidates came from closed party lists rather than incorporating local leaders as other parties did. However, its relatively wide presence in rural areas and its control of the central government allowed this party to gain control over 121 municipalities (39 percent of the total) (O'Neill 2005: 142). These results, therefore, made clear to parties the need to react swiftly and adjust to the realities of a new political scenario and new institutions, by creating ties between national and local politics and decentralizing and democratizing party structures. In other words, this did result in strengthening the electoral dimension with some degree of responsiveness and increasing accountability.

The second period (1997–2002) was characterized by the slowing down of PP by the center in an attempt to reclaim some of the lost political spaces. The election of President General Hugo Bánzer Suárez of Nationalist Democratic Action (Acción Democrática Nacionalista; ADN) in 1997[35] brought a halt to decentralization as PP was seen as a dubious political reform promoted by ADN's opponents, although ADN was also aware of the popularity of this reform and its seemingly irreversible character. As a result, Bánzer did not directly alter PP, but instead reduced its impact through fiscal and political restraints. Financially, the flow of resources to municipalities was reduced in favor of regional governments. Politically, decentralization was adjusted toward regional prefects and away from municipalities (Bohrt 2001: 61). Thus, it was not a coincidence that all prefects appointed by Bánzer were ADN members (Oporto 1998: 40), some of them his close relatives (O'Neill 2005). Also, taking advantage of the constructive censure vote, the dominant parties made political maneuvers to weaken MNR and its allies. For instance, MNR's control of municipal governments fell from 39 percent to 27 percent just a year later. Another opposition party, the Free Bolivia Movement (Movimiento Bolivia Libre; MBL), lost almost 70 percent of its municipalities. Meanwhile, ADN and its main ally, the Revolutionary Left Movement (Movimiento de la Izquierda Revolucionaria; MIR), doubled and quadrupled the number of their municipalities respectively, despite their small share of the 1995 vote. According to Ayo, ADN's effort to recentralize power was made in the form of a "party-oriented centralization of decentralization" (1999: 150). In August 2001, Bánzer was forced to resign due to a terminal illness and was replaced by his vice president, Jorge ("Tuto") Quiroga, who approached decentralization with caution while maintaining an ambiguous agenda. In summary, in this period some of the democratic gains at the grassroots were reversed, including a disregard for electoral decision and diminished participation and accountability.

The third period (2002–2010) is one of transformation with a growing debate on the role of subnational governments, the emergence of ethnopolitical movements, regional and indigenous claims for higher autonomy, and renewed strength of the central government. During his second mandate, Sánchez de Lozada—the man who had energetically promoted PP—disregarded it as a political priority. Although he did not curtail the reforms, he did little to push them forward either. After his forced resignation, his successor Carlos Mesa attempted to return to the decentralization agenda, particularly addressing some of its shortcomings related to the intermediate level, but failed in the attempt. Despite the instability at the national level, municipal elections were carried out without major difficulties in 2004. As mentioned earlier, an innovative element was the implementation of a constitutional amendment allowing candidates to compete under the umbrella of citizen groups (*asociaciones ciudadanas*) or representing indigenous groups (*pueblos indígenas*) in order to break the monopoly of political parties (see Romero 2005).[36] As result, more than 900 indigenous and citizen groups expressed their interest in registering candidates, and more than 400 managed to do so. The number of registered lists at the local level grew enormously, from 18 in 1999 to almost 450 in 2004 (Romero 2005: 26; Bazoberry Chali 2005). In this election, the decay of the three largest traditional parties (MNR, ADN, and MIR) became clear as each one obtained less than 15 percent of the vote. Also, two out of three indigenous groups that participated—albeit in a small fraction of municipalities—got at least one candidate elected, a better performance than that of citizen groups, where more than half the candidates failed to gain a seat (Romero 2005: 83). There were, nonetheless, some outstanding victories for independent candidates, such as those in large cities. But the biggest winner of this election was MAS, which consolidated its national position with 17.1 percent of the votes.

In 2005, following the interim government of Rodríguez Veltzé, President Evo Morales retook the PP agenda, this time emphasizing indigenous autonomy and territorial organization. Therefore, although decentralization was retaken with renewed energy, the goals were and continue not to be entirely clear as of my work on this chapter. PP's original design has been maintained in place, but as discussed previously, the contestation has moved to the intermediate level and has been characterized by a bitter confrontation between the central government and prefectures. Moreover, in 2006, political parties, including the resilient MNR and ADN and emerging MAS, still controlled three-quarters of the municipalities in Bolivia (76.5 percent), although MAS was by far the dominant force, controlling one-third of all municipalities (31.5 percent). Also, despite the poor performance of citizen groups, with mayors in only one-sixth of the municipalities (17.1 percent), their presence confirms the arrival of electoral alternatives. In addition, although the percentage of municipalities controlled by indigenous groups is small (6.4 percent), this is another sign of the penetration of ethno-political movements in the political system. In 2010, MAS-IPSP achieved another outstanding electoral victory, doubling its local presence through the election of 220 mayors (two-thirds of the municipalities in Bolivia). The rest of the municipalities were shared between surviving parties and several ad hoc citizen and indigenous groups. The outcomes of this subnational election, therefore, suggest that although the monopoly of traditional parties over political processes has been broken, which is an important improvement, the dominance of a single party, in this case MAS-IPSP, could be detrimental to the health of democracy in the future. Moreover, a new decentralization law was approved in July 2010—the Framework Law of Autonomies and Decentralization (Ley Marco de Autonomías y Descentralización)—that builds on the basic structure and precepts of PP but also adds new elements such as the incorporation of indigenous autonomies and the modification of some of the attributions and responsibilities of the intermediate level, defined in the new constitution as "autonomous departmental governments." Although the specific details have not been laid out, this law is another example of the center's intention to reorient the decentralization agenda toward a larger institutional restructuring of the state congruent with MAS's long-term political objectives. Evidently this new legislation will have great implications for the future of decentralization in Bolivia.

PP's Democratic Contribution, Emerging Local Leadership

A final important contribution of PP has been the promotion of new forms of local leadership. Prior to PP, most leaders emerged during their mandatory community service, but with limited possibilities to project themselves beyond the local sphere. Decentralization, via the election of thousands of local authorities, changed local leadership practically overnight. Leaders were not only given specific functions as part of PP's institutional design, but, most importantly, they received formal recognition by the state as mayors, CV members, OTB representatives, indigenous authorities, and other positions. But this emerging local leadership had to compete fiercely with local political elites and their clienteles. As the process consolidated, the new political leadership mixed with the abundant social leadership. Further, traditional forms of power and organization were suddenly transformed into formal structures recognized by the state, for example, the election of indigenous leaders as municipal authorities. The origins of some of Bolivia's dominant parties, such as MAS, are examples of this change of paradigm. In contrast to the oldest and for some well-established parties built from the top down by political and intellectual elites, these emerging parties were built from the bottom up in response to specific demands of grassroots organizations and social movements and with strong support from their local and municipal areas of influence. Municipal democracy also allowed the emergence of personalized forms of leadership (Mayorga 1997), which contributed to further deterioration of political parties by giving preference to local personalities, who were often independent candidates, rather than political structures and platforms.

Decentralization also created a prime opportunity for local leaders to build their political careers. The municipal arena became the training ground for future regional and national leaders. For example, five out of the nine departmental prefects elected in 2005 had previous municipal experience, including three of them that served as mayors. In 2010, five governors elected had prior municipal experience and another two were MAS representatives to the AC. Local leadership has also reached other instances of political power in Bolivia. For example, while only a small fraction of congressmen elected in 2005 had some sort of formal municipal experience having served as mayors and councilors (Figure 7.3), most of them had previous experience as community leaders (84 percent), union (*sindicato*) representatives (44 percent), or in coordinating social movements (18 percent). But the most symbolic cases of ascending leadership in Bolivia are, perhaps, those of President Evo Morales and Silvia Lazarte, president of the Constituent Assembly. Morales began his political career as a sports delegate under the *cargo* system in the Chapare region and later became a community leader for coca farmers. The election of Lazarte, a Quechua social leader also from the Chapare region and former municipal councilor of Chimoré, as president of Bolivia's Constituent Assembly

Figure 7.3 Previous Experience of Bolivian Congressmen/Senators

Source: Author's own data based on a sample of 108 congressmen and senators in 2006.

was clearly a symbol of the arrival of minority groups into power and that Bolivia's democracy has been altered for good.

Popular Participation and Quality of Democracy

As discussed throughout this chapter, the implications of PP for the quality of democracy in Bolivia, along the lines of what Levine and Molina propose in this volume, are extensive and diverse. On the one hand, the participatory essence of decentralization, exemplified by its name, Popular Participation, has clearly contributed to enhancing the quality of democracy in this country. The opening of local political spaces—many through electoral means—for participation, contestation, and negotiation has finally broken the hegemonic powers of a traditionally centralist and discriminatory state. The many innovative aspects of this reform, such as the introduction of CVs, OTBs, and other participatory mechanisms, have also made the state, at least at the local level, directly accountable to the citizenry. This does not mean that Bolivia is exempt from corruption, clientelism, and other political vices at the grassroots, but rather that society has new tools to combat and deter this kind of behavior, perhaps in a more effective way than in the more complex national scenario where accountability remains elusive. Through direct interaction, municipal governments have also demonstrated a good degree of responsiveness toward social demands, something that has placed them as the most trusted public institution in this country (Mendoza-Botelho 2009). PP has also fostered the emergence of a new kind of leadership that has gone beyond the local sphere and now occupies spaces of power that in the past were reserved to an exclusive elite. This new leadership, evidently, is crucial at the time of consolidating and enhancing a greatly needed democratic culture, something that might eventually translate into solid and responsive institutions.

On the other hand, the overall dominant political culture, one that tolerates corruption and still favors opportunism and clientelism, is still prevalent and has permeated many local institutions. This idea suggests that a deeply embedded political culture cannot be changed from the policy side alone. Moreover, the future of decentralization, and therefore that of local and departmental governments, still depends on the goodwill of a powerful central government that seems to have decided to regain lost political spaces and control. Also, despite the many social and political gains, PP has not been able to tackle some of the most serious problems faced by this society, such as widespread poverty and inequality, unemployment, a nonresponsive state with limited bureaucratic capacity, and chronic gender discrimination that continues to exclude women from active involvement in the civic and political life of this country. This last point questions how much the quality of democracy has improved for half the population.

National vs. Local: The Elusive Quest
to Build Democratic Institutions

In this chapter, I have presented the issues surrounding quality of democracy in Bolivia in two distinct but complementary sections. The first one offered a broad national overview of the evolution of democracy in this country since its reinception in 1982. For those familiar with Bolivia, it is clear that substantial progress has been made in consolidating democracy and its institutions—the electoral decision dimension—something particularly difficult for this highly complex, multiethnic, and socially and regionally divided society. The process has been difficult and at times filled with conflict. But this democracy has survived the difficult tests that it had to face, and it is notable that the rule of law has prevailed even during periods of high political crises and social unrest—the responsiveness element. Despite these positive aspects, it is also evident that the new kind of democracy being built in Bolivia is far from being consolidated, and the question of its quality becomes an imperative in an ever-changing political scenario. Much remains to be done. Despite the regular use of electoral means—the democratic game—the many and fair demands of Bolivian citizens for a more just and inclusive society still do not receive an adequate response from the state. The inception of forms of direct consultation, such as referenda, has not changed the way in which the popular will is subject to the interpretation and manipulation of those who control power in their pursuit of particular political objectives. Moreover, the efforts to build transparent and independent democratic institutions seem to have been reversed during the last decade, a situation that jeopardizes many of the political and social gains. Also, Bolivia is still highly dependent on other countries, economically and ideologically, regardless of the source of influence—the element of sovereignty.

In a comparative context, the empirical observations are congruent with Levine and Molina's Index of Quality of Democracy for 2005, which was the year of the transition to Evo Morales, that places Bolivia below the median of Latin American countries—tenth out of seventeen countries (this volume Chapter 2). Although the levels of electoral decision, participation, and responsiveness are relatively good, the other two dimensions, accountability and sovereignty, are disappointing, thus confirming the heterogeneity of the quality of democracy in this country. In other words, although democracy functions well in certain areas, it fails notably in others. Moreover, Bolivian democracy is highly sensitive to contextual issues, such as economic downturns or political crises, and the rule of law has been tested many times to the limits. A new exercise of this type would help to observe how much Morales and MAS have contributed (or not) to enhancing democracy in this Andean nation, considering that this particular interpretation of the quality of democracy might differ from alternative forms of assessing democracy, such as the collective views of indigenous and other social groups.

But this chapter also brought to light the experiences of a highly promising reform, Popular Participation. Parallel to the more complex, ideologically polarized, and regionally divided scenario, citizens have received a partial response to their most basic social and political needs in the form of active local governments (*municipios*) and in the institutional design put into place to allow direct participation in local public affairs. This transformation has not only generated a new sense of citizenship, but has also fostered an unseen process of social and political activism and growing accountability of public institutions from the citizenry. Despite many drawbacks and limitations, PP has become not only a viable alternative for democratic participation, but also a source for a new kind of leadership, one that hopefully will enhance the quality of democracy and its basic institutions in the future.

Notes

1. Jorge Quiroga constitutionally assumed the presidency in August 2001 after President Hugo Bánzer had to resign due to a terminal illness.

2. The "Punto Fijo" (Fixed Point) pact refers to the tacit agreement between Venezuela's main parties that began in 1958 and dominated the political life of this country for over thirty years.

3. The oversimplification of this analysis provides a broad overview of the national democratic process in Bolivia. Evidently more scholarly work needs to be done to fully understand the evolution of the quality of democracy in this period.

4. But, as in any other transitional country, there were a few isolated incidents that did not damage the legitimacy of the electoral process.

5. SAFCO Law 1178 (1990) and Ombudsman Law 1818 (1997) were later added to the 2008 Constitution as a section.

6. In the popular view, Chile is still seen as Bolivia's antagonist since the Pacific War of 1879 when Bolivia lost its access to the Pacific coast.

7. Estimate is based on data from the LAPOP Project for 2005.

8. Historian James Dunkerley refers to this process as "Bolivia's third revolution" (2006, 2007).

9. Corte Nacional Electoral de Bolivia (CNE), "Resultados del Referéndum Nacional y Constitucional," 2009, http://www.cne.org.bo/ResultadosRNC2009/.

10. The turnout was 84.5 percent of all registered voters (Corte Nacional Electoral de Bolivia 2006).

11. Because the position of prefect was absent from the previous Constitution, President Mesa had to resort to a legal subterfuge to call for regional elections. Presidential Decree 27988 of 2005 (later transformed into Law 3015) established that the president would designate as prefects those candidates that obtained a simple majority in departmental elections. This decree, kept in place by his successors, therefore, was a political compromise and a promise to be fulfilled rather than an actual enforceable law.

12. Some of the most important state revenues come from the taxation and commercialization of hydrocarbons, particularly exports of natural gas to neighboring countries.

13. Law No. 3850 of May 12, 2008.

14. In La Paz, the prefecture went to Pablo Ramos, former dean of Bolivia's largest university (University of San Andrés), who left his seat in the municipal council of the city of La Paz representing MAS; and in Cochabamba he appointed the former vice minister for Internal Affairs (Régimen Interior) and presidential delegate in Cochabamba, Rafael Puente, also representing MAS, who shortly after resigned and was replaced by MAS congressman Jorge Ledezma, also directly appointed by Morales. D.S. 29688 and D.S. 29689 of December 2008.

15. D.S. 29711.

16. The Bolivia country reports are available at www.freedomhouse.org.

17. Freedom House, 2008 Bolivia Country Report, http://www.freedomhouse.org/template.cfm ?page=251&year=2008.

18. Gobierno de Bolivia, 1994, *Ley de Participación Popular, La Paz, Bolivia*. Ley No. 1551 del 20 de abril de 1994. Translated by Altman and Lalander 2003.

19. See Ayo (2004); Behrendt (2002); Blanes (1998); Graham (1997); Gray-Molina (2001); Kohl (2002). Other more intricate reasons also mentioned in the literature include the potential future political gains of political parties (Grindle 2000; O'Neill 2005); the intention to reduce the migration flow from the countryside to urban areas and abroad (Peirce 1997; Van Cott 2000); the need to restrain "political adventures" similar to those of the terrorist group Shining Path in Peru (Ayo 2004); and the intention to weaken and even break national unions (Altman and Lalander 2003). See also Laurent Thévoz, "Decentralization in Bolivia: A Model Under Construction," Center for International Earth Science Information Network (CIESIN), Columbia University, 1999, www.ciesin.org/decentralization/English/CaseStudies/SDC_Bolivia.html.

20. For additional information, see Ayo (1999); Faguet (2004); Fundación Friederich Ebert e Instituto Latinomericano de Investigaciones Sociales (FES-ILDIS) (2004); Graham (1997); Grindle (2000); Mayorga (1997); Mendoza-Botelho (2009); Seligson, Moreno Morales, and Schwartz Blum (2005).

21. According to Gray-Molina, social investment at the local level increased "fivefold" and public investment grew from US$32 million in 1994 to US$128 million in 1995 and close to US$250 million in 2002 (2002). By 2000, municipal governments were responsible for approximately 40 percent of public investment and 60 percent of all social investments. Kohl also observes that from 1994 to 1996, municipalities were responsible for the creation of more than 32,000 direct and indirect jobs (2002: 464).

22. For example, the MIP in the Aymara Altiplano and Evo Morales's party, MAS, in the Cocalero region of Chapare.

23. Councilors and mayors are elected directly by citizens running under the umbrella of political parties, citizen groups (Agrupación Ciudadana), or representing indigenous community and ethnic groups. Similar to the national process, if mayors do not obtain more than one-half of the votes, they are elected indirectly by the council from among its members, thus giving space for after-election bargaining and the traditional use of clientelistic politics (Andersson 1999). The municipal council's primary roles are the legislation of local norms and the monitoring of the executive, including the approval of budgets. For the most part, this instance has proven to be an effective control mechanism and has allowed the representation of traditionally marginalized groups such as indigenous peoples and women.

24. Personal interview with Diego Ayo, La Paz, Bolivia, October 15, 2006.

25. For additional information, see Albó (1999); Ayo (1999 and 2001); Blanes (1998); Hadenius (2003); Hiskey and Seligson (2003); World Bank (1999). For a perspective on indigenous municipalities, see Albó (1997, 1999).

26. Law No. 22028.

27. In addition to prefectures, another deliberative organ was created at the intermediate level, the Departmental Councils (Consejos Departamentales), although their functions have been of little relevance to the overall decentralization process.

28. Including a large, open town meeting (*cabildo*) of one-quarter million people in Santa Cruz in January 2005 that put pressure on President Mesa for the signing of decrees granting more autonomous powers to departments and the election of prefects. See "El cabildo de Santa Cruz fue masivo y convocó a la unidad," *El deber* (Santa Cruz, Bolivia), January 1, 2005; "El mayor departamento de Bolivia proclama un gobierno regional autónomo del poder central," *El mundo* (Madrid), January 1, 2005; Peña and Jordán (2006).

29. In simple terms, the *cargo* system, which is most common in rural areas, is an expected community service from members, normally for a period of one year. The tasks and names in Spanish—including Quechua, Aymara, and other languages spoken in Bolivia—assigned to this responsibility vary, but are related to the needs of the community and adapted to their geographic location.

30. The walling-in (*tapiado*) is a very symbolic kind of demonstration in Bolivia. Normally protesters gather outside the municipal or any other state building, each one carrying one brick. Then, demonstrators place their bricks one by one at the main entrance, "building" a wall that blocks access to the offices, thus symbolizing a communal effort and unity in the protest and a visible physical expression of their contempt.

31. Albó uses the notion of "p-i" to incorporate, as part of the same category, indigenous groups that normally share a distinctive set of characteristics, such as the same language and traditions, and mixed (*mestizo*) rural groups, despite the fact that all his respondents identify themselves as indigenous.

32. In very simplistic terms, the Ayllu is a community unit of the high Andes where land and social responsibilities are shared. This ancestral form of organization requires the participation of all members in community duties (mutual aid), ranging from basic agricultural tasks to more complex administrative and political ones.

33. "Los alcaldes malversaron más de \$US 12 millones," *Los tiempos,* Cochabamba, Bolivia, sec. B4, March 6, 2002.

34. For additional information, see Altman and Lalander (2003: 89); Ayo (1999); Bazoberry Chali (2005); and Machicado Barbery (2004).

35. Although this was General Bánzer's second term in office, this was his first democratic period, as his previous presidency (1971–1978) was the result of a coup d'état.

36. According to Law 2771, citizen groups require the signatures of at least 2 percent of voters in the municipality to register candidates, while indigenous groups have only to demonstrate their condition as such.

8

Nicaragua: *Chapiolla* Democracy

Salvador Martí i Puig

FROM THE INSURRECTION THAT OVERTHREW THE SOMOZA dynasty in 1979 to the present day, Nicaragua's journey has been one of the most distinctive in recent Latin American history. In the course of a few short, but distinct, periods, it has experienced (1) a revolutionary phase of popular mobilization and state transformation from 1979 to 1984; (2) the creation of a system featuring Liberal and corporate elements from 1984 to 1990; (3) an experiment with a phase of neoliberal democracy from 1990 to 2006, which included episodes of instability with shifting rules of the game; and (4) since 2006 the return to power of Daniel Ortega in an environment of uncertainty, one marked by the politicization of certain institutions and the elimination of opportunities for political pluralism.

Since Nicaragua's first multiparty election in 1984 and its first competitive election in 1990, democracy has progressed, and continues to progress, though not always in a straight line, and not without continuing uncertainties. Civilian-military relations have undeniably improved, human rights violations have diminished, and civil liberties have expanded. However, the first decade of the twenty-first century has seen a politicization of a number of institutions that are crucial to the quality of democracy, as will become evident below.

To obtain an accurate picture of the quality of the country's democracy, the present account employs the theoretical model proposed by Levine and Molina (Chapter 1). In Levine and Molina's index of the quality of democracy in Latin American countries (see Table 2.7, Chapter 2) Nicaragua shares the bottom of the ranking with three neighbors (Guatemala, El Salvador, and Honduras), with one nation with an entrenched armed conflict (Colombia), another suffering increasing polarization (Venezuela), and the country with the distinction of having had the longest-lasting authoritarian dictatorship in the region (Paraguay).

I begin with a short outline of Nicaragua's history, then turn to the five dimensions that the above-cited authors highlight in studying the quality of democracy: electoral choice, participation, accountability, responsiveness to the will of the people, and sovereignty. The chapter ends by synthesizing this analysis to draw conclusions on the assets and liabilities of Nicaragua's political regime.

Historical Overview

Covering Nicaragua's political and social history is an exercise in contortionism. While continuity and stability have never been strong points of Latin America's political systems, discontinuity and conflict seem to have been the norm in Nicaragua.

The twentieth century began for that Central American nation in the crosshairs of imperial pretensions by the United States, which maintained a contingent of US Marines in the country from 1910 to 1934. It was in this context that one of Nicaragua's key historical figures emerged, in the person of Augusto César Sandino, a Liberal general who played a major role in the civil war. He refused to accept the Washington-sponsored peace agreements between Liberals and Conservatives, and withdrew to the mountains in the northern part of the country to wage a guerrilla war against what he considered an unacceptable situation.

Sandino fought the National Guard, a new armed force established by the United States, between 1927 and 1934, and the US Marines, sent to Nicaragua in hopes of putting an end to the party-based civil wars that had plagued the country. Sandino's life was cut short, however, by the ambitions of one of the most emblematic, powerful, and hated kingpins (*caudillos*) in Nicaragua's history, Anastasio Somoza García, who took over the presidency in a coup d'état in 1936, inaugurating a family dictatorship that lasted forty-three years. This reign ended when a guerrilla group, calling itself Sandinistas in homage to the earlier anti-imperialist guerrilla leader, brought down the dynasty.

During its four decades in power, the Somoza family regime became known as a "sultanate," "patrimonial," "mafiacratic," and "kleptocratic" regime, in that (1) it was a regime based on an individual rather than a party; (2) its political elites were not the traditional socioeconomic elites; (3) the Somoza family personally dominated the armed forces and the police; (4) the regime systematically used force and repression to maintain order; and (5) the state was used as a means of accumulating wealth and subverting the "logic of the market" (Wickham-Crowley 1992). Given the nature of the regime, the only possible form of opposition was guerrilla warfare. The Sandinista National Liberation Front (Frente Sandinista de Liberación Nacional; FSLN) coalesced in 1961 and became an important force. Growing action by the FSLN, increasing repression by the regime, and the assassination of the opposition leader Pedro Joaquín Charmorro, who was editor of the newspaper *La Prensa* and member of a distinguished conservative family, in January 1978, finally led to the collapse of a regime that had been increasingly on the defensive (Martí i Puig 1997).

Thus, in mid-July 1979, the Somoza regime collapsed, and the insurrection led by the FSLN, which had skillfully created a broad coalition encompassing most of the opposition organizations, remained the only plausible source of leadership. This was the start of one of the most attention-getting and disquieting political experiments in Latin America's history: the People's Sandinista Revolution.

The revolutionary process in Nicaragua, like all revolutions in surrounding countries, melded and synthesized multiple objectives around three basic issues: (1) democracy and the mobilization of the people, (2) national sovereignty, and (3) development. Upon these three pillars a new institutional and symbolic structure began to rise, accompanied by innovative and intensive agricultural development policies, a profound transformation of the productive structure, and the assumption of a new position in the international arena. Gaining a full understanding of the results of this process is a complex task, for it is one riddled with contradictions. The experience of the Sandinista revolution cannot be fully grasped without considering the impact of the financial, political, and military aggression rapidly unleashed by a coalition led primarily by the administration of US president Ronald Reagan.

The war that unfolded in Nicaragua, as of the beginning of the 1980s, limited, shaped, and finally transformed many of the initial projects of the revolutionary regime. Among the many changes emerging from the war was the 1987 Constitution, which created a liberal democratic institutional structure, which was consolidated with the elections of 1990.

Since the 1990s, there has been a modicum of institutional stability, despite profound changes in the relationships between political forces, and numerous impasses and conflicts involving the three branches of government, notably the 1992 battle between the executive and legislative branches and the struggle between the executive and judicial branches in 1998 and 2002.

Elections

After gaining power in 1979 through an insurrection, the FSLN committed itself to holding elections within five years. Although practically no one welcomed this announcement—some considered it a treasonous concession to the bourgeoisie, others regarded it as a lie—elections did, in fact, take place.

Contested elections were held in 1984. In 1990, in competitive elections, an opposition bloc won power and assumed the reins of government. Later, there would be three more general elections—in 1996, 2001, and 2006—in addition to a series of municipal, regional (Caribbean coast), and Central American elections. All of these, despite some variation in quality, have been considered acceptable by national and international observers. The most controversial were the municipal elections of 2008 and the presidential election of 1996.

From the 1990 to 2006 elections, a dual electoral dynamic has been evident. The presidential elections, on the one hand, have featured extreme polarization between the FSLN and an anti-Sandinista bloc. On the other hand, in nonpresidential elections, in which a smaller percentage of the population has voted, there has been a certain dispersion of the anti-Sandinista vote among different groups. The FSLN obtained 40.82 percent, 37.75 percent, and 42.3 percent of the vote in the three presidential elections up to 2001, with the opposition garnering majorities of 54.73 percent, 52.03 percent, and 56.3 percent. Unlike the results of local elections, in which third parties have participated, the FSLN has succeeded in being the largest minority since 2000. This process is examined in greater detail in the section below.

The 1990 Elections

Many analysts regard the 1990 election as a foundational event, since, although it was the second election under the so-called revolutionary regime, it was the first competitive election. An anti-Sandinista coalition, known as the National Opposition Union (Unión Nacional Opositora; UNO),[1] opposed the FSLN in that election and prevailed. The key elements of the UNO program were the dissolution of the Sandinista People's Army, the abolition of mandatory military service, a general reprivatization of the economy, deregulation of the national wage system, a reversion to land reform, and a reform of existing legislation—in short, an end to the Sandinista revolution.

For the Sandinistas, the prospect of holding and winning clean elections would mean the survival of the institutions arising out of the 1979 insurrection. The campaign took place under conditions that could be called totally normal if allowances were made for (1) the immensely abnormal fact of being a nation under attack by counterrevolutionary Contra forces, (2) being the target of aggressive warnings by senior US officials regarding the country's future fate in the event of a Sandinista victory, and (3) the effects of an economic crisis accentuated by the US financial and trade embargo.

On February 26, the day following the election, when 50 percent of the vote had been counted, Daniel Ortega, the FSLN candidate, announced the trend in the returns. At midday, the Supreme Electoral Council issued its final report: of the 1,101,397 votes cast, 54 percent were for the opposing UNO coalition, with 44 percent for the FSLN.

The results surprised international analysts and observers, as well as the participating political parties themselves. Most predictions and surveys during the previous year had given the Sandinistas a substantial lead.[2]

As a result of the election, Violeta Barrios de Chamorro assumed the presidency, and the Liberal politician Virgilio Godoy became vice president. Parliamentary representation is apportioned on a proportional basis; thus the UNO obtained an absolute majority in the National Assembly, with fifty-one out of the ninety-two seats, while the FSLN retained thirty-nine. Of the other contenders, only two parties gained seats. The geographical distribution of the vote revealed two patterns, which were repeated in the 1996 and 2001 elections. The first was a difference between the rural and urban vote, with rural areas favoring the Sandinistas (by approximately 15 percentage points more than the national average), except in the departments of Managua, Granada, and Masaya. The second was the presence of regional electorates with clear preferences. The interior and Atlantic coast departments, Chontales, Boaco, Jinotega, Matagalpa, the North Atlantic Autonomous Region (Región Autónoma del Atlántico Norte; RAAN), and the South Atlantic Autonomous Region (Región Autónoma del Atlántico Sur; RAAS), to this day vote overwhelmingly for anti-Sandinista candidates, while the northeast, Estelí, León, Nueva Segovia, Madriz, and Chinandega, vote solidly for the Sandinistas. The departments near Managua's metropolitan area and in the southeast, Managua, Masaya, Granada, and Rivas, are more competitive. The only department that shifted from majority Sandinista support in 1990 to an anti-Sandinista majority in 1996 and 2001 was Río San Juan.

The 1996 Elections and the Alemán Administration

In 1996, with the approach of the end of one of the longest presidential and legislative terms on the subcontinent, a total of six years and nine months, all of the political parties launched campaign activities. Unlike the quick-moving political parties, the Supreme Electoral Council (Consejo Supremo Electoral; CSE), which is responsible for ensuring that the technical infrastructure necessary for elections is in place, was mired in internal conflict.

The two pillars of the electoral system—the electoral law and the CSE—were widely criticized: the CSE for its failure to operate efficiently, and the electoral law, which had been changed in the 1995 constitutional reform despite a lack of consensus, for its overly politicized provisions for managing elections; its ambiguous treatment of voter rolls, which were yet to be created and faced serious problems in the rural interior of the country, where armed conflict had taken place; and its excessive leeway in allowing election results to be contested.

There were high expectations for the election, in which over twenty parties participated, with over 1 percent of the voters running as candidates on tickets in elections for various levels of government. The election, in addition to covering the presidency and the National Assembly, included mayors, municipal councils, and the Central American Parliament. Although many studies found a large proportion of citizens apathetic and frustrated about the country's politics and institutions, one phenomenon emerged to mobilize potential voters: polarization. As the campaign proceeded, it became clear that only two parties had any chance of winning—the FSLN and the Constitutionalist Liberal Party (Partido Liberal Constitucionalista; PLC), which represented the coalition known as the Nicaraguan Liberal Alliance (Alianza Liberal Nicaragüense; ALN). Thus, the contenders were at opposite ends of the political-ideological spectrum. Led by Ortega and Arnoldo Alemán, respectively, the two parties waged completely different types of campaigns. The PLC focused on its leader and deployed an aggressively anti-Sandinista rhetoric—a strategy notably similar to the UNO coalition's 1990 campaign. However, it differed in that the candidates also attacked the Chamorro administration aggressively.[3]

The FSLN candidate conducted a campaign notable for its moderation. Knowing that no political party could threaten its support on the left, the FSLN decided to seek the political center. It was conciliatory, calling for unity and putting itself forward as "the government of all." Propelled by this discourse and promising to end mandatory military service, the state-run economy, and property confiscations, as well as to combat US aggression, the FSLN was pulling even with their PLC competitors in surveys of voter intentions, and had 200,000 supporters working for them by the end of the campaign.

There was considerable turmoil in the final days of the campaign. On the one hand, the anti-Sandinista forces conducted an aggressive negative media campaign against the FSLN, recalling the years of revolution and linking them with the counterrevolutionary war, rationing, and the economic crisis, while featuring statements by the Cardinal of Managua on the Day of Reflection (the day prior to elections).The FSLN, meanwhile, continued its conciliatory message.

On election day, October 20, civic spirit was strongly in evidence. People voted in massive numbers, and the atmosphere was orderly and peaceful, despite the difficulties in transportation for those who lived far from polling places, a process that was slow and complex—ballots had to be deposited in six different ballot boxes—and the fact that many of the polling places opened late. Eventually, however, problems began to emerge. On the morning of October 21, the CSE announcement of projected results was disrupted by a series of disagreements, leading to a suspension of the press conference and a postponement of the announcement. At 5:00 in the morning, a televised announcement of results was also suspended. Projections at that point were based on 25 percent of the votes and predicted a comfortable PLC victory. Later, citizens were informed that the results would not be made public until there was a clear, definitive count. In the end, the CSE took nineteen days to announce its provisional election results. Meanwhile, various political parties and delegations of election observers began issuing accusations and counteraccusations that there had been fraud in the days following the election.

There were undoubtedly significant irregularities, mostly in the departments of Matagalpa and Managua, where the officials of the Electoral Departmental Council were members of the PLC. The irregularities were of various types, ranging from logistical problems due to the fact that the ballot boxes for the entire department of Managua were deposited in a single building to the manipulation of data, the retransmission of false results by telephone to the CSE, and lost ballot boxes. There was no evidence, however, of widespread fraud, since the two instruments needed to carry out the election—control of the voter rolls and the final count—were not controlled by the same political party. Nevertheless, the CSE failed to operate properly, the different delegations of official and independent observers contradicted each other, and mutual accusations between the leaders of the different parties were rampant.

Finally, on November 8, the CSE's National Computation Center announced the definitive results. The FSLN and PLC presidential candidates garnered most of the votes, and since the PLC had an absolute majority, there was no need for a second round. Alemán obtained 51 percent of the vote, with Ortega registering 37.7 percent. The third-party candidates were far behind: the Conservatives with 4 percent, the party that was heir to the Chamorro administration with 2.2 percent, and Sergio Ramírez, of the Sandinista Renovation Movement (Movimiento Renovador Sandinista; MRS), with 0.4 percent. The National Assembly vote was also split. Despite the proportional representation system and a somewhat greater split in the votes, forty-two of the ninety seats went to the PLC and thirty-six to the FSLN.[4] Nearly all of the mayoral elections were won either by the ALN (two-thirds) or by the FSLN (one-third).

Publication of the results, however, did not put an end to the climate of mutual accusations, or to declarations of victory by multiple candidates at the local level. The most unfortunate effect of the confusion in the electoral process was the swift delegitimization of the institution that had enjoyed the greatest credibility—the CSE.

The elections did nothing to lessen the intensity of the political scene. On the contrary, the discontent caused by the handling and resolution of the electoral dispute harmed the credibility of institutions as a whole. Perhaps because of this institutional weakening, the subsequent five years prominently featured pacts between various political bosses (*caudillos*) to the detriment of the rules of the game, the common good, and the country's institutions.

The October 20, 1996, election of Alemán to the presidency marked the beginning of a period of major political and institutional tension. The president quickly showed himself to be a leader with pronounced *caudillista* tendencies, which worked against previous efforts to consolidate institutions. Unlike the preceding president, Chamorro, however, Alemán had a solid majority in the National Assembly, causing a significant erosion of power on the part of the opposition.

The Alemán administration ultimately deepened, rather than resolved, the major issues that had been on the table since 1990: the persistent conflicts regarding property confiscated during the revolution; the institutional fragility—and extreme politicization—of all state entities; the erratic formulation and implementation of public policy; social polarization and agitation; and, above all, clientism. These five years included numerous accusations of corruption, poor management by the government,[5] and the president's demagoguery in negotiations with the International Monetary Fund over having Nicaragua included in its Highly Indebted Poor Countries Initiative and reducing the country's foreign debt. The most important political news of the five-year term, however, was the signing of a political agreement by then-president Alemán and Ortega in January 2000—known as the pact—which I will discuss below.

The 2001 Elections

The 2001 elections arrived in a climate of protest and social discontent provoked by the signing of the pact. As might have been expected, given the conditions of the new electoral law, only three parties—the PLC, the FSLN, and the Conservative Party of Nicaragua (Partido Conservador Nicaragüense)—were allowed to participate. The regional parties Yapti Tasba Masraka Nanih Aslatakanka (YATAMA; literally "Sons of Mother Earth") and Partido Multiétnico por la Unidad Costeña (PAMUC) were able to run in RAAN and RAAS. Once again, however, the vote was concentrated among the PLC and FSLN candidates, and a climate of polarization again emerged, along with demonstrations and a ramping-up of tension in the media. The FSLN had the largest number of demonstrators, while the PLC and various other anti-Sandinista parties used the mass media to show images of the war of the 1980s and of rationing, hoping to scare voters with the prospect of the so-called revolutionaries regaining power.

Once more, although the surveys had predicted a technical tie, the results left no doubt. Enrique Bolaños of the PLC received 1,216,863 votes to Ortega's 915,417, with the conservative candidate far behind at 29,233 votes.[6] A second round was therefore unnecessary, and it was clear that the polarized pattern based on the two ideological extremes was well entrenched, since the emerging third parties had gained almost no traction. More than a decade after the first competitive election, the political dynamic seemed to have crystallized in an unbalanced two-party system, where the weight of the advantage lay on the side of the forces whose principal focus was their opposition to the FSLN.

The 2006 Election and the Return of the FSLN

The 2006 election differed from the other elections held since 1990. This difference lay primarily in the fact that, during 2005 and the first half of 2006, the pattern of polar partisan opposition between FSLN and anti-Sandinistas shifted to a configuration that included two other major parties that had split off from those led by Ortega and Alemán.[7] The new parties were a reaction to the *caudillista*, pact-oriented, and top-down politics of the FSLN and PLC.

The FSLN ran their perpetual candidate, Ortega, who was opposed by the MRS candidate. The PLC ran José Rizo, who until 2005 had been vice president in the Bolaños administration, since the party's leader, Alemán, having been arrested and due to various judicial proceedings, was unable to run. The dissident Liberals ran Eduardo Montealegre, under the ALN banner (a PLC splinter group).

This scenario—with four players and a high degree of polarization—was unprecedented in the country's recent history. Thus, beginning in early 2006, there seemed to be a possibility of change in the political dynamics that had prevailed since the revolution. The basic question in the 2006 campaign was to what extent the divisions within the Liberal and Sandinista camps would lead to change in the two traditional major parties—the FSLN and the PLC. Polls soon showed that most Sandinista voters would remain faithful to the FSLN, since this was the only party with a nationwide organization; it had major financial resources, as well as strong leadership recognized at the grassroots level; and it had been able to appropriate the traditional symbolic elements of the Sandinista tradition and capitalize on them. The depth of the schism in the Liberal ranks represented an additional question mark. Most analysts suspected that the division of the vote between the ALN and the PLC would be uneven, and that, in the end, one of the two—resumably the ALN—would harvest the "useful vote," that is, the anti-Sandinista vote. It was therefore thought—and surveys bore this out—that the FSLN would not win the presidency on the first round, and that the election results on November 5, 2006, would function like a primary for the anti-Sandinista bloc.[8] In the election, however, the Sandinista, Ortega, prevailed with 38.07 percent of the vote, and the FSLN obtained a simple majority in both the National Assembly and the Central American Parliament.

There are three reasons for the FSLN victory. First, a new split appeared in reaction to the pact, superimposing itself on the old Sandinista vs. anti-Sandinista division. This overturned the previous two-party configuration, preventing the concentration of votes in two polar choices, a pattern characteristic of the previous elections. The new fragmentation favored the hardcore FSLN constituency, which, although it lost some of its members to the reemerging MRS, was for the most part *Danielista*. This meant that Daniel Ortega would win, although with a smaller margin than in any of the previous elections. On the Liberal side, although there remained nearly total support for Enrique Bolaño, as had been the case in 2001, when he gained 56.3 percent support, the constituency split almost evenly between the PLC and the ALN, with 26 percent and 29 percent, respectively.

Ortega's victory was also due to the fact that the electoral law that was in force, as another result of the pact, allowed for a presidential win with 40 percent of the votes—or with 35 percent if the difference between the winning candidate and the runner-up was over five points, which is what occurred in this case. The third factor in the victory was the FSLN's de-ideologized discourse, which called for peace and reconciliation.

Other Elections: Municipal and Regional

Besides the presidential election, there were municipal elections, which had been split off from the national election in 1996, in 2000, 2004, and 2008, as well as elections in the RAAN and the RAAS. Although these elections might appear to be of secondary importance, they have proven consequential, since they established different balances of power between the parties. They also served to seemingly punish behavior by national administrations—although 2008 seems to have been an inflection point.

In the municipal elections of 2000, which was the first time the municipal elections did not coincide with the presidential election, and 2004, the anti-Sandinista vote was divided between the two historical forces on the right, the Liberals and the Conservatives. Thus, the vote was less concentrated. The Conservative Party obtained 13.3 percent of the vote in 2000, with the Alliance for the Republic (Alianza para la República; APRE) receiving 9.2 percent. In addition, the FSLN fared well in both of those elections, especially in 2004, when it associated itself with a group of independent candidates running under the National Convergence (Convergencia Nacional) banner and won 87 mayoralties out of the country's 153. This meant that it had mayors in fourteen of the seventeen departmental capitals, including Managua (where it had also won in 2000). Thus, as of the middle of the decade, at the local level, the FSLN ran 71 percent of the population's public services.

The 2008 municipal elections marked a notable change, with an episode that increased the political polarization prevalent since 2007. They showed that Ortega was still capable of negotiating with the Liberal political boss (*cacique*), Alemán, and of controlling agencies and branches of the government—most importantly, the CSE.[9] Concern emerged over various actions by the CSE, ranging from the CSE's nullification of the legal status of the Conservative Party and the MRS to its restrictive policy on accrediting international observer commissions. The electoral campaign, moreover, was tense, with numerous incidents. Because of this, the elections turned into a sort of plebiscite on Ortega's two years in office, with Managua at the epicenter of the conflict.

According to official—and highly controversial[10]—figures, the FSLN won 105 mayoralties,[11] including Managua and León, as well as all of the top departmental posts except for Granada, Boaco, and Bluefields, while the opposition prevailed in 37 municipalities. In the days following the election, there were intense street confrontations between Sandinistas and anti-Sandinistas. The opposition called for civil disobedience, and FSLN supporters took to the street to discourage any demonstrations of resistance. The secretary general of the Organization of American States, José Miguel Insulza, issued statements expressing concern about the street violence and the opposition's protests.[12]

This coda to the election process was a blow to the credibility of the electoral institution and to vertical accountability—particularly serious matters, given that horizontal accountability was also jeopardized by the Pact signed in 2000, as will be seen in the following section.

In terms of the coast region elections, RAAS and RAAN have parliamentary systems in which voters first elect representatives of regional councils and then elect the head of the regional executive branch. In these areas, the elections, which have been held every four years since 1990, were peaceful and free of irregularities. The PLC obtained hegemony in the RAAS, and over the last decade a coalition of the FSLN and YATAMA has coalesced in the RAAN (Früling, González, and Setter Buvollen 2007: 227–271).

Accountability and Responsibility

In considering the quality of democracy—and of democracy *tout court*—it is important to mention a central feature of Nicaragua's political life: the plasticity of the rules. This feature—not thoroughly consistent with even a minimal definition of democratic institutional structure—is the product of the *caudillo*- and pact-based nature of Nicaragua's political dynamic that dominated the entire twentieth century and continues today. In this section, we shall see how institutions have failed, since 1979, to ensure accountability. Politicians have altered the rules of the game to suit their purposes, creating a protean political arena in the process. The resulting message has been "Don't bother to follow the rules," since they will prove ephemeral, and will almost never do what they are intended to, namely, reward or punish—and thus shape the behavior of—political actors.

Negotiations Between Elites and the Creation of Postrevolutionary Institutions

The February 1990 elections had three immediate consequences, making this a crucial point in the country's history. They strengthened pluralism, channeled partisan activity into the framework of rules established by the 1987 Constitution, and reshaped the interplay of political and social forces. In this scenario, political actors confronted two major challenges: first, that of defining an institutional framework for the country's political life; and second, dealing with the disappearance of the military arena. They were compelled to find methods, perspectives, and styles different from their habitual ones. Force through war would no longer be the central instrument, but, rather, the *pact*.

In terms of the institutional framework, the electoral process itself helped consolidate the mechanisms that arose out of the political process launched in 1979, since the opposition FSLN gained power in the context of the constitutional framework of 1987, not as a result of a military takeover of the Sandinista government, as originally endorsed by the US government. Nevertheless, the *institutional pact* remained a viable option.

The questions at issue in the pact included Chamorro's assumption of office as a result of the legal structure created by the 1987 Constitution; respect for, and integrity of, the armed forces and the police; the legal security of urban and rural property allocated during the FSLN's reign; and the demobilization of the Contras. The pact was limited in scope, elitist in nature, and reflected the common interests of a segment of the FSLN and a segment of the UNO.[13] This pact governing the transfer of executive power (Pacto de Transición del Poder Ejecutivo; PTPE) was intensely controversial and quickly led to deep rifts in all of the political parties—both within the UNO and in the FSLN.

Only shortly after the conclusion of the PTPE did the question of reforming the 1987 Constitution reappear on the political agenda. The reform proposal pitted the legislative and executive branches against each other, since it diminished the power of the president. The reform was ultimately ratified by 63 percent of the National Assembly in October 1994 and February 1995.

The most significant constitutional changes concerned the election of the president and the powers of the National Assembly. Under the reform, outgoing presidents were excluded from running again immediately, and total time in presidential office was limited to two terms. In addition, close relatives of the president, defined to the fourth degree of consanguinity, were prohibited from running. The electoral process itself was also changed through the introduction of a clause that mandated a second round for the two leading candidates if neither had received at least 45 percent of the valid vote in the first round. The National Assembly gained a more central role in developing and approving the national budget and in determining the tax burdens, preventing the president from making unilateral decrees regarding taxation. It also acquired the authority to approve, modify, or reject executive branch state-of-emergency decrees and to authorize the use of the nation's armed forces outside the national territory. In short, the reform shifted power toward the legislative branch, and made the second round a part of the institutional design of elections.

The Pact of 2000 and Its Consequences

The election of Alemán as president signaled the beginning of a period of marked political and institutional tension. Moreover, since he had a solid majority in the legislature, he was able to neutralize the constitutional reforms of 1995.

As was indicated earlier, the most consequential political event of the Alemán administration was the pact between the Sandinista and Liberal forces. Signed in January 2000, it established major agreements that were to be of decisive importance for the country's political life. It had two fundamental elements. First, it created two-party control—with representation based on the size of the parties' constituencies—of the state's three key institutions: the Office of the Comptroller General of the Republic, the Supreme Court, and the Supreme Electoral Council. Second, it changed the electoral law and its administration to restrict political representation for third parties. Thus, the pact made significant changes in both the Constitution and the electoral law.

In the judicial realm, along with altering the composition of the Supreme Court, the reforms gave Alemán and Ortega privileges that made it more difficult for the National Assembly to impose judicial sanctions on them or to annul the president's immunity, since such measures now required an absolute majority. Furthermore, they created a legislative seat for President Alemán once he left office, to be assumed at the end of 2001, thus providing him parliamentary immunity. Given that serious charges of illicit enrichment were pending against him, this was a significant move. The pact also provided similar immunity for the runner-up to the presidency, Ortega, who was charged with abusing his stepdaughter.

On the electoral front, significant changes included the lowering of the first-round threshold for winning the presidency, from 45 percent to 40 percent—lowering it to 35 percent when the difference between the leader and the runner-up exceeds 5 percent. Many analysts saw this change as a concession to Ortega on the part of Alemán, since it is common knowledge that the Sandinistas—who are the best organized party in the country, and have the most supporters—find it difficult to put together large coalitions capable of winning in a second round, although their ability to do well in the first round is clear to all (they garnered 41 percent of the vote in 1990 and 38 percent in 1996). As to the proportional formula for the election of deputies to the National Assembly, the 1996 formula—of "highest remainder"—was replaced by the D'Hondt formula, which limits the benefits of proportional representation to those parties receiving the highest number of votes. Another change was a provision permitting people who had renounced their Nicaraguan citizenship and subsequently reclaimed it to run for office. The law had previously prohibited this, to exclude Nicaraguans who had gone into exile during the revolution and become American citizens (Dye, Spence, and Vickers 2000).

For municipal elections, the residency requirements for mayoral elections were modified to require that candidates reside in the municipality in which they run. This change, along with a statutory change in the boundaries of the municipal district of Managua, from which certain outlying neighborhoods were removed, excluded independent candidate Pedro Solórzano from running for mayor there.

These changes, along with the onerous new requirement that, as a prerequisite to obtaining legal status, aspiring parties submit signatures equivalent in number to 3 percent of all voters, and that they obtain 4 percent of the votes nationally to maintain this status, make Nicaragua's electoral law one of the most restrictive in Latin America. The new law also prevents grassroots groups from running mayoral candidates, and it subjects electoral coalitions to the same 3 percent and 4 percent requirements that apply to new parties. As if this were not enough, the new law requires parties to have obtained their legal status twelve months prior to the election in which they intend to participate, if the election is a national one, and six months before in the case of municipal elections. Furthermore, if such a party failed to receive 4 percent of the vote in the local elections in which it participated, for example, the November 5, 2000, elections, it was excluded from the subsequent elections in November 2001.

It is hardly surprising that most of the country's social and political actors reacted negatively to the pact. The nine small parties with seats in the National Assembly, which together held fifteen of the ninety-three seats in 1996, opposed these measures and conducted publicity campaigns to expose the political motives behind the new reforms. They argued that the partisan control exerted over the Supreme Court, the CSE, and the Comptroller General politicized these institutions and eliminated their autonomy, to give greater power to the two dominant parties. The pact was also criticized by many independent figures, who viewed the measures as a setback to the pluralistic dynamic that had prevailed in Nicaragua since the 1980s. Mariano Fiallos, former chair of the CSE, stated that although some of these restrictive measures could be found in the electoral systems of other Latin American nations, no other country had such a restrictive overall set of conditions. Moreover, the motivations of the PLC and the FSLN in establishing the pact went far beyond the governance issue purported to be its rationale. In reality, the rules were designed to establish a de facto two-party system, shutting the door on all other parties and giving the two existing parties control of the government's institutions, while blocking civil society from playing a partisan role. Public opinion quickly registered opposition to the pact. In a survey in Managua in December 1999, 67 percent indicated that they believed the pact reflected the two major parties' desire to divide up the offices between themselves. Another national survey showed that 61 percent thought the pact benefited only the two major parties, while a mere 8 percent believed that it benefited the country as a whole.

The pact has nevertheless remained in force for a decade, but with the unexpected result that the FSLN has largely held control of the government. In 2000, when the pact was signed, Alemán believed that it would be a tool to perpetuate Liberal hegemony, and that the FSLN would tolerate this, since its subordinate position in the country's political dynamic would still allow it to obtain a significant share of the resources. Following the split in the Liberal ranks in 2005, however, and Ortega's electoral victory of 2006, it has, in fact, been the FSLN that has succeeded in controlling the government, and thus in reforming and interpreting the rules as it wishes—as Alemán did in his heyday. This situation has led to discussions on a new constitutional reform, which has been in the air since 2007, and there has even been talk of reorganizing the various state entities. This debate is, of course, being conducted outside the established institutional channels.

Participation

The Political Parties

Until 2006, Nicaragua had a de facto two-party system, with the FSLN and the anti-Sandinistas occupying these two roles. This dynamic, as has been noted, was interrupted in 2005. During the three five-year periods following the 1995 elections, however, political relations between the FSLN and their opponents were neither harmonious nor peaceful. In this section, I shall attempt to explain the dynamics of the conflict within the parties and to describe the most important operative political forces.

The FSLN. The FSLN, as a party, has overcome the major dilemmas that it faced after its defeat in 1990, although the solution has involved significant organizational conflicts and rifts, and losses of human and moral capital. Particularly notable among the former is the breakaway of Ramírez, the writer and former president from 1984 to 1990, giving rise to the MRS.[14]

The rupture of 1995 marked a new period for the Sandinistas. The FSLN began creating a type of political party that resembled many others in the region: geared toward winning elections and organized around the central figure and personality of its leader. The FSLN organized itself around electoral activities, with the focus on its secretary general, Ortega, thus reinforcing the Nicaraguan political culture associated with the idea of the strong central figure or strongman (*hombre fuerte*) (Martí i Puig and Santiuste 2006).

Since the first half of the 1990s, the FSLN has become a true political party, organized around achieving political power through elections and by negotiation in various political arenas, often including agreements with individuals who have been its most vocal (and most conspicuously denounced) opponents.

This has involved a continual process of compromise with members of other parties, and has almost invariably led to a dual rhetoric: the pragmatism of the negotiator and the ideals of the revolutionary. It is this duality, with the emergence of turbulent internal conflict—almost always ending in splits, desertions, expulsions, and squabbles among party officials—that has most eroded the credibility and political capital of the FSLN.

Even today, in many working-class areas—as well as in many rural areas, particularly in the Pacific region—the FSLN is the only party with an organizational structure. Thus, despite its mutation, it represents, for marginalized areas, a scarce resource of solidarity and connectedness for communities. Since 2000, it has been the most powerful party at the local level, maintaining a solid organizational network based primarily on unions, neighborhoods (the Nicaraguan communal movement; Movimiento Comunal), and students (the Nicaraguan Student Union; Unión Nacional de Estudiantes de Nicaragua).

The FSLN's ability to conduct intense electoral campaigns is also attributable to the resources it receives from economic groups with Sandinista affinities, the so-called Sandinista bourgeoisie, and from local public funds. Since 1996, the FSLN has made an effort to run all of its candidates as part of an alliance, to counteract its political isolation, and has espoused messages of "love, reconciliation and forgiveness." It has also altered its moral positions, for example, the case of therapeutic abortion, aligning itself with the most conservative sectors of the Catholic Church.

The Sandinista Renovation Movement and allies.   The Sandinista Renovation Movement (MRS) represents an alternative to the Sandinistas that grew out of the initial 1995 split in the FSLN. It performed disastrously in the 1996 elections, and did not run in 2001—when some of its members even supported the FSLN. It reemerged in 2005 with the new name Herty Alliance–MRS (Alianza Herty–MRS), having brought on board the popular Sandinista ex-mayor Herty Lewites, whom the FSLN apparatus had attempted to ostracize. With Lewites's candidacy, the Sandinista electoral structure again split in two, with each side retaining a number of revolutionary Sandinismo heavyweights. The MRS, for its part, enjoyed the support of three leaders (*comandantes*) of the historic Dirección Nacional (the real authority during the revolution), Henry Ruiz, Víctor Tirado, and Luís Carrión, in addition to that of two guerrilla commanders, Dora María Téllez and Mónica Baltodano.

With the unexpected death of Herty Lewites, a ticket had to be improvised. The result was the vice presidential candidate Edmundo Jarquín and the singer/songwriter Carlos Mejía Godoy. The MRS campaign centered more on issues of honesty and combating corruption than on traditional issues of the left, and it received a more favorable reception in the international media than within Nicaragua.

The party's weak point has been its lack of a nationwide organization, although it has a substantial presence in Managua and in some of the departments in the center of the country (Masaya, Carazo).

The Liberal Constitutionalist Party. Since the start of the 1990s, the Liberal Constitutionalist Party (PLC) has been the largest of the anti-Sandinista parties. It was from this base that Alemán, the party's leader, in 1996, and Bolaños, Alemán's vice president, who had not previously been an important figure in the party, in 2001, won the presidency. In 2006, with Alemán in prison, José Rizo ran with José Antonio Alvarado. Both were representatives of the country's traditional Liberal party (the PLC), had held governmental posts in the past decade, had been active anti-Sandinistas during the 1980s, had opposed the conciliatory rhetoric of Chamorro during her administration, and had symbolic connections with the Somoza-linked PLN.

The party's greatest assets are Alemán's leadership, the solidity of its organization, and its position in the institutional power structure. It has a presence throughout the country and is the dominant party in the interior and in the RAAS. Alemán is also its weak point, however, since the US government no longer considers him a valid interlocutor, given that judicial proceedings are pending against him for corruption, resulting in major internal party conflicts. On the other hand, the prominence, within the party, of his daughter, María Dolores Alemán, who currently serves as a deputy in the National Assembly, is a potential source of political capital.

The other anti-Sandinistas. In the early 1990s, when the ideological groups that had formed the UNO coalition—which included Liberals, Conservatives, Social Democrats, Christian Democrats, Socialists, and Communists—were still separate entities, attempts at unification had been unsuccessful. These entities included the National Project (Proyecto Nacional; PRONAL), APRE, ALN, and others. As the elections of October 1996 approached, however, new parties emerged: the populist Arriba Nicaragua and the Partido de la Resistencia Nacional (PRN), which attempted to use the support of the rural population in the interior that had been the social base for the counterrevolution, demanding satisfaction for earlier transgressions. However, except for the PLC, there was no effort to create a party identity, develop a strong organizational structure, or consolidate networks of loyal supporters and clients.

Since then, anti-Sandinista third parties have achieved little success, despite support, at times, from the administration: the PRONAL was promoted by Chamorro's son-in-law in 1996; the APRE, which ran candidates in the 2004 local elections, was supported by the Bolaños administration; and the ALN was led by Eduardo Montealegre, formerly a minister in the Alemán and Bolaños administrations.

The ALN had the explicit support of the outgoing president, the country's business sector, and the newspaper *La Prensa*, as well as the US government, but it was unable to prevail over Alemán's PLC in the 2006 elections. The ALN campaign rhetoric, with the slogan "planting opportunities," centered on foreign investment and job creation, but the conspicuously elitist style of the candidate and of the group close to him was a recipe for defeat. The party's failure to connect with important sectors of the population, which have strong attachments to the populist liberalism promoted by Alemán's coreligionists, and the absence of a strong party organization in the field, especially in rural areas, led to an unimpressive electoral performance—although it succeeded in garnering 26 percent of the vote.

Protests and Social Movements

Alongside party politics, unconventional forms of political participation have played a significant role in Nicaragua during the last two decades. In fact, political conflict has often taken a disruptive form. It is therefore important to understand the emergence and dynamics of popular movements.

Immediately following the FSLN's defeat at the polls, as the Chamorro administration began to put its neoliberal program into operation, the unions—of various political stripes, though most importantly those that were Sandinista in orientation—regained a prominent role. After nearly eleven years of paternalistic relations with the state, they changed direction to confront the policies of the new president. At the same time, they began to seek autonomy from the party apparatus that had nurtured them in the past.[15]

The unions, like many other organizations linked to the FSLN, were not preoccupied with the question of autonomy. They never believed that the FSLN would lose the elections, and thus did not focus on ensuring their own legal or financial future. With the defeat of the FSLN, all of the union organizations with links to them, in a survivalist effort, organized into the National Worker's Front (Frente Nacional de Trabajadores; FNT) to create a solid union bloc. From that point forward, relations between the FSLN and the unions became more tense and more complex. Bureaucratic management styles and the practice of installing leaders were criticized. The FNT, whose overall priority was now to confront the policies of the new administration, became the administration's principal opponent. The non-Sandinista unions, which coalesced around an organization known as the Permanent Congress of Workers (Congreso Permanente de los Trabajadores; CPT), initially supported the new president, but later distanced themselves from her.

Still, what began as a labor conflict often ended up as an insurrection. At one point the demonstrations threatened to verge into civil conflict, as violent confrontations between demonstrators and armed anti-Sandinistas became widespread. This made a negotiated solution essential. The FSLN leaders played an important role in seeking an accord to end the social upheaval. For nearly five years, the FSLN became a mediator between the government and the politically mobilized population. During this time, the government and the unions launched a negotiation process (the Concertación) that involved several phases, including setting a minimum wage and committing to certain privatization initiatives.[16]

Particularly notable in this situation was the fact that the unions, which years earlier had been split based on their position on the Sandinista regime, found themselves on the same side of the negotiating table defending similar interests, while the former officials of the revolutionary government and the "yuppies" of the new executive branch were going into business (Stahler-Sholk 1994: 77). In the process of conflict and negotiation in the wake of privatizations, the unions were increasing in autonomy, and—independent of party loyalties—class differences were playing a significant role.

In this new environment, with the redefinition of the state's role and the breakdown of party membership and loyalties, certain union leaders grasped the importance of bringing together a union movement capable of confronting the new business class, some of whom were Sandinistas, and combating neoliberal policies.[17]

Unions were not the only participants in this effort, however. Other social actors emerged and assumed leading roles, as well. This included neighborhood groups that joined together in various associations, ranging from grassroots church groups to the communal movement. The collective objective was to protect against the emergence of a *sauve qui peut* (every man for himself) society. This organizational capacity of Nicaraguan society is an essential key to understanding the massive popular resistance to the drastic adjustment policies in place and to the growing precariousness of the population's economic and social situation. As a United Nations report stated, "Seventy-five percent of Nicaraguan families live below the poverty line, and 44 percent are in extreme poverty. . . . Faced with this increasing social pauperization, it is significant that there have not been more social outbursts. . . . Probably a determining factor in this resistance is Nicaraguans' deeply rooted tradition of organization, social discipline, and solidarity."[18]

The increasing difficulties of daily life, especially toward the end of the 1980s and in the first half of the 1990s, broke down the barriers separating the private and public spheres. The deep economic crisis, the massive layoffs of public employees, and the drastic cuts in social services guaranteed that the decisions made in the public arena would be felt forcefully within households, and that social actors who had previously played a subordinate role would become more active.

It is precisely this environment that spawned the emergence of a key variant in the country's political life: a political culture of mobilization drawn from the legacy of the revolutionary period. However, the mobilizations that flourished during the first half of the 1990s declined noticeably starting in 1997, and particularly after the pact of 2000.

With the signing of the pact, the dynamic of the movement changed, and over the next decade mobilizations were driven less by unions and neighborhood organizing efforts against governmental policy than by civil society—citizens organized into networks, many associated with or supported by nongovernmental organizations (NGOs)—protesting the erosion of accountability under the Alemán-Ortega pact, as well as the increasing control over and intervention in NGOs on the part of the Alemán administration, most conspicuously in the wake of the devastations of Hurricane Mitch (Kampwirth 2004).

Over time, various sectors of civil society—especially the feminist and civil liberties movements—have become more active and combative. Two types of mobilizations have occurred in this context. First, there have been those formed in reaction to the morally and socially conservative policies on reproductive health promoted by the Liberals and by the FSLN itself,[19] and second, street demonstrations organized to protest the erosion of freedom and rights caused by the politicization of the judicial system and the state in general. The latter of these two types of mobilization have taken on major importance since Ortega assumed the presidency. Ortega has undertaken a campaign of harassment against NGOs that are supported by international cooperation organizations, claiming that criticisms and complaints against the government's actions violate national sovereignty and are destabilizing the government and undermining its authority. This charge relates specifically to the episode (cited above) that followed the local elections of November 2008.

Last, the Ortega administration has created a new so-called participatory mechanism known as the Citizens' Power Councils. Their makeup is reminiscent of the Sandinista Defense Committees of the revolutionary decade, although a more detailed analysis of their structure and behavior shows that they are actually parastate organizations structured hierarchically and controlled by the FSLN—their overall head is the wife of Ortega—whose aim is to distribute funds and resources under targeted social policies and to keep loyalties in place. This type of organization generates a top-down relationship rather than bottom-up participation, since it attempts to motivate and control the participation of the faithful as well as latecomers to the cause, generating policies of patronage.

Response to the Popular Will: Public Policy

Starting with the 1990 elections, the government's priorities were to pacify and demobilize the irregular troops present in the country, stabilize and integrate the economy in the global market, and transform institutions. To accomplish this, the new administration abandoned its statist policy, emphasized the market economy, opened the economy to the outside world, and drastically reduced social services.[20]

This involved a profound transformation of the Nicaraguan state and its role in society. The ability to satisfy social demands was now a function not only of political institutions, but of the combined effect of intervention by a wider range of actors.[21] For precisely this reason, the political dynamic that began during the 1990s provoked resistance from many sides, leading to an atmosphere of intense political conflict and an environment of recurrent instability and crisis, although the continuity of the institutional structure installed through the 1987 Constitution remained intact (Close 1988, 1999).

The new political order did little to meet the demands of the population, which was—and remains—mostly poor, and which had been the focus of Sandinista policy. The initial neoliberal period, from 1990 to 1993, saw zero growth. Between 1994 and 2007, growth in annual gross domestic product (GDP) was a respectable 3 percent to 7 percent.[22] This was associated with limited reductions in poverty, although even in 2000, 69 percent of the population was poor—less than US$2 daily per person—and 42 percent was indigent—under US$1 daily per person.[23] In 2006, the incidence of poverty dropped to 45 percent, and indigence levels to 30 percent.[24] However, the three center-right governments between 1990 and 2006 never made poverty reduction their priority. Rather, they concentrated on generating economic growth, hoping that the benefits would trickle down within the society. Only the Sandinistas seemed to recognize the devastating effects of poverty in Nicaragua. Nevertheless, the return of Ortega to the presidency in 2006 has not brought a substantial change in public policy, despite the campaign promises of 2006.

The 2006 campaign, in addition to attempting to attract a sector of the business community with promises of credits and subsidies, appealed to the poor Sandinista voter, and called for a shift in social policy. The proposed change was to emphasize targeted social policy, to be implemented through three programs, Zero Hunger, Zero Usury, and Zero Unemployment, and was based on the ostensible intention to reestablish a small-scale welfare state with policies of universal health and education. In practice, however, such policies have been very limited, due to the lack of budgetary resources and a reduced capacity to implement new programs. Adding to this situation was the fact that the macroeconomic policies that had been in place since 1990 were continued, including participation in the Central American Free Trade Agreement–Dominican Republic (CAFTA-DR).[25] Most recently, the initial years of the Ortega administration did not improve the economy. Instead, growth slowed from 4.2 percent to 3.9 percent; production of corn and beans fell by 8.7 percent and 4.2 percent, respectively; and there was 10.7 percent inflation, accompanied by a 24.8 percent increase in the cost of the basic basket of consumer goods.[26]

Given this scenario, international cooperation has been vital to the country's economy ever since the 1980s. Among developing countries, Nicaragua has one of the highest levels of international aid per capita in the world. It received US$618 million in 2003, representing a transfer of US$178 per capita in cooperation aid (13.1 percent of GDP and 68 percent of public investment, according to World Bank data).[27] The added elements of chronic trade deficits and low levels of foreign direct investment explain Nicaragua's reliance on international aid, including multilateral aid, bilateral aid, and aid based on decentralized NGOs to cover its fiscal deficit. This fact is every bit as important in terms of the country's sovereignty, as I discuss in the next section, as it is for public policy.

Sovereignty

Sovereignty is not an element that is generally considered when analyzing the quality of democracy. Levine and Molina, however, spotlight this issue, citing it as a prerequisite to the conduct of public policy (2006). Although traditionally considered an all-or-nothing concept, sovereignty can be a continuum. Accordingly, these authors define the concept as the extent to which political decisions are actually made by elected officials, noting: "The less autonomous a government is with respect to external forces (military or financial or diplomatic) and internal forces (religious, military), the lower the quality of democracy" (Levine and Molina 2006: 24).

From this perspective, three elements should be taken into account in Nicaragua's case: first, the state's capacity to maintain legal control over government forces and maintain a presence throughout the national territory; second, the capacity of democratically elected authorities to discipline different officials within the government, particularly among the police and the armed forces; and third, the influence of foreign actors—above all, governments.

Taking these in order, the Nicaraguan government maintains a presence throughout the national territory, although it varies in intensity among the country's three macroregions (Pacific, interior, and Caribbean coast) and between urban and rural areas. In rural portions of the country, this presence is clearly less pronounced than in cities. Regionally, the presence is strongest in the Pacific region, diminishing in the interior, and even more noticeably diminished in the Caribbean coast region, where there are notable deficiencies. In some municipalities (such as San Juan del Norte on the Costa Rican border), public services are provided by the neighboring country, and the currency used is the colón of Costa Rica, not the córdoba of Nicaragua. It is on the Caribbean coast that drug-trafficking cartels have gained a stronger presence, using this area as a transit zone.

With regard to the second element, the government has been able to control and maintain the absolute loyalty of both the army and the national police. This situation, uncommon in the region, derives from the ability to bring discipline to forces that, during administrations of the 1980s, were highly politi-cized—witness names such as the People's Sandinista Army and the Sandinista Police. In Nicaragua, moreover, these two institutions enjoy wide public sup-port, in contrast to the situation in neighboring countries. This is due in great part to their effectiveness in combating citizen insecurity, which is a major threat to sovereignty in the neighboring countries. This success owes much to the close involvement that the national police have had with working-class sectors of the population, whereby the police operate as a ground-level community policing force in high-risk neighborhoods, working in cooperation with neigh-borhood groups.

Finally, in terms of the presence and intervention of foreign actors, it is worth noting the importance of foreign cooperation in the country's economic and social development (as cited in the preceding section), and the traditional hegemonic presence of the US government in domestic political affairs—in some cases supporting the government, such as between 1990 and 2006; in oth-ers working against it, for example during the 1980s; and in yet other cases keeping a certain distance, as has been true since 2007. Beginning in 1990, however, the US presence has assumed a subtler form than in earlier periods, and since the 1990s, its influence has been felt primarily during election peri-ods. Each time, since 1990, that Nicaraguan presidential elections have drawn near, US ambassadors have aligned themselves clearly with the anti-Sandinista candidates. This was prominently in evidence in 2006—to the point that the American Chamber of Commerce of Nicaragua and then–US ambassador to Nicaragua Paul Trivelli pressured the two Liberal candidates to agree on a sin-gle candidate in order to prevent Ortega from winning in the first round of elec-tions. The United States was not the only source of foreign intervention in 2006, however, with the FSLN publicly highlighting its close relations with Hugo Chávez of Venezuela.[28] In short, the role of foreign actors in pressuring con-tenders in Nicaragua's domestic political arena has been, and continues to be, a recurrent phenomenon.

What Type of Democracy? What Quality of Democracy?

For the quality and evolution of Nicaraguan democracy, the period since 1990 has been a positive one, although there have been ups and downs in nearly all specific aspects, as will be considered below.

Electoral choice is probably the area in which Nicaragua most closely re-sembles the other countries of the region. Every five years, Nicaragua holds elections for the presidency, the National Assembly, and the Central American Parliament. In addition, since 1990, elections have been held every four years in the autonomous regions of the Caribbean coast to elect their respective representatives. Since 2000, there have also been quadrennial elections. Elections have therefore been an important element of democratization and participation. Alternations between administrations of opposing ideological camps have also been a staple. In 1990, the FSLN surrendered power to the opposition UNO coalition, and in 2006, after three ideologically similar governments, the FSLN again took power, under its old leader. Municipal and regional elections have served as a political barometer during presidential terms, and have also represented a limited degree of political decentralization in a country with a strong centralist tradition. In this regard, the most important problem has unquestionably been that of accountability and responsibility.

As noted, one of the major problems of Nicaraguan democracy has been the continual modification of the rules of the game, changes that reflect the interests of the political *caudillos*, especially with regard to the two most important sources of rules: the Constitution and the election law. Moreover, since the signing of the pact, the government—along with all of its presumed autonomous agencies—has become politicized. Thus, in the last decade, horizontal accountability has become practically a dead issue. Compounding this serious deficiency have been the controversial actions of the CSE during the 2008 municipal elections, where its clearly partisan pro-Sandinista actions posed a serious threat to democracy and further limited vertical accountability.

Levels of abstention in presidential elections have been only moderate—in contrast to municipal and regional elections, where, based on overall census figures, between 50 percent and 60 percent of the citizenry participates. Rates of abstention in the highly polarized national elections have been minimal: 24.6 percent in 1990, 24.4 percent in 1996, 13 percent in 2001, and 33 percent in 2006, although the actual abstention rate in the 2006 election is estimated to have been much lower, since the census inflated population figures, and emigrants living in Costa Rica and the United States were unable to vote. Any consideration of participation must take into account the importance that political parties—particularly the two major ones, the PLC and FSLN, which are hierarchical and *caudillista*[29]—traditionally have in the country's political dynamic. Since the signing of the pact, that dynamic has largely been controlled by the parties, leaving little room for nonparty influence by smaller groups.

Street-level social mobilization in Nicaragua is also important. Since the 1980s, when the revolutionary regime organized large demonstrations, street protests and takeovers of public spaces have become common tools in Nicaraguans' repertoire of collective action. Various sectors of the society have taken on significant roles—not only community movements or organized working-class groups operating through unions, but also large-scale, middle-class organizations working through networks of NGOs. Over the past decade, this latter type of activism has drawn on the feminist movement and on a number of citizens' movements—initially, during the Alemán administration, to protest the pact, and currently to protest certain measures adopted by the Ortega administration.

Limitations in the state's capacities—in terms of availability and management of resources, and possibilities for global involvement and negotiation—have restricted the government's response to citizen demands. Moreover, Liberal administrations that held power between 1990 and 2006 further restricted the role of the state in favor of the market, opening up the economy and drastically reducing social services. Given this overarching commitment by the Nicaraguan state to the so-called neoliberal market-driven and multicentered sociopolitical matrix (Garretón et al. 2003), its response to social demands has been extremely limited. The socioeconomic and human development figures of the past decades indicate little capacity to create wealth, and even less capacity to combat poverty. The Ortega administration promised a new role for the state beginning in 2007, but the only changes, to date, have involved the implementation of targeted social policies with limited impact.

Last, with regard to sovereignty, there are contradictory signals. The government maintains full control of its security forces, and it has succeeded in maintaining a notable presence throughout the national territory, with areas of the Caribbean coast region being the rare exception. It has also shown itself capable of keeping crime rates and violence low, in contrast to neighboring countries such as El Salvador, Honduras, and Guatemala. At the same time, foreign government influence on the country's political life—with the ever-present importance of the United States and the surging influence of Venezuelan interests in recent years—is merely a new chapter in a long-running story. The vital importance of international cooperation in combating poverty and promoting development inevitably leaves Nicaragua vulnerable to such outside influences.

While Nicaragua's democratic history gives reason for optimism, there is no scarcity of problems. Some of these are structural—problems of sovereignty, a historically weak state incapable of effective response to social problems, and deficiencies in the government's approach to an increasingly competitive globalized economy. In addition to these challenges are problems more situational in nature, though these owe much to the political culture of the country and could ultimately become entrenched in the political system and undermine Nicaragua's democracy. These include political polarization; the politicization of institutions, which has gradually eroded the accountability of the state and its representatives; and a political dynamic that leaves power in the hands of the two major parties—each controlled by its chieftain, who treats the party as his personal fiefdom: a duopoly of the nation's political life. One might venture, as did Close and Martí i Puig (2009), that Nicaragua has developed a type of democracy appropriately described by the Nicaraguan term *chapiollo*, which, in addition to meaning "autochthonous to Nicaragua," means "simple," "popular," and, at times, "of poor quality."

Notes

1. UNO was an electoral coalition structured solely on the basis of a political council, in which each of the thirteen participating parties had one vote and one representative, independent of its size or the size of its constituency.

2. To understand the result of the election, four elements must be understood: (1) the profound economic crisis produced by the Contra war, along with certain errors on the part of the FSLN; (2) the persistence of a state of war; (3) the impact of the adjustment policies on broad segments of the population; and (4) the arrogant behavior of certain Sandinista leaders, in tandem with the reappearance of a dynamic marked by clientism, which, due to the specific circumstances involved, antagonized citizens.

3. Alemán was the only one of the twenty-one presidential candidates who refused to sign a document promoted by then–vice president Julia Mena, entitled "Nicaragua's Commitment to a Minimum National Agenda," encompassing nine guidelines on governance, legal security, and poverty reduction—a set of proposals that all other candidates, regardless of party affiliation, endorsed.

4. The remaining seats were four for the Christian Path; three for the Conservative Party; two for the National Project; and one each for MRS, UNO-96, and the Independent Liberal Party.

5. The government's negligence in the wake of the Hurricane Mitch disaster was important in this respect.

6. A similar situation occurred in the other elections, though the Conservatives gained three times more votes—a phenomenon that reflected the crossover of two-thirds of Conservative votes to the Liberals in the presidential contest.

7. For an analysis of the conflict between Bolaños, who served as president in 2002 and 2004, and Alemán, see Martí i Puig (2008).

8. Because of this reasoning, no Liberal leader took seriously the proposal by the American Chamber of Commerce of Nicaragua, which suggested that the most popular Liberal candidate should head a united ticket called Unity for Nicaragua, designed to prevent the possibility of an Ortega victory in the first round.

9. According to a number of sources, the reasons for these decisions, and for Ortega's control of electoral authority, come from the fact that of the seven magistrates who make up the CSE, three remained faithful to the FSLN and three to the PLC, while one (the chair) was one of the political operatives involved in the pact, and therefore protected the interests of Ortega and Alemán. Meanwhile, of the CSE's nine central positions, five are, in effect, Sandinista, three are controlled directly by the chair of the CSE, and one is a PLC stronghold. Finally, of the seventeen departmental delegations, twelve are led by FSLN officers and five by Liberal leaders. Moreover, under the electoral law, the 11,808 polling places are staffed by, among others, members of the two parties that came in first and second in the last election (in this case, the 2006 election). For the municipal election of 2008, these members belonged to the FSLN and ALN, and, as of November 2008, the ALN was not allied with Eduardo Montealegre, but rather with individuals associated with the FSLN.

10. See, for example, www.voto2008.org, a website created by the followers of Montealegre, which shows what they believe to be the true district-by-district election results for Managua.

11. It should be noted that in seven municipalities on the Atlantic coast, no elections were held.

12. The Nicaraguan NGO Ethics and Transparency (Ética y Transparencia), which sponsored a commission of national observers, stated three days after the election that this was the "least transparent and most conflict-ridden election in our history," point-

ing to a large number of anomalies and irregularities in at least 32 percent of the country's polling places, and claiming that these represented serious breaches, all detrimental to the opposition.

13. During the ten years of Sandinista rule, the dynamics that typified Nicaragua's long political history persisted, as the interests of the country's most prominent families—which had members on both sides—continued to play a significant role (Vilas 1992: 27–29). This intersection of interests between *exiting* and *new* political elites, and their consociationalist style, led to a gradual political reunification of the traditional dominant sectors, relatively independent of the ideological and party conflict that had split the country's society for over ten years.

14. The MRS included an important group of ex-FSLN party members. This marked the split in the Sandinista party, despite the fact that the paltry showing of the MRS in the 1996 elections—with 0.44 percent of the presidential vote and 1.33 percent in the National Assembly—returned the symbolic patrimony of Sandinismo almost intact to the FSLN.

15. One union leader stated in an interview: "During the revolution, we never needed to fight for social causes such as food kitchens, transportation, clothing, medicine. These were gifts from the Sandinista Front. In exchange, we supported the government: we organized workers' brigades to harvest coffee, teach literacy, perform military service. . . . Now, everything is different. From here on, we don't get anything unless we fight for it."

16. The unions accepted the privatization plan designed by the government, on the condition that 25 percent of the privatized state enterprises be ceded to workers in the various unions. This gave rise to a new form of property, the so-called Workers' Ownership Area (Área de Propiedad de los Trabajadores; APT).

17. The reaction of the executive branch was always to criminalize the protests. For example, the vice minister of the presidency, Antonio Ibarra, said in 1991: "The unions are made up of terrorists. They live on outrage, they are out of control, they function as mobs, as peasants. . . . They are partiers, troublemakers, and rebels. . . . They are not a loyal opposition, they have enormous destructive potential, and they jeopardize everyone's interests."

18. United Nations Dispatch, "Desarrollo y democracia en movimiento: PNUD-Nicaragua," 1994, p. 155.

19. In October 2006, days before the presidential elections, there was a convergence in some of the underlying conflicts among Ortega's FSLN, the organized women's movement, and those who had been opposed to the feminist movement. The result was the abolition of what in Nicaragua had been known as "therapeutic abortion," that is, abortion to save the life of a pregnant woman. The unanimous votes of the FSLN congress members proved decisive. For a detailed analysis of the feminist movement, see the work by Kampwirth (2009).

20. Beginning in 1990, academic and media interest in Nicaragua diminished. In the past decade, few analysts have focused on the country. Exceptions to this are the work of Anderson and Dodd (2005); Close (1999); Close and Deonandan (2004); see also David R. Dye, "Retazos de democracia: La política nicaragüense diez años después de la derrota," 2001, www.hemisphereinitiatives.org; and "La democracia a la deriva: La política caudillista de Nicaragua," 2004, www.hemisphereinitiatives.org.

21. This type of change, according to some theorists, has led to the appearance in Latin America of a new "sociopolitical matrix" that is not based on the centrality of the state, but rather on the interaction between the state and the market. The consensus term for this has become the "neoliberal market-driven and multicentered" matrix (Garretón et al. 2003: 93–100).

22. Central Bank of Nicaragua, gross output at constant prices, 1960–1999, www
.bcn.gob.ni/estadisticas/macroeconomia/I-PRODUCCION/1-2.pdf; and *Anuario de es-
taíisticas económicas, 2001–2007*, www.bcn.gob.ni/publicaciones/anuario/anuario2007
.pdf, accessed August 31, 2008.

23. United Nations Economic Commission for Latin America and the Caribbean
(ECLAC), *Social Panorama of Latin America, 2005*, http://www.eclac.org/publicaciones/
xml/4/24054/PSI2005_Cap1_Pobreza.pdf, pp. 70–71, accessed on August 31, 2008.

24. Poverty data are from www.unicef.org/infobycountry/nicaragua.html, accessed
on September 21, 2008.

25. Although called the Central American Free Trade Agreement–Dominican Republic, the agreement is between the United States and Costa Rica, El Salvador,
Guatemala, Honduras, and Nicaragua, as well as the Dominican Republic.

26. Carlos F. Chamorro, "FUNIDES advierte sobre tendencia económica 2008,"
Confidencial 562, November 25 to December 1, 2007, http://www.confidencial.com
.ni/2007-562/economia_562.html, accessed on August 21, 2008.

27. See World Bank website: http://ddp-ext.worldbank.org/ext/ddpreports/viewshared
report?&cf=&report_id=13609&request_type=viewadvanced&hf=n&dimensions=26.

28. The Venezuelan government supported the FSLN's mayoral candidates through
the AMUNIC association of municipalities by providing 304,000 liters of oil in 2006 at
almost no cost, and Chávez promised major investments if the FSLN won the elections.

29. A word signifying an authoritarian, often political-military, type of leadership.

9

Colombia:
The Effects of Violence

Erika Moreno

COLOMBIA IS A NATION OF SHARP CONTRASTS. IT HAS BOASTED
a relatively long history of electoral and party politics, with some of the oldest
political parties in the region. The National Front pact[1] (Registraduría Nacional
de Colombia) that gave way to democratic practices in the late 1950s produced
stable electoral outcomes and a centrist two-party system, unlike most of its
neighbors. Yet democracy remains under siege. Years of interparty violence
gave way to a tricornered fight, pitting armed groups on the left and right against
drug traffickers and the state. A decade into the twenty-first century, Colombian democracy has yet to live up to its promise.

In many respects, the Colombian case provides a stark example of the rift
between basic definitions of democracy, which often focus on contestation, and
the quality of democracy. The quality of democracy is weak even though the
long-entrenched two-party system has given way to a more plural setting lately
(see Leal Buitrago and Ladrón de Guevara 1990; Moreno 2005; Pinzón de
Lewin 1987; Pizarro 1997). A twelfth-place ranking on Levine and Molina's
index of quality of democracy puts Colombia just slightly ahead of El Salvador
and just below Nicaragua, two countries recovering from the ravages of internal conflict (Chapter 2). There is no question that violence has had measurable
negative implications for Colombia's ability to deepen democratic practices beyond basic contestation.

This chapter explores Colombia's political evolution and places its ranking
into perspective. The quality of Colombian democracy faces many challenges,
particularly along the dimensions of sovereignty and electoral decision. Most
of the remaining dimensions of Colombian democracy, including participation
and accountability, are somewhat less clear-cut and often feature aspects that
seem conducive to strengthening the quality of democracy alongside those that
detract from it.

Undermining Sovereignty

Sovereignty stands as one of the weakest aspects of Colombian democracy. Beyond the usual cast of characters present in any democracy, including parties and interest groups, Colombia holds the rather unfortunate distinction of having numerous armed pressure groups weighing in on public policy. Leftist guerrillas, paramilitary organizations, and drug traffickers populate the landscape and threaten almost every aspect of society. Table 9.1 illustrates some of the most easily measured effects of the conflict. In addition to substantial murder and kidnapping rates, the data highlight high rates of internal displacement due to the conflict. For example, 310,387 people were displaced in 2005, compared to 85,000 recorded in 1995; this amounts to an almost fourfold increase in ten years. Although it is hard to disentangle the extent to which these violence indicators are the result of politically motivated crimes or common delinquency, they speak to a broader problem of insecurity caused by rampant violence and the inability of the state to establish security nationwide.

In Colombia's tricornered conflict, armed actors from the left and right and drug traffickers challenge the state for political influence. The conflict has made victims of hundreds of thousands of people over the course of nearly six decades. The roots of modern Colombian violence can be traced back to the 1940s, at the start of La Violencia (the Violence), which lasted from 1947 to 1957, a period of undeclared partisan war that claimed at least 300,000 lives in the span of a decade (Berquist, Peñaranda, and Sánchez 2001; Dix 1987). Following a brief period of military dictatorship, the country reintroduced a limited form of democracy under the National Front accord in 1957. While the consociational pact put an end to partisan warfare, it did not put an end to violence. Widespread social changes, brought on by the modernization of Colombian society in the 1940s and 1950s, brought a host of new demands that were never fully addressed by the political class (Dix 1987). Some of the actors involved in the partisan conflict found new purpose in guerrilla organizations formed in the latter half of the twentieth century. For example, the Revolution-

Table 9.1   Selected Violence Indicators, 1995–2005 (percentage of population in parentheses)

Year	Displaced	Kidnapped	Murdered
1995	85,000 (.23)	1,068 (.003)	25,398 (.07)
2000	317,375 (.80)	3,682 (.009)	26,540 (.07)
2005	310,387 (.72)	800 (.002)	17,331 (.04)

Sources: Displacement figures from CODHES, www.codhes.org; kidnapping figures from the Departamento National de Planeacion, www.dnp.gov.co/paginas_detalle.aspx?idp=562; murder figures from the Instituto Nacional de Medicina Legal y Ciencias Forenses, www.medicinalegal .gov.co.

ary Armed Forces of Colombia (Fuerzas Armadas Revolucionarias de Colombia; FARC) were guerrillas recruited heavily from the ranks of Liberal party forces (Marulanda 1991; Osterling 1989).

Although the FARC represents the oldest continuing guerrilla organization in Colombia and Latin America, it is not alone in perpetuating violence. A host of other leftist guerrillas, including Quintín Lamé, the National Liberation Army (Ejercito de Liberación National; ELN), and the April 19 Movement (Movimiento 19 de Abril; M-19), among others, took the stage starting in the 1960s, spurred by the example of the 1959 Cuban revolution (Castañeda 1994). Leftist guerrillas vary in terms of ideology, with some favoring Marxist (e.g., FARC), Maoist (e.g., ELN), or indigenous (*indigenista*) rhetoric (e.g., Quintín Lamé). [2] Nonetheless, the appeal of armed leftist groups has changed to reflect new concerns over time. The FARC and ELN continue to operate in vast areas of Colombia two decades after the end of the Cold War.

To counter leftist guerrillas, right-wing paramilitary organizations sprang up to provide protection in regions not effectively policed by the state. Although the paramilitary forces that exert control over parts of Colombia have a range of goals, they are united in opposition to leftists. Today the United Autodefenses of Colombia (Autodefensas Unidas de Colombia; AUC) is the single largest armed actor in the conflict (Berquist, Peñaranda, and Sánchez 2001).

Leftist guerrillas and paramilitary forces have both exerted significant pressure on public officials, either through direct intimidation or violence, some of which is captured in official statistics like those summarized in Table 9.1. For instance, kidnapping reflects a widespread problem affecting the polity. Included among a long list of high-profile kidnapping figures are Ingrid Betancourt, the former Green Party presidential candidate, who was released in 2008,[3] and former presidents Alvaro Gómez and Ernesto Samper. Threats and efforts to intimidate public officials are common. However, the reach of the AUC and other such forces goes beyond murder and kidnapping. It is not uncommon for local public officials to be *interviewed* by one or more armed groups before running for office. It is also fairly common for armed groups to demand so-called taxes (*boleteo*) in rural areas or protection fees (*vacuna*) from public officials and citizens alike (Berquist, Peñaranda, and Sánchez 2001; Cubides 2001).[4]

Colombia is also infamously known for its drug trade. The presence of a sizable and multifaceted illicit drug industry alone signals serious problems for state sovereignty.[5] The flow of money from the drug trade provides resources for both guerrilla and paramilitary forces alike (Berquist 2001; Reina 2001).[6] The presence of such a lucrative industry also has long-term implications for elections. Not surprisingly, drug traffickers have also sought to play a direct role in politics. Concerns about the growing influence of drug cartels are fueled by revelations like those uncovered by the Judicial Process 8000 (Proceso 8000). The investigation sparked by this process implicated some of the highest-ranking officials of then-president Ernesto Samper's 1998 campaign in accepting donations from drug cartel leaders and cast a dark shadow over the administration for years (Berquist 2001).

State sovereignty is also undermined, as large sections of the country are beyond the control of central state authority, often falling under the influence of one or another armed group. Efforts to lure armed actors to participate in the peace process have yielded significant concessions from the state. For instance, a section of Colombia the size of Switzerland (Zona de Distensión) was ceded to leftist guerrillas in 1999. In 2004, the state also provided the AUC control over the northern region of Córdoba (Zona de Despeje).[7] In both cases, ceded territories were eventually returned to so-called state control even though armed actors continued to operate openly. As remarkable as these steps sound, they are merely public recognition that the state lacks control of vast regions of the country.

In recent decades, the increasingly high-profile presence of US military and drug enforcement agencies has also spurred questions regarding Colombian sovereignty. For many obvious reasons, the United States maintains an interest in the fragile Colombian state and several of its armed actors. The United States has several decades' worth of experience weighing in on Colombian policy decisions, especially in dealing with the drug industry. In 1999, the US military presence in Colombia expanded under the auspices of Plan Colombia, which launched a binational military and strategic policy to battle the drug trade. Transfer of equipment and the presence of US military personnel caused a great deal of controversy in Colombia as well as the United States. Although Plan Colombia allocated billions of dollars in aid and equipment to the Colombian military and security forces, future support is expected to decline. Critics of US involvement in Colombia have little to celebrate since the US plans to set up as many as seven new military bases across Colombia to spearhead its hemispheric presence in Latin America.[8] Even with increased US presence in Colombia, the biggest threats to Colombian sovereignty are homegrown.

The ongoing internal armed conflict has endangered the integrity of the electoral process through attacks on candidates and parties and through the threat of violence directed at voters. It is evident that decisions made by political figures are subject to a variety of checks by armed and illicit actors. As long as Colombia remains mired in this tricornered conflict, pitting left- and right-wing groups, drug traffickers, and the state against each other, sovereignty will continue to remain elusive.

Quality of Electoral Decision

As this volume illustrates, the presence of democracy and the quality of democracy are not identical concepts. A key dimension for judging the quality of

Colombian democracy holds that elections be free, fair, frequent, and competitive, and that they lead to the designation of officials who have real power to act (Levine and Molina Chapter 1). In this section, I posit that while Colombian elections may have been contested and competitive on several levels, they have not been completely free or fair.

Competition and the Two-Party System

Competitive elections are a staple of Colombian politics, at least since the dismantling (*desmonte*) of the National Front in 1974, which opened up national elections beyond the two traditional parties (Liberal and Conservative Parties).[9] The National Front, which institutionalized party alternation and parity until 1974, emerged from negotiations between the Liberals and the two main factions of the Conservative Party and was endorsed via national referendum. Alternation was introduced to ensure that both parties had access to the presidency and executive branch for specified terms. Parity requirements meant that both parties were restricted from gaining more representation in Congress or other governmental posts (Latorre 1974; Taylor 2009).

While the National Front constrained the political space to the two largest parties, it meant an end to a period of dictatorship following years of internecine party violence (La Violencia*)*. Beginning in 1974, efforts were made to roll back the main restrictions on party competition under the National Front pact. The most drastic efforts to open up contestation (*desmonte*) occurred in the years between 1974 and 1979, when parity requirements were removed, and continued until the ratification of the 1991 Constitution (Dix 1980; Dix 1987; Taylor 2009).[10] The basic contours of the post–National Front electoral system included regular elections to the bicameral Congress every four years in March, two months after the first round of presidential elections.[11] Until 1991, representatives to both chambers of the Colombian Congress were elected in proportional representation districts that mirrored departmental boundaries.[12] Although individuals were elected in proportional representation (PR) contests, Colombian law did not limit the number of lists parties could submit in each district. This allowed parties to submit multiple lists in each congressional district, historically reflecting the presence of factions within the two main parties. These features led to the creation of personal-list PR or, probably more accurately, effective SNTV (single nontransferable vote) (Cox and Shugart 1995) until the multilist strategy was replaced in 2003 (Botero 2006). Personal-list PR (or effective SNTV) gives voters a wide range of choices within parties, including independent candidates within parties, but has the effect of reducing the cohesiveness of the parties that participate in it. While it might seem counterintuitive for parties to submit multiple lists to compete against each other, as well as the other parties, the peculiarities of Colombian electoral law provided strong incentives (and rewards) for large parties that engage in list proliferation.

Although there were important elements of competitiveness throughout, including fierce intraparty competition, the electoral process supported two-party hegemony for decades. While parity requirements under the National Front reduced interparty conflict,[13] they tended to increase intraparty competition since partisans competed against each other for a limited number of seats (Dix 1987; Hartlyn 1988; Martz 1999; Osterling 1989). The possibility of submitting multiple lists for congressional races prior to 2003 was—at least initially—a means to avoid difficult choices at the nomination stage. Access to the party label, at least during the National Front, was largely determined by faction heads—often prominent national party figures with previous political experience. Rather than choose from among factions representing some of the most prominent families, running official and unofficial lists allowed party leaders to lay responsibility at voters' doorsteps. It was a compromise position that, while it did not mollify critics of those in charge at the national level, allowed for a simple democratic solution and converted the general election into an effective primary for both major parties (Dix 1980; Martz 1999; Osterling 1989).

During the early stages of the National Front period, factions within both parties were driven by ideological or familial ties. The National Front period saw conflicts within the Liberal Party between followers of Julio César Turbay Ayala, Carlos Lleras Restrepo, and the Lopistas (followers of Alfonso López Michelson), often reproducing those conflicts at the legislative and subnational levels. Similarly, the Conservative Party was split between the Laureanistas (followers of former president and ultraconservative Laureano Gómez) and Ospinistas (followers of Mariano Ospina Pérez).[14] Nonetheless, over time, the factions lost their ideological and purely familial overtones, and became atomized as their ranks swelled with newcomers (Latorre 1974). Factions are clearly distinguishable during the early National Front years, but, as time passed, lists became vehicles for individuals that at times lacked a supporting cast of copartisans or cofactionalists. Lists representing different wings of each party were also used as an unofficial primary for aspiring presidential candidates (see Martz 1999). Thus, contests at the legislative level were decisive in resolving conflicts at multiple levels of electoral competition (see Moreno and Escobar Lemmon 2008).

Competition is an important aspect of democracy, and Colombia seems to have found ways to foster this quality even during the National Front period. Yet, even high levels of competition cannot overcome failings in other aspects of electoral decision.

Table 9.2 illustrates intraparty competition from 1958 to 2002 in the lower chamber. As the table demonstrates, the average number of lists submitted in each district by Liberals and Conservatives is always greater than one. While the average number of lists submitted varies over time, the table highlights that intraparty competition increases within the Liberal Party over time. Meanwhile, for the Conservatives the average number of lists ranges from 3 to 5 lists per dis-

Table 9.2 Mean Number of Lists Submitted to Lower Chamber Contests, 1958–2002

Year	Liberals	Conservatives	Total
1958	1.56	3.11	2.63
1964	5.95	4.21	6.03
1966	5.95	5.05	6.53
1968	4.95	4.81	6.72
1970	5.76	5.20	9.59
1974	4.23	2.88	7.97
1978	5.19	3.29	11.09
1982	5.94	4.13	12.38
1986	4.31	3.75	11.16
1990	6.60	3.86	11.41
1991	6.91	1.91	14.64
1994	8.56	2.61	18.97
1998	8.39	1.76	20.30
2002	10.12	1.72	27.45

Source: Registraduría Nacional, Colombia.

trict until 1990, when it drops to an average of 1.72 lists per district. The Liberal Party alone progressed from 28 total lists per district in 1958 to well over 300 per district in 2002, with the mean number of lists competing in each district rising from 1.56 in 1958 to over 10 in 2002, the final year of the multilist strategy. The increasing number of lists does not, however, correspond to an increase in the number of seats available in the lower house, as average district magnitude decreased from about seven prior to 1991 to about five.[15] Rather it reflects intense intraparty competition (see also Pizarro 2002). While the Conservative Party tended to have higher levels of intraparty competition early on, intraparty competition is clearly present in both parties.

In the following section, I explore some of the factors that limit the freedom and fairness of the electoral decision facing voters.

Freedom and Fairness:
Restrictive Democracy and Its Implications

The Colombian two-party system was firmly established well before the National Front. The National Front strengthened the system of two-party hegemony while allowing, and even fostering, high levels of intraparty competition. Yet, in order to fully address the needs of a rapidly modernizing society while meeting the goals of deepening democratic practice, a political system must have the flexibility to incorporate underrepresented segments of society. Multiparty politics is one means of accomplishing that goal. In that respect, Colombia was sorely lacking (Hartlyn 1988). Restrictions placed on multiparty competition fed critiques that the National Front created a restrictive democracy (Dix 1980; Escobar 2002; Leal Buitrago and Ladrón de Guevara 1990). In the most narrow sense, a restrictive democracy refers to the entrenchment of the two-party system. Most critiques of this sort, however, underscore the concern that the National Front had caused a deep divide between the political class (*país político*) and the public (*el pueblo*). Thus, restrictive democracy refers to the marginalization of new groups, interests, and voices in exchange for the perpetuation of a nineteenth-century elite in positions of power.

In spite of the many dramatic sociodemographic changes that had occurred in Colombia, it still seemed to many that power continued to reside in the hands of an old and entrenched political elite.[16] Many of the same social forces that contributed to the violence prior to the National Front were still present, in expanded form, in the post-Front era. Rapid urbanization, combined with its social and political ramifications, continued apace in Colombia during the 1940s and beyond (Berquist, Peñaranda, and Sánchez 2001; Dix 1980; Taylor 2009). Society had changed markedly during the twentieth century while Colombia's two parties continued to operate like exclusive nineteenth-century country clubs. The National Front allowed for a return to competition, but it was unable to give voice to twentieth-century Colombian society (Escobar 2002; Giraldo 2003; Latorre 1974).

Pressure to open up the political system, including calls to put an end to restrictive democracy, triggered efforts to rewrite the rules of the game. Unfortunately, the slow process of rewriting the rules only began after a series of violent protests. Calls for the end of National Front restrictions on presidential races were taken seriously after the leftist M-19 guerrilla group was formed to protest the results of the 1970 race. General Gustavo Rojas-Pinilla's failed 1970 presidential bid served as an indictment of the political system (Dix 1987).

Despite the effort to re-create and expand democracy in the post–National Front period, Colombia has still not been able to create an environment that fosters peaceful forms of dialogue among diverse groups. Formal measures to allow for freer and fairer elections have not been accompanied by widespread societal agreement. Serious fissures in Colombian politics and society fed armed insurrection for much of its modern history. The tricornered conflict continues to loom large as many of the armed groups have acted with impunity.[17] Threats to aspiring and incumbent officeholders, as well as voter intimidation in the form of direct threats or various forms of extortion, are as common as attacks on infrastructure and state authority (Berquist 2001).[18] In that context, it is virtually impossible to judge the Colombian electoral process as entirely free or fair.

There have been many efforts to pacify the country, ranging from institutional reform to peace talks to concessions on state presence. Results have been mixed. Reforms that allowed armed groups on the left to form political parties were unsuccessful in bringing about peace. The creation of new parties like the

M-19 and the Patriotic Action (Union Patriotica; UP), the political wing of the FARC guerrillas, led to massive retaliation by armed right-wing groups and the deaths of thousands of supporters and candidates (Motta Motta 1995).[19] Both parties perished along with the hope of drawing an end to the violence.

Some have suggested that Colombia's restrictive democracy engendered violent responses across society, including leftist guerrillas and their right-wing counterparts, the paramilitaries. The bottom line is that Colombia's problems did not start after the National Front (see Taylor 2009 for a thorough treatment of this argument). But the truth is that intolerance to opposing viewpoints and political violence preceded the democratic period in Colombia. Thus, the presence of regularly scheduled elections did not deepen democratic practice.

The Presence and Quality of Enlightened Voters

Levine and Molina's definition (Chapter 1) requires that voters act in an informed manner to make meaningful decisions about their representatives. Not surprisingly, the ongoing conflict in Colombia has had important implications for the quality and access of information available to its citizens. The ever-present threat of violence carries over to all segments of Colombian society. This is especially true for those who work in the field of journalism. According to Freedom House's Index of Press Freedom, Colombian print and broadcast media were rated as "partly free" throughout the 1990s and 2000s. The available data suggest that Colombia's poor rating in the 1990s was partly a function of repressive actions directed at the media, including the killing of journalists. The partly free rating is the direct result of political pressures and controls on media, especially for broadcast media, between 1996 and 1999. From 2002 until 2006, the primary contributor to Colombia's partly free designation was political pressure and control on media content, including harassment or violence against journalists and self-censorship.[20]

Table 9.3 provides a numerical summary for Colombia's press freedom scores and provides a comparison to the rest of the region. The total score given by Freedom House can range anywhere from 0 to 100. Scores ranging from 0 to 30 are considered free; 31 to 60 qualify as partly free; and 61 to 100 qualify as not free. While the regional average puts press freedoms in the range between 33 and 40, Colombia's scores range from 49 to 63. In other words, Colombia's press freedoms are at least 16 to 23 points worse than the regional average. Obviously there are cases that contribute much higher and lower scores to the regional average, so this does not suggest that Colombia is the worst offender in this realm. It does, however, suggest that the internal conflict continues to overshadow efforts to deepen democratic practice in Colombia through a free media.

The pressures placed on the media have significant implications for the quality and diversity of information available to citizens. The potential for censorship and self-censorship is high and negatively affects the quality of the

Table 9.3   Press Freedom in Colombia and Latin America, 1994–2008

Year	Colombia Score	Latin America[a] Average Score
1994	49	36.88
1995	48	36.84
1996	54	34.00
1997	55	35.44
1998	55	35.44
1999	60	35.81
2000	59	35.50
2001	60	34.19
2002	60	33.56
2003	63	36.13
2004	63	36.88
2005	63	37.59
2006	61	38.44
2007	57	38.78
2008	59	39.16

Source: Freedom House, Freedom of the Press Historical Data, 1980–2008, http://www.freedom house.org/template.cfm?page=274.

Note: a. Includes data on the following countries: Antigua and Barbuda, Argentina, Bahamas, Barbados, Belize, Bolivia, Brazil, Chile, Colombia, Costa Rica, Cuba, Dominica, Dominican Republic, Ecuador, El Salvador, Grenada, Guatemala, Guyana, Haiti, Honduras, Jamaica, Mexico, Nicaragua, Panama, Paraguay, Peru, St. Kitts and Nevis, St. Lucia, St. Vincent and the Grenadines, Suriname, Trinidad and Tobago, Uruguay, Venezuela.

electoral decision. The irony is that Colombia has a laudable history with competitive elections, even during the period of two-party hegemony, yet it has not been able to gain traction on improving the quality of electoral decision, owing largely to the effects of the conflict and the limits it places on segments of society like the media.

Institutional Reform and Efforts to Improve Participation

Robust political participation sustains democratic practice by providing vital feedback to those in positions of power and authority. Participation also serves to measure the level of interest and commitment to democratic procedures, outcomes, and culture. Whether you place the focus on formal or informal mechanisms of participation, Colombia tends to fare poorly. For instance, since the end of the National Front, turnout in legislative elections reached a high of 57 percent in 1974, with a low of 33 percent in 1978 and 1991; turnout in presidential elections has never exceeded 59 percent.[21] (See Tables 9.4 and 9.5.) The last two presidential races saw turnout rates of 45 percent in 2006 and 49.2 percent in

Table 9.4 Turnout in Colombia's Congressional Lower House Elections, 1970–2010 (as a percentage)

Year	Turnout
1970	51.9
1974	57.1
1978	33.4
1982	40.7
1986	43.6
1990	55.3
1991	33.0
1994	36.1
1998	45.0
2002	42.5
2006	40.5
2010	32.2

Source: Registraduría Nacional, Colombia.

2010 during the first round. These figures stand in stark contrast to the 65 percent congressional turnout rate during the 1958 elections that marked the start of the National Front. Although low turnout rates can be attributed to the absence of mandatory voting laws, which are otherwise common across Latin America, low participation in elections points to broader problems in the polity. Exhaustion with the system of two-party hegemony was chief among the explanations

Table 9.5 Turnout in Colombia's Presidential Elections, 1970–2010 (as a percentage)

Year	Turnout
1970	52
1974	58
1978	37
1982	49
1986	43
1990	43
1994 (1st round)	34
1994 (2nd round)	43
1998 (1st round)	52
1998 (2nd round)	59
2002	47
2006	46
2010 (1st round)	49.2
2010 (2nd round)	44.5

Sources: Pinzón de Lewin (1987); Registraduría Nacional, Colombia; IDEA Voter turnout summaries, http://www.idea.int/vt/country_view.cfm?country=CO#pres.

for low turnout in national contests (see Pizarro 2002). But even today as the party system accommodates itself to new players like former president Alvaro Uribe's Party of Social and National Unity (Partido de la Unidad Nacional) and Antanas Mockus's Green Party (Partido Verde) alongside much weakened versions of the Liberal and Conservative Parties, formal participation has not markedly improved.

Critiques of National Front–era restrictions and their long-term consequences provided a compelling rationale for institutional reform. As a response, the state embarked on several efforts to provide new opportunities for participation since 1974. However, these efforts at reform did not begin in earnest until the passage of Law 58 of 1985. Under the 1985 reforms, organizations that submitted a party platform, proof of organization, and a minimum of 10,000 members were recognized by the state and awarded media access, franking privileges, and access to government printing offices (see Moreno 2005; Pinzón de Lewin 1987). These measures were tied to the larger peace process and provided a means to reward those who participated in the conventional political arena. The 1991 Constitution further altered the electoral code by allowing the creation of political movements, which are temporary grassroots alternatives to the two major parties. Law 130 of 1994 provided even more incentives for party creation by creating a system of limited public financing for legally recognized parties and movements.[22]

Continued calls for reform were often broached in academic circles, in public, and in the midst of peace talks with armed actors. Internal pressures to provide more access points for the citizenry, along with external calls by international financial institutions to decentralize authority, led additional reforms. Law 1 of 1986, for instance, allowed for the direct election of mayors across the country. This represented a dramatic break with the past since mayors had historically been appointed by governors who were, in turn, appointed by presidents. What is more, the 1991 Constitution further extended political decentralization by providing citizens with opportunities to elect governors. While these reforms dramatically increased citizen input in local- and state-level government, additional legislation passed in 1994 introduced recall measures for local officials.[23] Law 134 of 1994 offers voters a chance to remove sitting mayors or governors. Although recall measures are rarely used, they do represent an effort to provide opportunities for citizen participation.

Additional measures of direct democracy were instituted during the 1994 electoral reform, including the formalization of national plebiscites and referenda to approve or strike down projects proposed by the president or legislative bodies. Popular initiatives also allow members of civil society to engage in the legislative process by introducing bills to appropriate legislative bodies at the national or subnational level. The 1994 law also included measures to encourage the creation of open, local town hall meetings, allowing the public to participate (*cabildo abierto*), and primaries for several of the major parties.

While the impetus to expand participation has motivated institutional reform, the effects are less than clear. On the one hand, turnout rates for the first mayoral elections in 1988 averaged 68.5 percent, among the lowest recorded rate of abstention for any election since the National Front. On the other hand, the first set of gubernatorial elections, held in 1991, averaged a turnout rate of nearly 40.1 percent, which is comparable to turnout rates at the national level for the period (Registraduría Nacional). Participation in other aspects of the political process, like the open town hall meetings, is far more difficult to measure.

Formal participation has lagged in spite of new avenues for citizens to participate. Yet informal political participation, such as demonstrations and peace rallies, has become more prominent in recent years. Social mobilization in Colombia is noteworthy because it demonstrates a strongly held desire to foster positive change in spite of the threat of violence. Social mobilization has manifested itself in the form of massive street demonstrations, cross regional peace rallies, and impromptu referenda.[24] Widespread exhaustion with politics as usual and the decades-old tricornered conflict have been the primary motivators for mobilization. Ultimately, these mass movements reflect well on the society's ability to organize and place pressure on the state for improved accountability.

Accountability

Accountability entails many dimensions, including informal social mobilization and formal institutions aimed at subjecting public officials to citizen control or sanction. Colombian society has built a thick web of social organizations that strive to hold the government accountable. What is more, institutional reforms in the post–National Front era have attempted to create a variety of mechanisms for formal accountability (see Moreno, Crisp, and Soberg Shugart 2003; O'Donnell 1999). Despite these developments in Colombia's political and social structures, Colombia, like its neighbors, still maintains a poor showing with respect to accountability (Levine and Molina Chapter 2). Yet, the growing web of social mobilization and efforts to create formal mechanisms for accountability provide some room for hope.

Social accountability, which relies exclusively on citizens and social movements, is an important aspect of accountability. In recent decades, Colombia has seen a dramatic growth in the size and number of social organizations, many of which are tied to peace-building efforts (Berquist 2001). While the scale and role of such mobilizations have changed somewhat between 1986 and today, Colombian society has certainly played an increasingly active role in shaping the political debate.

The search for a peaceful resolution to the ongoing internal conflict is an important leitmotif for social mobilization in Colombia. Under the direction of then-president Virgilio Barco, who was in office from 1986 to 1990, a peace initiative was launched to begin direct negotiations with the M-19 guerrillas following high-profile kidnappings, including that of former presidential candidate Alvaro Gómez Hurtado. Several sectors of society mobilized initially to support a negotiated solution, including the Catholic Church. While the first few manifestations of this sort were limited to the capital, Bogotá, they soon spread to include large cities like Medellín, Cali, and some of the most conflict-ravaged zones of the country, like the Urabá and Magdalena Medio regions.[25] As peace negotiations began to successfully demobilize leftist guerrillas and a new Constitution promising peace as a right of citizenship was enacted, new mobilizations, mainly between 1988 and 1994, emerged to demand complete fulfillment with the peace process.

Between 1993 and 1999, Colombia experienced a significant scaling up of social mobilization. A notable example of such mobilization occurred in 1996, when twenty-seven children from various organizations across Colombia formed the Children's Movement for Peace (Movimiento de los Niños por la Paz) along with the assistance of UNICEF, the Catholic Church, the Colombian Red Cross, the Boy Scouts, YMCA, and WorldVision. The movement sought to provide assistance and opportunities to children across the country affected by the internal conflict. In addition to pressing elected officials to turn schools and parks into peace zones, creating recreational opportunities for children, and providing increased protection in and around school zones, this organization quickly became a national player. Among its most notable achievements was the articulation of a Children's Mandate for Peace and Rights, which turned out over 2.7 million children and 10 million adults to the polls in October 1997 to support peace-building efforts.[26] Yet, this organization did not cease its operations with the Children's Mandate for Peace and Rights; it continues to provide an informal mechanism for children to support other children affected by violence through workshops. What is more, several municipalities across Colombia have created the position of Child Mayor, which serves as a liaison to the municipal councils and advocates for peace on behalf of children.[27] Obviously this organization benefited from receptive public and external support, but its dramatic expansion and national reach are indicative of the manner in which civil society was changing to meet the challenges of its decades-long armed conflict.

In addition to the growth of organizations like the Children's Movement for Peace, regional dialogues took hold throughout the country. In the latter half of the 1990s, the depth of social mobilization grew by incorporating a more diverse group of people, regions, and activities. The Committee for the Search for Peace (Comité de Busqueda de la Paz), the National Conciliation Commission (created by the Episcopalian Church), a host of NGOs, and regional associations gained prominence. The No More Campaign of 1999 (No Más) successfully brought together more than 2.5 million people in forty marches between April and September 1999 and in excess of 8 million more in October 1999 to protest kidnappings.[28]

At the start of the new millennium, Colombia had a combination of national-level and grassroots organizations that have tapped into a public zeitgeist targeting the internal conflict, lawlessness, and corruption. A shortlist of some of the most active grassroots groups includes the Association of Workers and Peasants of Carare (Asociación de Trabajadores y Campesinos de Carare; ATCC), Peace Communities (Comunidades de Paz), and efforts undertaken by the indigenous Nasa communities found in Cauca. National organizations like No More (No Más), Planet of Peace (Planeta Paz), Peace Colombia (Paz Colombia), and the Peaceful Path of Women (Ruta Pacífica de las Mujeres) are also prominent. Colombia's tricornered conflict has spurred the largest growth of autochthonous expressions of civic engagement in Colombia's long history. As such, these mobilizations provide some hope of improved accountability into the future.

Efforts to institute checks on elected—and unelected—officials have spurred interest in creating and strengthening formal accountability, including the judicial branch. Colombia is one of a handful of countries that has overseen the construction of constitutional tribunals to conduct judicial reviews (1991 Constitución National de Colombia). The 1991 Constitution also introduced the concept of allowing individual citizens the right to claim redress in the judicial system against public officials or individuals representing public offices (*acción de tutela*). It is important to note that any individual could request an *acción de tutela* without needing to hire a lawyer, and results are required to be quick—usually decisions are rendered within ten days—and definitive. Citizens may initiate an *acción de tutela* against health agencies for malpractice, educational agencies if they were denied a spot in public schools, or any governmental office if they were mistreated or believe they were denied services or are victims of corruption. Surveys conducted in 2001 suggest that Colombians are familiar with this option and find it to be the most effective means of redress, especially in cases where they claimed to be victims of corruption.[29]

The 1991 Constitution also created the human rights ombudsman (Defensoría del Pueblo) office. The ombudsman is another mechanism for individuals to seek redress from public officials. What is more, the ombudsman can initiate legal action against state officials on behalf of citizens, thereby reserving some important proactive powers to pursue violations of citizen rights. Although appointment and dismissal decisions for all of these offices still remain in the hands of elected officials, the potential for judicial review, citizen-initiated action, and ombudsman-initiated action is present.

Although creating formal avenues of accountability is important, it is obviously only part of the equation. The question of whether or not formal mechanisms of accountability have translated to substantive societal change remains subject to considerable debate. Take for instance, the creation of the Human Rights Ombudsman Office in 1991. The ombudsman is selected by Congress from a list of three candidates provided by the president. Terms are limited to four years and funds are drawn from the national budget, which some have argued tends to limit independence of action from elected officials (see Moreno, Crisp, and Shugart 2003; Uggla 2004). Cases brought to the attention of the ombudsman often deal with a range of public services, rights, and entitlements. For instance, in the year 2000, complaints involving the public health system and the right to petition public officials totaled 2,625 and 2,041 cases, respectively, whereas cases of humanitarian protection and life totaled 1,954 and 1,119 cases, respectively (Defensoria del Pueblo 2001). Efforts at institutional reform notwithstanding, extrajudicial killings continue to go unpunished in 98.5 percent of the cases reported.[30] The presence of high levels of violence and intimidation naturally limits the effectiveness of these sorts of institutional changes. Nonetheless, there is reason to hope that the combination of an active citizenry—as evident in growing levels of social mobilization—and formal mechanisms may one day yield an improvement in accountability.

While the internal conflict limits the effectiveness of institutional reforms and can tire out even the most committed social activist, the growth and longevity of informal social mobilization provide a ray of optimism for Colombian democracy. Thus, while Colombia has a long way to travel before it can claim more than just a long history of contestation, there are reasons to remain hopeful that it can flourish into a quality democracy.

Conclusions

Colombia is home to a long history of electoral competition, even during the restrictive National Front era, and has some of the region's oldest political parties. If democracy could be defined exclusively in terms of contestation, then Colombia easily qualifies. More demanding definitions of democracy, like those proposed by Levine and Molina, question the quality of Colombian democracy for many good reasons (Chapter 1). The presence of an ongoing armed conflict has eroded the promise of Colombian democracy, as envisioned in the late 1950s. As a result, the state and its public officials are unable to act as sovereigns. The tricornered fight has seriously undermined the ability of the state to act independently of armed actors, violence, and intimidation. The quality of electoral decision is also undermined by the way in which pervasive violence undermines free and fair elections, despite a long history of competition. As it stands, there are many factors working against Colombian democracy. What is worse, rates of participation in Colombia, especially formal participation, are low, and it ranks poorly on accountability.

Even in spite of its many weaknesses, there are rays of hope. For instance, efforts to create formal avenues for participation and accountability may yet yield fruit. If nothing else, at least these efforts at institutional reform create a means to channel popular sentiment. However, in the end the success or failure of those reforms will rest on the strength and depth of society's willingness to use them to their advantage. The last few decades have demonstrated that the people (*el pueblo*) are finding new ways to organize and place pressure on the political system. Whether through protests, demonstrations, pressure on public officials, or the use of legal instruments like the *acción de tutela*, the citizenry is making itself heard. The emergence of widespread social mobilization and the creation of grassroots and national political organizations bode well for the future.

Change is under way in Colombia. The long-entrenched two-party system has given way to a more plural setting as of late (see Leal Buitrago and Ladrón de Guevara 1990; Moreno 2005; Pinzón de Lewin 1987; Pizarro 1997). The second round of the 2010 presidential elections, which included candidates from the Party of Social and National Unity and the Green Party, is one indication of that change. Competition is still an important feature of the Colombian political system, yet the challenge lies in its ability to deepen democratic practice beyond contestation. As is the case for El Salvador and Nicaragua, the quality of democracy in Colombia will improve only when the conflict ceases to inflict more wounds. Whether that will even happen is, of course, in the hands of Colombia's besieged citizens.

Notes

1. The National Front (1958–1974) was a pacted agreement between Liberals and Conservatives, which required parity in Congress and government offices and alternation for the presidency. Thus, elections determined which representatives of each party were permitted to have a seat at the predivided Liberal-Conservative-only table (see Hoskin 1971).

2. *Indigenista* rhetoric refers to the pro-indigenous ideology that emphasizes indigenous communities, identity, and way of life. Variations on this theme are evident across the region, from Mexico to Peru.

3. Betancourt was released after nearly seven years of captivity.

4. The *boleteo* is a form of extortion primarily in rural areas by leftist guerrillas and paramilitaries alike. The term is derived from *boleta* (a note), indicating a threat to property owners and commonly used during the period of La Violencia. The *vacuna* (immunization) is a payoff to groups in exchange for protection against violence, kidnapping, or other threats.

5. Colombia's multifaceted illicit drug industry includes cocaine, heroin, and marijuana production (see Reina 2001).

6. BBC Mundo, "No hay congresistas a nuestras ordenes," August 8, 2005, http://news.bbc.co.uk/go/pr/fr/-/spanish/latin_america/newsid_4747000/4747367.stm.

7. BBC Mundo, "AUC entra zona de despeje," August 28, 2005, http://news.bbc.co.uk/hi/spanish/latin_america/newsid_4192000/4192092.stm; BBC Mundo, "No hay congresistas a nuestras ordenes," August 8, 2005, http://news.bbc.co.uk/go/pr/fr/-/spanish/latin_america/newsid_4747000/4747367.stm.

8. BBC News, "What Future for U.S. Backed Plan Colombia?" June 12, 2010, http://news.bbc.co.uk/2/hi/world/latin_america/10208937.stm.

9. The National Front pact ended decades of internecine party-based conflict, known as La Violencia, in Colombia. The National Front created a system of alternation between the two major parties, as well as the source of many future grievances.

10. Electoral reform continued into the next two decades with major changes occurring in 1986, allowing for the direct election of mayors and relaxation of party registration rules (see Moreno 2005). Subsequent reforms deepened efforts to decentralize the political system, allowing for the direct election of governors and other subnational offices.

11. Immediate reelection was only introduced under the aegis of outgoing president Alvaro Uribe. President Uribe would have attempted a third term in May 2010 had it not been for the Supreme Court ruling that declared a third term unconstitutional (see Felipe Botero, "Flash Report: A Key Decision," Andean Democracy Research Network, 2010, http://blogs.ubc.ca/andeandemocracy/2010/03/12/flash-report-on-colombia-a-key-decision/).

12. In 1991, the new Constitution altered the rules for electing members to the upper house by creating a single nationwide district, electing 100 members. Two additional seats were added to provide minority representation for indigenous populations in Colombia.

13. The Constitutional Reform of 1968 removed the parity requirement for subnational offices, notably state assembly and municipal council elections.

14. Laureanistas were succeeded by Alvaristas, led by Laureano Gómez's son Alvaro Gómez Hurtado. The Ospinistas were succeeded by the Pastranistas-Ospinistas, which includes former president Andres Pastrana.

15. The Chamber of Deputies continues to be elected from multimember department-level districts. District magnitude varies from 2 to 18, although the overall number of deputies in the chamber fell from 199 to 161 after the adoption of the 1991 Constitution. Not surprisingly there is some association between the number of seats in a district (DM) and the number of lists. Low-magnitude districts (DM less than or equal to 2) feature three to twelve lists with an average of seven, whereas high-magnitude districts (DM 17–29) contain 18–286 lists, with an average of 131.

16. Scions of some of the country's most notable political families have held prominent positions, elected and unelected, for many decades following the creation of Colombia's two main parties. Indeed, the fact that many familial factions existed in Colombia for so long is a testament to the maintenance, in the minds of many, of a political elite.

17. Colombia's oldest guerrilla group, the FARC, has its roots in the period of La Violencia. Originally composed of Liberal Party guerrillas, the FARC persisted even after the undeclared civil war ended in the 1950s. The brand of leftist ideology maintained by the FARC predates the Cuban revolution and survives even in the post–Cold War world.

18. In reference to threats to officeholders, see BBC News, "What Future for U.S. Backed Plan Colombia?" June 12, 2010, http://news.bbc.co.uk/2/hi/world/latin_america/10208937.stm.

19. See Radio Nacional de Colombia, "ONU denuncia patron de ejecuciones extrajudiciales e impunidad en Colombia," May 27, 2010, http://www.radionacionaldecolombia.gov.co/index.php/ultimas-noticias/nacionales/onu-denuncia-qpatron-de-ejecuciones-extrajudicialesq-e-impunidad-en-colombia.html.

20. The Press Freedom index did not begin to provide nuanced numerical scores or data on categorical designations, including the effects of laws, political pressures, repression, and economic influences on the media, until after 1993.

21. In that instance, the turnout rate was recorded only in the second round of the presidential contest.

22. Legal recognition required that parties submit a platform, proof of organization, and either a minimum of 50,000 signatures, votes in the previous election, or winning one representative to Congress (Ley Electoral 130 de 1994, Art. 3; Resolución 369 de 2000 Consejo Nacional Electoral).

23. Recall measures require that at least 40 percent of the total valid votes that elected the official in question request a recall. The official can then be recalled if at least 60 percent of the voters who participated in the previous election vote in favor of the recall.

24. The 1990 seventh ballot (*septima papeleta*) is a prominent example of impromptu referenda. In this case, the unofficial paper ballot cast by Colombians during national elections called for the convocation of a constituent assembly. Although the informal referendum was triggered by political elites, it was a relatively spontaneous show of support for change. Other forms of informal political participation have stronger grassroots support and are discussed more fully in the subsequent section.

25. Carlos Fernandez, Mauricio Duran, and Fernando Sarmiento, "Peace Mobilization in Colombia 1978–2002," *Conciliation Resources,* 2004, http://www.c-r.org/our work/accord/colombia/peace-mobilization.

26. UNICEF, "Social Mobilization," http://www.unicef.org/cbsc/index_42347.html.

27. Carlos Fernandez, Mauricio Duran, and Fernando Sarmiento, "Peace Mobilization in Colombia 1978–2002," *Conciliation Resources,* 2004, http://www.c-r.org/our work/accord/colombia/peace-mobilization.

28. Carlos Fernandez, Mauricio Duran, and Fernando Sarmiento, "Peace Mobilization in Colombia 1978–2002," *Conciliation Resources,* 2004, http://www.c-r.org/our work/accord/colombia/peace-mobilization.

29. Mitchell Seligson, "Transparencia y buen gobierno en cuatro cuidades en Colombia: Una encuesta de percepcion cuidadana," 2001, http://sitemason.vanderbilt .edu/lapop/COLOMBIABACK.

30. See Radio Nacional de Colombia, "ONU denuncia patron de ejecuciones extrajudiciales e impunidad en Colombia," May 27, 2010, http://www.radionacional decolombia.gov.co/index.php/ultimas-noticias/nacionales/onu-denuncia-qpatron-de-ejecuciones-extrajudicialesq-e-impunidad-en-colombia.html.

10

Venezuela:
The Impact of
Recent Electoral Processes

Valia Pereira Almao and Carmen Pérez Baralt

THE NATIONAL CONSTITUTION OF THE BOLIVARIAN REPUBLIC OF Venezuela of 1999, proposed by President Hugo Chávez and passed by a national referendum, defines the Venezuelan state as democratic, social, abiding by the rule of law, fair, affirming political pluralism (article 2), and, at the same time, establishes that the government will always remain democratic and participative, and that elected officials are subject to recall, among other characteristics (article 6). Furthermore, the decisions taken through the following means of participation by the people are binding on the state (article 70): elections, referenda, popular consultations, recall, legislative initiatives, citizen assemblies.

At first glance, these traits show a democracy in development, where citizen participation is focused on substantial political matters, not only on the selection of rulers. Venezuelan democracy, however, has experienced significant challenges in recent years, particularly since the referendum on constitutional reform that took place in December 2007, which was rejected by a narrow margin. There has been a turn toward greater personalization and concentration of power around the president, and a serious push toward the transformation of Venezuela into a socialist country according to the model of twenty-first–century socialism that Chávez's government is trying to develop. These challenges have unfolded throughout several electoral processes from 2007 to 2009: the constitutional reform referendum of 2007, which attempted to formally transform Venezuela into a socialist Bolivarian republic; the regional elections of 2008 for state and local government, in which the opposition advanced substantially, even if the government obtained the majority of positions; and the 2009 referendum for the constitutional amendment to allow unlimited reelection to elected offices, including the presidency.

Those referenda and elections carried out in Venezuela from 2007 to 2009 have provided spectacular moments for the Venezuelan political process.

Through them, revealing traits about the characteristics of this country's democracy may be learned. The goal of this chapter is to consider the impact those electoral events have had on the democratic political system, seeking to pinpoint some indicators that would determine if Venezuelan democracy has been affected in a positive or negative way. This objective is to be pursued in the framework of a wider discussion about the dimensions that indicate the quality of democracy, as discussed by Levine and Molina (Chapter 1).

Methodology

President Chávez has put forward his proposal for change toward participatory democracy as being a drastic departure from the previous model of representative democracy. This new model is meant to reject the negotiations and agreements between political opponents that were characteristic of politics in what Chávez refers to as the "Fourth Republic," which is his term for Venezuelan democracy between 1958 and 1998. Since 2000, negotiation and agreement have been replaced by polarization. It is expected by government forces that participative democracy, as established in the 1999 Constitution, should result in an increase in the quality of democracy. Whether this has been the case has to be determined at the political level, particularly looking at the electoral events to see if their quality has increased or decreased.

Since 2006 Chávez has stated clearly and repeatedly that his goal is the transformation of Venezuelan society into a socialist society. If the process that has been developing since then represents part of a transition to socialism, then analysis of the political events that have occurred since that time may give some indication of whether such socialism is truly democratic, and about its consequences for the quality of democracy under the new conditions. As suggested by Bobbio (1995), socialism may be presented in equalitarian-authoritarian or equalitarian-libertarian versions, but only the latter is geared toward democracy as it is understood in this volume.

The starting point for this chapter is the approach by Levine and Molina (Chapter 1) according to which the level of quality of democracy can be determined by measuring a set of procedural requisites of democracy and of the rights directly associated with them, which bind those who govern, public institutions, and voters to the effect that political decisions should be taken in accordance with popular consent. Levine and Molina classify the different procedural requisites of democracy in five conceptually distinguished, but interrelated, dimensions: electoral decision, participation, responsiveness, accountability, and sovereignty (Chapter 1). In this chapter, we have considered, through qualitative and quantitative analyses, indicators corresponding to three of these: electoral decision, accountability, and responsiveness.

Assessing the Impact on the Quality of Democracy of the 2007–2009 Electoral Events

Electoral Decision

Electoral decision includes the following minimum elements in a democracy: free, frequent, and impartial elections and universal suffrage (Levine and Molina 2007a). In Venezuela the right to vote is universal, and there have been frequent electoral processes. Nonetheless, an evaluation of their impartiality and of the levels of liberty and guarantees of political rights that surround them presents problematic aspects that we analyze in this section with particular reference to the role played by the National Electoral Council (Consejo Nacional Electoral; CNE), the state agency that organizes and supervises elections in Venezuela as the head of the Electoral Branch of Power, which is constitutionally coequal with the executive, legislative, and judicial branches. The CNE is supposed to be independent and autonomous in relation to other national powers. This is a fundamental premise, because only in this way can it guarantee the impartiality of the electoral processes and the acceptance of its results by all parties. One of the issues that interfere with the autonomy of the CNE is the method of selection of the members of its board of directors. The National Assembly has selected this board with a clear interest in political control, and that shows through the CNE's actions and decisions.[1]

The CNE accepted some petitions made by the opposition, who promoted the "no" vote for the referenda of 2007 and 2009, among which were the following: auditing over 50 percent of the voting results produced by the voting machines against the counting of the paper ballots issued by those machines to the voters and placed in a ballot box for control purposes in each voting precinct, tests of the permanent ink used to prevent multiple votes by the same person,[2] and ensuring the presence of witnesses at the voting precincts. These agreements between the CNE and the opposition sought to create conditions that would make participation acceptable to the latter, and that would prevent a boycott like the one that occurred for the parliamentary elections of 2005. In fact, the mainstream opposition participated in the electoral events under analysis.

Using available information, particularly that collected by nongovernment organizations (NGOs) and academic research teams, we assessed the degree of impartiality by the CNE during the electoral processes that occurred in the period considered. We looked at the following six issues, which are discussed below:

1. The CNE's impartiality regarding referenda wording;
2. The CNE's impartiality regarding the accompanying explanatory statement about the referenda;

3. The ability of citizens to be nominated as candidates and potentially elected by popular vote;
4. Forcing the competing blocs to comply with the norms to create equilibrium in the use of political advertisement in mass media;
5. Counting votes and publishing the electoral results;
6. Maintaining tolerance between the government and the opposition.

The first issue we examined was the CNE's impartiality regarding the wording of the issues to be submitted to referenda. According to the rules (article 5) approved by the CNE for the referendum of 2007: "The question object of the referendum will be proposed to the electors in the same terms and conditions as it was approved by the National Assembly, at the opportunity of the approval of the constitutional reform."[3] The CNE adopted the same criteria for the issues raised at the 2009 referendum, except that this time the question was laid out in a diffuse manner, the only argument being that the review of the question would be solely technical, not substantial.[4] Both criteria led to the acceptance of the questions in the manner in which they were to be established by the proponents, that is to say, the government.

The question posed to the voters in the 2007 referendum on constitutional reform was worded as follows: "Do you approve the Constitutional Reform project with its Titles, Chapters, Transitional Regulations, Derogatory and Final, presented in two blocs and sanctioned by the National Assembly *with the people's participation* and based on the initiative of the President Hugo Chávez?"[5]

The question posed to the voters in the 2009 referendum on constitutional reform was worded as follows: "Do you approve the amendment of articles 160, 162, 174, 192 and 230 of the Constitution of the Republic, presented by the National Assembly, *which expands the political rights of the people* with the end of permitting that any citizen exercising a function subject to popular vote, *may be nominated for the same position,* for the established constitutional period *with his or her possible election depending exclusively on the popular vote*?"[6]

For the 2007 referendum, the CNE admitted the original question as it was approved by the National Assembly. That wording presented a clear bias toward a positive answer to the reform, since the expression "with the people's participation" assumes that the people have already deliberated on the issues. The National Assembly did organize some public meetings on the constitutional reform, but participation was mostly limited to social and political organizations that supported the government, deliberately excluding the rest of the organizations that tried to bring their arguments and petitions to the national legislative branch. A number of public protests and skirmishes occurred as a result.

The question for the 2009 referendum stated the issue in terms of the political rights of the people—that any elected officer may be reelected with no limit to his or her term in office, which biases the question and is incorrect. The

2009 referendum question presented the government's argument for indefinite reelection as part of the question, by stating that it would be the people with their vote who would always decide if reelection would proceed. This excluded the argument of the opposition, according to which indefinite reelection is not democratic in countries with weak institutions because the incumbents would be able to use the resources of the state to their benefit, and in time accumulate an excessive advantage over their opponents. In the question, words from critical sectors were avoided: "indefinite reelection," "reiterated," and "successive," referring rather to nominations for the same position. This careful editing presented the proposal in the most favorable terms, thereby avoiding any hint that the amendment was an attempt to ensure the perpetuation in power of the president, as was alleged by the opposition. The CNE, as the agency charged with overseeing the impartiality of the electoral process, could have asked the National Assembly to modify the wording of the questions so as to correct the biases and search for a neutral phrasing, which would not refer to the arguments of either one of the two blocs of contenders. But the CNE did not do so, because it did not analyze and evaluate whether or not the wording was in fact neutral and impartial. The admission of the biased questions, as they were presented, is evidence of the partiality of the CNE with the proponents of the 2007 constitutional reform and the 2009 constitutional amendment.

The second issue refers to the fact that popular consultation in the referendum in 2007 involved a separate statement for the voters to read with detailed information about the modifications to the Constitution that were involved in the referendum decision. This was necessary due to the large number of articles of the Constitution that were included in the referendum. This was not the case for the 2009 referendum, because the constitutional issues to amend were included in the question itself.

The initiative for the constitutional reform of 2007 was taken by the president of the Republic, with the objective of submitting to the approval of the voters a wide range of changes to the Constitution that were intended to adapt it to his socialist project. These changes included giving constitutional acceptance to several forms of social property while diminishing the legal protection of private property, reinforcing communal power[7] under control of the presidency and parallel to the elected functionaries at regional and local levels, greater concentration of power at the national executive level, and indefinite presidential reelection, among others. During the debate in the National Assembly, new propositions for reform were added to the ones that were put forward by the president.[8]

The first controversy emerged around the way in which the referendum proposals should be voted on: should these be presented in one block (acceptance or rejection of the constitutional reform), or should each article be voted on separately, such as the opposition demanded? President Chávez repeatedly refused to separate the reform proposal into parts. The CNE agreed and explained that it could not be divided into parts because that was the way in which the proponent himself had put it forward.

Nevertheless, as discussion advanced, public rejection of the reform escalated dangerously and the president decided to separate it into two blocks for its presentation to the voters, thus distinguishing those included by the National Assembly from those put forward by the president. The CNE agreed again, without voicing objections. The modifications proposed by the president were laid out as block A, and those put forward by the National Assembly as block B, so that they were voted on separately in two blocks.

The CNE was not willing to harmonize the demands of the opposition and of the president in such a way as to maintain an impartial stance. Instead it accepted Chávez's proposition of separating the proposed modifications into two blocks, with the understanding that the presentation was part of the reform proposition made by Chávez. The crux of the matter here is that the CNE understood that the proponent (i.e., Chávez, the government) decided the terms of the presentation of the reform to the voters—although the CNE maintained the opposite opinion in the recall referendum of 2004—when in reality such a thing must pass through the filter of impartiality and equality of treatment that should surround all democratic electoral processes, and which includes giving due consideration to the arguments put forward by the opposition.

The third issue is respect for citizens' political right to be nominated as candidates and potentially elected for offices subject to the popular vote. Using the opportunity of the regional elections of 2008, the Comptroller General disqualified 272 persons, which involved their loss of political rights, arguing that they were responsible for committing administrative irregularities while in exercise of public charge. That decision is contrary to article 23 of the American Convention on Human Rights and articles 65 and 42 of the Constitution inasmuch as political incapacitation may only stem from a final decision by a court of law in a criminal trial. The majority of those disqualified came from the opposition, and some of them were the front-runners in their own regions, according to most opinion polls. These included Leopoldo López, candidate for mayor of the Metropolitan District of Caracas, and Enrique Mendoza, candidate for governor of Miranda state, among others.

The CNE obtained a supporting ruling from the Supreme Court of Justice and on this basis maintained the disqualifications. These disqualifications, used to reduce the possibilities of success for the opposition in some important governorships and mayoralties, amount to a clear act of political discrimination. That the CNE consented to them raises further questions about its impartiality. It also shows the political bias and weakness of the institutions called to guarantee the system of human rights in the country, such as the Supreme Court of Justice.

The existence of and compliance with laws that establish political rights have long been considered a part of the minimal procedural requisites of democracy (Dahl 1989b), as well as an indicator of the quality of democracy (Diamond and Morlino 2005; O'Donnell 2005), particularly when that indicator is analyzed in relation to the specific elements of the democratic political process, such as free and impartial elections (Levine and Molina 2007b: 25). That is the reason why the violation of the right of individuals to be candidates and to be elected by the disqualifications noted above constitutes a serious weakening of Venezuelan democracy.

The fourth issue involves requiring the competing sides to comply with the norms that help to create equilibrium in the use of political advertisement in the mass media. In democratic electoral processes, mechanisms of information are of critical importance both for those who stand as candidates and for voters. This is so for several reasons: first, because the right of candidates to communicate to the public their opinions and arguments is admitted, since this aspect is critical to their ability to compete and to achieve power and political positions; second, because this ensures the right to vote in an informed way, both from the point of view of a citizen's own interests and because of the consequences that would be derived from their voting decisions. Therefore, in a democracy, freedom of the press, multiple sources of information, the right to decide in an informed manner, and the right to air and disseminate ideas by the competing parties are all considered part and parcel of the institutional guaranties to have equal opportunities to formulate preferences, manifest them, and receive equal treatment from the government (Dahl 1989b: 14–15).

One of the decisions taken by the CNE was to regulate the amount of propaganda allowed for or against the two referenda under consideration. This was done in the name of ensuring equity in the ability of the competing parties to make their case to the public. Observation of the extent of compliance and enforcement of this regulation in the electoral campaign provides a direct way of measuring the disposition and effort of the CNE in the maintenance of the guarantee of equity about advertisements placed in the media. Compliance with this rule can be measured, and therefore we have chosen this as an indicator of the willingness of the CNE to enforce its rules regarding political propaganda.

We draw on the quantitative analysis of political advertisements by government and opposition in the media for the 2007 referendum carried out by the civil society watchdog group Súmate during the twenty-six days of the campaign. Súmate analyzed media advertising during one week of the campaign (January 26 to February 2, 2009).[9] These studies allow a comparison of the amount of propaganda in selected newspapers with the rules established by the CNE for such purposes: each party (the No supporters and Yes supporters) was allowed one-half page in newspapers of standard format and one page in tabloid-format newspapers; see Table 10.1.[10]

Table 10.1   Amount of Paid Ads in Selected Daily Newspapers (cm per column) for the 2007 and 2009 Referenda

	VEA[a]		Ultimas Noticias[a]		El Universal[b]		El Nacional[b]	
	2007	2009	2007	2009	2007	2009	2007	2009
Bloc Yes	6,008	4,113	6,404	4,193	6,968	3,640	5,720	416
Excess[c] Yes	1,952	3,021	2,348	3,101	1,560	2,184	312	0
Bloc No	4,056	0	4,485	156	4,964	0	6,534	0
Excess[c] No	—	—	429	—	—	—	1,126	—
Total published	10,064	7,134	10,889	7,450	11,932	5,824	12,254	416

Sources: Súmate 2008, 2009.

Notes: The analysis by Súmate for the 2007 referendum covers the twenty-six days of the formal electoral campaign; the analysis by Súmate for the 2009 referenda covers only the last week of the electoral campaign, specifically January 26 to February 2. The newspapers analyzed are published in Caracas, the Capital District, but have national circulation.

a. Page format is of tabloid type, measuring 26 cm per 6 columns, representing a total of 156 cm per column. The National Electoral Council (CNE) established the limit of one daily, tabloid-type page per newspaper for paid propaganda for each electoral option. Thus, for each week, the total of permitted propaganda was 1,092 cm per column.

b. Standard page format measures 52 cm per 8 columns, representing a total of 416 cm per column, thus one half-page is 208 cm per column. The CNE established a limit of one-half page daily per newspaper of standard type for paid propaganda for each electoral option. Thus, for one week the total area of allowed propaganda was 1,456 cm per column.

c. Indicates the amount of paid ad space in centimeters per column that exceeded the limits established by the CNE.

The data in Table 10.1 show that there was no compliance with the rules that the CNE had established about paid propaganda in the media. The CNE did not enforce its own rules to correct the lack of equilibrium in paid newspaper ads, and neither the media nor the competing parties complied with these rules.[11] The sector with the greater excess in paid newspaper propaganda, in relation to the CNE's standards, was the Yes sector (progovernment). Table 10.1 also shows that the No bloc spent less than the Yes bloc in both referenda, but particularly in 2009.[12]

The Yes bloc showed an excess over the allowed media space in its propaganda for the referendum of 2007 in both the progovernment press (*Vea* and *Ultimas Noticias*) and the pro-opposition media (*El Universal* and *El Nacional*), a situation that is repeated for the referendum of 2009, this time with the exception of *El Nacional*. It is important to point out that the excess of propaganda of the Yes bloc increases considerably for the referendum of 2009. The Yes bloc spent more money to buy publicity space than the No bloc. This demonstrates the persistence of a clear imbalance that the media rules promulgated by the CNE supposedly were to correct. Further, it shows a consistent and repeated lack of efficacy and willingness by the CNE in applying its rules and controlling propaganda inequality.

The CNE's inability and unwillingness to enforce its own regulations favored the government in the two referenda, and in this way limited both the rights of those who backed the No bloc to compete fairly and the right of the voters to be informed in a balanced way.

The fifth issue relates to vote counting and publication of the electoral results. Precise final figures for the results of the referendum of 2007 remain unknown: the CNE only published partial results.[13] The results posted at the web page of the CNE do not contain abstention figures or numbers of void votes, nor are the data discriminated by states. The CNE reports only provide the overall number and percentages of votes obtained by each option. Because of that deficiency in data, the results that are displayed in Table 10.2 are the ones offered by the president of the CNE during a press declaration as the final results, although

Table 10.2   Results for the Referendum for 2007 Constitutional Reform

Results for Block A:
Articles 11, 16, 18, 64, 67, 70, 87, 90, 98, 100, 103, 112, 113, 115, 136, 141, 152, 153, 156, 157, 158, 167, 168, 184, 185, 225, 230, 236, 251, 252, 272, 299, 300, 301, 302, 303, 305, 307, 318, 320, 321, 328, 329, 341, 342, 348

Option	Votes	Percentage
Yes	4,404,626	49.35
No	4,521,494	50.65
Total valid votes[a]	8,926,120	

Results for Block B:
Articles 21, 71, 72, 73, 74, 82, 109, 163, 164, 173, 176, 191, 264, 265, 266, 279, 289, 293, 295, 296, 337, 338, 339

Option	Votes	Percentage
Yes	4,360,014	48.99
No	4,539,707	51.01
Total valid votes[b]	8,899,721	

Source: CNE 2007, "CNE Proclaimed Definitive Results About the Constitutional Referendum," Caracas, July 12, 2007, http://www.cne.gov.ve/noticiaDetallada.php?id=4354.

Notes: a. There were 9,045,344 counted votes, but 199,155 were declared null. Also, 43.95 percent abstained.

b. There were 9,045,064 counted votes, but 145,239 were declared null. Also, 43.85 percent abstained.

in reality they are incomplete. Table 10.2 shows the data released for the 2007 referendum; Table 10.3 shows the data released for the 2009 referendum.

The informational subregistry that the CNE maintains in relation to the electoral data of the 2007 referendum contrasts with the rest of the electoral processes and referenda, for which definitive and complete data have been published. This continuing information gap for 2007 makes electoral analysis difficult, fuels the doubts about the credibility of the results, and appears as a bias and a lack of respect for the expression of popular will because it keeps the public from being informed as it should be about the results of the one and only nationwide election that the government has lost. The CNE has provided no explanation for the delay in the publication of the final results of the 2007 referendum.

The sixth and final issue discusses the attitude of tolerance between the government and the opposition. The way in which opponents treat each other during the electoral process is yet another indicator that may be included in the dimension of electoral decision and concerns. In a democratic society, if the actors are not antisystem and have accepted the rules of the democratic game, then the recognition of others as competitors and their respectful treatment as citizens are a requisite of tolerance and plurality that helps to reduce tensions among candidates and is preparation for the eventual alternation in power.

It is generally understood that there is tolerance in the treatment of opponents when actors in an electoral competition recognize and treat each other as legitimate competitors. This constitutes an element of democratic culture among the participating actors, which works out in favor of political stability, because it helps to settle differences and power conflicts in a peaceful way. An atmosphere of this nature backs up the conditions of freedom and equal treatment that Dahl considers a requirement for democratic competition (1989b). On the contrary, a relationship in which contenders are treated in dichotomous terms, as either friends or enemies (Schmitt 1984), leads to an authoritarian definition of the competition among the actors, because the goals are focused on the elimination and domination of the other, as well as on his/her nonrecognition as a subject, which corresponds with the ways of settling differences and conflicts in nondemocratic societies.

Table 10.3   Results for the 2009 Referendum

Option	Votes	Percentage
Yes	6,310,482	54.85
No	5,193,839	45.15
Total valid votes[a]	11,504,321	

Source: CNE 2009, Resolution No. 090116-0010, Caracas, January 16, 2009.
Note: a. There were 11,710,740 counted votes, but 206,419 were declared null. Also, 29.67 percent abstained, a total of 4,941,439.

The indicator we have chosen is more specific in relation to the electoral processes than assessments of tolerance in the overall culture of society, as proposed by Inglehart (2003) and Inglehart and Welzel (2005). We codify references made about the adversary in the main closing speeches of the electoral campaign about both referenda, which represent synthesized moments of the electoral process.

It is customary in Venezuelan electoral processes that the competing parties each stage massive rallies in the capital city, Caracas, as main events for closing their campaigns. In 2007 both the government and opposition blocs organized campaign closures of this kind in Caracas. But in the case of the 2009 referendum, the government prevented the opposition from holding its closing event in Caracas. The three applications submitted by the bloc for the No position for a permit for this activity were rejected by the mayoralty of Libertador municipality—Mayor Jorge Rodriguez, from the PSUV, backed up by the Ministry of the Interior and Justice.[14] Permits were only given to the bloc of the Yes position. Facing this impediment, the No bloc resorted to segmented campaign closures, with substitute activities—hikes, organization workdays, and press conferences—all carried out by political parties, groups of students, and civil organizations. The opposition was able to mount closing concentrations in other important cities, including Maracaibo, Barquisimeto, Mérida, and San Cristóbal. The Yes bloc staged its closing event in Caracas as well as additional cities of the country.

During the closing activities of the 2007 campaign, President Chávez depicted the opposition as an adversary to do away with, an ally of a foreign enemy power, according to which the arena of confrontation was a war among nations. The message was that friends would vote Yes for Chávez, and those voting No were enemies who supported Bush. That type of treatment visualizes an opponent as an enemy and traitor to the homeland. For the 2009 referendum, Chávez characterized the opposition as bourgeois, in contrast to his supporters: the people. He also regularly criminalized the opposition, referring to them as bandits and outlaws working against the institutions of the people. In both cases, Chávez denied the opposition the condition of actors that legitimately competed in a democratic process. They were his enemies, and the enemies of the people. Rhetoric of this kind, which frames the election in warlike terms, constitutes an obstacle to civility and democratic tolerance. This rhetoric can be seen in the following extracts for the 2007 and 2009 referenda by both Chávez and the opposition.

The following are statements made by Chávez at the main closure in Caracas on November 29, 2007:

> We are confronted with the imperialist's pawns. . . . Our true enemy is the United States empire. This Sunday we will give another knock out to Bush. . . . Let no one forget that this is, deep down, the content of this battle, a battle that has already been going on for 500 years. . . . Those who vote for the Yes, will be vot-

ing for Chávez, those who vote for the No, which will be the minority, will be voting against Chávez. Whoever votes for No will be voting for Bush. If the Yes option wins on Sunday . . . and the oligarchy and the piti-yanquis [small Yankees] here let loose violence . . . there will be 100 years of war in Venezuela.[15]

The next statements are from three speakers of the opposition at their closure in Caracas on November 30, 2007:

"You may stay until you respect the Constitution . . . Mr Comandante President, but lead as a democrat. If not, the people will meet you in the streets." —Jon Goicochea, student leader

"The country wanted the unification of all of us who are against the reform and we achieved it! . . . Does anyone here trust the CNE?"—Freddy Guevara, student leader

"The greatest mountain of votes on Venezuelan history is going to get moving . . . the only thing to fear is fear itself."—Manuel Rosales[16]

In the closing for the 2009 referendum on February 12, Chávez had this to say:

On Sunday you will decide my political destiny . . . whether Hugo Chávez leaves or does not leave . . . the chavistas (pro Chávez) go to vote for Chávez, to vote for the Yes. I will stand firm and obey whatever the people say. . . . There will be a new constitutional doctrine. It will be done as the people dictate, not according to what the bourgeoisie says. . . . Do not make a mistake . . . imagine what would happen if those bandits were to govern the country.[17]

The opposition, unable to meet in Caracas, as described above, held closings in various cities between February 9 and February 13. Here is what Julio Borges of the MPJ had to say at a press conference of the parties MPJ, UNT, MAS, and COPEI:

Vote with conscience [for a] leap towards the future; eradicate violence. Make Venezuela a country of peace. . . . Taking opportunistic advantage of the elections of 2012 . . . [Chávez hopes to imitate] Cuba, where people vote, but do not elect. . . . The role of the military of the Republican Plan . . . [is] not to mingle into the work of the members and presidents of the voting precincts boards. . . . [The] government must explain the use it will give to the money of all Venezuelans, for its own benefit.[18]

A press conference of student leaders continued in this way:

We have lived difficult weeks . . . against a government that has used in a very abusive way PDVSA's resources to impose its will over the voters. Mayor Jorge Rodríguez discriminated against us on the 20th and 23rd of January, 07,

10, 11 and 13 of February. . . . The only route that they may not deny us is the route of the No. We continue to act throughout the country.[19]

In a closing campaign rally in Maracaibo, Zulia's state governor, Pablo Pérez, spoke: "The vote is the tool to change Venezuela. We do not want a communist regime, nor to finish with Zulia's history . . . Here no one will know for whom did you vote, so you vote without fear. . . . We must defend the vote."[20]

In the opposition's closing meeting for the 2007 referendum, the speakers considered themselves a unified bloc of voters against the reform, and the adversary was referred to as the president, which would signal that they regarded their political adversaries as competitors in a democratic contest.[21]

Something similar occurred, but in a more tacit manner, with the opposition's closing speeches of 2009. Speakers stressed the need to turn out and vote and made direct comparisons with Cuba, portraying the government's project as the imposition of a model from a foreign country. In both instances of the opposition's closures, the frequent references to fear and to abuse of the public resources by the Yes bloc refer to the uneven treatment to which they have been subjected as enemies. It is evident that the perceived inequality and the treatment received as perceived enemies to be eliminated have taken their toll among the opposition leaders, producing distrust and fear in the face of official institutions. In the Yes bloc for both referenda, several aspects of democratic civility were infringed. The electoral dispute is depicted as a military battle, with the opposition as enemies to be defeated and done away with. This militarist conception detracts from the quality of Venezuelan democracy by promoting intolerance against political adversaries. The CNE did not intervene during the referenda campaigns of 2007 and 2009 to try to establish a democratic relationship between the competitors. It did not restrain the extreme verbal attacks the government side directed at the opposition. The rest of the public powers of the country did nothing in this respect either.

Accountability

In countries with institutional weakness, such as strong personal leadership; a weak party system; and limited independence among the public powers, including the electoral power, measuring the illegal use of public resources in an electoral campaign is difficult because the tendency is for the group in power to use public resources for its advantage in a surreptitious manner. Despite these difficulties, measurement of this phenomenon is useful as an indicator of democratic quality. Whether the government uses public resources to its advantage connects with the dimension of accountability that Levine and Molina put forward as one of the dimensions of quality of democracy, specifically regarding horizontal accountability: whether democratic checks and balances prevent or punish abuse of power and the guarantee of the rule of law (2007a: 31). We propose to examine the extent to which public resources were used in an even-handed manner by examining the amount of public television airtime that was given to the government position as opposed to the opposition in both referenda. The data come from research carried out by scholars from the University of Gothenburg in Sweden and the Andres Bello Catholic University in Venezuela, and performed during the electoral campaigns for the referenda of 2007 and 2009.[22] Their methodology consisted in establishing the political orientation of the news broadcasted by the selected public and private television and radio stations (in favor of Yes, in favor of No, or neutral). The results are detailed in Table 10.4 for television and Table 10.5 for radio.

Table 10.4   Distribution of TV Messages for and Against the 2007 and 2009 Constitutional Reforms (as a percentage)

TV Station	Message Orientation	Referendum 2007 (observed period November 19 to 25)	Referendum 2009 (observed period January 22 to February 4)
Globovisión[a]	In favor of Yes	14	7
	In favor of No	75	59
	Neutral	11	34
RCTV[a]	In favor of Yes	7	3
	In favor of No	84	91
	Neutral	9	5
Televen[a]	In favor of Yes	50	39
	In favor of No	35	39
	Neutral	15	21
Venevisión[a]	In favor of Yes	37	44
	In favor of No	50	49
	Neutral	13	8
TEVES[b]	In favor of Yes	90	100
	In favor of No	0	0
	Neutral	10	0
VTV[b]	In favor of Yes	90	93
	In favor of No	0	0
	Neutral	10	7
Canal i[a]	In favor of Yes	30	42
	In favor of No	50	37
	Neutral	20	21

Sources: Grupo de Monitoreo de Medios (Media Monitoring Group), University of Gothenburg (Sweden), and Catholic University Andrés Bello (Venezuela), 2007, http://200.2.14.175/ucabnuevo/Infocracia_CIC/recursos/gmm.pdf; Media Monitoring Group, University of Gothenburg (Sweden) and Catholic University Andrés Bello (Venezuela), 2009, "Television Channels," http://infocracia.info/blog/wp-content/uploads/2009/02/monitoreo-television.pdf.

Notes: a. Private TV channel. Globovisión does not have complete national coverage. RCTV had national coverage and was closed by a decision of the government at the beginning of 2007, converting it to a cable TV station, accessible only to those who pay for private access through cable or dish.

b. Public channel, financed by the state, with national coverage.

Table 10.5 Distribution of Radio Messages for and Against the 2007 and 2009 Constitutional Reform (as a percentage)

Radio Station	Message Orientation	Referendum 2007 (observed period November 19 to 25)	Referendum 2009 (observed period January 22 to February 4)
Radio	In favor of Yes	93	75
Nacional[a]	In favor of No	0	13
	Neutral	7	10
YVKE	In favor of Yes	71	73
Mundial[a]	In favor of No	2	2
	Neutral	27	25
Unión	In favor of Yes	39	24
Radio[b]	In favor of No	43	46
	Neutral	18	28
Radio	In favor of Yes	21	12
Caracas	In favor of No	76	74
Radio[b]	Neutral	3	14

Sources: Grupo de Monitoreo de Medios (Media Monitoring Group), University of Gothenburg (Sweden), and Catholic University Andrés Bello (Venezuela), 2007, http://200.2.14.175/ucabnuevo/Infocracia_CIC/recursos/gmm.pdf; Media Monitoring Group, University of Gothenburg (Sweden), and Catholic University Andrés Bello, 2009, "Radio Channels," http://infocracia.info/blog/wp-content/uploads/2009/02/monitoreo-radio.pdf.
Notes: a. Public radio broadcast, financed by the state, with national coverage.
b. Private radio broadcast.

The two public television channels, Venezolana de Televisión (VTV) and Televisora Venezolana Social (TEVES), and the two public radio stations, Radio Nacional and YVKE Mundial, showed a complete lack of equilibrium and allocated time in a way that distinctly favored the Yes option. Private radio stations and TV channels were also lacking in equilibrium and favored the No option, but they did broadcast information in favor of Yes in a greater proportion than that observed by the public media in the case of No. For both referenda, the main public television channel with nationwide coverage, VTV, and TEVES broadcast no information at all favoring the No option during the period under observation. The disproportion noted here has important implications. This is not only a matter of lack of equilibrium in the transmission of information, which includes also private media, according to Tables 10.5 and 10.6. It further reveals a disproportionate use of state resources for the promotion of one side in the debate, the progovernment option. It is in this last sense that this indicator provides us with a clear signal that horizontal accountability is not working in Venezuela when it comes to guarantees of equal access to public resources for both the government and the opposition.

Another aspect of abusive use of public resources in the country is represented by the profuse broadcast of presidential speeches during election periods. Here we emphasize the fact that the president's speeches are broadcast free, simultaneously, and compulsorily by all radio and television networks, in a process known in Spanish as *cadenas* (literally *chains*).[23] Table 10.6 provides data from an analysis of these presidential speeches done by Reporters Without Frontiers that show that the largest average of minutes per speech occurred during 2008, precisely when different organizations and political parties protested to the CNE against the illegal use of such broadcasts and of the public media by Chávez to promote his regional and local candidates.[24] Prior to 2007 the highest average of minutes per speech occurred in 2003, when Chávez faced a recall referendum—finally held in 2004—another moment of challenge for the regime when public resources were massively deployed in its favor.[25]

Although Chávez suspended his Sunday television program, *Aló Presidente (Hello President)*, on October 5, 2008—once the formal period of the regional campaign of that year was already quite advanced—he continued to use his advantageous position as president to campaign in favor of the candidates of his party, the PSUV. Their ability to win rested on his leadership, and his efforts to promote these candidates included frequent appearances in different states and cities, as well as a large number of public speeches. Well before the starting date of the campaign[26] (September 23, 2008), and throughout it, the president worked hard for PSUV candidates,[27] making an illegal and abusive use of public resources.[28] Among the expenses incurred were those for use of the presidential airplane, ground transportation, security, use of the state media, and as noted earlier, taking advantage of the presidential prerogative to require obligatory transmission of presidential broadcasts on public and private radio and television. The CNE did nothing to restrain or, in any way, to punish this blatant use of public resources by the president.

President Chávez's electoral campaign did not stop on the last formal day of campaigning for the regional elections of November 23, 2008. His political campaign continued unabated with the announcement of the constitutional ref-

Table 10.6   President Chávez's Obligatory National Broadcasts (2003–2008)

Year	Number of Chains	Duration (hours)	Average Minutes per Chain
2003	203	168	50
2004	375	124	20
2005	217	109	31
2006	182	92	31
2007	164	119	44
2008	154	190	92
Total	1,295	802	

Source: Reporters Without Frontiers (Reporteros sin Fronteras).

erendum for establishing indefinite reelection for the president. According to Súmate, from November 24, 2008, until February 13, 2009, which was the last day of the 2009 referendum campaign, the president made eighteen obligatory broadcasts, two *Hello President* programs on Sundays, fifty-four special programs, and four press conferences, for an estimated total of 246 hours of exposure on state TV channels (2009). This figure does not include many occasions in which those programs were of compulsory transmission through mandated obligatory national broadcasts in the rest of the country's private communications media.

The preceding analysis confirms the hegemonic and almost exclusive access by the Yes bloc to public television and radio media, financed by the state, which should have reflected the plurality of the country but were deployed to favor one side only.[29] The democratic political culture of the involved actors is clearly marginal. Those managing these public media—including the president—did not comply with the democratic precepts related to the equalitarian use of the media owned by the state. The CNE was weak in enforcing informative equilibrium, and the relevant state agencies did not do what was conducive to that goal.

Responsiveness

In the majority of the twelve electoral processes of different kinds carried out since 1999, the government has won. The results of such elections have been accepted by the contenders, although there have been criticisms about the lack of transparency and equity in some of them, particularly in relation to the presidential recall referendum of 2004.

In the 2007 vote for the constitutional reform, the opposition won with the option of the No, and Chávez was forced to accept the defeat after several hours of the results being known, both by the CNE and by his own party followers. Although Chávez accepted the results, he did so with harsh words against the opposition and resisted abandoning the issues of the reform.[30] The behavior of the government following its 2007 defeat has been to avoid complying with the popular will as expressed in the referendum, which shows a significant lack of responsiveness as well as a lack of respect for the 1999 Constitution still in place.

Despite having been rejected by the population, many provisions of the defeated 2007 constitutional reform were soon passed into law by the National Assembly. Governors and mayors elected from the opposition were stripped of many of their powers by a reform in the Decentralization Act, and a new centralist structure of power was put in place through the Federal Council of Government Organic Act (Ley Orgánica del Consejo Federal de Gobierno 2010).

State economic intervention and the Chávez brand of socialism for the twenty-first century have been entrenched in new legislation, also in spite of having been defeated in 2007 by popular vote. Among the legislation being discussed at the time of writing (2010) in the National Assembly, some clearly is an attack on private property, particularly business property, for example the project for the Reform of the Law of Regularization of Urban Settlements, which would not allow private property over terrain occupied by houses in the popular areas,[31] and the project for the Social Property Law, which pretends to incorporate social or collective property to stimulate social equality.[32] Both bills seek to enact into law provisions contained in the constitutional reform requested by the president in 2007, and defeated in the referendum.

Although the national government formally accepted the results of the regional and local elections of 2008, opposition governors and mayors have been subjected to harassment, and their resources and legal powers have been sharply curtailed. Manuel Rosales, elected mayor of Maracaibo, the second largest city of the country, was indicted for corruption in a judicial case that had already been discarded by the Attorney General's Office in 2004, and fled the country to exile in Peru. Antonio Ledezma, the mayor of the Capital District of Caracas and its suburbs, was stripped of most of his budget and powers. These powers were transferred to a new Sole Authority for the Capital District (Autoridad Unica del Distrito Capital) appointed by the president, and Mayor Ledezma has been subjected to constant threats and boycotts by the central government.

The Venezuelan case shows that formal recognition of electoral results is not sufficient to ensure a democratic result. The areas gained by the opposition must be respected, and those elected must be allowed to govern. The national government's noncompliance with the popular will, as expressed in the election of opposition mayors and governors, is not democratic behavior. It violates the principle of majority rule and infringes on democratic civility in relation to the acceptance of the achievements of the opponents. It negates the admission of democratic pluralism and the legitimacy of political differences. Clearly, there is no compliance with the mandate of the popular will. These authoritarian traits contribute to strengthening the thesis that defines the Venezuelan political system as electoral or competitive authoritarianism (Hidalgo 2009; Kornblith 2007).

Conclusions

The analysis of a range of indicators of quality of democracy in the electoral processes carried out from 2007 to 2009 in Venezuela produces discouraging results about the levels of the quality of democracy in the country. The elections of this period reveal a substantial weakening of the democratic character of the

Venezuelan political system. This judgment rests on the several points discussed below.

One of the essential requisites for an electoral competition to be truly democratic is an equitable balance in the conditions of participation of the contenders. The absence of such a balance during the electoral campaigns of the referenda of 2007 and 2009 and of the regional elections of 2008 is clearly visible in the difficulties the opposition experienced in standing as candidates with the issue of disqualifications, delivering their message to the people due to unequal media access, and being allowed to govern even when elected. These difficulties are particularly evident when compared to the progovernment side, which counted on the full resources of the state. The CNE showed a clear partiality toward progovernment sectors and a consistent unwillingness to maintain a democratic balance in the electoral contest.

Despite the results of the 2007 referendum, which rejected the constitutional reform put forward by Chávez and the National Assembly, the government operated in a consistent way to contradict the popular will expressed in the ballot box. Many of the rejected constitutional changes were implemented through ordinary legislation, and others by executive decree. This reveals a low level in one of the dimensions of quality of democracy: responsiveness. In the same way, restrictions on resources and removal of the power to govern experienced by opposition-elected governors and mayors also manifest a disrespect of the popular will, a case of lack of responsiveness, and a disregard for the minimal requirements for democracy.

A high level of democracy requires impartiality in the electoral process, respect for popular will as expressed in the ballot box, and tolerance and respect for the opposition. None of these conditions were fulfilled by Venezuela during the period under analysis.

In combination, the shortcomings of Venezuelan democracy reviewed here indicate the existence and development of important authoritarian traits, whose further persistence over time—were this to happen—would transform Venezuelan democracy into little more than a formal statement of intentions without roots in the actual political process, and would put in doubt the democratic character of the socialist project put forward by the Chávez government.

Notes

1. The National Assembly had chosen the five members of the board of directors of the CNE, still active for the referendum process of 2007, the year before, through mechanisms that on paper would guarantee their political independence. But the parliament, integrated exclusively by representatives of the progovernment sector as a result of the pullback on the part of the opposition at the elections of 2005, selected four progovernment members and one pro-opposition member.

2. One finger of the voter is dipped in this ink after voting, and the stain lasts for several days.

3. CNE, "Referendum for the Constitutional Reform," Caracas, 2007, http://www.cne.gov.ve/divulgacion_referendo_reforma/; CNE, "Resolution No. 071024-2826," Caracas, October 24, 2007.

4. The director of the CNE, Janeth Hernández, stated that the only thing that the electoral arbitrator could do with respect to the issues posed in the 2009 referendum was a technical review, because she could not do it for content due to a sentence of the Constitutional Chamber of the Supreme Court of Justice (No. 1,139 of July 5, 2002) that does not allow a different kind of consideration; see Venezolana de Televisión, Janeth Hernández: "CNE definirá este viernes fecha del referendo por la enmienda," Caracas, January 14, 2009, http://www.vtv.gov.ve/noticias-nacionales/13308.

5. CNE, "Referendum for the Constitutional Reform," Caracas, 2007, http://www.cne.gov.ve/divulgacion_referendo_reforma/.

6. CNE, "Referendum to Sanction the Constitutional Amendment 2009," http://www.cne.gov.ve/divulgacion_referendo_enmienda_2009/.

7. "Communal power" refers to the nationwide network of communal councils promoted by the government as the new way of organizing the people at community levels. These communal councils are linked directly to the presidency and are not formally integrated into municipal or state governments.

8. The modifications proposed by the National Assembly were more generic: no discrimination for any cause (article 21), the confirmation of the right to housing (article 82), and the need to adapt the legislation in municipal matters to the new geometry of power (article 173). They also included a change in the percentages of votes required for approval of the referenda (articles 71 to 74), along with procedural issues related to the appointment of judges for the Supreme Court of Justice, the National Electoral Council, and other offices. The most polemical proposals of this bloc were to establish a parity vote of employees, workers, students, and professors in the autonomous universities (article 109), and to expand the range of guarantees that could be suspended during states of exception, states of alert, and emergencies (articles 337 and 338).

9. There are no similar observations of newspapers for the regional elections of 2008.

10. See CNE, Resolution No. 071024-2826, Caracas, October 24, 2007; CNE, Resolution No. 090116-0010, Caracas, January 16, 2009.

11. In addition to the reports labeled by Súmate (2008, 2009) as "Camatagua," there are other studies of communication media about the Venezuelan electoral processes, including the referenda of 2007 and 2009, such as the media analysis done by the NGO Electoral Eye (Ojo Electoral) (2008) and the Media Monitoring Group (Grupo de Monitoreo de Medios) organized by the Catholic University Andrés Bello and the University of Gothenburg. Although these studies differ in the methodology employed, they also point to the lack of equilibrium in the propaganda among the media analyzed. See Ojo Electoral, "Informe final: Observación y Referendo sobre la Propuesta de Reforma Constitucional, December 2, 2007," http://www.ojoelectoral.org/admin/informes/Informe%20Final%202D%202007%20Anx.pdf; Grupo de Monitoreo de Medios (Media Monitoring Group), University of Gothenburg (Sweden) and Catholic University Andrés Bello (Venezuela), 2007, http://200.2.14.175/ucabnuevo/Infocracia_CIC/recursos/gmm.pdf; Media Monitoring Group, University of Gothenburg (Sweden) and Catholic University Andrés Bello (Venezuela), 2009, "Television Channels," http://infocracia.info/blog/wp-content/uploads/2009/02/monitoreo-television.pdf; Media Monitoring Group, University of Gothenburg (Sweden) and Catholic University Andrés Bello, 2009, "Radio Channels," http://infocracia.info/blog/wp-content/uploads/2009/02/monitoreo-radio.pdf.

12. Súmate's research for 2009 included in the sample eight regional newspapers, corresponding to the states of Lara, Zulia, Mérida, and Anzoátegui (two newspapers per state). The bloc for the Yes vote published its propaganda during the week under analysis in six of them, and exceeded the limits established by the CNE in two newspapers: *El Informador* of Lara state (an excess of 1,936 cm per column and *Panorama* of Zulia (excess of 7,184 cm per column). The bloc for the No vote was absent in the regional press that was analyzed by Súmate in the last week of the 2009 referendum campaign.

13. One week after the referenda took place, the president of CNE, Tibisay Lucena, declared that results from 2,000 more ballot boxes had not yet been included in the count—this represents about 200,000 voters, but she stated that "the irreversible tendency announced last Sunday, has maintained itself and these are the final results," see Consejo Nacional Electoral, "CNE proclaimed definitive results about the Constitutional Referendum," Caracas, July 12, 2007, http://www.cne.gov.ve/noticiaDetallada.php?id=4354. The results that might have stemmed from the count of these 200,000 votes remain unknown.

14. Partido Socialista Unido de Venezuela, the president's party.

15. Radio La Primerísima, "Marea roja invade Caracas, acuerpa a su líder y proclama Sí a la reforma socialista," Caracas, November 30, 2007, http://www.radiolaprimerisima.com/noticias/general/22341.

16. *El Universal,* "And we filled it up without busses," November 30, 2007, http://www.eluniversal.com /2007/11/30/pol_art y-la-llenamos-sin_619458.shtml.

17. Lugo-Galicia, Hernán, "Chávez confía en que sus seguidores no le fallarán," *El Nacional,* Caracas, February 13, 2009, p. 3; José G. Martínez, "El domingo ustedes deciden mi destino político," *La Verdad,* Maracaibo, February 13, 2009, p. A8.

18. Elvia Gómez, "No one may be indifferent facing the referendum of Sunday," *El Universal,* Caracas, February 10, 2009, pp. 1–2.

19. Gustavo A. Gil, "Government forbade the march that was going from Catia to Petare," *El nacional,* Caracas, February 12, 2009, sec. A2.

20. María Galbán, "Primero Justicia: To Vote and Participate Are the Keys," *La verdad,* Maracaibo, February 14, 2009, p. A5; María Galbán, "Pablo Pérez Affirms That the Vote Is the Instrument to Change Venezuela," *La verdad,* Maracaibo, February 13, 2009, p. A6.

21. In other moments, some opposition leaders have treated Chávez as part of the expansionist intention of Cuba or as a follower of Cuban socialism or of Fidel Castro's ideas. This demonstrates a consideration of the other as part of a foreign intervention against national sovereignty.

22. Grupo de Monitoreo de Medios (Media Monitoring Group), University of Gothenburg (Sweden) and Catholic University Andres Bello (Venezuela), 2007, http://200.2.14.175/ucabnuevo/Infocracia_CIC/recursos/gmm.pdf; "Television Channels," University of Gothenburg (Sweden) and Catholic University Andrés Bello (Venezuela), 2009, http://infocracia.info/blog/wp-content/uploads/2009/02/monitoreo-television.pdf.

23. In Venezuela the law provides for compulsory broadcasting of the presidential speeches by radio and television stations, as well as speeches by other high-ranking public officials, when so requested by the state for dealing with issues of national interest. These compulsory and universal broadcasts are called "chains." "Issues of national interest" have been interpreted in a very permissive way.

24. Reporters Without Frontiers (Reporteros sin Fronteras), "El referendo constitucional: Un paisaje mediático ensombrecido por la polarización y el exceso de alocuciones presidenciales," 2009, http://www.rsf.org/Referendum-constitucional-un.html.

25. Paragraphs from a letter sent by the NGO Active Citizenship (Ciudadanía Activa) to the CNE, dated August 27, 2008, concerning irregularities prior to the campaign

for regional elections that year: "As established in CNE's chronogram, the rules for this event should have been approved on the 28th of May and published before 19th June. Up to date, the regulation for advertisement and propaganda is unknown." (See María de Oteyza, ed., Letter to Rector Tibisay Lucena, President of the CNE, from Civil Association Active Citizenship, Caracas, August 28, 2008, www.ciudadaniaactiva.org.) "We ask ourselves if CNE did not notice the visit of President Chávez to Winche, of Petare, a few weeks ago, with the candidates of the Metropolitan Area, in a military vehicle with car plates GHP-029? It is difficult to believe that CNE did not get to know of his visit to Zulia State, last Saturday 23 of August, when the president cheekily said 'Although officially the electoral campaign has not been declared, it has started. That is why I came personally to attend the invitation that Di Martino made me. I come to ratify all my support to Juan Carlos Di Martino (and to the other pro-government candidates to mayors). All those who are with Chávez, have to vote for them.'"

26. The only independent CNE director, a nonsympathizer of the government, Vicente Diaz, stated the following to the media (Asociación Civil Queremos Elegir 2008, http://queremoselegir.org/presidente-utiliza-los-recursos-del-estado-a-favor-del-psuv/): "On Channel 8 they are permanently dedicated to promoting all the candidates running for the United Socialist Party of Venezuela (PSUV). We see how program directors at VTV direct those spaces, which are paid by all Venezuelans, with T-shirts and hats of the PSUV, which is prohibited by the Constitution. Additionally, the President of the Republic permanently uses the resources of the State and programs such as *Hello President*, to promote candidacies and a political party such as PSUV." He also stated that it is a responsibility of the electoral power and the general comptroller of the Republic to correct that irregularity. The other CNE directors attributed his declaration to a personal opinion, noninstitutional, and not belonging to the CNE.

27. Zulia was a state often visited by Chávez during the electoral campaign of 2008, where he was particularly active in the promotion of his candidates and harsh in his treatment of his opponents. In an official event in this state with businessmen from the region, transmitted by the media, Chávez said that the then-governor of the state and candidate for mayor of Maracaibo, the state capital, Manuel Rosales, leader of the main opposition party A New Time (Un Nuevo Tiempo; UNT), and his mafias, intended to kill him and he asked the Attorney General and the Supreme Court to put Rosales on trial and in prison, adding: "I am heading the operation and that operation is called Manuel Rosales you are going to prison." He also said, "You have as a governor, a mafia capo, but as of the 23rd of November you will have a patriot as governor, such as it is Giancarlo Di Martino, a real Zulian, who loves Zulia, is committed to Zulia, to morality, reason, truth, to Maracaibo, to La Chinita, to the aborigines, and to history." (See Heison Moreno, "Chávez: Estoy decidido a meter preso a Manuel Rosales," Press Web YVKE, ABN; Radio YVKE Mundial, October 25, 2008, http://www.radiomundial.com.ve/yvke/noticia.php?13890.) In spite of Chávez's efforts, Rosales won the race for mayor of Maracaibo. Soon after, he was indicted by the attorney general and fled to exile in Peru.

28. Starting on October 12, the electoral travels of the president led him to make twenty-four trips to fourteen states (five times to Zulia; three times to Carabobo; two times each to Sucre, Falcon, Nueva Esparta, Barinas, and Miranda; and once to Yaracuy, Guarico, Cojedes, Aragua, Bolívar, Táchira, and Anzoátegui). In his speeches in Zulia and Carabobo, he recognized that the fight was tough, saying that his candidates to the governorships were now level with those of the opposition. "This is a campaign for the rest of life, I am going to show up even in their soup . . . until I am dead then," he said on October 13 in Yaracuy. See Laura Helena Castillo, "2008 Campaign: Adán Chávez, Manuel Rosales and 'Mafioso' Were the Words Most Pronounced," *El nacional,* Caracas, November 17, 2008, p. A3.

29. The civil association Electoral Eye (Ojo Electoral) presented the following data, which reinforce what has been said about the bias of public communications media. Their methodology distinguishes between explicit messages (proselytizing propaganda) and implicit messages (which defend indirectly a certain option), and considers the rules outlined by the CNE for explicit televised propaganda (two noncumulative minutes, which added up to fourteen weekly minutes, by channel, for each option). They found that in the last week of the campaign, Venezolana de Television (VTV), a public channel, financed by the state and with national coverage, broadcast forty-two minutes of explicit messages favoring the Yes option, ten minutes favoring the No option, 500 minutes of implicit messages (nonregulated by CNE) favoring Yes, and none favoring No. That was the largest bias in favor of any option found by this study, which included the private communication media (2008).

30. Chavez's position about this defeat is well documented. For example, "It was a shitty victory and our defeat was a courageous one," said Chávez in a press conference surrounded by high military ranks (Libertad Digital [Digital Liberty], "Fue una victoria de mierda y la nuestra una victoria de coraje," 2007, http://www.libertaddigital.com/mundo/Chávez-fue-una-victoria-de-mierda-y-la-nuestra-una-derrota-de-coraje 1276318942/). Additionally, Chávez stated: "Not one comma of this proposal do I take back. I will continue bringing the proposal to the Venezuelan people. This proposal is alive, it is not dead. It could not be [done] as for now but I maintain it and will keep fighting for it" (María Lilibeth DaCorte, "Chávez Announces 'Second Offensive to Approve the Reform," *El universal*, June 12, 2007, http://www.eluniversal.com/2007/12/06/pol_art_Chávez-anuncia-segu_627973.shtml).

31. Asamblea Nacional, "Aprobada en primera discusion, reforma a Ley de Regularización de Asentamientos Urbanos," 2009, http://www.asambleanacional.gob.ve/index.php?option= com_content&task= view&id=21584&Itemid=27.

32. Asamblea Nacional, "Ley de propiedad social recoge los principios de democracia, solidaridad y justicia social," 2009, http://www.asambleanacional.gob.ve/index.php?option= com_content&task=view&id=21743&Itemid=27.

11

The Quality of Democracy: Strengths and Weaknesses in Latin America

Daniel H. Levine and José E. Molina

THIS CHAPTER DRAWS ON THE CASE STUDIES PREPARED FOR THIS volume to provide a closer look at the experience of democracy in eight countries: Argentina, Bolivia, Brazil, Chile, Colombia, Nicaragua, Mexico, and Venezuela. These cases range from countries whose democratic experience began only late in the last century—like Nicaragua, which celebrated its first competitive election in 1990, maintaining an unbroken string of democratic elections in an open social and democratic context since that time—to others like Chile, Brazil, and Argentina, with lengthy democratic trajectories marked by numerous breakdowns and restorations. Mexico provides a unique case of a civilian one-party authoritarian regime that has evolved without institutional rupture into a competitive democracy.

In an important group of our cases, the democracy was reconstructed in the wake of extended military rule, specifically in Argentina, Brazil, and Chile; and in Nicaragua, democracy was established in the aftermath of devastating civil war. Only three of the cases analyzed here show continuity of civil institutions. Mexico has moved progressively from a hegemonic one-party state to competitive democracy. Colombia has maintained institutional continuity in a context of severe and extended violence that has undermined the possibilities of holding officials accountable and of holding them to standards of responsiveness to popular will. Venezuela is now into the second decade of a revolutionary process that has diminished institutions, undercut the transparency of public processes and the accountability of leaders, while profoundly polarizing the country.

In this section we consider each of these cases in terms of our five core component dimensions of analysis and in order of their ranking on our index of quality of democracy. References in this chapter to the ranking of individual countries on each of the dimensions of quality of democracy or to the overall ranking of the quality of their democracy are based on the general index and evaluation outlined in exploratory form in Chapter 2. We close with a comparative overview and some judgments about the future of democracy in the region.

Chile

Since the transition to democracy in 1989, the Chilean political system has shown many signs of a rapid and successful recovery of democracy. The Concertación agreements among democratic political parties provided a necessary underpinning for democratic stability in the transition period. As Chile's democracy has survived and consolidated, there have been important areas of improvement, including the slow but steady transformation of civil-military relations and assertion of civilian authority, equally steady attention to curbing violations of human rights, and the reform of the Pinochet-era Constitution of 1980. With the constitutional reform of 2005, the quality of democracy has been considerably advanced, and Chile has resumed its place as one of the high-quality democracies of the region. In spite of these elements of progress, important problems remain, and some have grown since the restoration of democracy. These include decline in citizen confidence in political parties, growing public apathy and disinterest in politics, and a continued social deficit with bases in the country's very unequal distribution of income.

Ruiz argues that although substantial progress has been made in restoring democracy and reversing the institutional legacy of military rule, the level and quality of Chilean democracy could be much strengthened by a number of concrete reforms. The electoral decision dimension is a case in point. The index presented in Chapter 2 suggests that Chile's high ranking among the region's democracies rests above all on the strength of its electoral processes, which are clean and impartial, and on the solidity of its institutions, which provide an effective system of checks and balances on the exercise of power, through mechanisms of both horizontal and vertical accountability. Since the restoration of democracy, there have been eighteen elections at different levels (twenty if we include second-round voting), and conditions of voting have become much more free and fair since the 1988 referendum, which was conducted while the country was still under military rule. The electoral process has also been extended to many arenas, such as local government, that had been managed by appointment under military rule. But as Ruiz points out, the representativity of elections remains conditioned to laws from the military period. Moreover, many Chileans were exiled during the seventeen years of military rule, and have no access to suffrage.

There are also concerns with regard to the dimension of participation, above all the steady increase in electoral abstention in the face of a long tradition of high participation before the military period. Ruiz suggests that Chileans may be experiencing some degree of electoral fatigue and that reduced enthusiasm for and interest in politics may be a normal consequence of the return of democratic and competitive politics as more of an everyday occurence, no longer a cause to be fought for. A relatively low proportion of Chileans are registered to vote and the electoral system continues to favor minorities, in this case the parties of the right.

In terms of the responsiveness dimension, Chile looks better. The two overwhelming issues in Chilean society and politics since the end of military rule continue to be human rights and the status of the prevailing economic model. Both are clearly legacies of military rule, and considerable progress has been made on each front, although a notable social deficit remains. The social deficit is especially visible in areas of education, health care, and social security, issues that have all been front and center in national politics in the past decades. Ruiz underscores the need for further work on these issues, along with a loosening of the restrictive electoral system left in place by Pinochet.

Chile has made particularly notable strides since the return of democracy in the dimensions of accountability and sovereignty. In terms of accountability, Ruiz points to the restoration of an independent and respected judiciary and its capacity to deal with cases of official corruption and malfeasance along with lingering human rights concerns. She also underscores the renewed viability of other oversight institutions. Vertical accountability, which relies on electoral sanctions, is less strong given the very low volatility of votes across elections in Chile. This reflects the continued weight of the Concertación agreements and the fears that civilian division might open renewed doors for the military. Renewed and strengthened civilian control of the military is central to Chile's strong showing on the sovereignty dimension. This has been a slow but steady process and much remains to be done, including, as Ruiz points out, reforming the system of military justice, further limiting military power in states of emergency, and regaining control of the military budgets, which continue to benefit from a guaranteed share of income from national copper exports.

Argentina

Argentina's most recent transition from military rule to democracy has also been one of the strongest in many years. Democracy was reestablished in 1983 following the multiple disasters associated with military rule: the repression by the military and its vast abuses of rights, the Falklands war, and multiple problems associated with human rights abuses and failures of justice. Those who doubted the survivability of Argentine democracy had plenty of reason and long experience on their side. But to the surprise of many, as Jones and Micozzi describe, Argentine democracy has indeed survived and has managed to control the military—and, uniquely in Latin America, even tried and imprisoned leaders of the last military juntas; has restored justice; has recovered the historical memory of the victims of repression; and has survived a series of economic crises, including the catastrophic economic collapse of 2001, which included a month in which four presidents succeeded one another in short order. The explanation for this surprising durability lies in the reaction of citizens to the extremisms of the previous period, in the discrediting of the military, and in what Levitsky has termed the "organized disorganization" of the Peronist Party (Partido Justicialista), which has retained its ability to aggregate interests and construct coalitions around public policies despite persistent internal divisions (2005).

Argentina is located in the upper-middle rank of Latin American countries in terms of quality of democracy.[1] In the critical dimensions of electoral decision and participation, Argentina ranks among the highest in the region. High levels of education and respect for political rights have helped to strengthen the process of electoral choice, which has remained vibrant despite repeated economic crises and failures of leadership. Argentina also has a relatively high level of representativity. An important element here is that Argentina is first in the entire region in proportionality of gender representation, one of our indicators of the extent to which different sectors of the population participate in a proportional and fair measure through their legislative representatives; see Chapter 2, Table 2.3. The fact the Argentina ranks first on this measure is due to the adoption and rigorous implementation of gender quotas in the slates of candidates that parties present for elections to the national legislature. These obligatory quotas require that female candidates be mixed with male candidates in proportions required by the law—in Argentina this is 30 percent, a minimum of one woman for every two men in the list. This, combined with a system of proportional representation that works with closed and blocked lists (Jones 1998), has been effective in promoting the representation of women in the Congress. For this reason, countries that have adopted such measures, like Argentina and Costa Rica, occupy the highest rankings in the region in terms of the proportionality of gender representation, as can be seen in Chapter 2, Table 2.3.

Argentina's lowest ranking comes in the area of accountability. This ranking reflects continuing problems with its judicial system and with the viability of the formal mechanisms established to ensure accountability for institutions and public officials. Persistent citizen pressure via movements and protests has not been translated into effective institutions, and, in general terms, reported citizen participation in political organizations is on the low end of the regional scale.

Argentina's results on the sovereignty dimension are particularly noteworthy and reflect successful efforts to control a military institution that has played a central role in national politics for much of the last century. The discrediting of the military as a result of the dirty war and the fiasco of the Falkland Islands conflict were critical in this regard. The recent trial and conviction of high military officers, and the derogation of laws of "due obedience," which supported a defense of "only following orders" in cases of human rights abuses, are signs of this new level of civilian control. At the same time, Argentina's continuing fiscal and debt troubles pose ongoing problems for the nation's economic sovereignty.

Mexico

Mexico's transition from one-party hegemony to competitive democracy begins in the 1980s with the slow erosion of the electoral and institutional power of the Institutional Revolutionary Party (Partido Revolucionario Institucional; PRI). The transformation of the political system from one in which state and party were effectively fused into a competitive political system with competent and independent institutions had its first definitive expression with the victory of the National Action Party (Partido de Acción Nacional; PAN) in the elections of 2000, which marked the first time in national history in which an opposition party assumed power peacefully. Since that time, each national election and many regional and local elections have been increasingly competitive, with a notable reduction in the presence of one-party enclaves (Gibson 2005).

Mexico falls in the middle rank in Latin America in terms of the overall quality of democracy, along with Argentina, Panama, the Dominican Republic, and Brazil. The recent trajectory of Mexico's electoral institutions has done much to improve this ranking. The record of national elections and the role played by the institutions that manage and supervise elections have been one of the strengths of Mexican democracy in the first decade of the twenty-first century. Levels of electoral participation are relatively low, as are opportunities to vote and participation in political party and campaign activities. If progress in electoral processes is the signal strength of Mexican democracy, accountability is its weakness. As is the case with most of the countries in the region, Mexico's lowest ranking is on this dimension, a result that reflects historically low institutional control over the central government and the weakness of institutions intended to exercise control functions. As Fox notes, Mexico finds itself trapped in a "low accountability equilibrium" in which institutions like the police and judiciary remain unreformed, authoritarian practices persist in state society relations, and authoritarian subnational enclaves survive (2007).

Mexico ranks relatively high on the sovereignty dimension, a reflection of the strength of its economy and a long tradition of civilian control of the military. With respect to responsiveness, the degree to which the population believes that the government is or is not responsive to popular desires and needs, Mexico is once again located in the middle rank, reflecting a long-term accumulation of popular distrust in politics and politicians. As Holzner shows, this leads in some instances to apathy and withdrawal, phenomena exacerbated by many neoliberal reforms that have dismantled institutions and arenas that historically served many sectors of the population as access points to the political system.

Bolivia

Since the return of electoral democracy in 1982, Bolivia has made substantial progress consolidating this process. As in much of the region, an important part of the effort has centered on procedural aspects related to electoral and party politics at the national level. But Mendoza-Botelho demonstrates that a critical aspect of the progress that has been made in establishing, consolidating, and extending democracy in Bolivia and enhancing its quality lies at the grassroots level. Fifteen years into the implementation of decentralization, or Participación Popular, as it is widely known, have shown that despite its many limitations and drawbacks, this institutional reform not only has transformed the political system as a whole, but also has opened many spaces for political participation, civic activism, and the emergence of a new civic-minded local leadership. A new generation of leaders has emerged from hitherto unrepresented groups at the regional and local levels. This has fueled the creation of new movements and political parties, such as those that have swept Evo Morales to power. Once in power, Morales and his coalition have striven to extend and consolidate these aspects of the political system. The depth and extent of this process make contemporary Bolivian democracy a particularly important case for grasping the potential impact of institutional reforms in creating conditions for a different, and potentially higher-quality, kind of democratic political life.

Brazil

The index presented in Chapter 2 shows that the strengths of Brazil lie in the areas of participation, responsiveness, and electoral processes, although as Montero demonstrates, none of these areas is without its problems. Montero highlights important ways in which Brazilian experience demonstrates how the political aspects of democracy and the socioeconomic outcomes of democratic rule may not run in the same direction or even be part of the same process. He shows how deterioration in key aspects of democracy, such as the reduction of horizontal accountability due to corruption, can occur simultaneously with success in socioeconomic policies.

The dimension of electoral decision is one of Brazil's strong points, given a good level of respect for political rights, which have been gradually strengthened since the return of democracy in the mid-1980s. Montero notes that what studies of public opinion reveal as a coherence between votes and the interests of certain social sectors is possibly an effect of the fact that in terms of cognitive resources of the electorate, Brazil holds a privileged position compared to other countries of the region. Another strength of Brazilian democracy is the level of participation in politics by its citizens. This owes much to the country's federal structure and to other innovations that Montero describes, which in combination multiply the possibilities for participation.

Accountability stands out as a weakness: the most damaging elements in this area are corruption and the lack of judicial efficacy in controlling corruption. Brazil is also relatively weak in the area of societal accountability: despite the rich variety of organizations in civil society, participation in community activities reached only 14 percent of the population according to the 2005 Latinobarómetro survey (see Chapter 2).

Nicaragua

Democracy in Nicaragua arose out of a most unpromising history. Fixing a start date for Nicaraguan democracy is controversial. Did it begin with the Sandinista revolution that took power in 1979, overthrowing a long-lived family dictatorship and initiating a broad spectrum of democratizing elements, including the opening and empowering of the population, albeit in the context of a hegemonic party? Or should we mark the beginning of democracy in 1990, the date of the first competitive post-Somoza elections that opened an as yet unbroken string of competitive and, until recently, clean elections? Given our concern with procedural democracy, we have taken the second date, although we recognize the fundamental contribution of the Sandinista revolution to the construction of democracy, not only through its stimulus to popular participation and the opening of public spaces, but also through its important contributions to the spread of public education, which raised the capacity of ordinary people to make informed political judgments (Anderson and Dodd 2005).

In general terms, Nicaragua is located in the lower middle of our rankings of quality of democracy for the region. The most notable strengths of Nicaraguan democracy lie in its electoral processes, in participation (including electoral participation) and in the vigor of its civil society. Nicaragua's ranking on this dimension is reinforced by scores for cognitive resources, strengthened by decades of popular education following the revolution. The country also presents a relatively high level of representativity; Nicaragua's overall ranking is diminished by low levels on the dimension of accountability. Rankings on the dimension of sovereignty reflect the country's economic progress but also the continued weight of the Sandinista army in the political process.

There are significant difficulties with accountability. Martí i Puig shows that Nicaragua's problems of accountability are rooted in the malleability of norms, which undermines the efficacy of institutions and raises questions about their impartiality. The plasticity of norms permeates the entire institutional structure and has recently penetrated the electoral arena, as for example in the 2000 pact between Daniel Ortega and Arnoldo Alemán that changed the rules of the political game in ways that favored the principal parties, while reducing access to the electoral system. Martí i Puig writes that these changes "made the new Nicaraguan electoral law one of the most restrictive in Latin America." This raises troubling questions about the future of the electoral process and the institutions charged with overseeing elections.

Colombia

In many respects, the Colombian case provides a stark example of the rift between basic definitions of democracy, which often focus on contestation, and analysis that centers attention on the quality of democracy. Despite a record of periodic elections and the notable continuity of its formal democratic institutions, decades of intensive political violence and the pervasive influence of drug trafficking have undermined the quality of political processes in Colombia to the point that it is common now to consider that Colombia falls below the minimal levels required to qualify as a democratic country (Diamond, Hartlyn, and Linz 1999; Mainwaring, Brinks, and Pérez-Liñán 2007: 139). Our index also suggests that Colombia has a low-quality democracy. This low placement rests above all on Colombia's poor performance in terms of electoral decision and sovereignty.

Moreno shows in detail that democracy remains under siege in Colombia, as decades of what began as interparty violence have devolved into a semipermanent three-cornered struggle among armed groups on the left and right, drug traffickers, and the state. This continued struggle has undermined not only the sovereignty of political rulers, who struggle to control the territory of the nation, but also the quality of electoral decision, participation, and accountability. Despite this situation, it is important to note that societal mobilization in Colombia, while not high, still ranks fifth in the region in terms of societal accountability. As Moreno suggests, this societal mobilization has borne fruit already, for example in major constitutional reforms that opened up access and participation, in citizen movements for peace, and in the visible decay of the entrenched two-party system in favor of a more pluralist political setting.

Colombian democracy is above all electoral. There is regular and vigorous electoral competition, but this is not sufficient to raise the quality of Colombian democracy beyond a moderate ranking. Even electoral politics are badly hurt by the violence and intimidation of armed groups, in more than a few cases also by the repressive actions of state agents, as well as by the pervasive corruption that undermines efforts at accountability. Another factor that contributes to Colombia's low ranking on the dimension of electoral decision is that the country is very weak on press freedom, which is under constant pressure from the violence perpetrated by the guerrillas, by drug traffickers, and by the country's paramilitary organizations, who combine to hem in and intimidate the press. These same groups also exercise regular acts of intimidation in elections and on the actions of elected public officials throughout the country.

Accountability is an area in which almost all countries of the region score low—Uruguay and Chile being exceptions—so the fact that Colombians continue to press for accountability in the face of such notable obstacles is important. Regarding sovereignty, it should be taken into account that considerable sections of the country remain under the control of guerrillas and other forces and not under the effective control of the central government. The presence of these irregular forces and the fact of a military that often escapes civil control have created a situation in which it is clear that the greatest problems of Colombian democracy lie in the creation of effective sovereignty and in the difficulties that elected and legitimate officials face in the effort to govern the country (Murillo and Osorio 2007).

Venezuela

Venezuela has been widely recognized as a democracy since the ouster of the country's last military regime in early 1958. The advent of Hugo Chávez as president in 1998, and the subsequent processes of constitutional and political reform undertaken in the country, led many to hope for a renewal and deepening of the country's democracy. But there is considerable evidence of democratic decay in the Chávez years. Growing doubts about the freedom and impartiality of elections, along with the overwhelming dominance of the national executive over all other branches, have led many analysts to doubt the country's democratic credentials. Freedom House, in its 2009 report, no longer considers Venezuela an electoral democracy.[2] Further, Venezuela is classified as a semi-democracy by Mainwaring, Brinks, and Pérez-Liñán (2007); Smith (2005: 283); and Smith and Ziegler (2008). Schedler argues that Venezuela should be classified as an "electoral authoritarianism" rather than a democracy (2006).

Beginning with the recall referendum of 2004, growing doubts have been raised not only about the quality of Venezuelan democracy but about its democratic character as such (Hidalgo 2009). There is considerable governmental pressure intended to curb citizen dissent. Kornblith documents how the government elaborated a list of citizens who signed the petition to recall President Chávez and that these citizens were subjected to pressure to renounce their signatures (2005, 2007). Those who refused to do so were blacklisted from public employment and subjected to a range of other pressures. As Pereira and Pérez note, since that time, and particularly in the campaign surrounding the proposed constitutional reform of 2009, public employees have been the object of systematic pressure to vote and campaign in favor of the government (see also Jatar 2006; Pereira Almao and Pérez Baralt Chapter 10). Emblematic of this effort is the call by Rafael Ramírez, head of the state petroleum company, PDVSA, in a closed-circuit broadcast to employees during the presidential election of 2006, exhorting them to vote for Hugo Chávez because, according to him, PDVSA was "red red" (*roja rojita*). In the face of the scandal this remark caused, the president affirmed his support for this official, who has remained in his position as of 2010.

By 2005 Venezuela already displayed serious problems with respect to the freedom and impartiality of electoral processes and equally serious problems concerning freedom of the press. Given the controversy that surrounds this question, we have preferred to retain Venezuela in our list of democracies for 2005, but the data presented in Chapter 2 suggest strongly that even if Venezuela is still considered a democracy, it is a low-quality democracy and one in the throes of significant decay above all because of the deterioration in the quality and impartiality of electoral processes and of accountability. These elements of democratic decay have been exacerbated by the government's policy of disqualifying leading opposition candidates. During the regional elections of 2008, several candidates were leading in the polls at the time of their disqualification, which was on the grounds of alleged administrative irregularities. These disqualifications, which carried with them a loss of political rights, were carried out by the comptroller general of the Republic without any judicial sentence, although these are required by the Constitution and by the Inter-American Convention on Human Rights.

In terms of the impartiality of electoral processes, there has been a notable increase in the abusive use of public resources and mass media by the state to make its official campaign, as Pereira Almao and Pérez Baralt make clear (Chapter 10). This has involved not only state-run media, but also public buildings and publicly owned vehicles that display official propaganda. In the campaign surrounding the 2009 referendum, various PDVSA trucks paraded through Caracas painted with official propaganda. Independent media continue to exist in Venezuela and maintain an editorial position of opposition to the government. But these are coming under growing pressure, and the most important among them, the only one with national reach, Radio Caracas Television, was forced to close in May 2007 when the government refused to renew its concession. At the time of writing, Globovisión, another important media operation and news service, was also under intense governmental pressure.

As Pereira Almao and Pérez Baralt demonstrate, from 2005 to the time of writing, the situation has deteriorated. The opposition can still win elections, as was the case in the constitutional reform referendum of 2007, and in some regional elections in December 2008, including the mayoralties of Caracas and Maracaibo, the two largest cities in the country. But these events need to be taken with a grain of salt. The winner of the mayoralty of Maracaibo and the principal national opposition leader, Manuel Rosales, is now exiled in Peru, and the mayor of Caracas, Antonio Ledezma, was effectively stripped of all his powers and resources, which were transferred by a new act of the National Assembly to an official appointed by the president. So there are elections, but whether these elections are sufficient to make Venezuela a democracy becomes less clear with every passing day.

Comparative Dimensions and Issues for the Future

The recent period of democratization in Latin America has been more extensive and long-lasting than any in the history of the region (Smith 2005). The nations of the region have replaced military governments with civilian regimes, as in the case of Argentina, Brazil, Chile, and Uruguay; dislodged civilian authoritarian regimes in Mexico and Peru; opened the door to peaceful democratic political processes in Nicaragua, El Salvador, Guatemala, and Peru; and set in motion far-ranging initiatives to promote citizen participation in Bolivia. Even Paraguay, which for so long was dominated by a hegemonic party, has recently elected an opposition candidate as president. To say all this is not to see the world through rose-colored glasses, believing that everything that occurs is for the best in this best of all possible worlds, but rather to recognize the facts of transition and stabilization of democracies, facts that affirm the strong appeal and enduring power of democracy reinforced by new institutions and support from citizens and social movements.

The case studies collected in this book underscore—for the region as a whole and for each country—areas of democratic strength and weakness in very specific ways, and thus move the debate away from simple dichotomies—democracy or dictatorship, liberal or illiberal democracy—to a more nuanced understanding of the multidimensional character of democracy. Taken together, they also direct our attention beyond the simple attribution of democracy to a level of development or socioeconomic status of the population, leading us to consider variations in the quality of democracy once minimal thresholds have been surpassed. Finally, our analysis makes possible a clearer understanding of transformations within democracy or of decay without institutional rupture, such as seems to be the case in Venezuela.

Looking across the region as a whole, the most notable elements of democratic strength are to be found in the dimensions of electoral decision and sovereignty. Positive results on electoral decision are rooted in the very holding of free and impartial elections, the extension of public education, and the development of independent sources of information accessible to the public. Despite continuing economic problems and the ongoing weight of the external debt, relatively high levels on our dimension of sovereignty are sustained by the evidence of increasingly extensive and secure civilian control of the military. The most notable democratic deficit across the region is clearly on the dimension of accountability. Even in countries like Uruguay, Costa Rica, and Chile, which generally have high rankings, and which share the top spot in Freedom House's ranking in this area, the dimension of accountability remains a source of weakness.

Although it can be misleading to speak of average rankings in such a diverse region, it is nonetheless noteworthy that if we take the five dimensions of our index of quality of democracy measured on a scale running from 0 to 100, by far the lowest average score for the seventeen countries included in our index comes on the dimension of accountability, with a score of 28.6. The next lowest is participation, with a score of 48.5. Further, without exception in each country considered individually, the dimension with the lowest scores is precisely that of accountability; see Chapter 2, Table 2.7. Consideration of this result and the historical and qualitative analyses presented by the authors of the individual chapters in this volume strongly suggests that accountability is the dimension that presents the most serious problem for democracy in the region. For this reason, it is important to continue to insist on the need to reinforce institutions and practices that monitor and control the exercise of power. This may appear to be a trivial conclusion, but it is not.

In the face of the urgent need to consolidate democracy during the 1990s, much scholarship on Latin America, inspired by neo-institutional approaches to democracy, stressed the importance of enhancing levels of governability by adopting electoral systems that would increase the likelihood that presidents could count on a majority in both chambers of the national legislature (Mainwaring and Shugart 1997; Shugart and Carey 1992). Institutional design of this kind was intended to avoid the possibility of executive-legislative deadlock that might lead to a breakdown of democracy in countries with weak institutions and high levels of polarization, as occurred in Peru in the early years of the Fujimori presidency, leading to the self-generated coup of 1992.

The problem with efforts to reinforce governability by increasing the likelihood that the president has a legislative majority is that in the process of accomplishing this goal, they often weaken the ability of legislatures to exercise effective oversight and control of the executive. In a region like Latin America, where there is a well-established tradition of strong leaders and personalization of political power, institutional arrangements that enhance the likelihood of a one-party majority in favor of the president do much to undermine the possibilities of effective horizontal accountability. These considerations suggest that, as we indicated at the beginning of Chapter 1, given the general consensus that the current wave of democracy in Latin America is stronger and more durable than others, the time has arrived to think seriously about institutional arrangements that can empower and protect the autonomy of legislatures and judiciaries relative to the executive power of presidents. When consolidation is the priority, it makes sense that governability and the concern to ensure a strong presidency and to avoid deadlock should also be high on the agenda. But when priorities evolve beyond mere survival and improvement of the quality of democracy becomes a central goal, then it makes sense to shift the focus of analytical attention and practical action to efforts to reinforce accountability and to provide for greater autonomy for legislative and judicial powers, while at the same time creating means to enhance the possibility of citizen control through vertical and societal accountability. The indicators presented in Chapter 2, Table 2.4, make it clear that considerable room for improvement exists in all three areas of accountability: horizontal, vertical, and societal. Achieving this end should be a central concern for scholars and reformers in the future.

In general terms, the accountability deficit rests on a mix of institutional, attitudinal, and behavioral elements. With rare exceptions, the institutions formally charged with accountability and oversight, such as the judiciary, legislative commissions, and agencies like ombudsmen or public defenders, lack the power, resources, and backing needed to carry out their functions successfully. In most cases, national electoral agencies show the best results, although at the subnational level problems persist. A related theme, highlighted by Martí i Puig for Nicaragua, concerns frequent changes in the rules of the game that make it difficult for institutions or their agents to operate effectively or to establish any kind of tradition of institutional control. For these reasons, much of the weight of ensuring accountability falls on citizen campaigns and public pressure—societal accountability—whose effectiveness is reduced in many cases by deep and persisting social, economic, and ethnic inequalities. Other factors that weigh against the exacting of institutional accountability include the persistence of subnational authoritarian enclaves, reinforced by endemic violence, corruption, and official impunity in many regions that undercuts any kind of real access to justice and rights. The concept of a low-level equilibrium trap, which Holzner uses for Mexico, in which institutions like the police and judiciary remain unreformed, authoritarian practices continue to permeate state-society relations, and subnational enclaves persist, unfortunately applies equally well to numerous other cases.

The dimension of participation also presents generally low levels, which is surprising given the record of social movements and political participation during the decades leading up to the democratic transitions.[3] Many of the organizations of that period persist, but they are often fragmented and dispersed with weaker connections to political institutions than in the past. Low- or intermediate-level participation may reflect the demobilization and general decay of many movements following the return to political democracy. But at the same time it is important to remember that in hard economic times sustained participation requires energies and resources that may simply not be available given the exigencies of the daily struggle for personal and family survival.

The low average level of participation on our index, which is 48.5 for the region as a whole, can be attributed primarily to the weight of one of the elements of the index, which is reported citizen participation in parties and political campaigns. Ranked on a scale of 0 to 100, the average on this specific indicator of participation is only 6.3, and all countries—with the sole exception of the Dominican Republic—fall below 10; see Chapter 2, Table 2.2.[4]

Within the general analysis of participation, attention to issues of representativity provides an indication of the extent to which participation is open and is balanced among different sectors in accord with their presence in society as a whole. In this regard the situation in the region is positive. For political representation in general, mechanisms of proportional representation work to ensure that parties and those elected in their name have a legislative presence that accurately reflects electoral results. With respect to legislative representation by gender, there has been considerable effort throughout the region to promote the participation of women and to reduce the weight of historical and social forces that inhibit an active role for women in political leadership. The primary tool used to achieve these goals has been the application of gender quotas for lists of candidates. Of the seventeen democracies we have analyzed, eleven have established some kind of obligatory gender quota as part of their electoral legislation.[5] The effect has been positive, elevating the parliamentary presence of women in significant ways. This is particularly true in countries like Argentina and Costa Rica, where such quotas have more tradition and greater institutional backing. This effort to counter discrimination against women is also having evident effects on the presence of women as presidential candidates, and in the election of various Latin American women to the presidency of their country in recent years. These do not appear to be isolated cases. To the contrary, they are clear indications of a positive change in the quality of democracy. To be sure, much remains to be done, but these results are the product of a long-term cultural and institutional effort to counter discrimination on the basis of gender with evident success, at least within the political elite.

As we noted in Chapter 2, the available scholarly literature suggests that overlap is likely among the various dimensions of the quality of democracy. This should be no surprise, given the multiple points of contact among them in practice. A statistical analysis of the correlations among the dimensions outlined in Chapter 2 affirms that such overlap exists, but that the level of overlap is moderate at most. This means that we can affirm that the dimensions of quality of democracy can and should be considered independently of one another, although there are, to be sure, important connections among them. Although some correlations are negative, they are not statistically significant. Therefore, based on the data we present, it is not possible to affirm that improvement in any one dimension implies deterioration in another. We believe it is highly encouraging that the correlation among our dimensions suggests that efforts to improve quality in one dimension neither imply nor require deterioration in others. To the contrary, it is probable that improvement in any one area contributes to raise the level of the others.

The pattern of strengths and weaknesses that we have found suggests a number of important themes for the future, areas in which the nations of Latin America could reinforce their democracies, and themes on which future studies could fruitfully concentrate attention. Among these are investment in reinforcing institutions and mechanisms of control and accountability, including the creation and reinforcement of an independent judiciary; movement toward eliminating the all-too-common impunity of police and armed services (and eliminating the special legal regimes that guarantee such impunity in some cases); and reinforcing freedom of information and of the press, along with freedom of assembly, that together constitute the basis of a free and open public space in which demands for accountability can be presented and public pressure mobilized.

One issue that does not appear directly in our index but which has had a visible impact in more than a few cases concerns violence. The persistent presence of violence—whether from armed insurrectionary movements, drug traffickers, or ordinary criminality—has a debilitating effect on the capacity of citizens to participate freely in social and political life. Although the worst periods of civil war and naked political repression are happily in the past, many Latin American countries remain plagued by extensive violence, a violence with debilitating impact on institutions and political life that is exacerbated by the impunity of police and security officials (Fuentes 2006), and by continued high levels of corruption tied to this impunity. Violence can never be fully eliminated, but measures to curtail its worst excesses would do a lot to improve the quality of ordinary life and, in this way, enhance the ability of ordinary citizens to participate fully in civil society and politics.

The region's demonstrated strength in electoral decision and sovereignty, particularly relative to control over the military, offers a promising base for the future and can be reinforced to the extent that free and fair elections are maintained and extended to all levels of the political system. Strengthening of decentralization—unfortunately now being reversed in cases like Venezuela—along with concrete measures to reduce the barriers to organization and extend the limits of effective citizenship, would also strengthen the possibilities for control and accountability.

Any agenda for future scholarship that arises from the studies collected in this volume would benefit from centering attention on the elements of strength and weakness to which we have pointed. We need to develop measures of accountability that are more sensitive and varied. The cases gathered in this volume make it clear that not all forms of participation are equal: some are more costly and therefore less available to ordinary citizens, while others may be more effective. Because not all types of participation are equal, future studies should concentrate on developing concepts and indicators that discriminate among kinds of participation.

Analysis of these dimensions will contribute to improving the quality of democracy and acquiring a more complete and dynamic understanding of its most problematic points. Particular democratic regimes may succeed or fail, but the central point is if—and how—the grounds for democracy are strengthened. If there are setbacks or erosion of key elements of democracy, can democrats do a better job the next time? Can they create higher-quality electoral processes that will prove more viable in the face of difficulties? The analysis and case studies presented here give us grounds for hope and point clearly to areas where future work will reap rewards.

Notes

1. See Chapter 2 for Argentina's placement in the indices by Freedom House, Polity IV, and our own.

2. The 2009 Freedom House report analyzes data from 2008. See Freedom House, "Freedom in the World 2009: Global Data," 2009, http://www.freedomhouse.org/uploads/fiw09/FIW09_Tables&GraphsForWeb.pdf.

3. The average for the seventeen countries is the second lowest (48.5), just ahead of accountability.

4. In this case, the number shows the percentage of respondents from the Latinobarómetro survey of 2005 who stated that they worked often or very often for a candidate or political party. One can wonder whether it is this specific indicator that produces the appearance of scant participation in politics, especially if it is compared with the other components of our dimension of participation. But if we compare this result with a similar indicator, such as the question we use to measure participation in mechanisms of societal accountability—how frequently the individual engages in work on community issues—we find the results are similarly low (19.3 percent as average). This suggests that in general, citizen participation in activities linked to politics is effectively low, and our indicator reflects the situation accurately.

5. The situation in each country can be seen in the information presented by the Quota Project of IDEA International, which is a global database on election quotas for women, http://www.quotaproject.org/index.cfm.

Bibliography

Abente, Diego. 2007. "The Quality of Democracy in Small South American Countries: the Case of Paraguay." Working Paper 343. Kellogg Institute, University of Notre Dame.

Abers, Rebecca Neaera. 2000. *Inventing Local Democracy: Grassroots Politics in Brazil.* Boulder, CO: Lynne Rienner.

Adler Lomnitz, Larissa, Claudio Lomnitz Adler, and Ilya Adler. 1993. "The Function of the Form: Power Play and Ritual in the 1988 Mexican Presidential Campaign." Pp. 357–402 in Daniel H. Levine, ed. *Constructing Culture and Power in Latin America.* Ann Arbor: University of Michigan Press.

Agüero, Felipe. 2006a. "Democratización y militares: Breve balance de diecisiete años desde la transición." Pp. 313–336 in Manuel Alcántara and Leticia Ruiz, eds. *Chile: Política y modernización democrática.* Barcelona: Ediciones Bellaterra.

——. 2006b. "Democracia gobierno y militares desde el cambio de siglo: Avances hacia la normalidad democratica." Pp. 49–68 in R. Funk, ed. *El gobierno de Ricardo Lagos: La nueva via chilena hacia el socialismo.* Santiago de Chile: Universidad Diego Portales.

Ahnen, Ronald. 2007. "The Politics of Police Violence in Democratic Brazil." *Latin American Politics and Society* 49 (1) (Spring): 141–164.

Albó, Xavier. 1997. "Alcaldes y concejales campesinos/indígenas: La lógica tras las cifras." Pp. 7–26 in *Indígenas en el poder local.* La Paz, Bolivia: S.N.P.P. (Secretaria Nacional de Participación Popular).

——. 1999. *Quotas en el poder local: Cuatro años después.* Cuadernos de Investigación 53. La Paz, Bolivia: Centro de Investigación y Promoción del Campesinado, PADER (Proyecto de Promoción al Desarrollo Económico Rural).

Albó, Xavier, and Franz Barrios. 2006. *El estado del estado en Bolivia: Informe nacional sobre desarrollo humano 2006.* Documento de Trabajo Enero 2006. Bolivia: Programa de las Naciones Unidas para el Desarrollo (PNUD).

Albó, Xavier, Tituyla Libermann, Armando Godinez, and Francisco Pifarre. 1990. *Para comprender las culturas rurales en Bolivia.* La Paz, Bolivia: Ministerio de Educación y Cultura, MEC-CIPCA-UNICEF.

Almeida, Alberto Carlos. 2001. "Ideologia e comportamento eleitoral: Evidências de que a ideologia não e importante para explicar o voto." Paper presented at the 15th

Annual Meeting of National Association of Post-Graduate Research in the Social Sciences (Associação Nacional de Pós-Graduação e Pesquisa em Ciências Sociais, ANPOCS), Caxambu.

———. 2006. *Por que Lula? O contexto e as estratégias políticas que explicam a eleição e a crise.* Rio de Janeiro: Editora Record.

———. 2008. *A cabeça do eleitor.* Rio de Janeiro: Editora Record.

Almond, Gabriel, and Sidney Verba. 1963. *The Civic Culture: Political Attitudes and Democracy in Five Nations.* Princeton: Princeton University Press.

Altman, David, and Aníbal Pérez-Liñán. 2002. "Assessing the Quality of Democracy: Freedom, Competitiveness and Participation in Eighteen Latin American Countries." *Democratization* 9 (2): 85–100.

Altman, David, and Rickard Lalander. 2003. "Bolivia's Popular Participation Law: An Undemocratic Democratisation Process?" In A. E. Hadenius and Elanders Gotab, eds. *Decentralisation and Democratic Governance: Experiences from India, Bolivia and South Africa.* Stockholm: Expert Group on Development Issues (EGDI), Swedish Ministry for Foreign Affairs.

Alvarez, Angel. 2009. "El consejo supremo electoral y los dilemas de la competencia electoral en Venezuela." *América Latina hoy* 51 (April): 61–76.

Alvarez, Sonia. 1993. "'Deepening' Democracy: Popular Movement Networks, Constitutional Reform, and Radical Urban Regimes in Contemporary Brazil." Pp. 191–222 in Robert Fisher and Joseph Kling, eds. *Mobilizing the Community: Local Politics in the Era of the Global City.* London: Sage.

Ames, Barry. 2001. *The Deadlock of Democracy in Brazil: Interests, Identities, and Institutions in Comparative Perspective.* Ann Arbor: University of Michigan Press.

———. 2002. "Party Discipline in the Chamber of Deputies." Pp. 185–221 in Scott Morgenstern and Benito Nacif, eds. *Legislative Politics in Latin America.* New York: Cambridge University Press.

Ames, Barry, Andy Baker, and Lucio Rennó. 2008a. "Split-ticket Voting as the Rule: Voters and Permanent Divided Government in Brazil." *Electoral Studies* 30: 1–13.

———. 2008b. "The Quality of Elections in Brazil: Policy, Performance, Pageantry, or Pork?" Pp. 107–136 in Peter R. Kingstone and Timothy J. Power, eds. *Democratic Brazil Revisited.* Pittsburgh: University of Pittsburgh Press.

Amorim Neto, Octavio. 2002. "Presidential Cabinets, Electoral Cycles, and Coalition Discipline in Brazil." Pp. 48–78 in Scott Morgenstern and Benito Nacif, eds. *Legislative Politics in Latin America.* New York: Cambridge University Press.

———. 2006. *Presidencialismo e governabilidade nas Américas.* Rio de Janeiro: FGV.

Amorim Neto, Octavio, Gary W. Cox, and Mathew D. McCubbins. 2003. "Agenda Power in Brazil's *Câmara dos Deputados,* 1989–1998." *World Politics* 55: 550–578.

Anderson, Leslie E., and Lawrence C. Dodd. 2005. *Learning Democracy: Citizen Engagement and Electoral Choice in Nicaragua 1990–2001.* Chicago: University of Chicago Press.

Andersson, Vibeke. 1999. *Popular Participation in Bolivia: Does the Law "Participación Popular" Secure Participation of the Rural Bolivian Population?* CDR Working Paper 99.6. Copenhagen: Centre for Development Research.

Andreev, Svetlozar. 2008. "Corruption, Legitimacy and the Quality of Democracy in Central and Eastern Europe and Latin America." *Review of Sociology* 14 (2): 93–115.

Angell, Alan. 2006. "Hechos o percepciones ciudadanas? Una paradoja en la evaluación de la democracia chilena." Pp. 165–198 in Manuel Alcantara and Leticia Ruiz, eds. *Chile: Política y modernización democrática.* Barcelona: Ediciones Bellaterra.

Arantes, Rogério B. 1999. "Direito e política: O Ministério Público e a defesa dos direitos coletivos." *Revista brasileira de ciências sociais* 14 (39) (February): 83–102.
———. 2003. "The Brazilian Ministério Público and Political Corruption in Brazil." Working Paper No. CBS-50-03. Centre for Brazilian Studies, University of Oxford.
———. 2005. "Constitutionalism, the Expansion of Justice and the Judicialization of Politics in Brazil." In Rachel Sieder, Line Schjolden, and Alan Angell, eds. *The Judicialization of Politics in Latin America*. New York: Palgrave Macmillan.
Araújo, Clara, and José Eustáquio Diniz Alves. 2007. "Impactos de indicadores sociais e do sistema eleitoral sobre as chances das mulheres nas eleições e suas interações com as cotas." *Dados: Revista de ciências sociais* 50 (3): 535–577.
Araya M., Eduardo, and Diego T. Barria. 2009. "E-participación en el senado chileno: Aplicaciones deliberativas." *Convergencia* 51 (Septiembre–Diciembre): 239–268.
Arzt, Sigrid. 2007. "The Militarization of the Procuraduría General de la República: Risks for Mexican Democracy." Pp. 153–174 in Wayne A. Cornelius and D. Shirk, eds. *Reforming the Administration of Justice in Mexico*. Notre Dame: University of Notre Dame Press.
Avritzer, Leonardo. 2002. *Democracy and the Public Space in Latin America*. Princeton: Princeton University Press.
Ayo, Diego. 1999. *Los desafíos de la participación popular*. La Paz: Centro Boliviano de Estudios Multidisciplinarios.
———. 2001. *El control social en Bolivia: Una reflexión sobre el Comité de Vigilancia, el Mecanismo de Control Social y demás formas de control social*. Santa Cruz: GNTP, LogoLink.
———. 2004. Descentralización y Participación No. 7. La Paz, Bolivia: Fundación Friederich Ebert e Instituto Latinomericano de Investigaciones Sociales (ILDIS). Plural Editores.
Baiocchi, Gianpaolo. 2005. *Militants and Citizens: The Politics of Participatory Democracy in Porto Alegre*. Stanford: Stanford University Press.
Baker, Andy, Barry Ames, and Lucio R. Rennó. 2006. "Social Context and Campaign Volatility in New Democracies: Networks and Neighborhoods in Brazil's 2002 Elections." *American Journal of Political Science* 50 (2) (April): 382–399.
Barbery Anaya, R. 2006. *Participación popular, descentralización y autonomías departamentales en Bolivia*. La Paz, Bolivia: Plural Editores.
Bazoberry Chali, Oscar. 2005. "Descentralización y participación ciudadana: El caso de Bolivia." *Documento de trabajo*. La Paz, Bolivia: Centro de Promocion del Campesinado (CIPCA).
Beer, Caroline C. 2003. *Electoral Competition and Institutional Change in Mexico*. Notre Dame: University of Notre Dame Press.
Beetham, David. 2004. "The Quality of Democracy: Freedom as the Foundation." *Journal of Democracy* 15 (4): 61–75.
Behrendt, Adam, ed. 2002. *Participatory Assessment of Key Issues for Bolivia's Decentralisation*. Santa Cruz, Bolivia: Grupo Nacional de Trabajo en la Participación (GNT-P) and Swedish International Development Cooperation Agency (SIDA).
Beltrán, Ulises, et al. 2006. *Estudio Comparativo de los Sistemas Electorales* (CSES). Mexico: Banco de Información para la Investiación Aplicada en Ciencias Sociales; Centro de Investigación y Docencia Económicas, http://hdl.handle.net/10089/3715.
Berg-Schlosser, Dirk. 2004. "The Quality of Democracies in Europe as Measured by Current Indicators of Democratization and Good Governance." *Journal of Communist Studies and Transition Politics* 20 (1): 28–55.

Berquist, Charles. 2001. "Waging War and Negotiating Peace: The Contemporary Crisis in Historical Perspective." Pp. 195–221 in Charles Berquist, Ricardo Peñaranda, and Gonzalo Sánchez G. eds. *Violence in Colombia 1990–2000: Waging War and Negotiating Peace.* Wilmington, DE: Scholarly Resources.

Berquist, Charles, Ricardo Peñaranda, and Gonzalo Sánchez. 2001, eds. *Violence in Colombia: Waging War and Negotiating Peace.* Wilmington, DE: Scholarly Resources.

Blais, André, and Agnieszka Dobrzynska. 1998. "Turnout in Electoral Democracies." *European Journal of Political Research* 33: 239–261.

Blanes, José. 1998. *La Paz, juntas vecinales y Comité de Vigilancia: Resumen ejecutivo.* La Paz, Bolivia: Centro Boliviano de Estudios Multidisciplinarios (CEBEM).

Bobbio, Norberto. 1995. *Derecha e izquierda: Razones y significaciones de una distinción política.* Madrid: Santillana S.A. Taurus.

Boeninger Commission. 2006. "Chile, Chamber of Deputies." *Boeninger Commission Report.* Santiago, Chile: Congreso de la República.

Bohrt Irahola, Carlos. 2001. *La decentralización del estado boliviano: Evaluación y perspectivas.* La Paz, Bolivia: Fondo Editorial de los Diputados.

Booth, David, S. Clisby, and C. Widmark. 1997. *Popular Participation: Democratising the State in Rural Bolivia.* Stockholm: Stockholm University.

Botero, Felipe. 2006. "Reforma política, personalismo, y sistema de partidos." In Gary Hoskin and Miguel García Sánchez, eds. *La reforma política de 2003: La salvación de los partidos políticos?* Bogotá, Colombia: Universidad de los Andes.

Bruhn, Kathleen. 1999. "The Resurrection of the Mexican Left in the 1997 Elections." In Jorge Domínguez and Alejandro Poiré, eds. *Toward Mexico's Democratization: Parties, Campaigns, Elections and Public Opinion.* New York: Routledge.

Cabrero Mendoza, Enrique. 1998. *Las políticas descentralizadoras en México, 1983–1993: Logros y desencantos.* México City: CIDE (Centro de Investigacion y Docencia Economica) Miguel Angel Porrúa.

Calvancanti, Rosangela Batista. 2006. "The Effectiveness of Law: Civil Society and the Public Prosecution in Brazil." Pp. 34–54 in Enrique Peruzzotti and Catalina Smulovitz, eds. *Enforcing the Rule of Law: Social Accountability in the New Latin American Democracies.* Pittsburgh: University of Pittsburgh Press.

Calvo, Ernesto, and Juan Manuel Abal Medina, eds. 2001. *El federalismo electoral argentino.* Buenos Aires: INAP/Eudeba.

Calvo, Ernesto, and Marcelo Escolar. 2005. *La nueva política de partidos en la Argentina: Crisis política, realineamientos partidarios y reforma electoral.* Buenos Aires: Prometeo.

Calvo, Ernesto, and Juan P. Micozzi. 2005. "The Governor's Backyard: A Seat-Vote Model of Electoral Reform for Subnational Multiparty Races." *The Journal of Politics* 67: 1050–1074.

Camp, Roderic Ai. 2004. "Mexico's Armed Forces: Marching to a Democratic Tune?" In Kevin J. Middlebrook, ed. *Dilemmas of Political Change in Mexico.* London: Institute of Latin American Studies.

———. 2007. *Politics in Mexico: The Democratic Consolidation,* 5th ed. New York: Oxford University Press.

Campbell, Andrea Louise. 2003. *How Policies Make Citizens.* Princeton, NJ: Princeton University Press.

Carraro, André, Ari Francisco Araújo, Otávio Menezes Damé, Leonardo Monteiro Monasterio, and Cláudio Djissey Shikida. 2007. "É a economia, companheiro! Uma análise empírica da reeleição de Lula com base em dados municipais." Working Paper No. 41. Brazilian Institute of Firms and Capital Markets (Instituto Brasileiro de Empresas e Mercados de Capitais, Ibemec).

Carreirão, Yan de Souza. 2002. "Identificação ideológica e voto para presidente." *Opinião pública* 8 (8): 54–79.

―――. 2007a. "Identificação ideológica, partidos e voto na eleição presidencial de 2006." *Opinião pública* 13 (2) (November): 307–339.

―――. 2007b. "Relevant Factors for the Voting Decision in the 2002 Presidential Election: An Analysis of the ESEB (Brazilian Electoral Study) Data." *Brazilian Political Science Review* 1 (1): 70–101.

―――. 2007c. "A Eleição Presidencial Brasileira de 2006: Uma Análise Preliminar." *Política e Sociedade* 10 (April): 91–116.

Carreirão, Yan de Souza, and Maria D'Alva Kinzo. 2004. "Partidos políticos, preferência partidária e decisão eleitoral no Brasil (1989–2002)." *Dados: Revista de ciências sociais* 47 (1): 131–167.

Casteñeda, Jorge. 1994. *Utopia Unarmed: The Latin American Left After the Cold War.* New York: Vintage Books.

Casteñeda, Jorge, and Marco A. Morales. 2008. "Progress, but to What End? 2007 Electoral Reform in Mexico." *Harvard International Review* 30 (1): 44–48.

Cea Egaña, José L. 2002. "Integración del senado y método electoral. *Ius y Praxis* 8 (1): 511–517.

CIDE (Centro de Investigación y Docencia Económicas). 2000. "Estudio Comparativo de los Sistemas Electorales (CSES)." Mexico, DF: Banco de Información para la Investigación Aplicada en Ciencias Sociales. Centro de Investiación y Docencia Económicas. http://hdl.handle.net/10089/3550.

―――. 2003. "Estudio Comparativo de los Sistemas Electorales (CSES)." Mexico, DF: Banco de Información para la Investigación Aplicada en Ciencias Sociales. Centro de Investigacion y Docencia Económicas. http://hdl.handle.net/10089/3687.

Close, David. 1988. *Nicaragua: Politics, Economics and Society.* London: Pinter.

―――. 1999. *Nicaragua: The Chamorro Years.* Boulder, CO: Lynne Rienner.

Close, David, and Kalowatie Deonandan, eds. 2004. *Undoing Democracy: The Politics of Electoral Caudillismo.* New York: Lexington Books.

Close, David, and Salvador Martí i Puig, eds. 2009. *Nicaragua y el FSLN, 1979–2009. ¿Qué queda de la revolución?* Barcelona: Edicions Bellaterra.

Conaghan, Catherine. 2005. *Fujimori's Peru: Deception in the Public Sphere.* Pittsburgh: University of Pittsburgh Press.

Coppedge, Michael, Angel Alvarez, and Claudia Maldonado. 2008. "Two Persistent Dimensions of Democracy: Contestation and Inclusiveness." *The Journal of Politics* 70: 632–647.

Córdova, Arnaldo. 1972. *La formación del poder político en México: Colección problemas de México.* Mexico City: Ediciones Era.

Cornelius, Wayne A., Todd A. Eisenstadt, and Jane Hindley, eds. 1999. *Subnational Politics and Democratization in Mexico.* La Jolla, CA: Center for U.S.-Mexican Studies, University of California–San Diego.

Cornelius, Wayne A., and David Shirk, eds. 2007. *Reforming the Administration of Justice in Mexico.* Notre Dame: University of Notre Dame Press.

Cox, Gary W., and Matthew S. Shugart. 1995. "In the Absence of Vote Pooling: Nomination and Allocation Errors in Colombia." *Electoral Studies* 14 (4): 441–460.

Craig, Ann L., and Wayne A. Cornelius. 1980. "Political Culture in Mexico: Continuities and Revisionist Interpretations." Pp. 325–393 in Gabriel Almond and Sidney Verba, eds. *The Civic Culture Revisited.* Boston: Little, Brown.

Crespo, José Antonio. 2004. "Party Competition in Mexico: Evolution and Prospects." Pp. 57–81 in Kevin J. Middlebrook, ed. *Dilemmas of Political Change in Mexico.* London: Institute of Latin American Studies, Center for U.S.-Mexican Studies.

Cubides, Fernando. 2001. "From Private to Public Violence: The Paramilitaries." Pp. 127–150 in Charles Berquist, Ricardo Peñaranda, and Gonzalo Sánchez G., eds. *Violence in Colombia: Waging War and Negotiating Peace.* Wilmington, DE: Scholarly Resources.

Dagnino, Evelina. 1998. "The Cultural Politics of Citizenship, Democracy and the State." In Sonia E. Alvarez, Evelina Dagnino, and Arturo Escobar, eds. *Cultures of Politics/Politics of Cultures: Re-visioning Latin American Social Movements.* Boulder, CO: Westview.

Dahl, Robert A. 1971. *Polyarchy: Participation and Opposition.* New Haven: Yale University Press.

———. 1989a. *Democracy and Its Critics.* New Haven, CT: Yale University Press.

———. 1989b. *La poliarquía: Participación y oposición.* Madrid: Tecnos.

———. 1998. *On Democracy.* New Haven, CT: Yale University Press.

———. 2002. *How Democratic Is the American Constitution?* New Haven, CT: Yale University Press.

Defensoría del Pueblo. 2001. *Octavo informe del defensor del pueblo al congreso de Colombia.* Bogotá, Colombia: Congreso de Colombia.

del Pozo, Blanca Elena, and Ricardo Aparicio. 2001. *Estudio sobre la participación ciudadana y las condiciones del voto libre y secreto en las elecciones federales del año 2000: Una aproximación a la magnitud de la inducción y coacción del voto.* Mexico City: FLACSO and IFE.

Desposato, Scott W. 2006. "How Informal Institutions Shape the Brazilian Legislative Arena." Pp. 56–68 in Gretchen Helmke and Steven Levitsky, eds. *Informal Institutions and Democracy: Lessons from Latin America.* Baltimore: Johns Hopkins University Press.

Diamond, Larry, Jonathan Hartlyn, and Juan Linz. 1999. "Introduction: Politics, Society, and Democracy in Latin America." Pp. 1–70 in Larry Diamond, Jonathan Hartlyn, Juan Linz, and Seymour Martin Lipset, eds. *Democracy in Developing Countries: Latin America,* 2nd ed. Boulder, CO: Lynne Rienner.

Diamond, Larry, and Leonardo Morlino. 2005. "Introduction." Pp. ix–lxiii in Larry Diamond and Leonardo Morlino, eds. *Assessing the Quality of Democracy.* Baltimore: Johns Hopkins University Press.

Díaz-Cayeros, Alberto. 2004. "Decentralization, Democratization and Federalism in Mexico." In Kevin J. Middlebrook, ed. *Dilemmas of Political Change in Mexico.* London: Institute of Latin American Studies, Center for U.S.-Mexican Studies.

Dietz, Henry. 1998. *Urban Poverty, Political Participation and the State.* Pittsburgh: University of Pittsburgh Press.

Dix, Robert H. 1980. "Consociational Democracy: The Case of Colombia." *Comparative Politics* 12 (3): 303–321.

———. 1987. *The Politics of Colombia.* New York: Praeger.

Domínguez, Jorge. 1999. "The Transformation of Mexico's Electoral and Party System, 1988–1997: An Introduction." Pp. 1–23 in Jorge Dominguez and Alejandro Poire, eds. *Toward Mexico's Democratization: Parties, Campaigns, Elections, and Public Opinion.* New York: Routledge.

Domínguez, Jorge I., and James A. McCann. 1996. *Democratizing Mexico: Public Opinion and Electoral Choices.* Baltimore: Johns Hopkins University Press.

Drake, Paul W., and Eduardo Silva, eds. 1986. *Elections and Democratization in Latin America.* San Diego: Center for Iberian and Latin American Studies, Center for U.S.-Mexican Studies, University of California–San Diego.

Dresser, Denise. 2008. "Mexico: Dysfunctional Democracy." Pp. 242–263 in Jorge I. Dominguez and Michael Shifter, eds. *Constructing Democratic Governance in Latin America*. Baltimore: Johns Hopkins University Press.

Dunkerley, James. 2006. "The Third Bolivian Revolution: Evo Morales in Historical Perspective." Seminar, Centre for Latin American Studies, University of Cambridge, October 9.

———. 2007. "Commentary: Evo Morales, the 'Two Bolivias' and the Third Bolivian Revolution." *Journal of Latin American Studies* 39: 133–166.

Dye, David R., Jack Spence, and George Vickers. 2000. *Patchwork Democracy: Nicaraguan Politics Ten Years After the Fall*. Cambridge, MA: Hemisphere Initiatives.

———. 2004. *Democracy Adrift: Caudillo Politics in Nicaragua*. Managua: PRODENI.

Eaton, Kent. 2006. "Decentralization's Nondemocratic Roots: Authoritarianism and Subnational Reform in Latin America." *Latin American Politics and Society* 48 (1): 1–26.

Escobar, Cristina. 2002. "Clientelism and Citizenship: The Limits of Democratic Reform in Colombia." *Latin American Perspectives* 29 (5): 20–47.

Fagen, Richard, and William S. Tuohy. 1972. *Politics and Privilege in a Mexican City*. Stanford: Stanford University Press.

Faguet, Jean-Paul. 2004. "Does Decentralisation Increase Responsiveness to Local Needs? Evidence from Bolivia." *Journal of Public Economics* 88: 867–894.

Feinberg, Richard, Carlos Waisman, and Leon Zamosc, eds. 2006. *Civil Society and Democracy in Latin America*. London: Palgrave Macmillan.

Fernandois, Joaquin, and Angel Soto. 2005. "El plebiscito de 1988: Candidato único y competencia." Pp. 371–399 in Alejandro San Francisco and Angel Soto, eds. *Camino a la moneda*. Santiago, Chile: Centro de Estudios Bicentenario.

Figueiredo, Argelina Cheibub. 2001. "Instituições e política no controle do executivo." *Dados: Revista de ciências sociais* 44 (4): 689–727.

———. 2003. "The Role of Congress as an Agency of Horizontal Accountability: Lessons from the Brazilian Experience." Pp. 170–197 in Scott Mainwaring and Christopher Welna, eds. *Democratic Accountability in Latin America*. New York: Oxford University Press.

Figueiredo, Argelina Cheibub, and Fernando Limongi. 1995. "Mudança constitucional, desempenho do legislativo e consolidação institucional." *Revista brasileira de ciências sociais*: 175–200.

———. 1997. "O congresso e as medidas provisórias: Abdicação ou delegação? *Cadernos de Pesquisa (CEBRAP)* 47: 127–154.

———. 1999. *Executivo e legislativo na nova ordem constitucional*. Rio de Janeiro: Editora FGV.

———. 2002. "Incentivos eleitorais, partidos e política orçamentária." *Dados: Revista de ciências sociais* 45 (2): 303–344.

FLACSO (Facultad Latinoamericana de Ciencias Sociales). 2006. *Efectos del sistema binominal: Una reforma necesaria*. Santiago, Chile: FLACSO.

Fox, Jonathan. 1994. "The Difficult Transition From Clientelism to Citizenship: Lessons from Mexico." *World Politics* 46: 151–184.

———. 1996. "How Does Civil Society Thicken? The Political Construction of Social Capital in Rural Mexico." *World Development* 24 (6): 1089–1103.

———. 2007. *Accountability Politics: Power and Voice in Rural Mexico*. Oxford: Oxford University Press.

Fox, Jonathan, Libby Haight, Helena Hofbauer, and Tania Sánchez, eds. 2007. *Mexico's Right-to-Know Reforms: Civil Society Perspectives.* Washington: Woodrow Wilson International Center for Scholars.

Franklin, Mark N. 2002. "The Dynamics of Electoral Participation." Pp. 148–168 in Lawrence Le Duc, Richard G. Niemi, and Pippa Norris, eds. *Comparing Democracies 2: New Challenges in the Study of Elections and Voting.* Thousand Oaks, CA: Sage Publications.

Friedman, Elisabeth Jay, and Kathryn Hochstetler. 2002. "Assessing the Third Transition in Latin American Democratization: Representational Regimes and Civil Society in Argentina and Brazil." *Comparative Politics* 35 (1) (October): 21–42.

Früling, Pierre, Miguel González, and Hans Setter Buvollen. 2007. *Etnicidad y nación: El desarrollo de la autonomía de la costa Atlántica de Nicaragua, 1987–2007.* Guatemala: G&G Editores.

Fuentes, Claudio. 2006. "Violent Police, Passive Citizens: The Failure of Social Accountability in Chile." Pp. 134–177 in Enrique Peruzzotti and Catalina Smulovitz, eds. *Enforcing the Rule of Law: Social Accountability in the New Latin American Democracies.* Pittsburgh: University of Pittsburgh Press.

Fundación Friederich Ebert e Instituto Latinomericano de Investigaciones Sociales (FES-ILDIS). 2004. *Municipalización: Diagnóstico de una década* (Tomos I y II). La Paz, Bolivia: Plural Editores.

Garretón, Antonio, Marcelo Cavarozzi, Peter Cleavres, Gary Gereffi, and Jonathan Hartlyn. 2003. *Latin America in the Twenty-first Century: Toward a New Sociopolitical Matrix.* Miami: North/South Center Press.

Gaventa, John. 1980. *Power and Powerlessness: Quiescence and Rebellion in an Appalachian Valley.* Oxford: Clarendon Press.

Gay, Robert. 1990. "Community Organization and Clientelist Politics in Contemporary Brazil: A Case Study from Suburban Rio de Janeiro." *International Journal of Urban and Regional Research* 14 (4): 648–666.

Gibson, Edward. L. 2005. "Boundary Control: Sub-national Authoritarianism in Democratic Countries." *World Politics* 58: 101–132.

———. 2008. "Subnational Authoritarianism and Territorial Politics: Charting the Theoretical Landscape." Paper presented at a meeting of the American Political Science Association, Boston.

Giraldo, Fernando, ed. 2003. *Sistema de partidos politicos en Colombia: Estado de arte 1991–2002.* Bogota: Centro Editorial Javeriana.

Goldfrank, Benjamin. 2007. "The Politics of Deepening Local Democracy: Decentralization, Party Institutionalization, and Participation." *Comparative Politics* 39 (1): 147–168.

Gómez Tagle, Silvia. 2004. "Public Institutions and Electoral Transparency." In Kevin J. Middlebrook, ed. *Dilemmas of Political Change in Mexico.* London: Institute of Latin American Studies, Center for U.S.-Mexican Studies.

Gómez Tagle, Silvia, ed. 1997. *1994: Las elecciones en los estados.* Vols. 1 and 2. Mexico City: Centro de Investigaciones Interdisciplinarias en Ciencias y Humanidades/ UNAM.

González Casanova, Pablo. 1965. *La democracia en México.* Mexico City: Ediciones Era.

———, ed. 1985. *Las elecciones en México: Evolución y perspectivas.* Mexico: Siglo XXI.

Graham, Carol. 1997. "Building Support for Market Reforms in Bolivia: The Capitalization and Popular Participation Programs." *The Deepening of Market Based Re-*

form: Bolivia's Capitalization Program. Washington, DC: Woodrow Wilson International Center for Scholars.

Gray-Molina, George. 2001. "Exclusion, Participation and Democratic State-building." In Laurence Whitehead and John Crabtree, eds. *Towards Democratic Viability: The Bolivian Experience.* New York: Palgrave.

———. 2002. "Popular Participation, Social Service Delivery and Poverty Reduction 1994–2000." Paper presented at the seminar on Citizen Participation in the Context of Fiscal Decentralization: Best Practices in Municipal Administration. Inter-American Development Bank Tokyo and Kobe, September 2–6.

Grindle, Merilee. S. 2000 *Audacious Reforms: Institutional Invention and Democracy in Latin America.* Baltimore: Johns Hopkins University Press.

Gutmann, Matthew. C. 2002. *The Romance of Democracy: Compliant Defiance in Contemporary Mexico.* Berkeley: University of California Press.

Hadenius, Axel, ed. 2003. *Decentralisation and Democratic Governance: Experiences from India, Bolivia and South Africa.* Expert Group on Development Issues (EGDI). Elanders Gotab, Stockholm: Swedish Ministry for Foreign Affairs.

Hagopian, Frances. 1996. *Traditional Politics and Regime Change in Brazil.* New York: Cambridge University Press.

———. 2005. "Brazil and Chile." Pp. 123–162 in Larry Diamond and Leonardo Morlino, eds. *Assessing the Quality of Democracy in Latin America.* Baltimore: Johns Hopkins University Press.

Hamilton, Nora. 1982. *The Limits of State Autonomy: Post-Revolutionary Mexico.* Princeton: Princeton University Press.

Hartlyn, Jonathan. 1988. *The Politics of Coalition Rule in Colombia.* New York: Cambridge University Press.

Hartlyn, Jonathan, Jennifer McCoy, and Thomas M. Mustillo. 2009. "La importancia de la gobernanza electoral y la calidad de las elecciones en la América Latina contemporanea." *América Latina hoy* 51 (April 2009): 15–40.

Hidalgo, Manuel. 2009. "Hugo Chávez's Petro-Socialism." *Journal of Democracy* 20 (April): 78–92.

Hilbink, Lisa. 2007. *Judges Beyond Politics in Democracy and Dictatorship: Lessons from Chile.* Cambridge University Press.

Hinton, Mercedes S. 2009. "Police and State Reform in Brazil: Bad Apple or Rotten Barrel?" Pp. 213–234 in Mercedes S. Hinton and Tim Newburn, eds. *Policing Developing Democracies.* New York: Routledge.

Hiskey, Jonathan T., and Shaun Bowler. 2005. "Local Context and Democratization in Mexico." *America Journal of Political Science* 49 (1): 57–71.

Hiskey, Jonathan T., and Mitchell A. Seligson. 2003. "Pitfalls of Power to the People: Decentralisation, Local Government Performance, and System Support in Bolivia." *Studies in Comparative International Development* 37 (4): 64–88.

Hochstetler, Kathryn. 2000. "Democratizing Pressures from Below? Social Movements in the New Brazilian Democracy." Pp. 167–183 in Peter R. Kingstone and Timothy J. Power, eds. *Democratic Brazil: Actors, Institutions, and Processes.* Pittsburgh: University of Pittsburgh Press.

———. 2008. "Organized Civil Society in Lula's Brazil." Pp. 33–56 in Peter R. Kingstone and Timothy J. Power, eds. *Democratic Brazil Revisited.* Pittsburgh: University of Pittsburgh Press.

Holzner, Claudio A. 2004. "End of Clientelism? Strong and Weak Networks in a Mexican Squatter Movement." *Mobilization: An International Journal* 9 (3): 223–240.

———. 2007a. "The Poverty of Democracy: Neoliberal Reforms and Political Participation of the Poor in Mexico." *Latin American Politics and Society* 49 (2): 87–122.

————. 2007b. "Voz y voto: Participación política y calidad de la democracia en México." *América Latina hoy* 45 (April): 17–46.

————. 2010. *Poverty of Democracy: The Institutional Roots of Political Participation in Mexico.* Pittsburgh: University of Pittsburgh Press.

Hoskin, Gary. 1971. "Dimensions of Representation in the Colombian National Legislature." In Weston Agor, ed. *Latin American Legislatures: Their Role and Influence—Analyses for Nine Countries.* New York: Praeger Publishers.

Houtzager, Peter, and Marcus J. Kurtz. 2000. "The Institutional Roots of Popular Mobilization." *Comparative Studies of Society and History* 42 (2): 394–424.

Htun, Mala, and Mark Jones. 2002. "Engendering the Right to Participate in Decision-making: Electoral Quotas and Women's Leadership in Latin America." Pp. 32–56 in Nikki Craske and Maime Molyneux, eds. *Gender and the Politics of Rights and Democracy in Latin America.* New York: Palgrave.

Hunter, Wendy. 1997. *Eroding Military Influence in Brazil: Politicians Against Soldiers.* Chapel Hill: University of North Carolina.

————. 2000. "Assessing Civil-Military Relations in Post-authoritarian Brazil." In Peter R. Kingstone and Timothy J. Power, eds. *Democratic Brazil: Actors, Institutions, and Processes.* Pittsburgh: University of Pittsburgh Press.

Hunter, Wendy, and Timothy Power. 2007. "Rewarding Lula: Executive Power, Social Policy, and the Brazilian Elections of 2006." *Latin American Politics And Society* 49 (1): 1–30.

Huntington, Samuel. 1991. *The Third Wave: Democratization in the Late Twentieth Century.* Norman, OK: University of Oklahoma Press.

Inglehart, Ronald. 2003. "How Solid Is Mass Support for Democracy and How Can We Measure It?" *PS: Political Science and Politics* 36 (1): 51–57.

Inglehart, Ronald, and Christian Welzel. 2005. *Modernization, Cultural Change, and Democracy: The Human Development Sequence.* New York: Cambridge University Press.

Jatar, Ana Julia. *2006 Apartheid del siglo XXI: La informática al servicio de la discriminación política en Venezuela.* Caracas: Sumate.

Johnson, Ollie A., III. 2008. "Afro-Brazilian Politics: White Supremacy, Black Struggle, and Affirmative Action." Pp. 209–232 in Peter R. Kingstone and Timothy J. Power, eds. *Democratic Brazil Revisited.* Pittsburgh: University of Pittsburgh Press.

Jones, Mark P. 1996. "Increasing Women's Representation via Gender Quotas: The Argentine Ley de Cupos." *Women & Politics* 16 (4): 75–98.

————. 1997. "Evaluating Argentina's Presidential Democracy: 1983–1995." Pp. 259–299 in Scott Mainwaring and Matthew Soberg Shugart, eds. *Presidentialism and Democracy in Latin America.* New York: Cambridge University Press.

————. 1998. "Gender Quotas, Electoral Laws, and the Election of Women: Lessons from Argentine Provinces." *Comparative Political Studies* 31 (February): 3–21.

Kampwirth, Karen. 2004. "Alemán's War on the NGO Community." Pp. 65–86 in David Close and Deonandan Kalowatie, eds. *Undoing Democracy. The Politics of Electoral Caudillismo.* New York: Lexington Books.

————. 2009. "Feminismos, anti-feminismo y la lucha del aborto terapéutico: La memoria y las consecuencias inesperadas de la revolución." In David Close and Salvador Martí i Puig, eds. *Nicaragua y el FSLN, 1979–2009: ¿Qué queda de la revolución?* Barcelona: Edicions Bellaterra.

Keck, Margaret. 1992. *The Workers' Party and Democratization in Brazil.* New Haven: Yale University Press.

Kerche, Fábio. 2007. "Autonomia e discricionariedade do Ministério Público no Brasil." *Dados: Revista de ciências sociais* 50 (2): 259–279.

Kingstone, Peter R., and Timothy J. Power. 2008. "Introduction." Pp. 1–14 in Peter R. Kingstone and Timothy J. Power, eds. *Democratic Brazil Revisited*. Pittsburgh: University of Pittsburgh Press.

Kinzo, Maria D'Alva. 2005. "Parties in the Electorate: Public Perceptions and Party Attachments in Brazil." *Revista brasileira de ciências sociais* 20 (57): 65–81.

Klesner, Joseph, and Chappell Lawson. 2000. "Adiós to the PRI? Changing Voter Turnout in Mexico's Political Transition." *Mexican Studies/Estudios Mexicanos* 17 (1): 17–39.

Kohl, Benjamin. 2002. "Stabilizing Neoliberalism in Bolivia: Popular Participation and Privatization." *Political Geography* 21 (4): 449–472.

Kooning, Kees, and Dirk Kruijt. 2003. "Latin American Political Armies in the Twenty First Century." *Bulletin of Latin American Research* 22: 371–384.

Kornblith, Miriam. 2005. "The Referendum in Venezuela: Elections Versus Democracy." *Journal of Democracy* 16 (1): 124–137.

———. 2007. "Venezuela: Calidad de las elecciones y calidad de la democracia." *América Latina hoy* 45 (April): 109–124.

Kurtz, Marcus. 2004. *Free Market Democracy and the Chilean and Mexican Countryside*. New York: Cambridge University Press.

Kurtz, Marcus, and Andrew Schrank. 2007. "Growth and Governance. Models, Measures and Mechanisms." *Journal of Politics* 69 (2): 538–554.

Latin American Public Opinion Project (LAPOP). 2007. "Brazil Survey 2007." Nashville, TN: Vanderbilt University.

Latorre, Mario. 1974. *Elecciones y partidos políticos en Colombia*. Bogotá: Universidad de los Andes, Departamento de Ciencia Política.

Lawson, Chappell, and Joseph Klesner. 2004. "Political Reform, Electoral Participation, and the Campaign of 2000." In Jorge Domínguez and H. Lawson Chapell, eds. *Mexico's Pivotal Democratic Election: Candidates, Voters and the Presidential Campaign of 2000*. Stanford, CA: Stanford University Press.

Leal Buitrago, Francisco, and Andrés Dávila Ladrón de Guevara. 1990. *Clientelismo: El sistema político y su expresión regional*. Bogotá: Tercer Mundo Editores.

Lemos-Nelson, Ana Tereza, and Jorge Zaverucha. 2006. "Multiple Activations as a Strategy of Citizen Accountability and the Role of the Investigating Legislative Commissions." Pp. 75–114 in Enrique Peruzzotti and Catalina Smulovitz, eds. *Enforcing the Rule of Law: Social Accountability in the New Latin American Democracies*. Pittsburgh: University of Pittsburgh Press.

Levine, Daniel, and José Enrique Molina. 2006. "Calidad de la democracia: Fortalezas y debilidades en América Latina." Paper presented at meeting of the Latin American Studies Association, Rio de Janeiro, June.

———. 2007a. "La calidad de la democracia en América Latina: Una visión comparada." *América Latina hoy* 45 (April): 17–46.

———. 2007b. "Calidad de la democracia en América Latina: Índice específico y evaluación comparada de los países." Paper presented at meeting of the Latin American Studies Association, Montreal, September 5–8.

Levitsky, Steven. 2005. "Argentina: Democratic Survival Amidst Economic Failure." Pp. 63–89 in Scott Mainwaring and Frances Hagopian, eds. *The Third Wave of Democratization in Latin America: Advances and Setbacks*. Cambridge: Cambridge University Press.

Levitsky, Steven, and Lucan Way. 2002. "The Rise of Competitive Authoritarianism." *Journal of Democracy* 13 (2): 52–65.

Levy, Daniel, and Kathleen Bruhn. 2001. *Mexico: The Struggle for Democratic Development*. Berkeley and Los Angeles: University of California Press.

Levy, Daniel, and Gabriel Székely. 1987. *Mexico: Paradoxes of Stability and Change.* Boulder: Westview.

Lijphart, Arend. 1994. *Electoral Systems and Party Systems: A Study of Twenty-seven Democracies, 1945–1990.* New York: Oxford University Press.

———. 1997. "Unequal Participation: Democracy's Unresolved Dilemma." *American Political Science Review* 91 (1): 1–14.

———. 1999. *Patterns of Democracy: Government Forms and Performance in Thirty-six Countries.* New Haven: Yale University Press.

Lipset, Seymour M., and Stein Rokkan. 1967. "Cleavage Structures, Party Systems and Voter Alignments: An Introduction." In Seymour M. Lipset and Stein Rokkan, eds. *Party Systems and Voter Alignments.* New York: Free Press.

Loosemore, John, and Victor J. Hanby. 1971. "The Theoretical Limits of Maximum Distortion: Some Analytic Expressions for Electoral Systems." *British Journal of Political Science* 1: 467–477.

Luna, Juan Pablo, and Elizabeth Zeichmesier. 2005. "The Quality of Representation in Latin America." *Comparative Political Studies* 38 (4): 388–416.

Machicado Barbery, X. 2004. *Acoso político: Un tema urgente que enfrentar.* La Paz, Bolivia: Garza Azul.

Magaloni, Beatriz. 1999. "Is the PRI Fading? Economic Performance, Electoral Accountability, and Voting Behavior in the 1994 and 1997 Elections." Pp. 203–236 in Jorge Domínguez and Alejandro Poiré, eds. *Toward Mexico's Democratization.* New York: Routledge.

———. 2003. "Authoritarianism, Democracy and the Supreme Court: Horizontal Accountability and the Rule of Law in Mexico." Pp. 266–305 in Scott Mainwaring and Christopher Wellna, eds. *Horizontal Accountability in Latin America.* Oxford: Oxford University Press.

———. 2006. *Voting for Autocracy: Hegemonic Party Survival and Its Demise in Mexico.* New York: Cambridge University Press.

Mainwaring, Scott. 1999. *Rethinking Party Systems in the Third Wave of Democratization: The Case of Brazil.* Stanford, CA: Stanford University Press.

———. 2003. "Introduction: Democratic Accountability in Latin America." Pp. 3–33 in Scott Mainwaring and Christopher Welna, eds. *Democratic Accountability in Latin America.* Oxford: Oxford University Press.

Mainwaring, Scott, Daniel Brinks, and Aníbal Pérez-Liñán. 2007. "Classifying Political Regimes in Latin America, 1945–2004." Pp. 123–160 in Gerardo Munck, ed. *Regimes and Democracy in Latin America: Theories and Methods.* New York: Oxford University Press.

Mainwaring, Scott, and Frances Hagopian, eds. 2005. *The Third Wave of Democratization in Latin America: Advances and Setbacks.* New York: Cambridge University Press.

Mainwaring, Scott, Rachel Meneguello, and Timothy J. Power. 2000. "Conservative Parties, Democracy, and Economic Reform in Contemporary Brazil." Pp. 164–222 in Kevin J. Middlebrook, ed. *Conservative Parties, the Right, and Democracy in Latin America.* Baltimore: Johns Hopkins University Press.

Mainwaring, Scott, Timothy Scully, and Jorge Vargas Cullell. 2010. "Measuring Success in Democratic Governance in Latin America." Pp. 11–51 in Scott Mainwaring, Timothy Scully, and Jose Vargas Cullell, eds. *Democratic Governance in Latin America.* Stanford: Stanford University Press.

Mainwaring, Scott, and Matthew S. Shugart, eds. 1997. *Presidentialism and Democracy in Latin America.* Cambridge: Cambridge University Press.

Manin, Bernard, Adam Przeworski, and Susan C. Stokes. 1999. "Elections and Representation." Pp. 29–54 in Adam Przeworski, Susan C. Stokes, and Bernard Manin, eds. *Democracy, Accountability, and Representation*. New York: Cambridge University Press.

Martí i Puig, Salvador. 1997. *Nicaragua 1977–1996: La revolución enredada*. Madrid: Libros de la Catarata.

———. 2008. "El regreso del FSLN al poder: ¿Es posible hablar de realineamiento electoral en Nicaragua?" *Política y Gobierno* 15 (1): 75–107.

Martí i Puig, Salvador, and Salvador Santiuste. 2006. "El FSLN: De guerrilla a oposición negociadora." In Salvador Martí i Puig and Carlos Figueroa, eds. *La izquierda revolucionaria en Centroamérica: De la lucha armada a la participación electoral*. Madrid: Libros de la Catarata.

Martz, John. 1999. "Political Parties and Candidate Selection in Venezuela and Colombia." *Political Science Quarterly* 114 (4): 639–660.

Marulanda, Elsy. 1991. *Colonizacion y conflicto*. Bogota, Colombia: Tercer Mundo Editores.

Massicotte, Louis, André Blais, and Antoine Yoshinaka. 2004. *Establishing the Rules of the Game: Election Laws in Democracies*. Toronto: University of Toronto Press.

Mayorga, René A.1997. "Bolivia's Silent Revolution." *Journal of Democracy* 8 (1): 142–156.

McAdam, Douglas, John D. McCarthy, and Meyer Zald, eds. 1996. *Comparative Perspectives on Social Movements: Political Opportunities, Social Structures, and Cultural Framings*. Cambridge: Cambridge University Press.

Melo, Marcus André. 2008. "Unexpected Successes, Unanticipated Failures: Social Policy from Cardoso to Lula." Pp. 161–184 in Peter R. Kingstone and Timothy J. Power, eds. *Democratic Brazil Revisited*. Pittsburgh: University of Pittsburgh Press.

Mendoza-Botelho, Martin. 2009. "Decentralisation, Social Capital, and Social Change in the Andes: The Case of Bolivia." Ph.D. dissertation, University of Cambridge.

Molina, José Enrique, and Janeth Hernández. 1999. "La credibilidad de las elecciones latinoamericanas y sus factores." *Cuadernos del Cendes* 41 (May–August): 1–26.

Molinar Horcasitas, Juan. 1987. "Regreso a Chihuahua." *Nexos* 3 (March): 21–32.

Morales, Mauricio. 2005. "Los partidos de derecha en Chile (1989–2001): Una radiografía a la coalición UDI-RN." *Revista derecho mayor* 4 (4): 187–221.

Moreno, Erika. 2005. "Whither the Colombian Two Party System: An Assessment of Political Reforms and Their Limits." *Electoral Studies* 24 (3): 485–509.

Moreno, Erika, Brian F. Crisp, and Matthew Soberg Shugart. 2003. "The Accountability Deficit in Latin America." Pp. 79–131 in Scott Mainwaring and Chris Welna, eds. *Democratic Accountability in Latin America*. New York: Oxford University Press.

Moreno, Erika, and Maria Escobar Lemmon. 2008. "Mejor solo que mal acompañado: Political Entrepreneurs and List Proliferation in Colombia." Pp. 119–142 in Scott Morgenstern and Peter Siavelis, eds. *Pathways to Power: Political Recruitment and Candidate Selection in Latin America*. University Park, PA: Pennsylvania State University Press.

Morlino, Leonardo. 2004. "'Good' and 'Bad' Democracies: How to Conduct Research into the Quality of Democracy." *Journal of Communist Studies and Transition Politics* 20 (1): 5–27.

Morris, Stephen D., and Charles H. Blake. 2009. *Corruption and Democracy in Latin America*. Pittsburgh: University of Pittsburgh Press.

Motta Motta, Hernan. 1995. *Acción parlamentaria de la UP*. Bogotá, Colombia: Senado de la República.

Munck, Gerardo, ed. 2007a. *Regimes and Democracy in Latin America: Theories and Methods*. New York: Oxford University Press.

———. 2007b. "The Study of Politics and Democracy: Touchstones of a Research Agenda." Pp. 25–37 in Gerardo Munck, ed. *Regimes and Democracy in Latin America: Theories and Methods*. New York: Oxford University Press.

Munck, Gerardo, and Jay Verkuilen. 2002. "Conceptualizing and Measuring Democracy: Evaluating Alternative Indices." *Comparative Political Studies* 35 (1): 5–34.

Murillo, Gabriel, and Freddy Osorio. 2007. "La calidad de la democracia colombiana: Perspectivas y limitaciones." *América Latina hoy* 45 (April): 47–68.

Navia, Patricio. 2004. "Participación electoral en Chile, 1998–2004." *Revista de ciencia política* 24 (1): 81–103.

Nicolau, Jairo Marconi. 1998. "A volatilidade eleitoral nas eleições para a câmara dos deputados brasileira (1992–1994)." Paper presented at the annual meeting of the National Association of Post-Graduate Research in the Social Sciences (ANPOCS, Associação Nacional de Pós-Graduação e Pesquisa em Ciências Sociais), Caxambu.

———. 2000. "Disciplina partidária e base parlamentar na câmara dos deputados no primeiro governo de Fernando Henrique Cardoso (1995–1998)." *Dados: Revista de ciências sociais* 43 (4): 709–734.

Nylen, William R. 2002. "Testing the Empowerment Thesis: The Participatory Budget in Belo Horizonte and Betim, Brazil." *Comparative Politics* 34: 127–145.

———. 2003. *Participatory Democracy Versus Elitist Democracy: Lessons from Brazil*. New York: Palgrave Macmillan.

O'Donnell, Guillermo. 1994a. "Delegative Democracy." *Journal of Democracy* 5 (1): 55–69.

———. 1994b. "The State, Democratization, and Some Conceptual Problems." In William C. Smith, Carlos H. Acuña, and Eduardo A. Gamarra, eds. *Latin American Political Economy in the Age of Neoliberal Reform: Theoretical and Comparative Perspectives for the 1990s*. Coral Gables, FL: North-South Center.

———. 1999. "Horizontal Accountability in New Democracies." In Andreas Schedler, Larry Diamond, and Marc F. Plattner, eds. *The Self-Restraining State: Power and Accountability in New Democracies*. Boulder, CO: Lynne Rienner.

———. 2003. "Horizontal Accountability: The Legal Institutionalization of Mistrust." Pp. 34–54 in Scott Mainwaring and Christopher Welna, eds. *Democratic Accountability in Latin America*. Oxford: Oxford University Press.

———. 2004a. "The Quality of Democracy: Why the Rule of Law Matters." *Journal of Democracy* 15 (4): 32–46.

———. 2004b. "Human Development, Human Rights, and Democracy." Pp. 9–92 in Guillermo O'Donnell, Jorge Vargas Cullell, and Osvaldo M. Iazetta, eds. *The Quality of Democracy Theory and Applications*. Notre Dame, IN: University of Notre Dame Press.

———. 2005. "Why the Rule of Law Matters." Pp. 3–17 in L. Diamond and L. Morlino, eds. *Assessing the Quality of Democracy*. Baltimore: Johns Hopkins University Press, The National Endowment for Democracy.

O'Neill, Kathleen. 2005. *Decentralizing the State: Elections, Parties and Local Power in the Andes*. Cambridge: Cambridge University Press.

Oporto Castro, Henry 1998. *El difícil camino a la descentralización*. La Paz, Bolivia: Instituto Latinoamericano de Investigaciones Sociales de la Fundación Friederich Ebert Stiftung (FES-ILDIS).

Osterling, Jorge P. 1989. *Democracy in Colombia*. New Brunswick, NJ: Transaction Publishers.

Payne, J. Mark, Daniel Zovatto, and Mercedes Mateo Díaz. 2006. "Participación electoral en América Latina 1978–2004." In Mark Payne, Daniel Zovatto, and Mercedes Mateo Díaz, eds. *La política importa: Democracia y desarrollo en América Latina.* Washington, DC: Banco Interamericano de Desarrollo and Instituto Internacional para la Democracia y la Asistencia Electoral. Appendix 2 on CD-ROM.

Pederson, Mogens. 1990. "Electoral Volatility in Western Europe: 1948–1977." Pp. 195–207 in Peter Mair, ed. *The West European Party System.* New York: Oxford University Press.

Peirce, Margaret Hollis. 1997. "Local Level Democracy and Decentralized Development: The Case of Bolivia's Popular Participation Plan." Paper presented at meeting of the Latin American Studies Association, Guadalajara, Mexico, April 17–19.

Peña, Claudia, and Nelson Jordan. 2006. *Ser cruceño en octubre.* Santa Cruz, Bolivia: Programa de Investigación Estratégica en Bolivia (PIEB), Editorial Gente Común.

Pereira, Anthony W. 2000. "An Ugly Democracy? State Violence and the Rule of Law in Post-authoritarian Brazil." Pp. 217–235 in Peter R. Kingstone and Timothy J. Power, eds. *Democratic Brazil: Actors, Institutions and Processes.* Pittsburgh: University of Pittsburgh Press.

Pereira, Carlos, and Bernando Mueller. 2003. "Partidos fracos na arena eleitoral e partidos fortes na arena legislativa: A conexão eleitoral no Brasil." *Dados: Revista de ciências sociais* 46 (4): 735–771.

Peres, Paulo S. 2000. "Sistema partidário, instabilidade eleitoral e consolidação democrática no Brasil." Paper presented at the annual meeting of the Associação Brasileira de Ciência Política (ABCP), São Paulo, November 20–24.

Peruzzotti, Enrique, and Catalina Smulovits. 2006a. "Social Accountability: An Introduction." Pp. 3–33 in Enrique Peruzzotti and Catalina Smulovitz, eds. *Enforcing the Rule of Law: Social Accountability in the New Latin American Democracies.* Pittsburgh: University of Pittsburgh Press.

———, eds. 2006b. *Enforcing the Rule of Law: Social Accountability in the New Latin American Democracies.* Pittsburgh, PA: University of Pittsburgh Press.

Peschard, Jaqueline. 2010. "Federal and Local Electoral Institutions: From a National to a Fragmented System." Pp. 68-91 in Andrew Selee and Jacqueline Peschard, eds. *Mexico's Democratic Challenges: Politics, Government and Society.* Stanford: Stanford University Press.

Picado León, Hugo. 2009. "Diseño y transformacion de la gobernanza electoral en Costa Rica." *América Latina hoy* 51 (April): 95–116.

Pitkin, Hannah F. 1967. *The Concept of Representation.* Berkeley: University of California Press.

Pinzón de Lewin, Patricia. 1987. *Los partidos politicos colombianos.* Bogotá, Colombia: Universidad de los Andes.

Piven, Frances Fox, and Richard Cloward. 1997. "Low Income People and the Political Process." Pp. 271–286 in Frances Fox Piven and Richard A. Cloward, eds. *The Breaking of the American Social Compact.* New York: The New Press.

Pizarro, Eduardo. 1997. "¿Hacia un sistema multipartidista? Las terceras fuerzas en Colombia hoy." *Análisis político* 31: 82–104.

———. 2002. "La atomización partidista en Colombia: El fenómeno de las microempresas electorales." In Gutiérrez Sanín, ed. *Degradación o cambio: Evolución del sistema político colombiano.* Bogotá: Editorial Norma.

Powell, G. Bingham. 2000. *Elections as Instruments of Democracy: Majoritarian and Proportional Visions.* New Haven, CT: Yale University Press.

————. 2004. "The Quality of Democracy: The Chain of Responsiveness." *Journal of Democracy* 15 (4): 91–105.

————. 2005. "The Chain of Responsiveness." Pp. 62–76 in Larry Diamond and Leonardo Morlino, eds. *Assessing the Quality of Democracy*. Baltimore: Johns Hopkins University Press.

Power, Timothy J. 2000. *The Political Right in Post-authoritarian Brazil*. University Park, PA: Pennsylvania State University Press.

Preston, Julia, and Samuel Dillon. 2004. *Opening Mexico: The Making of a Democracy*. New York: Farrar, Straus and Giroux.

Przeworski, Adam, Susan Stokes, and Bernard Manin, eds. 1999. *Democracy, Accountability, and Representation*. Cambridge: Cambridge University Press.

Reina, Mauricio. 2001. "Drug Trafficking and the National Economy." Pp. 75–94 in Charles Berquist, Ricardo Peñaranda, and Gonzalo Sánchez, eds. *Violence in Colombia 1990–2000: Waging War and Negotiating Peace*. Wilmington, DE: Scholarly Resources.

Reis, Fábio W., and Mônica M. M. De Castro. 1992. "Regiões, classe e ideologia no processo eleitoral brasileiro." *Lua Nova* 26.

Roberts, Kenneth. 2006. "Populist Mobilization, Socio-Political Conflict, and Grass Roots Organization in Latin America." *Comparative Politics* 38 (2): 127–148.

————. Forthcoming. *Changing Course: Parties, Populism, and Political Representation in Latin America's Neo-Liberal Era*. New York: Cambridge University Press.

Rock, David. 1987. *Argentina 1516–1987: From Spanish Colonization to Alfonsín*. Berkeley: University of California Press.

Rodríguez, Victoria Elizabeth. 1997. *Decentralization in Mexico: From Reforma Municipal to Solidaridad to Nuevo Federalismo*. Boulder, CO: Westview.

Rodríguez Arechavaleta, Carlos Manuel. 2010. "Democratization, Media and Elections: Electoral Reform in Mexico." *Policy and Society* 29: 65–75.

Romero Ballivián, Salvador. 2005. *En la bifurcación del camino: Análisis de resultados de las elecciones municipales 2004*. La Paz, Bolivia: Corte Nacional Electoral (CNE).

Ropelato, Daniela. 2007. "The Quality of Democracy: Participation and Its Dilemma: How to Go Beyond?" *Crossroads* 7 (1): 54–84.

Rose, Richard. 1984. "Electoral Systems: A Question of Degree or of Principle?" Pp. 73–81 in Arend Lijphart and Bernard Grofman, eds. *Choosing an Electoral System: Issues and Alternatives*. New York: Praeger.

————. 2004. "Voter Turnout in the European Member Countries." Pp. 17–24 in Rafael López Pintor and Maria Gratschew, eds. *Voter Turnout in Western Europe Since 1945: A Regional Report*. Stockholm: International IDEA.

Rubin, Jeffrey W. 1997. *Decentering the Regime: Ethnicity, Radicalism, and Democracy in Juchitán, Mexico*. Durham: Duke University Press.

Rueschemeyer, Dietrich. 2004. "The Quality of Democracy: Assessing Inequality." *Journal of Democracy* 15 (4): 76–90.

Sachs, Jeffrey, and Juan Antonio Morales. 1990. "Bolivia's Economic Crisis." *Developing Country Debt and Economic Performance*. National Bureau of Economic Research Report. Chicago: University of Chicago Press.

Sadek, Maria Tereza, and Rosângela Batista Cavalcanti. 2003. "The New Brazilian Prosecution: An Agent of Accountability." Pp. 201–227 in Scott Mainwaring and Christopher Welna, eds. *Democratic Accountability in Latin America*. New York: Oxford University Press.

Samuels, David. 2006a. "Sources of Mass Partisanship in Brazil." *Latin American Politics and Society* 48 (2) (Summer): 1–27.

————. 2006b. "Informal Institutions When Formal Contracting Is Prohibited: Campaign Finance in Brazil." Pp. 106–124 in Gretchen Helmke and Steven Levitsky, eds. *Informal Institutions and Democracy: Lessons from Latin America*. Baltimore: Johns Hopkins University Press.

Santos, Fabiano, and Márcio Grijó Vilarouca. 2008. "Political Institutions and Governability from FHC to Lula." Pp. 57–80 in Peter R. Kingstone and Timothy J. Power, eds. *Democratic Brazil Revisited*. Pittsburgh: University of Pittsburgh Press.

Schedler, Andreas. 2006. "The Logic of Electoral Authoritarianism." Pp. 1–23 in Andreas Schedler, ed. *Electoral Authoritarianism: The Dynamics of Unfree Competition.*" Boulder, CO: Lynne Rienner.

————. 2008. "The Mobilization of Distrust in Mexico." Pp. 232–246 in Larry Diamond, Marc F. Plattner, and Diego Abente Brun, eds. *Latin America's Struggle for Democracy*. Baltimore: Johns Hopkins University Press.

————. 2009. "Inconsistencias contaminantes: Gobernación electoral y conflicto postelectoral en las elecciones presidenciales del 2006 en Mexico." *América Latina hoy* 51 (April): 41–59.

Schmitt, Carl. 1984. *El concepto de lo político*. Buenos Aires: Folios Ediciones.

Schmitter, Philippe. 1997. "Civil Society East and West." Pp. 239–262 in Larry Diamond, Marc F. Plattner, Yun-han Chu, and Hung-mao Tien, eds. *Consolidating the Third Wave Democracies: Themes and Perspectives*. Baltimore: Johns Hopkins University Press.

Schonwalder, Gerd. 2002. *Linking Civil Society and the State: Urban Popular Movements, the Left, and Local Government in Peru, 1980–1992*. University Park, PA: Pennsylvania State University Press.

Seligson, Mitchell, Daniel Moreno Morales, and Vivian Schwartz Blum. 2005. *Democracy Audit: Bolivia 2004 Report*. La Paz, Bolivia: US Agency for International Development (USAID) and Catholic University of Bolivia.

Shefner, Jon. 2008. *The Illusion of Civil Society: Democratization and Community Mobilization in Low-Income Mexico*. University Park, PA: Pennsylvania State University Press.

Shugart, Matthew S., and John Carey. 1992. *Presidents and Assemblies: Constitutional Design and Electoral Dynamics*. Cambridge: Cambridge University Press.

Siavelis, Peter. 2004. Sistema electoral, desintegración de coaliciones y democracia en Chile. ¿El fin de la Concertación? *Revista de ciencia política* 24 (1): 58–80.

————. 2005: "La lógica oculta de la selección de candidatos en las elecciones parlamentarias chilenas." *Estudios públicos*, no. 98.

Singer, André. 1999. *Esquerda e direita no eleitorado brasileiro: A identificação ideológica nas disputas presidenciais de 1989 e 1994*. São Paulo: Editora Edusp/ Fapesp.

Smith, Peter H. 2005. *Democracy in Latin America: Political Change in Comparative Perspective*. Oxford: Oxford University Press.

Smith, Peter, and Melissa Ziegler. 2008. "Liberal and Illiberal Democracy in Latinamerica." *Latin American Politics and Society* 50 (1): 31–57.

Snyder, Richard, and David Samuels. 2001. "Devaluing the Vote in Latin America." *Journal of Democracy* 12 (1): 146–159.

Sola, Lourdes. 2008. "Politics, Markets, and Society in Lula's Brazil." *Journal of Democracy* 19 (2) (April): 31–45.

Spiller, Pablo T., and Mariano Tommasi. 2007. *The Institutional Foundations of Public Policy: A Transaction Theory and an Application to Argentina*. New York: Cambridge University Press.

Stahler-Sholk, Richard. 1994. "El ajuste neo-liberal y sus opciones: La respuesta del movimiento sindical nicaragüense." *Revista mexicana de sociología* 56 (3): 59–88.

Stepan, Alfred. 1988. *Rethinking Military Politics: Brazil and the Southern Cone.* Princeton: Princeton University Press.

Stokes, Susan. 1995. *Cultures in Conflict: Social Movements and the State in Peru.* Berkeley: University of California Press.

———. 2001. *Mandates and Democracy: Neoliberalism by Surprise in Latin America.* Cambridge: Cambridge University Press.

Súmate. 2008. "Proyecto Camatagua: Informe final." *Plan de vigilancia electoral 2009.* Caracas: Súmate.

———. 2009. "Proyecto Camatagua: Referendo para enmienda constitucional. Informe final." *Plan de vigilancia electoral 2009.* Caracas: Súmate.

Sunkel, Guillermo, and Esteban Geoffroy. 2001. *Concentración económica de los medios de comunicación.* Santiago, Chile: LOM.

Tarrow, Sidney. 1998. *Power in Movement: Social Movements and Contentious Politics,* 2nd ed. Cambridge: Cambridge University Press.

Taylor, Matthew M. 2008. *Judging Policy: Courts and Policy Reform in Democratic Brazil.* Stanford: Stanford University Press.

Taylor, Stephen. 2009. *Voting amid Violence: Electoral Democracy in Colombia.* Boston: University Press of New England.

Telles, Edward E. 2004. *Race in Another America: The Significance of Skin Color in Brazil.* Princeton: Princeton University Press.

Tendler, Judith. 1997. *Good Government in the Tropics.* Baltimore: Johns Hopkins University Press.

Tilly, Charles. 2007. *Democracy.* New York: Cambridge University Press.

Torcal, Mariano, and Scott Mainwaring. 2005. "La institucionalización de los sistemas de partidos y la teoría del sistema partidista después de la tercera ola democratizadora." *América Latina hoy* 41: 141–173.

Trinkunas, H. 2002. "The Crisis in Venezuelan Civil-Military Relations: From Punto Fijo to the Fifth Republic." *Latin American Research Review* 37 (1): 41–76.

Tuchschneider, David. 1998. "Decentralisation and Rural Development in Bolivia: In Search of a Model." Mimeo.

Uggla, Frederik. 2004. "The Ombudsman in Latin America." *Journal of Latin American Studies* 36 (3): 423–450.

United Nations Development Program. 2005. *Democracy in Latin America.* New York: United Nations Development Program.

———. 2008. *Human Development Report.* Santiago, Chile: PNUD.

Valenzuela, Arturo, and Lucía Dammert. 2006. "Problems of Success in Chile." *Journal of Democracy* 17 (4): 65–79.

Valenzuela, Samuel J. 2006. "Los derechos humanos y la redemocratización en Chile." Pp. 269–312 in Manuel Alcántara Sáez and Leticia Ruiz Rodríguez, eds. *Chile: Política y modernización democratic.* Barcelona: Ediciones Bellaterra.

Van Cott, Donna Lee. 2000. *The Friendly Liquidation of the Past: The Politics of Diversity in Latin America.* Pittsburgh: University of Pittsburgh Press.

———. 2005. *From Movements to Parties in Latin America: The Evolution of Ethnic Politics.* New York: Cambridge University Press.

———. 2008. *Radical Democracy in the Andes.* New York: Cambridge University Press.

Vargas Cullell, Jorge. 2004. "Democracy and the Quality of Democracy: Empirical Findings and Methodological and Theoretical Issues Drawn from the Citizen Audit of the Quality of Democracy in Costa Rica." Pp. 93–162 in Guillermo O'Donnell, Jorge Vargas Cullell, and Osvaldo M. Iazetta, eds. *The Quality of Democracy Theory and Applications*. Notre Dame, IN: University of Notre Dame Press.

Verba, Sidney, Kay Lehman Schlozman, and Henry Brady. 1995. *Voice and Equality: Civic Voluntarism in American Politics*. Cambridge, MA: Harvard University Press.

Verba, Sidney, Norman H. Nie, and Jae on Kim. 1978. *Participation and Political Equality: A Seven Nation Comparison*. Chicago: University of Chicago Press.

Vilas, Carlos. 1992. "Una patria para todos: Revolución, desarrollo y democracia en Nicaragua." Paper presented at the seminar "La democracia en América Latina: Actualidad y perspectives." Madrid: Universidad Complutense.

Wampler, Brian. 2007. *Participatory Budgeting in Brazil: Contestation, Cooperation, and Accountability*. University Park, PA: Pennsylvania State University Press.

———. 2008. "When Does Participatory Democracy Deepen Democracy? Lessons from Brazil." *Comparative Politics* 41 (1): 61–82.

Wampler, Brian, and Leonardo Avritzer. 2004. "Participatory Publics: Civil Society and New Institutions in Democratic Brazil." *Comparative Politics* 36: 291–312.

Wickham-Crowley, Timothy P. 1992. *Guerrillas and Revolution in Latin America: A Comparative Study of Insurgents and Regimes Since 1959*. Princeton: Princeton University Press.

World Bank. 1999. "A Strategic View of Decentralisation in Bolivia: Advances, Issues, Opportunities, and Recommendations." Project Evaluation Report, February. Washington, DC: World Bank.

———. 2007. *The Little Data Book 2007*. Washington, DC: World Bank.

———. 2008. "Brazil: Toward a More Inclusive and Effective Participatory Budget in Porto Alegre." *World Bank Report* No. 40144-BR. Washington, DC: World Bank.

Yashar, Deborah J. 2005. *Contesting Citizenship in Latin America: The Rise of Indigenous Movements and the Postliberal Challenge*. New York: Cambridge University Press.

Zaller, John R. 1992. *The Nature and Origins of Mass Opinion*. New York: Cambridge University Press.

Zovatto, Daniel. 2006. "Instituciones de democracia directa en América Latina." Pp. 241–261 in J. Mark Payne, Daniel Zovatto, and Mercedes Mateos Díaz, eds. *La política importa: Democracia y desarrollo en América Latina*. Washington, DC: Banco Interamericano de Desarrollo and Instituto Internacional para Democracia y la Asistencia Electoral.

Zovatto, Daniel, and Flavia Freidenberg. 2006. "Democracia interna y financiamiento de los partidos políticos." Pp. 197–238 in J. Mark Payne, Daniel Zovatto, and Mercedes Mateos Díaz, eds. *La política importa: Democracia y desarrollo en América Latina*. Washington, DC: Banco Interamericano de Desarrollo y Instituto Internacional para Democracia y la Asistencia Electoral.

Zucco, Cesar. 2008a. "The President's 'New' Constituency: Lula and the Pragmatic Vote in Brazil's 2006 Presidential Elections." *Journal of Latin American Studies* 40: 29–49.

———. 2008b. "Democracy in Poor and Unequal Polities: Preliminary Evidence from Brazil (and Beyond)." Princeton University. Mimeo.

The Contributors

Claudio A. Holzner is associate professor of political science at the University of Utah. He is the author of *Poverty of Democracy: The Institutional Roots of Political Participation in Mexico,* which examines the effect of neoliberal reforms and democratization on political participation. His research and publications have focused on political participation in new democracies and among immigrants in the United States.

Mark P. Jones is the Joseph D. Jamail Chair in Latin American Studies and chair of the Department of Political Science at Rice University. He has published widely on questions of electoral laws, legislatures, and other political institutions; political parties and party systems; and Latin American and Argentine politics.

Daniel H. Levine is professor of political science at the University of Michigan. He has published widely on issues of democracy, democratization, social movements, and religion and politics in Latin America. His books include *Conflict and Political Change in Venezuela, Religion and Politics in Latin America, Popular Voices in Latin American Catholicism,* and *Constructing Culture and Power in Latin America.*

Salvador Martí i Puig is professor of political science at the University of Salamanca, Spain, and a member of the Institute of International Relations of Barcelona (CIDOB-IBEI). He has been a research fellow in different universities in Latin America and Europe and has published extensively on issues of democratization and development and collective action and identity. His most recent publications include *Nicaragua y el FSLN (1979–2009), ¿Qué queda de* *la revolución?*, *Creadores de democracia radical*, *Movimientos sociales y redes de políticas públicas*, and *Pueblos indigenas y política en America Latina.*

Martín Mendoza-Botelho is assistant professor of political science at Tulane University. His research specializes in issues of political economy and institutional strengthening in developing countries, with emphasis on Latin America. Prior to his scholarly work, he served at the Organization of American States (OAS) in Washington, D.C., and the United Nations Children's Fund (UNICEF), among other organizations.

Juan Pablo Micozzi is assistant professor of political science at the University of New Mexico. His research interests lie primarily in Latin America, with specialization in the fields of legislative studies, institutions, research methodology, and the interaction of national and subnational units in multilevel political systems.

José E. Molina is professor at the Instituto de Estudios Políticos y Derecho Público, University of Zulia, Venezuela. Previously, he taught at the graduate and undergraduate levels in the Department of Political Science, University of Michigan, and was a visiting scholar at the University of Salamanca. His research interests center on comparative political behavior. He is the author of *Los partidos politicos venezolanos del siglo XXI* (coedited with Angel Alvarez), *El sistema electoral venezolano y sus consecuencias politicas*, and *Los sistemas electorales de América Latina*, along with numerous articles and chapters in English and Spanish.

Alfred P. Montero is associate professor of political science and director of the Latin American Studies program at Carleton College, Carleton, Minnesota. He has published extensively on such issues as the quality of subnational democracy in Brazil, the determinants of foreign investment flows in Latin America, and the political economy of the Spanish regional autonomy system in comparative perspective. His books include *Shifting States in Global Markets: Subnational Industrial Policy in Contemporary Brazil and Spain*, *Brazilian Politics: Reforming a Democratic State in a Changing World,* and *Decentralization and Democracy in Latin America.*

Erika Moreno is assistant professor at Creighton University. Her research focuses on Latin American democratic institutions, with special concern for the roles and interactions of common democratic institutions, including political parties and executives, and for aspects of democratic design that foster accountability in nascent and consolidating democracies. Her recent publications include articles in *Comparative Political Studies, Electoral Studies,* and *Legislative Studies Quarterly.*

Valia Pereira Almao is professor and researcher at the Instituto de Estudios Políticos y Derecho Público, University of Zulia, Maracaibo, Venezuela. She has published extensively on questions of political socialization and democracy in Venezuela. Her current work centers on Venezuelan politics and local government.

Carmen Pérez Baralt is researcher at the Instituto de Estudios Políticos y Derecho Público and director of the School of Political Science at the University of Zulia, Maracaibo, Venezuela. Her research centers on electoral behavior, and she has published extensively in journals in Latin America and the United States.

Leticia M. Ruiz Rodríguez is assistant professor at the Complutense University of Madrid. She has published widely on issues of politics, political parties, and democracy in Latin America. She is the author of *Partidos y coherencia and parlamentarios en América Latina,* coeditor of *Chile: Política y modernización,* and author of numerous articles on party political system dynamics.

Index

About the Book

IN CONSIDERING THE NATURE AND FUTURE PROSPECTS OF THE current wave of democracies in Latin America, analysis has shifted from a concern with regime change, transitions, and consolidation to a focus on the quality of these democracies. To what extent, for example, do citizens participate and influence decisionmaking? Are elections free and fair? Are there ways of ensuring government accountability? Do unelected power brokers exert undue influence?

Furthering this new approach, the authors of *The Quality of Democracy in Latin America* provide a rich, nuanced analysis—centered on a multidimensional theoretical foundation—of democratic systems in Argentina, Bolivia, Brazil, Chile, Colombia, Mexico, Nicaragua, and Venezuela.

Daniel H. Levine is professor of political science at the University of Michigan. He is author of *Popular Voices in Latin American Catholicism* and *Religion and Politics in Latin America*, among other works on democracy, social movements, and religion and politics in Latin America. **José E. Molina** is professor of political science at the Institute of Political Studies and Public Law at the University of Zulia. His publications include *Los sistemas electorales de América Latina* and *El sistema electoral venezolano y sus consecuencias políticas.*